OXFORD STUDIES IN SOCIAL AND CULTURAL ANTHROPOLOGY

THE PASTORAL CONTINUUM

OXFORD STUDIES IN SOCIAL AND CULTURAL ANTHROPOLOGY

Oxford Studies in Social and Cultural Anthropology represents the work of authors, new and established, which will set the criteria of excellence in ethnographic description and innovation in analysis. The series serves as an essential source of information about the world and the discipline.

THE PASTORAL CONTINUUM

The Marginalization of Tradition in East Africa

PAUL SPENCER

CLARENDON PRESS · OXFORD
1998

Oxford University Press, Great Clarendon Street, Oxford OX2 6DP
Oxford New York
Athens Auckland Bangkok Bogota Bombay
Buenos Aires Calcutta Cape Town Dar es Salaam
Delhi Florence Hong Kong Istanbul Karachi
Kuala Lumpur Madras Madrid Melbourne
Mexico City Nairobi Paris Singapore
Taipei Tokyo Toronto Warsaw
and associated companies in
Berlin Ibadan

Oxford is a trade mark of Oxford University Press

Published in the United States
by Oxford University Press Inc., New York

British Library Cataloguing in Publication Data
Data available

Library of Congress Cataloging in Publication Data
Spencer, Paul, 1932–
The pastoral continuum: the marginalization of tradition in East
Africa/Paul Spencer.
(Oxford studies in social and cultural anthropology)
Includes bibliographical references.
1. Pastoral systems—Africa, Eastern. 2. Herders—Africa,
Eastern. 3. Camels—Africa, Eastern. 4. Polygamy—Africa, Eastern.
5. Marginality, Social—Africa, Eastern. 6. Social change—Africa,
Eastern. 7. Africa, Eastern—Social conditions. 8. Africa,
Eastern—Economic conditions. I. Title. II. Series.
GN658.S64 1997 306'.09676–dc21 97-2310-5

ISBN 0-19-823375-2

1 3 5 7 9 10 8 6 4 2

Typeset by Best-set Typesetter Ltd., Hong Kong
Printed in Great Britain
on acid-free paper by
Biddles Ltd, Guildford and King's Lynn

To Diane

PREFACE

The three parts of this volume have evolved over an extended period. Earlier versions of some of the chapters have been published as articles elsewhere. In order to present these within a single framework, I have thoroughly revised and reworked this material, taking into account more recently published data and the further development of my own understanding. Chapter 1 appeared in an earlier form in *Production pastorale et société* (1984), but now retains only the broad thrust of the original article. Chapter 2 appeared in Clyde Mitchell's volume on *Numerical Techniques in Social Anthropology* (1980). Since then, the Africa-wide sample of polygyny data has been revised and extended, separating pastoral from non-pastoral societies, updating the technique, omitting the technical appendix, and drawing new conclusions. Certain sections of Chapter 3 appeared in Paul Baxter and Uri Almagor's edited volume on *Age, Generation and Time* (1978), but these now form part of a wider argument and have been suitably revised. Odd paragraphs of Chapters 7 and 8 appeared in an earlier article in *African Affairs* on 'Drought and the Commitment to Growth' (1974). In the course of preparing the present volume, the whole of Part III has developed from that brief article, taking on new directions as it responded to the trends that have since become more firmly established, and giving birth to Chapter 9. The justification for republishing earlier ideas lies in the work I have put into the revision in the 1990s, which has been (or feels) no less than the work for the original versions, and has brought the various strands much closer together. I would like to thank the editors of these volumes, the Secretary of The Royal African Society, and C. Hurst & Company (London) for permission to draw on these earlier articles.

This is a welcome opportunity to acknowledge the help of others who have contributed indirectly to this volume. Chapter 2 especially has been enhanced by the generosity of those who have responded to my requests for unpublished data, but other chapters have also been discussed with colleagues over the years. Here I wish to thank the following for their material and helpful comments: Uri Almagor, Kirsten Alsaker-Kjerland, Astrid Blystad, Paul Baxter, Monique Borgherhoff-Mulder, Lee Cronk, Keith Hart, Richard Hogg, Jan Hultin, Getachew Kassa, John Lamphear, Peter Little, Harald Muller-Kempf, David Parkin, Frank Stewart, Richard Tapper, Richard Waller, David Western and Fred Zaal. Personal communications and unpublished sources are acknowledged at relevant points of the text, and of course I claim full responsibility for any errors or misunderstandings. Beyond these, I would also like to express my gratitude to a large number of authors whose published writings are cited in Parts I and III. It is the stimulus of these works that has provided me with a wider perspective and the necessary incentive to re-examine my own findings from fieldwork among a small sample of East African pastoralists, notably the Maasai, Samburu, Rendille, and Chamus.

Here, it is the Chamus elders especially that I must thank for their engaging company and collaboration in helping me understand the nature of their society and history in my two brief visits as an extension of fieldwork, among the Samburu in 1959 and the Maasai in 1977. The Chamus are unique in sharing similarities with both of these societies, having been influenced by them at successive stages of their recent history; and it was almost inevitable that my own interest in the two societies should have extended to this area of overlap. It is the Chamus who form the topic for Part II of the present work, bridging the argument from Part I, which is concerned with traditional aspects of pastoral societies in East Africa, to Part III, which is concerned with the impact of recent change on these societies. It is precisely because the Chamus have a sense of their own history, in a way that is not evident in any other pastoral society I have studied, that they provide an extended case example at the centre of this work.

I must express my debt to David Anderson as a historian and Peter Little as an economic anthropologist, both of whom have also undertaken research among the Chamus. It was partly the stimulus of their recent analyses that led me to interrupt a second volume on the Maasai in order to refocus on Chamus data that had remained undisturbed in my notebooks for too long. Anderson's work concerned the earlier transformation of the Chamus irrigation system, Little explored the development of social differentiation under modern conditions, while my own findings complemented theirs in elaborating the development of Chamus social institutions and the cultural interplay between pastoralism and irrigation in their oral history. Here was a situation of adaptation on the borders of pastoralism that filled a gap in my researches elsewhere and a chance to explore the development and decline of a local tradition. This led me to consider problems that stretched beyond the Chamus to the wider region, and this provided the setting from which Parts I and III emerged.

In the course of preparing this work, the invigorating conditions of my employment at the School of Oriental and African Studies in London have provided the opportunity and urge to pursue my own special interest. Research among the Chamus was undertaken with the help of research grants from the William Wyse Studentship in Cambridge (1959) and the Social Science Research Council in London (1977).

I am of course very grateful to Oxford University Press for publishing this volume in its present form, and I owe a particular debt to my copy editor, Hilary Walford who has painstakingly gathered together an untidy stock of stray constructions and spellings and returned them to the herd.

Finally, I would again like to thank those who have been close to me during my periods in the field and at home. I am particularly grateful to Benet for his cover design. Above all, I wish to thank my wife, Diane Wells, for her generous support and understanding as chapters of this volume have been gestating, mutating, and devouring an unfair share of my attention.

School of Oriental and African Studies, London P.S.
1997

CONTENTS

PART II. OPPORTUNISM AND ADAPTATION TO THE PASTORAL NICHE: THE CASE OF THE CHAMUS OF LAKE BARINGO

LIST OF FIGURES

LIST OF MAPS

LIST OF TABLES

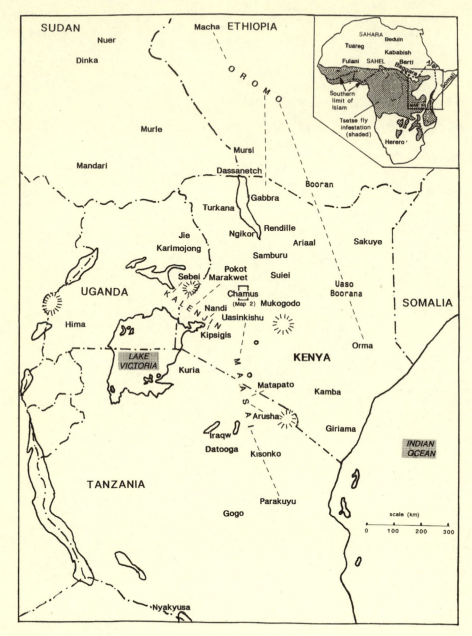

MAP 1. *The pastoral peoples of East Africa*

Introduction

Nomadism as a careful pastoral continuum is the least traumatic of human influences and as a form of husbandry utilizes areas which could not be utilized by man in any other way.

Unesco (1970: 35)[1]

pastoralists are no less affected by history and by national and global processes than farmers and city dwellers. As long as this is unrecognized and as long as the environmental, income, and food problems that plague dry regions of Africa are treated as unrelated, development solutions will continue to elude practitioners.

Little (1992: 180)

The two views of a pastoral continuum expressed in the above quotations represent the span of the present work. In East Africa, pastoral nomads have been depicted as the custodians of a self-contained way of life that has been largely unaffected by the spread of Western ideals or any notion of progress. They are thinly dispersed over the ecological margins where the terrain does not encourage further development and the problem of recurrent drought seems insurmountable. Meanwhile, the thrust of change has been concentrated in the more populated areas, and development (for want of a better term) is undoubtedly creeping towards these margins, bringing with it settlement and a precarious form of rain-fed agriculture that displaces pastureland formerly used by nomads. More ominously, there is an increasing spread of irrigation and flood–retreat agriculture around the permanent sources of water that have provided vital reserves on which pastoralists depend during the driest parts of the year, threatening their ultimate survival.

With the changing scene, there has been a trend within anthropology away from the study of traditional systems and towards problems of development and change, and this is certainly true of writings on pastoralism in this region. There have also been searching questions concerning the realities of unchanging traditions prior to colonial intervention when boundaries were fixed and customs and life styles were treated as immutable. To what extent did earlier studies (my own included) project a false image of established traditions of 'pure pastoralism' that merely reflected this protective regime and conspired in

---

[1] Cited by Grove (1974: 151). Cf. Barber (1968: 209 (citing G. Archer)).

the invention of a changeless order? Here, I wish to distinguish between any misplaced assumption of some fixed traditional order and the notion of 'tradition' as the expression of a meaningful life style to which pastoralists remain committed—a concept that yields guiding principles when men and women are faced with uncertainty. The situation prior to colonial intervention was clearly volatile and 'traditions' appear to have been modified with circumstance. However, the evidence from successful pastoralist cultures in particular suggests an institutionalized complex that adjusted to change; and the wisdom accredited to the elders was their ability to comprehend and to reinterpret the principles on which their traditions were based. The present work seeks to examine the evidence of this complex in order to understand better the nature of pastoral society in East Africa and the historical problem of accommodation to change. Here, the central case study is concerned with the development of tradition within a single society in its wider regional setting before, during, and since the colonial era. To pursue this argument, it is necessary to extend the notion of a pastoral continuum in two directions, on the one hand drawing attention to the continuity from the pre- through to the post-colonial, and on the other emphasizing the extent to which there are not and probably never were any pure pastoralists, wholly independent of other modes of livelihood or of their non-pastoral neighbours.[2]

As between cultivation, cattle, camels, sheep, and goats, every pastoral economy in East Africa involves some combination of these resources. However, in the right conditions, cattle have a unique value that places them above agriculture or other types of stock. Preferences vary with circumstance, and these are considered more fully in the following chapter, but, as a rule in traditional settings, the larger the herd of cattle, the less a stock-owner relies on alternative forms of livelihood.

The notion of a 'pastoral continuum' in the present work is clearly less sweeping than the 'cattle complex' identified by Herskovits (1926) which encompassed a broad band across the Sahel and down the eastern side of the continent to the south. The region considered here is bounded in the north by the influence of Islam. To extend into this northern area would impinge on a further continuum of beliefs and practices associated with camels and long-distance trading that have more affinity with the ethnography of the Middle East. The non-Islamic pastoralists live in a less demanding area than the Sahara, but paradoxically, because of the general absence of long-distance trading, they have been altogether more isolated. Economic and cultural self-sufficiency has characterized their life style. However, the boundary between these two very different types of pastoralism—within and beyond Islam—does not coincide precisely with the shift from camels to cattle. In West Africa, for

---

[2] Spencer (1973: 199–200); Berntsen (1979: 109); Hjort (1981a: 137); Kelly (1990: 82); Cribb (1991: 17–19); Galaty and Bonte (1991: 15–16); Barnard (1992: 27); Ndagala (1992: 174).

instance, long-distance trade and hence Islam penetrated into the cattle belt across the Sahel. In East Africa, these activities did not extend beyond the Somali to camel nomads further inland such as the Rendille, Gabbra, and Sakuye of Northern Kenya. Certainly, there are tenuous links in the oral traditions of these peoples claiming common origin with the Somali, but the rough terrain may account for the absence of long-distance trade in the past and hence of direct Islamic influence. These non-Islamic camel nomads may be regarded as living in a marginal zone on the boundary between two styles of pastoralism, where their land is too harsh for trading caravans and too dry for cattle, although they do have links with neighbouring cattle nomads. In the present work, then, the northern boundary is not between camels and cattle as such, but between Islamic trading and pastoralism largely unaffected by trade or Islam, and this cuts across the camel/cattle divide at the margins.

Along its southern and western flanks, the region is confined by the broad band of tsetse fly infestation that stretches across central Africa, severely limiting the extent to which cattle can play a dominant role in social exchange. These two factors—Islam to the north and east and tsetse to the south and west—define a broad region in which cattle have a central role to a greater or lesser extent. Map 1 shows the extent of this area and the location of the various pastoral peoples identified in this work. Where I refer to the 'pastoral continuum', this is a convenient tag for the non-Islamic (agro-)pastoralists of eastern Africa. It is not so much the cattle complex at large as the more limited cultural complex within this region that makes ethnographic comparison particularly fruitful.

It is evident from Map 1 that this work is somewhat selective in the number of pastoral societies it covers. Surveying the ethnography of traditional East Africa is rather like trying to construct an aerial map by peering through a layer of uneven cloud cover as the twilight gathers. In some parts, there is a clear view, and this may reveal enough to guess at least some of the uncertain details in neighbouring parts where the cover is hazy. Over the region as a whole, enough is visible to have a broad notion of what kind of features to expect even in areas where the view is wholly obscured. Each new study helps to lift the cover in some area, often revealing the unexpected and raising new questions. However, the new insights are offset by the gathering twilight, as indigenous patterns are increasingly lost from view. At best in making a survey of this kind, one is led to informed guesses, uncomfortably aware that lost traditions raise unanswerable questions, and beyond these that even the notion of the immutability of tradition is itself questionable.

In this work, the result is a piecemeal selection of societies for whom the ethnography is robust enough to give confidence, and hopefully representative of the region as a whole, as far as one can gather. Very broadly, they belong to five major clusters that each share the same language and traditions of origin or accretion: the Nuer and Dinka; the Maa (the Maasai, Samburu, Parakuyu,

Arusha—and the Chamus in Part II); the Oromo (notably the Booran and extending logically to the Rendille, who are outside the Oromo federation); the Karimojong–Jie–Turkana cluster; and the Kalenjin (the Kipsigis, Nandi, Pokot, Marakwet, and Sebei), who have been less studied than they deserve. In addition, there are others who fall within the scope of this study: the Dassanetch, pastoral Giriama, Gogo, Kamba, Mandari, and Mursi, and the outlying Hima and Nyakyusa; and yet more distant are certain Islamic pastoralists who provide a useful class for comparison. Map 1 indicates the distribution of these various groups.

The three parts of this work progress from tradition to change. In seeking to establish the resilience of tradition in Part I, the ethnographic present is preferred to an overloaded use of the past tense. This is not to deny the fact of change since some of the studies cited here were made, but rather to stress some of the more persistent principles that were visible at the time of fieldwork as against aspects that had lapsed. Only when the relevant points clearly refer to earlier times is use made of the past tense.

The first chapter sets out to correct a popular impression that the pastoralists of East Africa lack a spirit of enterprise. On the contrary, such a spirit typifies their approach to husbandry, and it is useful to compare ethnographic studies with this in mind. Traditional pastoralism is viewed as a family business, with problems of growth, ageing, and succession, comparable to developing family businesses elsewhere. The symbiotic balance between family and herd has to be maintained and the fragility of the family unit has to be offset by maintaining robust ties with the wider community. The whole argument—within the family and beyond—hinges on two persistent themes that typify this area: age systems and marriage, or more specifically polygyny. Polygyny sustains a more viable family enterprise, but it favours elders and delays the marriages of younger men, which can create rifts within the family. Age systems can be usefully examined with this in mind.

The next two chapters consider polygyny and age organization in greater detail, in an attempt to probe the relevance of hidden patterns. Polygyny is widespread throughout Africa, and the survey in Chapter 2 extends to non-pastoralist societies to highlight comparison with the pastoralists. In exploring patterns that are concealed within the figures, I would ask for a willing suspension of any disbelief in numeracy for the sake of sheer curiosity. Of special interest is the evidence of social differentiation implicit in the data. Thus, just as the popular assumption of a lack of enterprise among pastoralists is questioned in the first chapter, so the assumption of a deeply democratic equality is questioned in the second.

Chapter 3 is concerned with age organization, which is a teasing speciality of East African pastoralists. Attempts to disentangle the ramifications of these systems sometimes suggest that they must be unworkable because they defy logic. Yet the ethnographers who have actually seen them work appear least concerned with such doubts. Having argued in Chapter 1 that age systems are bound up with problems of succession in a developing enterprise, it is therefore logical to attempt to unravel the problem rather than simply to dismiss it as irrelevant or misunderstood—which is a surprisingly popular resolution of the whole tangle. Here, I would argue that this is more than just a curiosity with an appeal to the curious-minded. Age systems among these peoples dominate their social organization, their perception of time, and their mode of thought, and to dismiss age systems in any way is to disavow any interest in such cultures. This chapter focuses especially on one improbable case example, and its resolution touches on important aspects of age organization more generally. Although initiation plays an essential role in age systems, I would stress that the argument is deliberately geared towards the uninitiated, holding age-set geometry to a minimum and inviting the reader to reinterpret the evidence. If further proof is needed, it is hoped that this chapter at least will establish the historical depth and resilience of 'tradition' associated with institutions of age organization in this region.

The second part of this work provides an ethnographic account of the Chamus of Lake Baringo as one of several oasis economies in the region to whom destitute pastoralists could turn at times of severe crisis when their very survival was threatened. Historically, the Chamus have held a celebrated position in relation to the pioneering activities of Islamic ivory traders from the coast, followed by the first European explorers towards the end of the nineteenth century. However, they have been almost entirely overlooked in the anthropological literature. They are unusual among the pastoralists of East Africa in having a strong oral history of their pre-colonial evolution. This history straddles the pastoral continuum from a tradition of aboriginal foraging, through the development of irrigation agriculture (Chapter 4), to the assimilation of pastoralist institutions as they themselves came to rely increasingly on cattle (Chapter 5), and then to certain aberrations within this system with the spread of individualism following Independence in Kenya (Chapter 6). This study of the Chamus, therefore, brings the argument to the wider links between pastoralism and other forms of livelihood and introduces the historical problem of development. Pastoralism, polygyny, and age organization are relevant to these chapters, but so is the problem of post-colonial influences from beyond Chamus.

This leads in the third part to an overview of the dilemmas of recent change. In Chapter 7 the problems facing the Chamus are presented as a microcosm of those of the wider region. With growing populations and the spread of the commercial interests into remoter parts, pastoralists especially are caught in an ecological trap which is experienced as an endemic form of drought leading to a growing problem of refugees from famine. The confusion of causes and effects and the partial application of Western technologies lead to self-defeating attempts by development agencies to surmount the problem. In these attempts to limit the damage to the environment, there is little consideration of the relevance of indigenous practices for adapting to marginal conditions. Nor is there any concern for the extent to which the strength of consensus is geared towards containing the Tragedy of the Commons (the problem of over-exploiting community resources for personal gain). From this aspect, the analysis of Chapter 7 reverts to the central themes of Chapter 1.

The prosperity of a minority in parts of East Africa created by the market economy is the counterpart of rural drought and urban deprivation experienced elsewhere. This progressive polarization of society is considered in Chapter 8, with particular reference to theories of dependency in so far as they affect pastoralists as a peripheral underclass. Pastoralism is no longer an idealized form of existence, but it still offers a means for storing surplus wealth. With the increasing concentration of capital, pastoralism in the region ceases to be a small or local or nomadic business enterprise. Increasingly, the wealthy are taking control of the best pastoral land, and stockless pastoralists are being employed as their herders, reduced to a form of foraging the margins of the capitalist economy. In the more arid areas, the question facing the surviving nomadic pastoralists is one that concerns their future: for how long can they survive conditions of recurrent drought and diminishing resources?

Chapter 9 concludes this work by seeking to address this problem with reference to evidence of a comparable development in the history of the Islamic regions to the north. What pastoralists in East Africa are experiencing may not be altogether without precedent, but this brings into question the persistence of a way of life that ultimately may be forced to accommodate to new influences and wider enterprises as the boundaries of remoteness break down.

The pastoral continuum described here, then, may be viewed as a phenomenon that has its place within a wider historical framework, providing a wealth of material for an anthropological understanding of society. Meanwhile, it persists as a way of life in the most marginal areas. Indeed, in a world with depleting resources whose future is equally uncertain, it may even have a better chance of survival than many other sectors.

PART I

The Dimensions of Pastoral Society
in East Africa

1

Pastoralists and the Spirit of Enterprise

> The polygamous household of the Maasai may be compared to a joint stock company . . . The father of the family is the chief shareholder, the remaining shares are in the hands of his wives, who acquire them by giving birth to a son.
>
> Merker (1904: 333)

> They are our life. As the Government likes shillings, so we Samburu like cattle.
>
> *Kenya Land Commission, Evidence* (1933: 1602)

Traditional pastoralism in East Africa popularly conveys a leisurely way of life that contrasts with the spirit of enterprise shown by more progressive settled peoples such as the Kikuyu. This contrast is well illustrated in early accounts of trading between the pastoral Maasai and their agricultural neighbours. The Maasai benefited from this trade, but their men especially displayed a self-contained pastoralist life style and despised others who tilled the ground and traded their products. The actual trading was conducted between Maasai woman and visiting traders, and when these traders were men, this confirmed the visitors' lack of self-esteem in Maasai eyes.[1] Trading caravans risked being harassed by Maasai warriors (*moran*), who tended to dominate neighbouring agricultural peoples. Nevertheless, care was taken not to disrupt the trading itself, and the more persistent raids were directed against semi-pastoral peoples with cattle and no mutual trading arrangements. While Maasai men engaged in male activities, the women were protected by custom and continued to trade for their own domestic purposes, notably for grain to tide their families over the hunger of the dry season, and notably with neighbours that shared an uneasy peace with the Maasai.[2]

A reconstruction by Marris and Somerset of the trade between Kikuyu men and the Maasai in one area emphasizes the enterprise shown by the Kikuyu, who regarded their initiative with pride as an extension of their expanding

---

[1] Thomson (1885: 159); von Hohnel (1894: 284–5, 296); Merker (1904: 30); cf. Muriuki (1974: 107–9).

[2] Thomson (1885: 285–6, 308); von Hohnel (1894: 248); Merker (1904: 9); cf. Muriuki (1974: 86); Berntsen (1976: 6); Dahl (1979a: 170).

frontier economy.[3] The Kikuyu admired the Maasai with their abundance of stock as an ideal of cultural excellence, while the Maasai played an essentially passive and condescending role in response to the Kikuyu initiative. They would not exchange their cattle, and the Kikuyu were obliged to trade for small stock: sheep and goats. It was not that the Maasai had no eye for a bargain, but they placed little value on small stock compared with their cattle, whereas the Kikuyu valued sheep and goats highly enough to engage in the trade. It was the Kikuyu who took the trouble to respond to Maasai expectations, and they raised themselves in their own estimation through their enterprise. The traders who made most profit were those who built up a business as middlemen, reinvesting the gains in small stock among themselves to acquire manufactured products most valued by the Maasai. More enterprising still were the leading traders who built up a rapport with local Maasai, placing themselves in a key position to organize the trading caravans in the first place. By marrying off their daughters to Maasai and planting their sons as herdboys for Maasai, they could build up their own network of Maasai trading partners. The notion of a Kikuyu-centred enterprise adapting to new frontiers is very evident in this account, extending from an agricultural base towards a pastoral ideal. By contrast, the Maasai were passive beneficiaries at the end of a trading network that topped up their reserves during periods of hunger and introduced them also to a limited range of luxury items, but had no wider relevance. This trading lasted until the colonial intervention opened up more lucrative opportunities for the Kikuyu, and then, with Independence, further choices that were more lucrative still. The history of the development of Kenya has left the Maasai stranded, no longer emulated by their neighbours and unable to keep pace with the momentum of change. The obverse of Marris and Somerset's vignette is the dilemma facing all pastoralists in East Africa, and indeed those Kikuyu who failed to grasp the new opportunities for whatever reason.

   Yet the metaphors expressing the pastoralist point of view at the beginning of this chapter suggest some economic rationale. An alternative view has to be centred on the pastoralists themselves, taking account of their own patterns of aspiration and investment in social networks. Anthropological studies of African pastoralists have linked the high social regard for cattle with an acquisitive urge, valuing self-sufficiency and wealth as a means towards acquiring status. In the most celebrated work on this topic, Evans-Pritchard has noted that on cattle are concentrated a Nuer's 'immediate interests and his farthest ambitions. More than anything else they determine his daily action and dominate his attention.' Similar claims have been made for the Maasai, Baggara, Karimojong, Gogo, Turkana, and others.[4] This commitment to cattle has to be

---

[3] Marris and Somerset (1972: 25–43). Cf. Cowen (1982: 158). In a separate account by Leakey (1977: 479–96), trading by Kikuyu women follows a similar pattern.

[4] Nuer: Evans-Pritchard (1940: 40). Cf. Maasai: Hollis (1905: 288–9); Jie and Turkana: P. H. Gulliver (1955: 196–7); Baggara: Cunnison (1966: 31–2); Karimojong: N. Dyson-Hudson (1966: 81, 102–3); Gogo: Rigby (1969: 46, 53–4).

seen as a major premiss in these societies, bringing with it an irreducible set of values and an alternative spirit of enterprise that utilizes a different type of exchange and focuses on the dynamics of herd growth.

Bride-Wealth and the System of Exchange

The nature of marriage payments whereby stock are exchanged for women is a critical issue that goes beyond the immediate problems of family production and subsistence to those of community and reproduction. Associated with the growth of a herd is the need to establish a family, and hence the use of the herd to acquire wives. Details of the bride-wealth transaction vary between societies, but a single theme recurs: that cattle pastoralism in East Africa has to be regarded as a family enterprise and a vital aspect of this enterprise is marriage, or widespread polygyny, to be more precise. Two examples serve as ideal types to illustrate complementary aspects of the general pattern of this transaction: these are Evans-Pritchard's study of relations through marriage among the Nuer and Uri Almagor's more transactional approach among the Dassanetch.

The Nuer regard for their cattle provides a graphic model that is broadly representative of other pastoral societies in the region. In his first volume on these people, Evans-Pritchard stressed that the concentration of their concern for cattle had to be viewed as an aspect of relations between people. In the subsequent volume, he shifted his focus from relations between people through cattle to the exchange of cattle between men for women. Cattle were now held to be important *because* they brought wives. The cause of quarrels and troubles that had previously been blamed on cattle ('*Cherchez la vache*' . . .) was now cited as marriage in relation to bride-wealth (. . . *et la femme*).[5] It was a shift in emphasis from relations through cattle to a *system of exchange* with just two scarce commodities, both necessary for the symbiotic growth of family and herd.

Among the Nuer, a man's herd is depleted with every marriage, and as soon as this 'herd is large enough he, or one of his family, marries. The herd is thereby reduced to two or three beasts and the next few years are spent in repairing its losses.' However, the family has invested in a bride, and through her in future children. The daughters will be married out at a relatively early age to bring in more cattle, while the sons will only earn the right to a share of the herd for their own marriages at a much later age and after an extended period of tending the cattle as boys and defending them as young men. To coin an analogy with a family business, it is as if the family has a fund of capital that is invested alternately in brides and in cattle through an exchange aimed at perpetuating and with luck increasing the size of their venture: cattle bring in wives, wives breed children, children bring in cattle—as herdboys and as brides. Ideally there is a standard bride-wealth payment which reflects the

[5] Evans-Pritchard (1940: 16, 89; 1951: 90–1); cf. Cummins (1904: 154).

notion that all brides have the same potential fertility. Thus, while the Nuer family herd may be reduced to a bare nucleus after a marriage, it remains a reality in the capacity to restock: the outgoing cattle have been reinvested and not lost, and the exchange of women for cattle is a necessary part of this family development. The thrust of Evans-Pritchard's analysis is to emphasize that this is no commercial purchase and that the most important role of bride-wealth negotiations lies in creating and regulating relations between persons. The suitor may take several years to assemble sufficient cattle from his claim to a share of the family herd, extending to the settlement of debts owed them from previous marriages, and augmented by gifts from kinsmen and friends. The subsequent distribution of this herd among the bride's kin beyond her immediate family involves extensive discussion and payments during the successive stages leading up to her marriage.[6]

In emphasizing the compromises and negotiations of the marriage process among the Nuer, Evans-Pritchard drew attention to the individuality of each circumstance—the relations through cattle—in the process of developing new bonds. In coining the term *bride-wealth*, he rejected any suggestion of 'wife-purchase' as a Western construct. However, this argument glosses over the element of calculation and self-interest in the haggling, the delays, and even the seizures that can occur over the claims of more distant kin of the Nuer bride. In practice, the standard payment is more flexible than the ideal, and the amounts expected have decreased as cattle have become more scarce, and they may be lowered further still (or raised) according to the resources of the groom.

The Nuer pattern of marriage payment is quite common in this region. A comparable system has been reported, for instance, among the Dinka, among the Karimojong–Jie–Turkana cluster, and among the semi-pastoral Gogo, Mandari, and Mursi. These societies also observe the practice of soliciting gifts to build up the family herd for each marriage and then deplete it through the widespread distribution of bride-wealth, switching their investment between wives and cattle. It is also clear, as among the Nuer, that the actual amount paid is subject to negotiation, argument, and compromise, adjusting itself to the resources available to the groom (Jie, Turkana, Marakwet, and Mursi), or to the size of importance of the bride's group (Dinka, Karimojong, and Mandari), or to the relative scarcity of brides or cattle (Dinka, Gogo, Sebei, and Murle).[7] A tacit law of supply and demand appears to be in operation. The fact of this law implies a scarcity of brides and the operation of market forces in this respect. In

---

[6] Evans-Pritchard (1940: 20; 1951: 74, 79, 82–4, 89, 98–9); Howell (1954: 78, 97–8).

[7] Nuer: Evans-Pritchard (1951: 83); Howell (1954: 98–9); R. C. Kelly (1985: 119–20); Hutchinson (1996: 81–2). Jie and Turkana: P. H. Gulliver (1955: 197, 202, 229–38). Marakwet: H. L. Moore (1986: 63). Mursi: Turton (1980: 70–2). Dinka: Titherington (1927: 206); Howell (1951: 280–7); Lienhardt (1961: 25–6). Karimojong: Clark (1952: 176–7); N. Dyson-Hudson (1966: 51 n., 83–4, 91). Mandari: Buxton (1963: 50; 1973: 162–3). Gogo: Rigby (1969: 49–50, 227–8). Sebei: Goldschmidt (1976: 219). Murle: B. A. Lewis (1972: 112–20).

this context, Robert Gray has noted the extent to which ethnographers since Evans-Pritchard have preferred the more neutral 'bride-wealth' to the more market-oriented 'bride-price', and yet have also coined expressions and drawn parallels that are simply euphemistic ways of implying marriage as an economic arrangement. As Gray notes, the term 'economic' deals with an aspect of behaviour rather than with a type, and as such provides one way of looking at the element of choice in any system of exchange such as marriage transactions.[8] Certainly, during my own resocialization among the Samburu, I drew some decisive responses when I tried to convey Evans-Pritchard's argument as a way of expressing my own sympathy for the non-economic aspects of their system of bride-wealth. It was only when I conceded that the Samburu did perhaps pay for their wives with hard-earned cattle that the elders were satisfied that I had grasped their point of view and were then able to elaborate on it.

In contrast to the Nuer model of a negotiated transfer of cattle between families at marriage marking an alliance of sorts, Uri Almagor's model of marriage payments among the Dassanetch provides an alternative ideal type with a deferred and open-ended distribution of marriage cattle. This draws particular attention to the element of calculation and self-interest in selecting relationships that was discounted by Evans-Pritchard. As compared with the Nuer, there is a shift from an emphasis on the productive and reproductive capacity of the bride to the extension of the husband's network of friends formed through gifts in stock. Instead of a standard payment to be shared among the bride's kin, each of her kinsmen has a notional claim, and marriage into a large family is expensive; but such a marriage also provides the husband with an extended network of new allies in the mixed economy, and access through them to a wide variety of resources. Whereas the bulk of the Nuer bride-wealth is paid immediately before marriage, among the Dassanetch marriage payments are made over a prolonged period and only after the birth of the first child, typically one or two cattle each year but amounting over the years to as many as eighty head in exceptional cases. In this way, the payments take the form of discharging a marriage debt rather than offering a bride-wealth; and there is not even any negotiation regarding the extent of this debt or the pace of repayment beforehand. It is a matter of expectation rather than of obligation, with the extent of the network of 'wife-givers' implicit and ill-defined. Through these payments, the husband has an opportunity to work his way into this network selectively as suits him best. His strategy is first to fulfil the most pressing expectations for payment among the senior generation, establishing himself as a worthy 'wife-receiver' and building up his credibility in return for help while his family are young and dependent on others. Increasingly, with his credibility and family established, he can afford to be selective in responding to more distant expectations, cultivating trust among those that are strategically

[8] Hart (1986: 647–50); R. F. Gray (1960: 45–7, 53–6; 1964: 17); Burling (1962: 817).

placed to give him access to their own networks and resources, and risking the hostility of others who appear to offer less. The husband has to use his discretion through a mixture of calculated generosity and default: of gifts and bad debts. As a young man, his concern at first is to build up his herd in order to assert his independence and establish useful contacts among his wife's kin. As his range of allies expands, it is these alliances rather than cattle as such that become his greatest asset, and he invests his opportunities in consolidating and maintaining this network, extending it especially through the marriages of his daughters, where his token share of the marriage debt is offset by a decisive role in negotiating the debts due to others. In this way, an established elder develops his role as a broker whose closest allies are themselves brokers of a similar age. His network is a resource that he can call upon at any time, but not one that he can pass on to his sons. Like reputation or charisma, it is built up very personally and is not something that can be inherited. The capital he builds up is in reputation and credibility. In theory, he could translate this into a herd at any time, but in practice he allows his herd to diminish, trading on his good name in a network of credit, recycling, and directing cattle rather than hoarding them, until his reserves of energy decrease with age, and his ability to maintain his network and his credibility dwindles. This viewpoint provides a transactional model in which networks and careers are cultivated in tandem. Here too the analysis focuses on relations through cattle, but not as an end in themselves: the relations formed through marriage payments are perceived as a means to an end, and the system of exchange extends from wives and cattle to a selective network of power relations among men who direct these exchanges.[9]

The Nuer model is slanted towards the problems of a young suitor building up his herd and negotiating his first marriage from a position of weakness. The Dassanetch model extends also to the power of older men operating their networks in controlling marriages, redistributing cattle, and selecting and cultivating younger suitors as a further resource. As compared with the Nuer model, the Dassanetch analysis draws attention to the scope of individual initiative in building up a personal network through marriage. To the extent that there are compromises, concessions, and a residue of deferred payments in the ethnographic accounts of other peoples, this is to acknowledge the relevance of personal ties. Very generally, the bride's father is in a strategic position to act as broker, negotiating between the groom's family and his own kin, and this role is extended to her mother's brother among the Nuer and even to her mother among the Gogo.

The extent to which the wife-givers in other societies are also a resource for the groom varies, but this is especially marked among the Turkana, who appear to combine a marriage system that is comparable to Nuer practice in its customary expectation, although with a strongly individualistic slant, as among the

---

[9] Almagor (1978: 165–7, 174–232).

Dassanetch. Like the Dassanetch, each Turkana has to build up his personal network as an insurance against hard times, and older men emerge as the key brokers who build up credit through the circulation of stock rather than their accumulation. The Dinka and Karimojong have similar systems of marriage payment to the Nuer, but the actual scale of payment varies with the influence (Dinka) or the size (Karimojong) of the bride's descent group, and indirectly with the wealth of the groom. This creates a range of high- and low-status marriage alliances, with the bride's father in a key position to orchestrate the marriage on behalf of his kin, comparable to the Dassanetch ideal. Among the pastoral Giriama, the principal value of cattle is for bride-wealth, which is negotiated at the time of marriage, as among the Nuer; but there is a shift towards the Dassanetch practice of building up the herd as younger men, lodging a major part of it for security with a wide network of affines, and then allowing it to dwindle in old age as their sons marry.[10]

A further argument that takes a position somewhere between the two models has been put forward by David Turton and concerns the widespread practice of distributing bride-wealth beyond the immediate agnatic lineage of the bride. To the extent that a considerable portion of the bride-wealth is dispersed among a range of her non-agnatic kin—related to the bride through older women—it may be regarded as a form of deferred payment for the earlier marriages of these kinswomen and part of her father's ramifying network of alliance. In this way, even where the payment of bride-wealth is a condition for the removal of the bride and in this sense a direct exchange, as among the Nuer, this still contains a longer-term interest. The payment serves to honour earlier debts, and the marriage itself leaves a residue of future claims.[11]

The resources of these pastoralist ventures, then, are not just the uses to which cattle can be put, but also the fertility of their wives, the potentiality of their children, their credit elsewhere, and above all the skill of each family head in managing both his stock and his stock transactions. This is to accept the relevance of the economic argument, but also to recognize that any economic system is hedged around with moral boundaries that structure the perception of opportunity and limit the freedom of choice. Evans-Pritchard's model is a necessary complement to Almagor's. In economic anthropology, this is the difference between a formalist approach that emphasizes the aspirations of individuals and a substantivist approach that emphasizes the uniqueness of the institutional framework within any society, patterning behaviour and channelling expectations. Between these two models lies a whole range of

---

[10] Turkana: P. H. Gulliver (1955: 176); Broch-Due (1990: 148–51). Dinka: Howell (1951: 280, 287); R. C. Kelly (1985: 138–9). Karimojong: Clark (1952: 176); N. Dyson-Hudson (1966: 84); cf. P. H. Gulliver (1955: 233). Pastoral Giriama: Parkin (1991: 60–3, 66–8, 86, 95).

[11] Turton (1980: 70–2); cf. Evans-Pritchard (1951: 78). To Turton's argument, one may add that the process of inheritance also serves to spread the cattle widely, especially among successful polygynous families.

possibilities—a continuum—along which different points of view in the ethnographies and in the circumstances of each case can be placed. Within each society, the shape of the marriage transaction reflects the nature of the alliance.

Trust and the Morality of Exchange

While Nuer and Dassanetch marriage transactions differ fundamentally, both entail a measure of trust. The Nuer suitor needs to be trustworthy among his own kinsmen to build up a herd for marriage; the Dassanetch suitor needs to build his trustworthiness directly with his bride's kinsmen to be accepted as a sound investment. Each system concerns a different type of strategy that links community bonds to a measure of trust between individuals.

The two models reflect a dilemma between levels of immediate and ultimate interest. It is this dilemma that accounts for a certain contradiction in the literature on pastoralists, who are often portrayed as both compliant *and* individualistic. The Nuer, for instance, must assist kinsmen and yet at other times will risk breaking up their community by fighting these same men; they are 'deeply democratic' and yet find 'any restraint urksome'.[12] The resolution, of course, lies in the context. When a cow is at stake, then the owner becomes involved as an uncompromising individualist, but when the issue is broader he displays the façade of a moderate member of society whose interests blend into those of the wider community. Ultimately, the essence of community rests on a widely shared confidence that members are to be held accountable for their selfish acts. The topic of marriage payments is an intriguing illustration of this precisely because it links two highly emotive forms of property: both the Nuer and the Dassanetch are driven to extreme displays of self-interest on this issue, which ostensibly is critical to the continuity of community life.

To illustrate the importance of confidence in the institution of marriage payments, a third example may be cited which is broadly representative of the Maa- (or Maasai-)speaking peoples. The Samburu marriage system provides a model that draws attention to the credibility of the group rather than of individuals as a basis for trust. The formal bride-wealth in Samburu is a mere token as compared with the size of their herds, and its payment legitimizes the marriage, but has little economic significance. This is, however, augmented by a generalized marriage debt which, unlike Dassanetch practice, is not even notionally specified by custom. After marriage, the husband faces endless requests for cattle. At any time, a close kinsman of any of his wives may visit him and ask for a cow. To refuse would be to risk the anger of the visitor, which could have the effect of an unvoiced curse on the children of this wife, born or unborn. The husband may try to evade the request with promises, but he should not risk a curse by an outright refusal. Marriage in this type of

---

[12] Evans-Pritchard (1940: 49, 181, 183).

situation is an open-ended commitment to an indefinite series of payments. There is no fixed limit and there is in a sense a never-ending mortgage on each wife, with the wife-givers stipulating the rate of repayment. The husband and his affines are in direct competition for his cattle, and this leads to a general relationship of avoidance and hostility between them and ultimately between all exogamous clans, who are each surrounded with a wall of mistrust built on unfulfilled marriage payments. Thus, whereas the Dassanetch make allies by fulfilling the expectations of their marriage debt, the Samburu are faced with the ambiguity of always remaining obligated to the wife-givers and there is no basis for alliance—except within the clan, because their exogamy precludes misunderstandings over marriage payments.

There is, however, an important limitation on the ability of a wife's kin to exploit the husband's herd endlessly. If they are known to be excessive in their demands, then Samburu of other clans will be reluctant to marry their daughters, or for that matter to give such men their own daughters in marriage. There is in this way a widespread concern with 'marriageability', as they say—that is, with their reputation as reasonable wife-givers and worthy wife-receivers. Within the family, the patrilineage, and ultimately the exogamous clan, there is pressure on individuals to curb their demands for stock from the husbands of kinswomen. The Samburu claim that the number of cattle they give away for any marriage amounts to a very substantial herd over time, and they normally expect their wife-givers to err on the side of demanding too much. However, as wife-givers in their turn, they try to restrain themselves and their clansmen so as to maintain a reputation for reasonableness in such matters. In the final analysis, Samburu of all clans are caught up with a need to be seen as marriageable, and the ideal of community and trust becomes synonymous with being Samburu. The interests of the family merge into those of the lineage and clan, and ultimately into those of the Samburu as a whole.[13]

The notion of 'marriageability' among the Maa-speaking peoples corresponds to 'creditworthiness' among the Dassanetch and Turkana, and (as we shall see) to 'eligibility' for office among the Booran. These are community virtues that bind the individual in a system of exchange. The temptation to break away from community constraints should not be underestimated. In these remoter areas where resources are sparse, pastoralism encourages dispersal to exploit every patch of grazing. This gives the stock-owner considerable independence and flexibility, but it also makes him vulnerable at times when he needs help to search for stray animals, for instance, or to protect his herd or to share in herding arrangements. He is forced into some kind of community existence; and this is reinforced by the need for a local consensus on herd

---

[13] Spencer (1965: 29–36, 51–2). The Maasai have a similar marriage system, but with a distinct shift towards a close friendship between a suitor and his prospective father-in-law. A stronger sense of clanship among the Samburu corresponds to more mistrust between affines who belong to different clans (Spencer 1988: 25–9, 35–7).

discipline to exploit scarce water resources and to stem the spread of any local infection among the stock. These are short-term problems. With an eye to the longer term, the stock-owner needs to rely on others to spread the risks. He may loan out a substantial portion of his herd on trust to insure against a sudden local disaster and to redistribute food (but not capital) in exchange for prestige and ultimately credit.[14] Ultimately, he must nurture his reputation within the wider community, expressed in terms of eligibility for credit or marriage or office.

In this context, it is useful to conceive of a 'tribe' as a more inclusive unit, with a viability that the individual family or village simply does not have. This term is sometimes questioned on the historical grounds that the 'tribal' boundaries that were fixed by colonial authorities had been more transient in earlier times, and even that the very concept of 'tribe' is a relic of colonial rule. The clear thrust of the evidence, however, goes no further than the blurring of certain boundaries in pre-colonial times, leaving intact the existence of rela- tively self-contained ethnic groupings who maintained their own identities and cultures with a sense of integrity and pride. Between these groupings, there could be a certain trade, as we have seen, and also a diffuse network of dispersed clanship across tribal borders which became especially important for refugees seeking distant kinsmen in the wake of crisis. At such times, when local group- ings were threatened with annihilation, a certain regrouping could take place locally and the tribal boundaries and identities could shift or be redefined.[15] This appears broadly to have occurred in the Samburu–Turkana border area in the 1890s during the period of widespread epidemics and unrest, and also following the rout of the Sakuye in the 1960s, leading to a modification of boundaries subsequently.[16] But, modified or transformed, a tribal array has persisted throughout the region. In this way, the indigenous concept of 'tribe' appears to have merged into that of the colonial and post-colonial order rather than to have emerged out of it.

Here, 'tribe' is taken to imply a consensus to coexist, to intermarry, to extend credit, to support, and so on. In this sense it may be regarded as a moral community: a group of people with a strong sense of obligation towards one another that they do not extend to outsiders, and the boundary marks a shift in custom and the limit of this obligation.[17] Admittedly, among settled agro- pastoralists such as the Gogo, personal networks are more concentrated, boundaries are less pronounced, and there is a certain merging of cultures,

[14] e.g. Dinka: Titherington (1927: 176). Kipsigis: Peristiany (1939: 150). Nandi: Huntingford (1950: 52–5). Samburu: Spencer (1965: 28–9). Karimojong: N. Dyson-Hudson (1966: 85–6). Gogo: Rigby (1969: 50–3). Rendille: Spencer (1973: 37–40). Somali: I. M. Lewis (1975: 429). Sebei: Goldschmidt (1976: 129–34). Dassanetch: Almagor (1978: 146–51). Maasai: Galaty (1981: 72). Turkana: Broch-Due (1990: 149–51). Cf. Dahl and Hjort (1976: 134–7).
[15] Galaty and Bonte (1991: 17); Sobania (1991: 118, 124–9, 139–40); and especially Schlee (1989). Cf. also pp. 126, 132, and 222.
[16] Dahl (1979a: 16); Schlee (1989: 19–21); Lamphear (1992: 46).
[17] Cf. Evans-Pritchard (1940: 120–2); N. Dyson-Hudson (1966: 227–35).

bringing into question the usefulness of the concept of 'tribe'.[18] However, the more nomadic pastoralists range over a wide area, maintaining a dispersed network of ties, and this encourages a considerable uniformity of culture and expectation. As a result, where there is a border with a neighbouring tribe—as between the Samburu and Turkana—the contrast in culture and ethnic identity is especially sharp, corresponding to a break in the nomadic continuum. There is a change in marriage arrangements and other media through which there can be a build-up of trust and confidence in a system of exchange. Tribal boundaries are boundaries of mistrust, setting limits to customary expectation. In more uncertain situations and especially at times of extreme crisis, there may be a collapse of confidence and hence of community life, and individuals and their families have to rely to a greater extent on their own devices. In such circumstances any notion of 'tribe' as a moral entity is effectively in abeyance.

The Mix of Economy in Marginal Areas and the Strategic Role of Cattle

Among East African pastoralists, the use of cattle for marriage transactions provides a vivid illustration of Evans-Pritchard's view of material objects as the chain along which social relationships run, a concept that is also implied in the expression *property relations*.[19] But why necessarily cattle? None of these peoples subsisted exclusively as cattle nomads. Cattle are supplemented by other types of stock, and many stock-owners have a mixed agro-pastoral economy and range from semi-nomadic herders to fully sedentary farmers.

In an area where agricultural land is at best only marginal, the ideological bias towards cattle can be viewed at two levels. Economically, agriculture provides an alternative and often necessary food supply, but it is widely seen as altogether more arduous and unpleasant than cattle husbandry. With an erratic pattern of rainfall, cultivation is also unreliable, and the effort devoted to it early in the cropping season may be unrewarded as hunger spreads towards the end.[20] Cattle, on the other hand, are more resilient during drought and have a natural tendency to increase. At another level, there is the widespread attitude that extols the managerial skills of men in relation to the virtues of pastoralism, and trivializes the essential role of women in food production. To the extent that women are exchanged for cattle, this places them under the ultimate authority of men, like cattle; and, to the extent that they undertake the bulk of agricultural and domestic work, this confirms their subservient position. Drudgery is assumed to be the lot of women.

[18] Rigby (1969: 14–15, 236).
[19] Evans-Pritchard (1940: 89).
[20] Kipsigis: Peristiany (1939: 149–50). Nuer: Evans-Pritchard (1940: 40, 80); Howell (1954: 197–8). Dinka: Howell (1951: 245). Somali: I. M. Lewis (1961: 100). Baggara: Cunnison (1966: 22, 36). Karimojong: N. Dyson-Hudson (1966: 43). Gogo: Rigby (1969: 44, 54–5, 183). Booran: Baxter (1979: 76). Mursi: Turton (1980: 80). Cf. Sahel: Swift (1977a: 171).

Among the Dassanetch, for instance, the dry season is a time when grain and milk are scarce and men dominate in the management of domestic and political life, especially at their meat-feasting, while women are excluded from these feasts and are relegated to the periphery of social intercourse more generally. The women do attain greater equality with men during the three months following harvest, with an enhanced status as hostesses responsible for preparing and distributing food, and they may take a lively part in conversation. But there is no concept of conserving the grain supply during this time of plenty. The season is treated almost as an irrelevant interlude, and to this extent the bias against agriculture and the role of women is displayed. As a Dassanetch expressed this: 'What is land? Land is nothing. Today I cultivate here, tomorrow I cultivate in another place. Today land exists but tomorrow it vanishes. Cattle stay forever', and (as Almagor comments) 'create enduring relationships'—implicitly through women.[21]

However, this is to underrate the sheer necessity of agriculture for survival. Elaborating the argument, David Turton has suggested that the importance of cattle in the more sedentary areas is that they can be exchanged for food as a final resort when the harvests fail, providing a measure of insurance. Paraphrasing Evans-Pritchard's remark that 'a man who receives only one cow of the bride-wealth has in it the promise of a herd', Turton suggests that the real economic importance of a single animal for the Nuer is the promise of several sacks of grain in the event of crop failure.[22]

The combination of herding and cultivation is a way of spreading the risk, even in areas where there is less reliance on grain. Cattle can survive in years when crops fail, tiding the family over at a certain cost to the herd, either by slaughter or through exchange. When the crop is adequate, the herd has a better chance to grow. In areas where surplus grain is stored from one year to the next (not the Dassanetch), the surplus may be taken up in periods of hunger, and the mixed farmer does not face the prospect of depleting his herd to feed his family. This lessens the risk of a vicious downward spiral through successive years of drought and epidemic when his herd may dwindle beyond the threshold of need. The benign aspect of cultivation is that the investment is in labour rather than capital, and failure in one season does not have such a knock-on effect for the following year; and there is always the possibility of a surplus harvest as an investment for the future. The converse of failure, when cattle have to be sold for food, is the ideal of trading surplus grain for cattle, and ultimately cattle for wives.[23]

Agro-pastoralists face a spread of choice from free-range nomadism to a more sedentary commitment to farming. Strategies are likely to vary with

---

[21] Almagor (1978: 102–6, 142).

[22] Turton (1980: 81). Cf. Evans-Pritchard (1940: 88); Howell (1954: 197–8); and n. 23 below.

[23] Howell (1951: 245); Cunnison (1966: 36–7); Schneider (1968: 429, 435); Brandstrom *et al.* (1969: 18, 21); Rigby (1969: 54); cf. Mace (1993: 364–5, 367).

circumstance and especially over the life course. A young man with a relatively small herd and dependent family is likely to be tied down to farming. As the herd grows, so do the pressures towards nomadism, for mobility provides a means of dodging the worst effects of drought and the spread of disease among stock, leading to a healthier and more robust herd. As the family grows further and matures, so may the pressures towards dividing its labour between no-madic herding and sedentary cultivation. Times of transition between these strategies may be critically related to changes in the family itself that affect the balance between consumption needs and labour potential. Underlying chang-ing strategies and the task of survival from season to season is the overriding ideal of building up the herd. With a large herd, a slight risk of failure in the long term is preferable to the hard-won and uncertain benefits of farming.[24]

Generally, successful pastoralists in the past held a high reputation among their neighbours, who would emulate them when possible. Right across the Sahel region from Northern Nigeria eastwards and down into East Africa there are reports of cultivators who would take up cattle husbandry once conditions were right and they had the nucleus of a herd. This course was also followed by hunters and gatherers when they turned to herding for their rich neighbours as a step towards entering the pastoralist economy. When conditions were not right, then the reverse could take place. This is not simply a random fluctuation between life styles. There is still a definite preference for opting into the cattle economy voluntarily, and a risk of becoming stockless involuntarily and forced to search for some alternative ecological niche for survival.[25]

Historically, it is the nomadic pastoralists who have been best able to cope in such situations and even to benefit from the misfortunes of those who have been more vulnerable at times of political and economic instability. It is this robust adaptation of pure pastoralists that appears closely linked to the domi-nant status acquired by the Maasai in Kenya and Tanzania and by Hima pastoralist communities among their cultivator neighbours throughout much of western Uganda.[26]

Among the sedentary cultivators of this region are those that maintained peaceful relations with their pastoralist neighbours by avoiding cattle alto-gether, making them less vulnerable to stock raiding. Those who traded with the Maasai, for instance, confined their pastoralism to small stock—sheep and goats—and these were the most they could expect in exchange for their goods. Such societies are essentially beyond the present area of concern, but it is worth noting that their small stock tended to have a similar role to cattle elsewhere in

---

[24] Cf. Brandstrom *et al.* (1979: 31); Mace (1993: 364, 366–7).

[25] Fulani: Stenning (1959: 6–8). Dorobo: Spencer (1965: 286; 1973: 200). Fur: Haaland (1972). Northern Nigeria: Frantz (1975: 347). Somali: I. M. Lewis (1975: 437). Sahel: Lovejoy and Baier (1976: 157–8); Swift (1977*b*: 463). Maasai: Berntsen (1979: 109–10, 113–15). Chamus: Anderson (1984: 107; 1988: 244, 250). Oromo: Oba (1990: 40–1); H. Kelly (1990: 81).

[26] Steinhart (1979: 203); Packard (1981: 61, 72, 78–82); Ndagala (1990: 58).

relation to marriage transactions and other ritual festivities, and this gives them at least a marginal relevance.[27]

The Social Construction of Choice in Stock

The high value placed on cattle is matched by a relatively low regard for sheep and goats, and these animals have a closer association with the domain of women. Like grain, they provide an alternative source of food during the drier months and for lesser ritual feasts, preserving the herd of cattle. Because small stock breed more quickly, pastoralists who have lost cattle may seek to build up their flocks in order to re-establish a self-sufficient base from which to rebuild their herds of cattle in the longer term. In these ways small stock provide an important reserve. But as the flock grows so does the attention it requires, and the labour cost of maintaining a large flock of sheep and goats as against the reward in food is generally held to be inferior when compared with cattle. Like grain, small stock are viewed as a product for consumption rather than as an investment, whereas cattle offer an easier and more prestigious means of storing wealth.[28]

The very ease with which sheep and goats can breed means that relations expressed through the gift or slaughter of such animals are regarded as trivial: the flock is expected to replenish itself. Because cattle are scarcer and have more individuality than small stock, relationships expressed through gifts of cattle are additionally valuable, and a stock-owner has a perceptive awareness and a singular concern for each animal in his herd. In terms of their social value among predominantly pastoral peoples, then, cattle and small stock are of different orders, and to refer to small stock as small change in describing predominantly cattle-owning groups tends to gloss over this vital point.[29] It is not normally easy or cheap to convert from small stock to large. In gifts as in feasting, small stock have a lesser role, and to this extent, they belong to a separate sphere of exchange.

Paradoxically, it is because sheep and goats are less precious that they can also be endowed with a special role. The ritual value of certain token gifts is altogether less ambiguous precisely because they are not inherently valuable. Maasai women, for instance, cannot own cattle, and the ewe given as bride-wealth to the mother-in-law expresses a sensitive relationship. The context of the giving endows both the gift and the relationship with meaning that has no ulterior economic value. This is even more apparent in Dassanetch marriage payments, where small stock are used to space out the completion of a marriage

[27] Berntsen (1976: 5–6); R. F. Gray (1962: 486–9); Marris and Somerset (1972: 29, 40). Other accounts note the high value of cattle among the Kikuyu, because they are so scarce, but the emphasis on trading lies with small stock (Routledge and Routledge 1910: 44; Kenyatta 1938: 66–8, 167–8).

[28] Dahl and Hjort (1976; 1979: 10–28) provide a useful summary of the characteristics of the various types of stock. Cf. also Spencer (1973: 9–19); Almagor (1978: 95, 106 n.); Dahl (1979a: 37, 50–1). Cf. Cribb (1991: 28–30), whose data refer primarily to the Middle East.

[29] Cf. B. A. Lewis (1972: 32); Livingstone (1977: 212); Schneider (1968: 427; 1979: 101–2); Fratkin (1991: 47).

and may even be refused if a husband is felt to be lagging in paying off his massive cattle debt: once all the small stock have been given, he is in a stronger position to default on the remainder of his debt. Meanwhile, the prestigious role of the father-in-law as broker in this process of repayment is emphasized by the fact that he is given only small stock as his share and no cattle.[30] Turkana bride-wealth contains a large proportion of small stock precisely because it reaffirms the relationships of the groom to his more distant stock associates.[31] Economically, such gifts are mere tokens, but they extend the range of goodwill in a society that stresses the importance of constantly circulating stock through an extended social network. In such instances, the economic argument underpinning marriage payments—that the bride does have a price—does not apply, and it is the token gifts that reinforce the counter-argument, that these payments concern social relationships rather than self-interest.

Camels as an alternative form of large stock have a bearing on the margins of the present concern. They are comparatively new to northern Kenya and lie within a buffer zone between the Somali and hence Islamic influence along the east coast and the non-Islamic cattle pastoralists further inland that concern us here. While Somali influence has been generally increasing, there are also oral traditions of camel pastoralists, such as the Rendille and Gabbra, who have broken away from Islam and formed alliances with their western cattle-owning neighbours, linking them to the same pastoral continuum.[32] Camels are principally associated with the more arid lowland areas that are on the whole too hot and waterless for cattle. There, they can provide milk even in the height of the dry season, but they are also less docile to manage and have a higher mortality rate than cattle, and this can pose problems for maintaining a viable herd.[33] Camels and cattle, adapted to quite different environmental conditions and needing different regimes of management, do not mix together easily, but nor do they obviously compete.

Generally, various forms of stock are combined as an insurance against disaster in the more arid areas, rather as pastoralism combines with cultivation in the easier areas; and again this is only achieved through extra effort. Instead of the arduous routine of cultivation, mixed pastoralism involves sufficient manpower to mount separate herding routines for different forms of stock. Herding resources are especially stretched during the dry season when younger mobile herders are dispersed with surplus stock to distant undergrazed areas. Diversification of stock is another mixed strategy that offers more security and a better chance for the herds to multiply, but only at a cost.[34]

[30] Almagor (1978: 176, 182, 192–4).
[31] Gulliver (1955: 198–9, 230–1).
[32] Baxter (1954: 50–5); Spencer (1973); Schlee (1989: 6).
[33] Spencer (1973: 11); Dahl and Hjort (1976: 79–81); Hjort (1979: 152); Dahl (1979a: 49–50); Fratkin (1991: 44); Bollig (1992: 40, 43).
[34] Dahl and Hjort (1976: 135, 224–56; 1979: 18–28) and also R. T. Wilson *et al.* (1985) provide systematic surveys of aspects of the diversification of herds. With regard to diversification as a strategy for spreading risk in the Sahel, see Swift (1977b: 472–3), and Bernus (1990: 175).

The combination of cattle and camels as alternative types of large stock is of particular interest. Such peoples as the Ariaal, Gabbra, Turkana, and Pokot have acquired both, and in each instance this has entailed complex arrangements to adapt to the separate needs of the herds.[35] Related to the Ariaal are the Rendille, who illustrate further the dynamics of the continuum across an ethnic boundary. The camel-owning Rendille and the cattle-owning Samburu have quite separate languages and cultures and contrasting orientations towards their stock, but they also share a long-standing tradition of alliance. The slow growth of the brittle camel economy of the Rendille is reflected in their preference for monogamy and primogeniture, entailing the camel herd in a single line of inheritance to avoid fragmenting it into unviable units. Across the boundary, the Samburu cattle economy has easier prospects for growth, permitting polygyny and the dispersal of herds through inheritance.[36] Historically, the Ariaal straddled this boundary, comprising some wealthy stock-owners who had a family and herd on each side and divided their attention between them, interacting as Samburu in one and as Rendille in the other. So far as they were concerned, the boundary was not in space between two quite different ethnic groups, but in time depending on which family or herd they happened to be with, and they switched between the contrasting cultures associated with the two types of stock as the occasion demanded.

To the north of the Ariaal, the Rendille proper remained aloof from the Samburu, but they were both irrevocably linked in a symbiotic pact. The Rendille camel herds seemed to grow at a slower pace than the human population, and this was resolved through a steady trickle of stockless migrants and brides to the Samburu economy, where the cattle population grew at a fast enough rate to contain the Rendille overspill. The dynamics of this relationship are summarized in Fig. 1.1, illustrating the extent to which the flow of migration had become institutionalized across the boundary,

---

[35] Turkana: P. H. Gulliver (1955: 39, 198 n., 260); Storas (1990: 139); Lamphear (1992: 11, 31, 126). Ariaal: Spencer (1973: 130–45, 159–60); Fratkin (1991: 37–8). Gabbra: Torry (1976). Pokot: Bollig (1992: 35, 43–4).

[36] For fuller details of 'sharing' camels and problems of growth among the Rendille, and the Rendille–Samburu alliance, see Spencer (1973: 11–12, 36–40, 79, 130–45). My earlier suggestion that Rendille camel herds did not grow significantly was based on the testimony of Rendille and Ariaal informants. More recently, Shun Sato (1980: 30–1) has produced a more detailed study of Rendille herds that suggests an annual growth rate of 3.4%, which is certainly less than the typical growth rate reported for cattle, but is still higher than the expected growth rate of the human population. This suggests (although Sato does not) that my earlier model should be modified. Here, I would note that Sato's data were collected over a relatively limited period, and this does not allow for fluctuations in growth in the longer term. As against this estimate in 1976, one might place the very severe losses the Rendille were suffering during each of my three visits between 1958 and 1962. In all essential details, my provisional findings among the Rendille appear to be confirmed by a more systematic survey by Eric Roth (1993), suggesting little change. Certainly, statistics for cattle growth rates vary strikingly over time (Spencer 1973: 9–10), and the same could be true for camels.

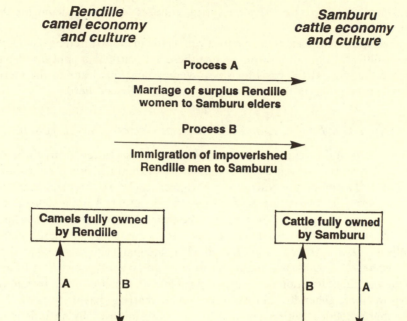

Fig. 1.1. *Migration from the Rendille to the Samburu, and the alternation of rights in stock*

The diagram indicates two parallel processes of migration to the easier cattle economy of Samburu. These were (A) the marriage of surplus Rendille women, and (B) the immigration of impoverished Rendille men. The problem facing the migrating men was not simply to adapt their pastoralism to a different kind of stock, but also to dispose of their few remaining camels before leaving, and then to acquire a herd of cattle on arrival. This was complemented by the problem of marrying a Rendille bride among Samburu for which either her (Samburu) groom had to find marriage camels, or her (Rendille) father had to accept cattle instead and then find someone to look after them. By convention, this problem was shared between groom and father-in-law, with the payment of equal numbers of camels and cattle. It was the resolution of these two problems that led to a complex alternation of rights in stock on each side of the camel–cattle divide, as shown in the diagram. In this arrangement, Rendille fathers-in-law loaned their cattle to Samburu to herd, and ex-Rendille emigrants 'shared' their few surviving camels with unrelated Rendille who tended them among their own herds. In each case, the original owner retained rights in the female descendants of these animals, but 'sharing' (*mal*) was a major institutional feature in Rendille, whereas cattle loans in Samburu were more a matter of convenience and trust. These arrangements are represented by the downward arrows in the diagram. Correspondingly, the upward arrows refer on the one side to the recalling of loaned cattle by ex-Rendille in order to build up their herds, and on the other side to the recalling of 'shared' camels so that Samburu grooms could pay for their Rendille brides. The recaller would normally be a kinsman or descendant of the original owner. In the case of camels especially, he might be invoking a 'sharing' that had been placed in a previous generation and was expected to continue in perpetuity through the female line. In this way, both Rendille and Samburu had a long-term economic interest in the persistence of their alliance despite marked linguistic and cultural differences between them.

maintaining the separate economies and cultures within a demographic continuum.

Camels and small stock, then, contrast with cattle in quite different ways that relate to different rates of growth. Among these, it is cattle that appear to have provided the most viable basis for stock-keeping, and this leads to the more general consideration of the symbiotic growth of family and herd.

Pastoralism as a Family Enterprise: Maasai Growth and Succession

Very generally in this region, cattle are a means towards a larger family through marriage payments, and the accumulation of wives complements the accumulation of stock. Among the Nuer, as we have seen, these are complementary as items of exchange, alternating between one and the other. Among some more purely pastoral groups where the herd is the prime source of food, wives and cattle are complementary in a more symbiotic sense, for family and herd should broadly increase together to support each other, and marriage payments tend to be drawn out.[37] The Maasai are an example of this type of society, and they provide a useful illustration of the problems of growth that are shared by family enterprises more generally. The Maasai system of marriage payments is similar to Samburu practice, with a nominal bride-wealth followed by an indefinite series of further gifts, but, in contrast to the Samburu, there is no effective clan support and the family head has to establish himself and his household on his own merits. Among the Maasai there is an acquisitive edge in their personal affairs. The stock-owner has an investment in his herd and family as a joint enterprise, and he is expected to 'tend' his family as he would his herd, keeping both in good care and under firm control, and instilling his dependants with a sense of commitment. There is no tolerance for a son who is not a devoted herdboy or a daughter who does not attract a worthy suitor. For the elders, husbandry is a dedicated task and this involves the whole family.

As the household grows, constraints on local pasture may encourage the Maasai stock-owner to divide his family and herd into separate units of production in order to extend the grazing opportunities, adjusting to the scarcity of pasture and the needs of different types of stock, and spreading the risk of local drought or disease. Each of these subsidiary units is largely self-contained under the control of a responsible member—ideally an adult son or younger brother—while the family head retains ultimate authority. Given this ideal of a growing family enterprise, the successful stock-owner will seek to pass on his success to his sons, using his influence to arrange their marriages, and even establishing them as polygynists. With polygyny and dispersal, there is no theoretical upper limit to the size of family and herd that can be built up apart

[37] See references in n. 7 above. With regard to the symbiotic pattern of growth among purer pastoralists, see Stenning (1958: 100–4); Dahl (1979*a*: 69–72); Cribb (1991: 38–9). The following aspects of the Maasai system are elaborated more fully in Spencer (1988: chs. 1, 2, and 13).

from the desire of his junior partners for full autonomy and herds of their own. In the long term, however, there has to be a limit in the extent to which the wealth accumulated in one generation can accrue to the next. Wealthy families also tend to be large, and the combined herd of a rich man is ultimately dispersed among any number of sons. As an ageing stock-owner loses influence or dies, the success of each son in building up his herd and family lies again essentially in his own hands.

The problem of family growth is one of development during the father's lifetime. Each son aspires to control his own enterprise in his own way, and he should be allowed this independence once he has married and shown himself trustworthy. Delegation to the next generation is seen as a necessary development of an expanding family, with the father always retaining the ultimate right to reassert his authority over any son who abuses his freedom. Sometimes, however, a son's independence is delayed even until he is a relatively mature elder. Faced with a possessive or mistrusting father, the son is expected to concur until considerable tension has built up between them and the case for separation is insuperable. At this point, he can appeal to respected elders outside the family, and the father should defer to their advice. If the son does not appeal, no one will interfere. In the most successful families, sons separate from their father amicably and the spirit of cooperation and unity survives his death, with brothers (his sons) continuing to live in close accord, but as independent stock-owners. At the first sign of tension between them, which is felt to be inevitable sooner or later, the brothers should agree to separate totally. By handling their dispersal with dignity, whenever that point may occur, the extended family can maintain their reputation and 'marriageability'.

It is revealing to compare this Maasai pattern with an analysis of family firms in a Western setting. The close similarities suggest that this cycle of development is quite typical of family enterprises in situations of general growth and by no means unique to pastoralists. A study by Burton Benedict identifies two major points of crisis in the development of the family firm among successful ethnic minorities.[38] The enterprise is typically established by a small businessman with the help of his wife and growing children. What one might term the *first-generation crisis* occurs as the sons reach adulthood and assume that they can handle the business on their own. An astute father will recognize their desire for greater independence and may hand over responsibility for new sectors or branches of the business. This enables the enterprise to grow further and perhaps diversify under the father's overall supervision. Within the business sector of a developing economy, fathers who cannot accommodate their

[38] Benedict (1968). In Benedict's example, there is an element of selective recruitment discarding certain sons (as the family outgrows the business) or eventually bringing in outside expertise (if the business outgrows the family). With limited division of labour, a pastoral economy is more demanding, and traditionally there were no realistic alternatives to the family enterprise for the sons; and no outsider could conceivably be brought in at an executive level.

children's reasonable aspirations and firms that do not expand are exposed to considerable risks. To insure against these hazards, there is also a network of intermarriage and associated credit arrangements between firms within the same ethnic community. Altogether, the boundary between family and business is ill defined: the firm is an integral aspect of the family and of kinship links. As the father ages and dies, the firm's further development depends on the continued loyalty and spirit of cooperation between his sons and the branches of his enterprise. This loyalty is less likely to be maintained among the succeeding generation—that of his grandchildren—who were not brought up together within a single household. As they in their turn mature, it is this loss of loyalty and the divergence of interest that poses the *second-generation crisis*, leading often to severing the formal link with the original enterprise, and the branches become independent firms in their own right.

The parallel with family development among the Maasai is striking, and this appears to be a general pattern among pastoralists in East Africa who talk, live, and marry through cattle. The obsession with cattle, the interplay of herd development with marriage payments, of marriage with family, of family with herd, and the principle of a spirit of trust to resolve minor disagreements are all summarized in the notion of a family enterprise. Sooner or later, even if the herd is not split, sons may want a measure of independence, and inevitably family development is punctuated with a number of potential crisis points, which characteristically vary from society to society. Among the Islamic pastoralists to the north, it is the marriage of each son that typically marks his right to a certain independence. In Dassanetch, this point is reached with the birth of the son's first-born. In Maasai, independence tends to be delayed and the death of the father is in principle the decisive point. The Oromo have a general practice of dispersing sons as a means of resolving rivalries between them and diversifying the household economy. A variety of indeterminate factors may affect the process of succession revealing the underlying ambivalence within and between generations. To draw the parallel with family enterprises elsewhere is no chance metaphor. Pastoralism *is* a family business, with its sights set on growth.[39]

Male Age Systems and the Problems of Generational Succession

Age organizations whereby peers are grouped together to form an age-set within a hierarchy of age-sets have been widely reported, but it is the pastoral societies of East Africa that are associated with the most extensive and elaborate concentration of age-set systems on record. The elaborations often extend to the alignment of generations, and this leads one to look more

---

[39] Nuer: Evans-Pritchard (1951: 14); Howell (1954: 190–3). Oromo: Baxter (1954: 50–1, 320); Dahl (1979*a*: 76, 104, 214–16); Hultin (1979: 285–6). Jie and Turkana: P. H. Gulliver (1955: 55, 135–5). Samburu: Spencer (1965: 60–2). Gogo: Rigby (1969: 187–200). Dassanetch: Almagor (1978: 66).

closely at the implications for family development and the problem of ageing and generational succession. The workings of age-set and generation-set systems, or more simply *age systems*, are considered more fully in Chapter 3. Here, the task is to find a place for this type of organization within the present argument.

The Samburu provide a useful example in which age-sets and family are closely interwoven. Their age system involves young men—*moran*—in a colourful and self-absorbed but separate existence as bachelors until about the age of 30. Meanwhile, the unacknowledged effect of this prolonged bachelorhood is to create a surplus of younger wives for older men, facilitating a high rate of polygyny. This arrangement contrasts with the more typical situation in Africa, whereby the extent of polygyny is rationed by high marriage payments bringing brothers into competition with each other and with their father over their excessive claims on the family herd. Samburu bride-wealth is low, there is no direct competition for marriage cattle, and anyway, with delayed first marriage, fathers are relatively old by the time their most senior sons marry. In this way, the conditions for a first-generation crisis are generally absent among the Samburu. Indeed, a boy cannot be initiated while his father's age-set are just two age-sets senior to the *moran* and responsible for administering the process of their gradual admission to marriageable elderhood. In these ways, the age system protects the family from inter-generational strains: the fathers are responsible neither for the delayed marriages of their sons nor for the duration of this delay. Any strain arising from a prolonged bachelorhood is diverted to relations between the *moran* and their formal patrons and is contained within the age system itself.[40]

Another example illustrates the channelling rather than the avoidance of a first-generation crisis. The Maasai, who are closely related to the Samburu and also have a low bride-wealth, contrast in other ways. Relations within the family are more ambivalent: the father has an almost unchallengeable authority, as we have noted, and there are fewer age-set restrictions on the son's early first marriage, tending to reduce the age difference between many men and their older sons as compared with Samburu. However, following the Maasai son's initiation into his age-set as a warrior, or *moran*, he is expected to join his age mates at a warrior village (*manyata*), and this marks a clean break from his former role as herdboy and lackey. The vicious circle that can too easily build up between an authoritarian father and his adolescent son is broken by a period of enforced separation. The *moran* son returns to the parental village after several years with a firm claim to adult status, although no automatic right to independence. From this point, it is in the father's interest to negotiate a suitable marriage for his son as a development of the joint family. Again this presents the age system as an institutionalized way of controlling

---

[40] Spencer (1965: 133–4; 1978: 137).

strains within the family which are more apparent among the Maasai than Samburu.[41]

It is characteristic of analyses of age systems, however, that they do not link up so tidily with family development. Evans-Pritchard's *The Nuer* is the prototype of functionalist holism; and yet an oddly neglected but carefully argued tailpiece denies any functional relevance of the Nuer age system. In a passage that makes it quite clear that functionalism is not to be taken as dogma, Evans-Pritchard argues: 'the political system and the age system do not seem to be interdependent. Both are consistent in themselves and to some extent overlap and influence one another, but it is easy to conceive of the political system existing without the age-set organization.' The success of the Nuer in raiding and expanding against the Dinka was associated with larger, more cohesive tribes and based on a more elaborate segmentary structure that remained largely intact under European rule; whereas the age system had little relevance for warfare and appeared to have broken down. Yet this argument is incomplete. In what ways did the political and age systems overlap and influence one another? And might not the survival of the age system *until* European rule imply a certain relevance for pre-European warfare after all? It has been widely noted that the segmentary organization displayed inconsistencies and contradictions that have led to various reinterpretations; whereas the age-set system at least appears to have been a consistent integrating feature at the tribal level, structuring respect for age seniority and creating close fellowship among age peers, and associated with particular wars and raids when age-sets would establish their reputation. Among the Nuer, the largest territorial unit for both raiding and age organization was the individual tribe. Among the Dinka, on the other hand, age-sets were more parochial and associated with subtribal leaders (spear-masters). Where growth led to local competition, a rival from the spear-master clan could attract followers by setting up a new age-set as a nucleus of an independent subtribe. Thus, the divisive Dinka 'age system' appears to have been as correlated with their systematic defeats as the more cohesive age system of the Nuer was with their successes.[42]

Following Evans-Pritchard, ethnographers in general have tended to discount the wider implications of age organization. A recurrent feature of the analysis of age systems in this region is the assumption that they are self-contained and self-explanatory. They may be seen as providing a set of peer bonds and a hierarchy of authority that cut across affiliations based on kinship

---

[41] Note that the Maasai *moran*'s sojourn at the warrior village does not mark his final break from his father's control, as my own earlier reading of the literature had led me to assume before undertaking fieldwork among the Maasai (Spencer 1976: 170).

[42] Evans-Pritchard (1940: 249, 253–7, 260); Howell (1951: 258); Lienhardt (1958: 103, 114–15, 131–2; 1961: 216); Gough (1971). It seems that a major first-generation crisis is avoided among the Nuer, with brothers agreeing to marry in strict order of birth, even after their father's death (Evans-Pritchard 1951: 80, 138, 141–3). Competition between them appears to develop in stages only after this point. However, there is too little information on whether this is influenced by their age system or any other pressures beyond the family.

and territory; but this stops short of identifying a direct relevance for the structure of the family in the broadest sense, which is just as concerned with unfolding tensions associated with age and authority.[43] Above all, this does not explain the highly elaborate rules underpinning these systems and to this extent it overlooks the place of such elaborations within the pastoral system. Certainly, there are other accounts of age systems beside the Nuer's that do not at first glance seem to have more than a very general relevance and one would hesitate to presume some deeper significance when the functionalist argument at best is only a working premiss. Nevertheless, where age systems appear to be a stable aspect of relatively stable societies, the search for some comprehensive explanation has an added impetus to account for the apparent resistance to change. Consider the following examples.

(*a*) Monica Wilson (1951) noted that older men married much younger women among the highly polygynous Nyakyusa, and their age villages served to reinforce the sexual avoidances between generations, notably between older men who had handed over power and their daughters-in-law. However, Wilson did not consider the possibility that this segregation between fathers and sons coupled with adelphic succession (between brothers) might also have served to reinforce the monopoly of the older men over cattle and hence brides. This calls into question whether ultimate power had ever been transferred to the junior generation at their 'coming out'.[44]

(*b*) Paul Baxter (1954, 1978) and Asmarom Legesse (1973) have provided independent accounts of the Booran *gada* age system. Baxter portrays *gada* as an engaging philosophical puzzle that is primarily concerned with expensive ritual commitments, but unimportant in daily life and only marginally relevant in political affairs. Legesse, on the other hand, has drawn attention to the role of the *gada* assemblies in governing the country and to the relevance of lineage loyalties in the periodic selection of councillors to these assemblies, but he discounts any further relevance of kinship. Yet both authors provide material that indicates the extent to which *gada* constrains the relationship between elders and their senior sons, reducing the possibility of a first-generation crisis for senior sons.[45]

(*c*) Philip Gulliver (1963) has presented the Arusha age and patrilineal systems as alternative arenas in the competition for power, discounting the possibility of any structured cross-linkages between them. Yet his own case material points to a firm control through the age system as a public domain that effectively contains the dramatic confrontations between rival patrilineages within the private domain: competition over land can be bitter,

---

[43] Evans-Pritchard (1940: 259–60); Bernardi (1952: 325–6; 1985: 147–9); Eisenstadt (1954: 102; 1956: 54); Legesse (1973: 229–30); Baxter and Almagor (1978: 9); Maybury-Lewis (1984: 136).

[44] M. Wilson (1950: 119, 128, 131; 1951: 22–30). For further discussion on the Nyakyusa, see pp. 120–3.

[45] Baxter (1954: 50–1, 54, 56, 65–6, 303, 320, 336; 1978: 152–3, 156, 177); Legesse (1973: 19, 25, 35, 48, 66, 99, 113–14, 159–60, 173, 221, 224–5). For further discussion on *gada*, see pp. 124–6.

but any violence would become a public issue for resolution by the relevant age-sets. At a more domestic level, as the Arusha family develops, Gulliver (1964) has also indicated the extent to which the age system reinforces the father's authority while the sons are still *moran* and then increasingly supports a degree of autonomy once they are elders, while the father through his age-set is forced into semi-retirement.[46]

(*d*) Neville Dyson-Hudson (1966) has described the cycle of conflict between generation-sets within the Karimojong age system, and yet he gives only a brief hint of any tension between generations of men within the family itself. Similarly, in Philip Gulliver's analysis of the Jie and Turkana, who have close affinities with the Karimojong, there is no attempt to link these two aspects of their social organization.[47]

Each of these instances is discussed more fully in Chapter 3, but the Jie deserve closer consideration at this point. Gulliver's analysis of the Jie provides a particularly clear statement dissociating the age system from other aspects of their society. He published two significant accounts of these people: on their age and generation organization (1953); on the dynamics of the extended family of males in relation to their herds (1955); and also, incidentally, a separate note on the independent domain of women as indispensible cultivators and food producers (1954). The irrelevance of the men's age system is stressed in the two major texts: 'Initiation and membership of age-sets has extremely little significance outside ritual affairs . . . [and] little direct connection with either kinship or property rights.'[48] These rituals concern periodic blessings linked to meat-feasting among men where seniority demands respect and stems from the order of initiation at about the age of 20, which is determined by an intricate set of rules. Even mild-mannered elders make a point of emphasizing their age seniority by harassing their juniors in a peremptory manner and demanding that they carry out menial tasks.

According to Gulliver's earlier account, asserting a pecking order in this way has no relevance outside the ritual context of the Jie age system. And yet a pecking order within the extended family is also implied in his later account in relation to the problems of building up substantial bride-wealth payments. It is surely significant that he lists an *identical* set of rules that govern the order in which brothers and cousins have rights in stock from the joint herd for their

[46] P. H. Gulliver (1963; 1964: 215–16, 228); Spencer (1976: 160–8). The systematic pairing of Arusha lineages at various levels of segmentation (P. H. Gulliver 1963: 110–12) precludes any collateral third parties who might have an incentive to mediate in any land dispute, and this could give an added significance to the role of the age system in containing violence.

[47] N. Dyson-Hudson (1966: 170–1); P. H. Gulliver (1953, 1955, 1958). (See also nn. 49 and 50 below, and pp. 99–119, for further details.) Cf. also Tornay (1979: 307–29), who acknowledges a certain role of age seniority among the related Nyangatom, but (like Gulliver) relegates the generational base of age grading to the sphere of religion and superstructure.

[48] P. H. Gulliver (1955: 11; cf. 1953: 163–5).

marriages. This occurs at about the age of 30, typically ten years or so after the same rules of precedence govern the order of their initiation into the age system. As against Gulliver's analysis, one is led to infer that the emphasis on young men's respect for seniority within the age system reinforces the ranking of brothers and cousins within the extended family. This is a highly polygynous society, and the age system appears to instil a queue discipline between close kin in their prolonged wait for marriage as the family herd fluctuates with each successive allocation of cattle for brides or of sisters for cattle. Within this regime the family survives the death of the father. Marriages of the next generation continue to be jointly arranged, sharing the heavy burden of bride-wealth. By maintaining this queue discipline, a first-generation crisis is avoided and the extended family continues to keep together as a joint enterprise. Eventually, it divides as the principal segments drift apart, at a point more or less corresponding to a second-generation crisis.[49]

This interpretation is further supported by Gulliver's linked account of the Turkana family and age system, again published in separate parts (1955, 1958). According to their oral traditions, the Turkana are descended from the Jie, having migrated to a harsher environment that led to a higher degree of dispersal and nomadism and the breakdown of their age organization, after losing respect for age and seniority. Correspondingly, the Turkana family does not normally build up into a large enterprise that survives the death of the stock-owner. In contrast to the Jie, the family is frequently confronted with a first-generation crisis as the father is challenged by successive sons seeking to assert their independence prematurely.[50] Thus there appears to be a breakdown both of constraints within the age system *and* of queue discipline within the family. The two appear to be positively linked among the Jie consistent with their absences among the Turkana.

Clearly, the various examples suggest that age systems have a variety of possible roles within different societies. A consistent thread, however, is of an institution controlled by older men that lessens strains within the paternal family between fathers and growing sons. The first generation crisis is defused by delaying the maturation of the sons; and this extends to late first marriages in the more polygynous societies, thereby diverting strains from the family where fathers, sons, and brothers compete indirectly for a limited number of brides.

Among the pastoral peoples of East Africa are three important exceptions to this model that test the more basic argument: the Turkana, the Cushitic-

---

[49] P. H. Gulliver (1953: 154, 160–3; 1955: 63–71, 86–9, 119–23). Cf. Lamphear (1976: 154–5). Lamphear (1976: 38) also notes that the age of initiation in Jie 'depends largely on the number of sons and the number of available livestock of his father'. In other words, richer families can afford early initiations for their sons, while poorer families may delay. However, this would apply also to their marriages for the same reasons, and hence early or late initiations would correspond to early or delayed marriages within each family.

[50] P. H. Gulliver (1955: 5, 135–46; 1958: 919–21). Cf. Lamphear (1992: 14, 17, 20–1).

speaking pastoralists in the north-east, and the outlying Hima in the west. The
Turkana have already been considered and the apparent breakdown of their age
system highlights the argument concerning the Jie. The Cushitic-speakers,
such as the Booran and Rendille, have a radically different type of family
structure based on primogeniture, favouring eldest sons and restricting
polygyny; and the Booran *gada* age system supports this characteristic feature,
controlling also the strains of succession between generations.

The Hima are widely scattered over western Uganda and beyond, on the far
side of Lake Victoria, where they have a tradition of close association with the
ruling dynasties of earlier times. They diverge from this model in nearly every
way. There is no age organization, no delay in first marriage, and a low rate of
polygyny. The first-generation crisis, as portrayed by Yitzchak Elam (1973), is
not of fully mature sons who are frustrated by the delay in marriage, but of
youths who are tempted to wander off to assert their freedom. It is in response
to this that a Hima father arranges an early marriage for each son, involving him
in a daily domestic routine that will tie him down. There is in this a distant
parallel with Maasai practice, whereby the marriage of each retiring *moran* is
arranged by his father as a logical development of his family. The extended
form of patriarchal control among the Hima in this respect appears no less
marked than among the Maasai, although it ties down much younger men.
However, in total constrast to any society considered so far, the Hima father has
sexual access to the wives he has arranged for his sons, and to this extent there
is a vicarious form of polygyny. The Hima are different from the other
pastoralists considered here, but in a way that lends support to the broad
model. The first-generation crisis among pastoralists is clearly more widespread than polygyny or age systems.[51]

Strategies for Growth

The notion of pastoralism as an enterprise dedicated to growth is expressed
in Ioan Lewis's claim that pastoralists are 'some of the thickest-skinned
capitalists on earth'. The terms 'cattle' and 'capital' in our own language
have a common origin as property and relate to 'stock' as a source of investment. The derivation of these terms from the Latin for 'head' or the chief
part of property bears coincidentally on a Maasai saying cited by Hollis: ' "One
cow resembles a man's head." They mean by this that if a man has a cow,
which he looks after and tends, it bears and by so doing enables him to live,
for he can marry and have children, and thus become rich.' Evans-Pritchard
has noted a similar attitude among the Nuer, as has Ian Cunnison among
the Baggara.[52] Cunnison's account also reveals an Islamic ethic towards pasto-

---

[51] Elam (1973: 186–9).
[52] I. M. Lewis (1975: 437); Hollis (1905: 298–9); Cunnison (1966: 31); Evans-Pritchard (1951: 89;
1956: 259). Cf. Schneider (1968: 441); Klima (1970: 109); Goldschmidt (1972).

ralism that is strikingly close to Weber's description of the calvinist spirit of capitalism:

Strong pressures exist on all men to acquire and maintain a herd. Balancing the belief that God is the ultimate dispenser of all things and that if one has no cattle then God has willed it so, there is the precept that initiative, careful husbanding of resources, and puritan thrift . . . are the requisites for building a herd. . . . By being industrious and thrifty, anyone with God's will, can own cattle.[53]

Pastoralism, then, is a major exception to Sahlins's contention that family-based economies spurn the accumulation of surplus. In elaborating his notion of a single 'domestic mode of production', Sahlins does not consider pastoralism in detail, but cites evidence assuming that youths were as indolent among the Maasai, for instance, as in non-pastoral societies: they were fighters as young men and only settled down as producers later when they acquired families of their own. This completely overlooks the point made by so many other writers that the aspirations of warriorhood in East Africa are to acquire cattle.[54] Here, bearing in mind what Cunnison refers to as 'the cattle urge' and Evans-Pritchard as an 'obsession' with cattle, one is tempted to take a cue from Robert Paine (1971) and coin the term 'rudimentary capitalism'—a single-minded devotion to the growth of the herd. The parallels with capitalism are intriguing, but a single term such as 'rudimentary capitalism' falls into the same trap as a 'domestic mode of production'. It highlights one aspect of pastoralism, and to this extent glosses over the various domains of interaction that comprise pastoralism in East Africa. To express this differently, pastoralism, like any other mode of livelihood, extends to a complex range of activities, but this is nevertheless a structured complexity and can usefully be broken down into components—domains—that are related, even opposed up to a point, and relevant to different contexts. The exchange of women and cattle is one of these, the parallel growth of the family and herd a second, and the activities of younger men a third.

One may identify two principal strategies for building up herds which I refer to here as *predation* and *peaceful husbandry* respectively. Predation depends upon the exploits of younger men as successful warriors to augment the herds through raiding, and it is they who effectively control this strategy. Peaceful husbandry depends on diligent herding and is controlled by the older men as individual stock-owners, with the younger men held responsible for defending the herds and maintaining the tribal claim to its territories and its vital resources of pasture and water.

The balance between these two strategies in the past can only be surmised. It seems likely that predation played an important role in times of famine and

[53] Weber (1930: 162–3); Cunnison (1966: 31).
[54] Sahlins (1974: 54) and Ingold (1980: 217). But cf. Maasai: Thomson (1885: 436); Kipsigis: Peristiany (1939: 163–4); Nuer: Evans-Pritchard (1940: 50); Karimojong: N. Dyson-Hudson (1966: 51); Samburu: Spencer (1973: 97); Turkana: Broch-Due (1990: 150–1).

political turmoil, and especially during periods of expansion among the Nuer, Maasai, and Oromo, enabling them to build up their herds rapidly. The classic example of the Nuer amounts to an ideal type, and Raymond Kelly's (1985) historical elaboration of Evans-Pritchard's and Lienhardt's analyses of this region incorporates various more recent interpretations. Oral traditions suggest that the swampy region of the central Nile basion was once occupied by agro-pastoralists from whom the Nuer and Dinka are now derived. In Kelly's model, these were proto-Dinka whose values were oriented towards their cattle, but they depended heavily on their crops. Cultivation above the flood level was a more land-intensive source of food, and this limited the land available for grazing during the wet season and hence the sizes of their herds. As the floods receded, cattle would be driven to the dry-season pastures, while the villages remained on the high ground. The development of larger communities among these proto-Dinka was inhibited by local rivalries, and any population growth led instead to the emergence of new groupings. The Nuer appear to have arisen as a localized mutation within this setting, relying on larger herds and wider collaboration. Whatever the reason for this initial switch, possibly a temporary demographic imbalance, it led to a succession of adaptations. With more cattle, the Nuer had less land for wet-season cultivation and hence a need to disperse. Larger herds also made it necessary to share more distant dry-season pastures, and hunger drove them to raid for more cattle. In ranging further afield, the tendency among the Nuer was to form alliances rather than raid one another and this led to the formation of larger fighting units and tribes. There was a certain jostling for land and advantage, but the major thrust was against the Dinka, who were only organized at a local level and were overwhelmed by the sheer numerical superiority of Nuer raiding parties. The urge to raid the Dinka was bound up with the emerging concept of Nuer identity as a separate people. The thrust of Kelly's analysis is to show how this had a snowball effect, especially eastwards, systematically encroaching on the eastern Dinka, expanding into their dry-season pastures, raiding them for cattle, driving them away from their wet-season land, adopting Dinka captives as Nuer, and thereby increasing the Nuer population and their need for yet more pasture and cattle. In concert with this trend, the Nuer superstructure adapted to limit the instabilities of larger political units, linking dominant lineages to a broader segmentary structure, extending the distribution of bride-wealth and the constraints on marriage, elaborating mechanisms of dispute settlement, and developing a more integrated age-set system. The effect on the Dinka was to confirm their weakness, making them even more dependent on cultivation and local pastures, more vulnerable to raids from rival Dinka, and less able to unite into wider alliances. In this way, rivalries between local Dinka communities limited the growth of their political system; while the shift towards external predation among the Nuer appears to have accompanied a transformation of their internal structure.[55]

[55] R. C. Kelly (1985: 103–5, 120–3, 157–60, 174–9, 194–226, and *passim*).

A particularly vivid insight into the predatory mode is given by John Lamphear (1992) in his oral history of the Turkana, who were one of the last peoples of the region to be pacified. The Turkana lived in an unusually arid area and raiding their neighbours for stock to maintain their herds may well have been a necessary means of survival as they expanded their territories southwards. In contrast to the Maasai, whose warfare appears to have been tightly organized through the age system in association with their Prophets, Turkana raiding was altogether more spontaneous but apparently no less impressive. Raids were initiated by war leaders in consultation with diviners whose joint reputations were established and maintained by their string of successes. The personal charisma of these leaders provided a driving force that attracted followers from a wider area, building up to an almost unstoppable force that needed to attain a quick and decisive victory before dispersing. The environment could not sustain a slow and organized build-up. The very spontaneity of this pattern meant that their enemies could not anticipate the thrust of any raid to muster their defence; and the wide dispersal of the Turkana did not lend itself to counter-raiding, as the British came to realize.[56]

Contemporary accounts of the Turkana stress the continued importance of raiding to establish their herds among young men, which stems from the poverty of their environment and competition within the family that was noted earlier. However, it is clear that this element of predation is (and presumably was) complemented by an elaborate web of mutual support as an aspect of peaceful husbandry, comparable with the Dassanetch pattern. The shift in Turkana away from the bonds of age organization and extended family has been towards individualism only in the sense that the independent stock-owner has more freedom to choose those with whom he will share his chances. It is a shift towards the importance of sustaining trust and confidence in a network of stock relations of all kinds, and the extensive chain of bride-wealth gifts and debts is simply one aspect of a broader pattern. It is not just that types of stock are diversified and loaned to those in need as a form of insurance, but that this is a major thrust of their economy, which extends to camels. The pared-down family enterprise is part of an informal network of mutual assistance, stretching across ecological zones that are suited to different types of stock and herding routine. Each stock-owner specializes within one of these zones up to a point, having dispersed a considerable portion of his herd and taken on herding responsibilities for others as part of a wider pattern of symbiosis. Ultimately, the success of such an arrangement hinges on the ability of each Turkana to build up his credibility. This is measured not so much by the size of his herd as the extent to which he is engaged in the constant transfer of animals for the

---

[56] Lamphear (1992: 22, 71–2, 86, 163–4). Cf. Hjort (1981*b*: 56–7) on the continuing southward migration of the Turkana; Merker (1904: 90–101) on the Maasai; and Hultin (1979: 292–3), who notes the increasing role of war leaders and local men of influence as the *gada* age system broke down in some outlying areas of the Oromo.

benefit of his network, displaying his trust in others and theirs in him. There is a fluid nature of association, and relations have to be constantly cultivated through gifts or they lapse. Security lies in being actively involved in this give and take at all times, and it is the most active stock-owners in this sense who attract further friends and increase their access to available resources, ranging from labour to distant wells and grazing. When disaster strikes, it is a well-connected victim who can most readily look to others for help, and their credibility in turn hinges on their ready response to his sudden loss.[57]

The Turkana survive as pastoralists in an unusually arid area, and it is by no means clear how far this symbiotic diversification of different types of stock is a direct adaptation to the pressures of their environment or a response to the need to contain the tendency towards predation, at least among themselves—an argument that echoes Durkheim's analysis of the causes of the division of labour in a remote setting.[58] The earlier analysis concerning other pastoralists in the region stressed the pattern of alliances beyond the family enterprise through various institutional arrangements which could be sustained only through peace and a spirit of trust and confidence. Among the Turkana, it is this element of wider collaboration in peaceful husbandry that is the more critical because of the fragility of the family enterprise and the continuing brittleness of their borders with neighbouring peoples.

A point to stress is that pre-colonial raiding between pastoral groups would only have affected the distribution of cattle and not the overall pattern of growth. Any desire to initiate raids following the formation of a new age-set, say, would shift over time from one tribal group to another with no clear winner. In fact, some of the fiercest rivalry during the period of Maasai pre-eminence appears to have been within the Maasai cluster itself, when the civil-war gains of one faction would have been the losses of another. Similar large-scale in-fighting also appears to have characterized relations within the Karimojong–Jie–Turkana cluster.[59]

While warriors from poorer families especially could have been more motivated to raid, it was the elders as stock-owners, and especially the wealthiest elders, who had most to gain from peace. A striking feature of accounts of warfare throughout the region is the local conventions that sought to govern it as a bounded domain, limiting the damage inflicted on other domains and on exchange relations between neighbouring peoples that extended from trading to a degree of intermigration and intermarriage. The most successful predators—including the Maasai, Turkana, Oromo, and Nuer—also comprised fed-

[57] P. H. Gulliver (1955: 196–222); Broch-Due (1990: 148–53, 165); Storas (1990: 138–9). Cf. Lamphear (1992: 253); Goldschmidt (1972: 190, 198–9); Almagor (1978: 108); and Parkin (1991: 58–70).

[58] Durkheim (1964: 269–70). Cf. Bates and Lees (1977: 825–6).

[59] Maasai: Waller (1976: 532–4). Jie and Karimojong: N. Dyson-Hudson (1966: 239–60); Lamphear (1976: 202–62).

erations aimed at limiting in-fighting.[60] To the extent that such federal arrangements held and the younger men could be restrained to keep their raiding
within limits, this would lessen the likelihood of reprisals and a wider escalation
of disorder when the herds would be doubly at risk—from raiding and from
restricted opportunities for grazing and migration.

There was also a very pragmatic reason for preferring peaceful husbandry.
This strategy appears to have been a far more efficient way of increasing herds,
at least in areas that were less arid than the Turkana district. Kelly's analysis of
the extreme instance of the Nuer accepts a natural annual growth rate through
calving of 3.5 per cent, whereas their period of maximum territorial expansion
(as a measure of predation) amounted to only 2 per cent per annum. A rough
estimate from my own notes on the Maasai suggests that typically a *moran*
would have had to rustle about seven cattle *each year* to compare with the more
successful years of peaceful breeding, whereas the majority of *moran* would
probably not have acquired that number by raiding in their entire careers as
warriors.[61] Peaceful husbandry would seem to have been the more realistic
strategy and associated with the control of the elders over younger men, while
predation was perhaps more significant in maintaining tribal prestige and
claims to territory during periods of unrest. Once Maasai expansion had
reached its territorial limit, it was peaceful husbandry with adequate defence
that probably held the more consistent promise of growth, and predation
appears to have been a deviant form from the elders' point of view, giving some
young men a better start, although at the expense of elders elsewhere. In this
way, the structure of conflict between older men who controlled ritual within
the age system and younger men who were constrained bore (and bears) on the
balance between the two strategies.

Within peaceful husbandry, there is a sub-domain that perhaps has the best
claim to the title 'rudimentary capitalism'. This is the employment of impoverished clients by stock-owners whose herds have outgrown their families,
helping to maintain the herds and accumulate yet more wealth. This has been
widely reported and is becoming increasingly widespread, but there is no
reason to assume that it is a recent innovation. The way into pastoralism for

---

[60] Nuer: Evans-Pritchard (1940: 131). Oromo: Baxter (1954: 53; 1979: 70). Dassanetch: Almagor (1979: 126–8, 141). Maasai: Jacobs (1979: 49). Meru: Fadiman (1982: 41–2). Turkana: Lamphear (1992: 14–15, 269). Cf. Peristiany (1939: 161); Galaty and Bonte (1991: 17); Sobania (1991: 118, 128, 135-6).

[61] R. C. Kelly (1985: 104, 227). Extrapolating from data collected among the Samburu, it seems likely that each ruling age-group of Maasai *moran* would comprise about 6% of the total population. With, say, about 12 cattle per person and a growth rate through husbandry of about 3.4% per annum (see n. 63 below), the natural growth rate per active *moran* in the population would be 12 × 3.4%/6%, that is 6.8 cattle per annum. Richard Waller (1976: 552) has collated data on cattle gains by Maasai *moran* working as levies for fourteen armed government punitive expeditions between 1893 and 1905. Under these very favourable conditions, which provided a quite unprecedented and unrepeatable advantage, the gains for each raid averaged 8.5 cattle and 25.3 sheep and goats per *moran*. Even assuming that certain *moran* could conceivably have been involved in every one of these expeditions, their annual gains would still have averaged only 9.1 cattle and 27.2 sheep and goats.

those who have no stock (and the way back for those who have lost theirs) is as herdsmen. There is less trust for non-kin, and reward for their services apart from their upkeep is meagre, but beyond this hard bargain lies the ultimate possibility of founding a herd of their own, notably if they can cultivate the trust of their patron. A variation of this arrangement occurs when poorer stock-owners with large families attach themselves to wealthy households, sharing the burden of herding in exchange for food and giving their own herds a better chance to grow.[62]

In this ideology of growth, there is a resilient optimism. A stockless herdsman expects ultimately to be rewarded. Just one immature ox could in time be large enough for some ritual meat feast and be exchanged for a young heifer or even an ageing cow, which in turn could be the founder of a herd. Growth is seen as life, propitious, and God-given; while loss is ill destined, malignant, and believed to imply a withholding of God's blessing, ultimately spelling disaster. Even a balance between these is regarded with some misgiving.

However, growth in pastoralism as elsewhere is bedevilled by an inherent contradiction, for it can be sustained only up to a point. The symbiotic balance sets a limit on the extent to which the cattle population can outgrow the human population and both are constrained by the poverty of their environment. A herd can become too large to manage, especially in semi-arid conditions.[63] The effort to build up herds and families implicitly brings stock-owners into competition, even in peaceful husbandry. One man's success in wives and cattle is a loss for others, since wives, grazing, and water will be harder to find. With a general increase of the total stock population, there is more hunger for the herds, a greater likelihood of some debilitating cattle epidemic, and widely shared hardship. Growth is an ideal that destroys its attainment. With no notion of diversifying capital outside the stock economy, a purely pastoralist enterprise has nowhere else to go other than up or down; and there has to be an upper limit on success. Even this does not allow for any degradation of the soil due to overgrazing, which implies diminishing herds in the long term. These are problems to which we will return in Part III of this work.

[62] Maasai: Native Labour Commission (1913: 196); Spencer (1988: 11); Kituyi (1990: 66, 149, 218). Dinka: Howell (1951: 246). Karimojong: N. Dyson-Hudson (1966: 50, 68–9, 85–6). Gogo: Rigby (1969: 54 n.). Rendille: Spencer (1973: 40). Oromo: Dahl (1979a: 77–9; 1979b: 272–3); Ensminger (1992: 114–21); Baxter (1993: 155). Babito *c*.1800: Packard (1981: 79). Samburu: Hjort (1981b: 53–8); Sperling (1987a: 6–7). The redistribution of children between households as temporary measures or fostering in the longer term may be regarded as means to the same end (Shell-Duncan 1994; Spencer 1988: 45).

[63] Spencer (1965: 11, 282–3); Cunnison (1966: 68–9); Goldschmidt (1972: 198); Dahl (1979a: 81). The growth rates of herds may vary considerably depending on the local conditions. Dahl and Hjort (1976: 61–6) consider circumstances that might give a growth rate even above 10%, but suggest that around 3.4% is more typical. Evidence collected among the Samburu reflects the close symbiotic relationship between the pastoralists and their herds, and suggests that in the longer term the cattle population can grow no faster than the human population, which was currently of the order of 2.3% (Spencer 1973: 10; and see ch. 7 n. 17). Cf. also Stenning (1959: 147–72) and Frantz (1975: 340) on the Fulani.

The Two Moods of the Sawtooth Profile

Two popular and contrasting views of pastoralism in East Africa together comprise an ecological balance of sorts between growth and loss, up and down. The first expresses an ecological concern over the mounting pressure of stock on the land that could ultimately lead to the destruction of the environment; and the second is the widely publicized effects of each serious drought as it decimates herds of cattle throughout the region. These are the dual aspects of their high-profit/high-risk 'rudimentary capitalism'. Together they describe a sawtooth profile of steady growth offset at irregular intervals by a sharp and devastating loss. The optimistic ideology of growth persists regardless of the evidence to the contrary, and it is dogged by the inevitability of the next downturn.

Tim Ingold (1980) has argued that this sawtooth profile of growth and disaster is especially characteristic of pastoralism. The natural growth of undomesticated herds in the wild is stunted by preditors, and the young and infirm are particularly at risk. Under domestication, culling is more selective, and younger and breeding stock are carefully protected, leading to an unnaturally rapid rate of growth towards the next crisis of overpopulation.[64] Clearly, any parallel between the sawtooth pattern and the boom and bust cycles of confidence in the market economy in which overheating alternates with a periodic collapse is superficial, for the underlying forces are quite dissimilar. Nevertheless, the metaphor of a rudimentary capitalism can be pursued in another way by comparing the changing fortunes of husbandry with the growth of Western capitalism as perceived by Max Weber (1930). His analysis identified a changing mood. Capitalism in its more exacting form arose out of an earlier more relaxed approach, regulated through a network of trust and established interests. With the transition to the more individualist form of capitalism, there was a new mood, a stern ethic linked to a sense of religious fervour, and a positive attitude towards initiative, innovation, and the use of time. This was the 'spirit of capitalism'. It did not last, but it bore the seeds of the more routinized capitalism as we know it today. Without attempting to follow Weber's analysis in detail, one can postulate here a '*laissez-faire* capitalism', an 'ethical capitalism', and 'modern capitalism'. Very loosely, there are parallels with all three among East African pastoralists today, but there is an interaction between a *laissez-faire* and an ethical approach instead of a transition from one form to another, with the third as a recent innovation, building up with the cash economy.

From the point of view of a *laissez-faire* approach, this corresponds to the slow upward growth along the sawtooth profile. Here, one has the popular view

---

[64] For a comprehensive critique of the literature on this pattern, see Ingold (1980: 32–48). Cf. Allan (1965: 315–18); Mbithi and Wisner (1973: 118); Spencer (1974: 419); Hjort (1982: 12–14); Cribb (1991: 24).

of day-to-day pastoralism with a vested interest that resists change. There is little scope for innovation in traditional terms, but rather established patterns ranging from herd management to exchanges involving stock, and a relatively comfortable existence for many. There is no concept that 'time' is a valuable resource that *must* be utilized, converting it into further capital through productive labour. In normal times and with shrewd management, the herd as capital will automatically increase, and pastoralism has the appearance of an indolent way of life that underutilizes its labour potential, rather as in Sahlins's vision of the 'domestic mode of production'. There is gain with no toil in the fields; and such work as is necessary can be undertaken to a considerable extent as a form of relaxed supervision and ideally by boys. The familiar claim that pastoralism is an easy and rewarding pastime evokes the image of elders with time on their hands gossiping, quite often even drinking these days, and of *moran* freed from essential herding duties. In this *laissez-faire* mood there is little obvious advantage to be gained from further effort, and no suggestion that the growth of one man's herd is at the expense of others.

As against this, there is an immediate switch to a more demanding mood at times of crisis: when stock have strayed or are threatened by a predator; when discipline breaks down among thirsty herds at a water point; when some epidemic is spread through an area by the movements of cattle; or when drought sets in and hunger prevails. At such times, there is a switch from husbandry to predation only in the sense that an uncompromising response is necessary to meet the predation of nature itself. It is the most active young men who hold the front line against crisis; but the expectations for vigilance and prompt action extend to the community at large in defence of their herds. When need is pressing, there is an ethical response in the sense that no time should be lost or opportunity missed and there is no tolerance for anyone— even a visitor—who does not respond to the call of the moment. Within each household, there is a shift of mood, a dedication to the survival of family and herd. If both can survive the rigours of drought and unexpected crisis, then their joint growth during easier times is assured.

The second mood is never far from the surface, and it shows a constant awareness of the possibility of a downturn from growth simply through negligence. Animals may be lost or threatened at any point without warning. Any straying cow may be the next growth-point in the herd, or even the last to survive; only God knows. Even when some informal gathering of elders has every appearance of being relaxed and underproductive, the gossip that one might associate with the *laissez-faire* mood and time to kill is by no means always idle. It gives each elder a better notion of a wide variety of facts that may be relevant when next he has to make some decision on where to send his herd for grazing or where to go when it is time to migrate. It is the elders who have the experience of managing their herds and families through previous episodes of hardship, and any shred of information gleaned in gossip may have significance for coping with the next episode. Also through gossip, each elder adds to the thrust of public opinion. Such relaxed conversation frequently draws attention to the hazards, the unexpected misfortunes of one elder, the habitual drunkenness of another and his immoral neglect of his herds, the miscalculations of a third who has recently migrated, the dilemmas facing a fourth, and so on. It is productive gossip, and it is couched in tones of convinced approval or disapproval.

The ethical mood intrudes on the *laissez-faire* mood as an undertone. It is backed by the uncompromising forces of public opinion which come to the surface in times of crisis. It is closely linked with the concern for reputation within the community. To the extent that pastoralism bears on marriage transactions, credits, and debts, individuals and families have to be very marriageable and creditworthy. The wider group is a moral community in a very stern sense. Everyone is expected to show a devotion towards family and herd, and a respect for local opinion. The Maasai show no tolerance for a man who is ungenerous with food or who squanders away his stock. The man who does not care would not get a wife: he is a wastrel. Among the Turkana, any lack of commitment is reflected in a failure to build up a personal network of associates, isolating the individual and placing him most at risk when disaster strikes.[65]

These two contrasting moods among pastoralists reflect the contradiction of growth noted earlier. It is as if there is a constantly nagging awareness of the sawtooth profile. The relaxed *laissez-faire* mood accords with the steady growth of herds without undue effort on the part of their owners, and this is seen as the benign face of normality. The sharp switch to an intensive concern for the herd or for even just one cow in a moment of crisis reveals an awareness of the cruel downturn of fortune that can strike at any time. This alternation is not so much the sawtooth profile in itself as a recurrent anticipation of the real thing. Weber portrayed the successive moods of capitalism as irreversible; whereas among these pastoral societies there appears to be a reversible mixture that shifts with context, and the ethical mood is switched on at every crisis.

Conclusion: The Hierarchy of Domains among East African Pastoralists

Accounts of pastoralism in East Africa provide a rich variety of ethnographic detail, but also the recurrence of certain themes that bear on pastoralism as a family enterprise in a demanding and competitive environment. Analytically, it is useful to identify clusters of activity appropriate to different situations. Among the Maasai, for instance, one may discern at least five domains within their traditional economy: peaceful husbandry controlled by the elders;

---

[65] Maasai: Spencer (1988: 249–50). Turkana: Broch-Due (1990: 153–4).

predatory raiding for cattle conducted by the *moran* as warriors; the trading of pastoral products for other goods undertaken by the women; and to these one may add the employment of stockless herdsmen in times of affluence when the herd had outgrown the family; and foraging as a last resort following some disaster to the herd.

Coining a term from economic anthropology, the traditional domains of pastoral economies may be regarded as *spheres of exchange*. Thus, the exchange of women for cattle persists as a strategic feature of peaceful husbandry and it relates to a broad network of credit and debt in stock. In Fig. 1.1 this network was shown to extend even to a complex of spheres of exchange that defines the relationship between two tribal groups. While the ramifications of the cattle–women exchange network are as wide as the possibilities of intermarriage, this sphere is constrained by local conventions in other respects, and this gives rise to a halo of borderline activities that cause concern. Unfulfilled pledges following a marriage are a source of friction. Divorce involves an attempt to reverse the flow of stock along the network which may be practicable only up to a point and leads to further friction. At the outer margins of marriageability, stockless clients who tend the cattle of richer men are despised, and even more despised is any wastrel who has squandered his herd and is reduced to some form of foraging. Crossing the boundary of this sphere, cattle are only exchanged for the sheep and goats as a regrettable necessity, or nowadays for cash, and again reluctantly unless it is to purchase more productive additions to the herd. To this extent, cattle-ownership remains an ideal, and the boundaries surrounding this traditional sphere of exchange persist, even if they are also flexible. The point at issue is not that the spheres are absolutely discrete or that boundaries separating them are in every case impenetrable—there may be ways round them or across them—but that any contravention is an anomaly. These are moral boundaries concerned with upholding tradition. Resentment following some breach of convention is also a critical concern over precedent, even arousing a certain apprehensiveness of misfortune. Innovations threaten to erode some aspect of tradition, undermining stability and ultimately the structure of status and power. In contrast to an amoral and free market system, the structuring of economic activities into broadly separate spheres is no less than the moral structure of society itself.

Among pastoral societies throughout the region, the contradiction between the domains of peaceful husbandry and predatory raiding suggests an alternative theoretical model. This is the neo-Marxist concern with the articulation between *modes of production* within any economic system.[66] These modes are associated, respectively, with the authority of a stock-owner over his family enterprise which is the nub of peaceful husbandry, and with relations of exploitation between predatory raiders and the producers on whom they prey. It was

[66] Asad (1979: 425–6); Meillassoux (1972: 98); Dupré and Rey (1973: 132); Foster-Carter (1978: 216).

the predatory mode that dominated in the relationship between the Nuer and Dinka. However, *within* any tribal group there tends to be a presumption that peaceful husbandry will prevail among elders as the dominant mode, although always with the possibility of more unsettled periods when the initiative may slip to younger men in their prime, asserting the predatory mode. At certain times, in protest against their domination by elders, women also may seize the initiative and muster their numbers to reverse the social order. On such occasions, they claim control over their own fertility and domestic affairs, and confront the elders with a further antithetical mode that briefly occupies the central arena.[67]

Various examples may be cited to elaborate ways in which modes of production and spheres of exchange overlap within the indigenous systems considered here. Where women are exchanged for cattle, for instance, the notion of a sphere of exchange extends to the propriety of relations between families and to the ideal of marriageability itself. From another point of view (broadly following Meillassoux), it is elders engaged in this exchange who claim to own both the women and the cattle as commodities, extending to their reproductive capacities, and this bears on *family enterprise* as a way of describing the dominant mode of production in these societies.[68] Again, in relation to age organization, the elaborate etiquette of sharing among age mates fits easily into the notion of each age-set as a sphere of exchange. From the point of view of the hierarchy of age-sets, on the other hand, this reveals the power of the elders to use this system to control younger men, the rate at which they mature, and ultimately the problem of succession between generations; and this has the characteristics of a mode of production (and reproduction) beyond the family.

Taking account of this vista of activities, the vexed notion of some 'pastoral mode of production' can be avoided. Pastoralists resort to a variety of modes, none of which is unique to pastoralism, just as they engage in various spheres of exchange. Exchange and production are overlapping concepts, and to refer to spheres of one or modes of the other is to shift the analytical focus from a value system that defines relations of trust and expectation between quasi-equal exchange partners in the first instance, to power relations and fundamental claims to property ownership between unequals in the second. Bringing together these analytical concepts expands the significance and complexity of the thresholds between domains. On the one hand, there are the ethical implications of anomalous transactions between spheres of exchange. On the other hand, the articulation between modes of production raises questions of a hierarchy of dominance between them. The boundaries are both ethically sensitive

---

[67] Spencer (1965: 228–9; 1988: 200–7); Rigby (1968: 159–60); Klima (1970: 89–94); Obeler (1985: 66); Ensminger (1987: 43).
[68] Cf. Meillassoux (1964; 1972: 100–1).

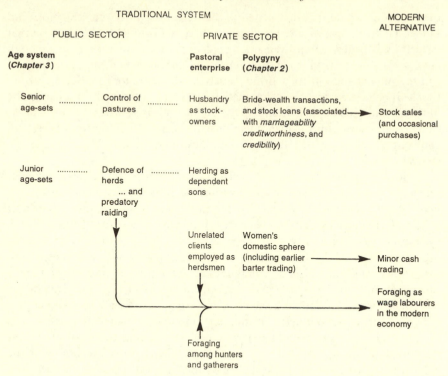

FIG. 1.2. *The configuration of domains typical among pastoralists in East Africa and the transition towards the cash economy*

and concerned with differentials of power. The analytical task initially is to identify the relationships between the domains which may involve a certain hierarchy of prestige (Bohannan 1955) or certain ambiguities that provide scope for exploitation and change, shifting the boundaries (Barth 1967).[69]

Fig. 1.2 suggests a typical configuration of domains that reasonably describes pastoralist societies such as the Maasai. With regard to the domains controlled by older men, polygyny is a supreme ideal and control over cattle and women is the means towards this end. One purpose of building a herd and raising daughters is for marriage, either in direct exchange or as a speculative investment.[70] To this end, peaceful husbandry is clearly preferable to predation in times of peace, and dominates in so far as younger men are dominated by

[69] Bohannan (1955: 62–5); Barth (1967: 165).

[70] Marriage may be regarded as a more speculative investment among the Maasai, Samburu, and Dassanetch, where the marriage payments are protracted as compared with a greater emphasis on direct exchange among the Nuer, Dinka, Jie, Karimojong, Turkana, Giriama, Gogo, and Mursi. See nn. 7, 9, and 13 for references.

elders. However, to the extent that younger men are at first impoverished and can assert their independence, predation offers a tempting alternative. Moreover, defence against predation is a necessary part of peaceful husbandry: the warriors who raid neighbouring tribes to augment their own herds must also be prepared to defend them, and the boundary between predation and peaceful husbandry is also in a sense intertribal. It is in this context that it is useful to note the existence of age systems as a characteristic feature of this region. Typically, these are linked to the tensions between older and younger men, both in the monopoly of the seniors over marriage and in containing the excesses associated with warriorhood among the juniors.

Turning to other domains, the employment of stockless clients as herdsmen is regarded as degrading and the rewards are meagre. However, if a client can emerge from several years of service with a small herd and a family of his own, then he will have transcended the boundary that marks him off from other stock-owners. The comparative rareness of this form of clientage reflects the ambiguous position of an outsider entrusted with the family herd. There can be no guarantee of his commitment and this limits the exploitation of labour beyond the family and hence the scope for inequality in pastoralist societies. It is in sedentary societies, relying on cultivation rather than herding, that various forms of supervision or share-cropping become more practicable, and this can lead to marked inequalities between those who control and those who work the land, developing surplus production beyond a family enterprise. In Chapter 2 some clear differences become apparent in the nature of inequality between pastoral and non-pastoral societies.

In so far as this model relegates women to productive and reproductive commodities for exchange, it should be stressed that this describes their position at the beginning of their adult careers. The rights they are granted are quite basic and even these may be abused by ruthless husbands, emphasizing their essential lack of freedom.[71] As they bear children and build up their own networks of support, women acquire a certain autonomy, but this still varies with circumstance and their ability to resist total domination. Their control over aspects of food production often extended in the past to trading, which provided a domain in which they held an inviolable position. Most inviolate of all are certain formidable widows with strong personalities who are respected for their assertiveness in managing their own families and possessions.[72] Yet significantly, when they negotiate directly with the elders and impinge on their domain, they subscribe to masculine values rather than asserting those of womanhood, and they are respected as quasi-elders. Gender relations vary, and a critical variable may well be the nature of nomadism. Where independent

---

[71] Dahl (1979a: 116–19); Wienpahl (1984: 195–202); Obeler (1985: 240–2); Ensminger (1987: 38–9); Spencer (1988: 33–5).

[72] Wienpahl (1984: 202); Obeler (1985: 270–1); Little (1987b: 95–6); Fratkin (1991: 70–1).

homesteads move frequently, as among the Samburu, elders can choose their neighbours and undermine (or facilitate) the networks of support formed by women. Where it is the village that migrates as a unit, as among the Rendille, and also in more settled agro-pastoral societies such as the Nandi, the opportunities for women to play a significant role in village continuity and kinship networks are considerably enhanced.[73]

Interspersed with pastoralists in earlier times were small groups of hunter–gatherers who foraged for survival and were generally despised. Some of the trading was with them, and they also provided a useful niche for pastoralists who had lost their herds in hard times and a source of labour in easier times as client herdsmen. More recently—towards the right of Fig. 1.2—wage labour has largely replaced these reserve sources of livelihood, shifting the foraging to the margins of the developing market economy, and trading with cash has replaced barter in kind.

The increasing use of cash illustrates the penetration of Western capitalism as an invasive and increasingly dominant mode of production. Nevertheless, the strength of the cash economy is no stronger than the confidence that can be placed on it, and in this respect it is the 'rudimentary capitalism' of pastoralism that has retained its tarnished ideal. It remains, however, that money has partially replaced cattle as a medium of bride-wealth in many parts and this has altered the balance of power between younger men who can more easily acquire cash and older men who to that extent have lost control and respect. Viewed over a longer period, as formal administration became established in the area, this strengthened the position of older men, who benefited from administrative support; and predation became a more deviant activity, although remaining a popular ideal among some younger pastoralists. With the development of alternative forms of employment for younger men especially, the balance of power with age has shifted back, away from the elders.

Fig. 1.2, then, suggests a structure of the domains broadly shared among the more polygynous pastoralists of this region with a hierarchy of priorities—that is, of means lower down in relation to ends higher up. In the private sector, luck and good judgement facilitate considerable differences of status, wealth, and polygyny. This is complemented by the age system in the public sector, which does not recognize inequalities between stock-owners or families as such, but only between older and younger age-sets.

The broad pattern of Fig. 1.2 becomes blurred in the north-eastern part of the region, which forms a buffer zone bordering on Somali–Islamic influence. The Oromo and Rendille contrast with the other pastoral groups considered here in various ways and also have certain characteristics, including their Cushitic languages, that are closer to the Somali. It was the Booran who dominated this area at one time and forged the Oromo federation, and, while

---

[73] Spencer (1973: 20–2); Obeler (1985: 41, 118–22). Cf. Elam (1973: 177–8, 195).

they set themselves decisively apart from their Islamic neighbours, they also have a sophisticated awareness of their own historical traditions. There is a sense of nationhood associated with a religious cosmology, with its own dynasty of ritual leaders derived from God and associated with holy places, a complex ritual calendar, and esoteric expertise. These beliefs and practices seem altogether more elaborate and grander in scale than those among any of their southern neighbours, even the Maasai. There is in the scale of this conception a certain affinity with Islam, and there are anomalous traditions of shifting affiliation between various quasi-Oromo and quasi-Somali groups in both directions. Taking the non-Islamic pastoral continuum as a whole, the Oromo (and Rendille) appear as an important but diverging branch. They do not fit the scheme summarized in Fig. 1.2. Their concern with primogeniture, concentrating wealth and prospective influence on the line of oldest sons, does not encourage polygyny or expensive bride-wealth commitments. In effect, the regard for lineage marriageability among the Maasai and for individual creditworthiness among Turkana corresponds to a concern for lineage eligibility for office among the Oromo within their uniquely complex age system, *gada* (which is echoed in attenuated form among the Rendille).[74]

When one compares the broad pattern of Fig. 1.2 with the practices of Islamic pastoralists to the north and north-east of this buffer zone, there is an even more striking shift in the ordering of domains. Age systems for men are absent and the focus shifts from relations between young and old to the corporateness of kin groups, the dominance of successful lineages within the framework of Islam, and the charismatic influence of successful individuals. Marriage appears altogether less stable and the theme of a calculated exchange of women for stock is muted.[75] To this extent, a non-economic interpretation of bride-wealth is altogether more appropriate. There is a shift in the ideals concerning economic exchange away from bartering for brides and towards a more routine form of trading. Among Islamic pastoralists, the spirit of enterprise is clearly integrated with the thrust of capitalism; and Lewis's comment on pastoral nomads as some of the thickest-skinned capitalists on earth appears to relate specifically to the Somali, for whom personal wealth merges into political power.

Among the Oromo and the Islamic pastoralists, then, there appears to be a certain inversion of the hierarchy shown in Fig. 1.2 and a greater prominence

[74] Baxter (1954: 62, 113; 1966: 233, 236, 247; 1978: 152, 159, 175; 1996: 184); Legesse (1973: 18, 32, 66, 170–1, 174, 221). See also Table 2.1 regarding polygyny rates.

[75] Somali: I. M. Lewis (1961: 138–9). Baggara: Cunnison (1966: 86, 90). Beja: Ornas and Dahl (1991: 62, 82–3, 88, 107–8). Cf., further afield, Fulani: Stenning (1959: 189); Kababish: Asad (1970: 57). I. M. Lewis (1962: 8, 15–16, 21, 34) indicates that bride-wealth among ordinary Somali is explicitly regarded as a reward to the bride's family for her upbringing (an economic explanation), whereas the proportion returned to her husband as her dowry is a gratuitous gift reflecting the status of her family and their relationship with the husband's family (a social explanation). From Lewis's sample data, it remains that the net marriage payment to the bride's kin averages at only 15% of a typical herd.

of the public sector based on privilege. Wealth is associated with power, lineage, and influence over others in public life. Patronage over low-born clients loyal to the family is high in their hierarchy, and husbandry is a means towards this end. Marriage may be highly desirable as a springboard to later wealth and power, but polygyny and high marriage payments are not pronounced ends in their own right.[76]

In the remainder of Part I, two topics that have a strategic position in Fig. 1.2 are examined in greater detail. These are polygyny (Chapter 2) and age systems (Chapter 3). It is by no means coincidental that the hierarchy within this figure broadly corresponds to that of age. The shortage of marriageable women because of polygyny also implies a delayed marriage for younger men; and this, like the contradictions between peaceful husbandry and predation, brings them into conflict with older men. In different ways, polygyny and age systems both order the seniority of men by age and are highly characteristic of this area. They are linked institutions that have a critical relevance for the persistence of tradition into modern times.

[76] Somali: I. M. Lewis (1961: 84). Baggara: Cunnison (1966: 31, 42). Cf. Fulani: Hopen (1958: 26); Stenning (1959: 120); Oromo: Legesse (1973: 170–1); Baxter (1978: 152); Dahl (1979*b*: 279).

2

Polygyny and the Manifestations of Inequality

The high value placed on polygyny among East African pastoralists has to be viewed against the extensiveness of this practice throughout Africa, which is reputedly the most polygynous region in the world.[1] Correspondingly, many ethnographic accounts are supported by numerical data indicating the distribution and scale of polygyny. This presents the opportunity to probe the data for hidden patterns, noting especially any differences between pastoral and non-pastoral societies.

That this chapter is primarily a statistical exercise does not place it beyond the anthropological aim of reaching out towards deeper ethnographic understanding. In one respect it even has an odd bearing on the pattern of discourse of pastoralists among whom I have worked. Counting is characteristic of normal conversation among the Maasai, for instance, extending from cattle to almost any topic. Their manner of speech refers constantly to numbers, marking the significance of their points. There is a very pragmatic awareness of the role of chance in their daily experience, and it is as if an attempt is made to make the hazards of their existence more certain by resorting to an idiom that attaches a ritual significance to quantification. This goes a step further when the turn of events has gone beyond normal expectation and there is a sense of crisis. A diviner may then be consulted to help cope with misfortune, relying on his ability to probe the uncertainties surrounding the mishap. In his hands, the pattern of numbers thrown up by chance is assumed to reveal the secrets of nature. In effect he seeks to replicate these mysteries, rather like tossing a coin in the air to find a lost coin. The diviner traces through the episode by systematically asking his oracle questions and casting pebbles on the ground at random to provide the answers. After each throw, he counts the stones with a view to discerning the meaning of the number thrown up by chance, according to an esoteric numerology. Numbers revealed in this way and chance events are seen to bear on some concealed pattern. The client is then given an interpretation that indicates his best course of action, and the numerical exercise has achieved its end.

Statistics may be regarded as another way of comparing experience with a theoretical model that has some of the mystique and faith of the diviner in order

---

[1] Clignet (1970: 17) notes that the Human Relations Area Files indicate a lower percentage of monogamous cultures in Africa than elsewhere, with three-quarters of the recorded societies characterized by a general polygyny.

to suggest solutions to problems of chance. In resorting here to statistical
argument, an alternative attempt is made to discern a pattern—a distribution of
probabilities—that replicates a perceived reality. It is not that pastoralists do
not have their own intuitive perception of averages and variation when they
express their notions of rich and poor stock-owners or of good and bad years—
see Chapter 1—but that diviners lead them along a different track, abandoning
the pragmatic perception of probabilities for an alternative logic. Statistics, on
the other hand, aim to pursue the logic of probabilities systematically, and
provides—rightly or wrongly—a powerful model in its own right, open to
public scrutiny in a way that the esoteric expertise of the Maasai diviner is not.

The present chapter is divided into three sections. *Section A* outlines two
types of inequality that are implicit in the surveys of polygyny over a wide range
of sub-Saharan societies. Readers who have followed the argument so far
should have little difficulty in grasping the trend of this elaboration. *Section B*
develops this approach further, but in doing so it resorts to certain statistical
concepts that may be less familiar to some. As a layman, I have tried to translate
my own understanding of the technical literature into an unsophisticated lay
language and to pursue an unfamiliar approach through a series of logical steps
with ethnographic illustration. This follows the development of my own understanding as I have toyed with this problem, and it leads to some quite
unexpected conclusions arising entirely from the data considered in the first
section. Readers whose curiosity does not extend to tackling the technicalities
of this section or who find themselves unable to follow the gist of the argument
are invited to skip directly to the next section. *Section C* summarizes the
relevant discussion to this point and concludes it in terms that should be
equally comprehensible for those who have taken either route, pursuing the full
argument or skipping the second section for whatever reason. Thus *Section B*
may be regarded as a central feature in the thrust of the present chapter, as a
technical option, as a challenge for any waverers, or as an irrelevance for those
who are allergic to numerical subterfuge. At worst, it need not detract from the
remainder of the chapter.

SECTION A. POLYGYNY PROFILES AND THE DIMENSIONS OF INEQUALITY

The Distribution of Polygyny in 87 African Samples

A representative view of the high regard for polygyny in Africa has been
expressed by A. Phillips in his *Survey of African Marriage and Family Life*
(1953).

Where the traditional outlook still prevails, the possession of a number of wives is
normally a mark of importance and success in life and—for this among other reasons—

is something which the average African man would gladly achieve if he could: in other words, monogamy is for the majority who are in fact monogamous, a matter of necessity rather than choice.[2]

In the same survey, Lucy Mair echoed the theme, but with a deliberate shift in emphasis, noting the extent to which polygyny has remained an ideal in those areas where it is still an economic asset rather than a liability, but dwindling in those areas where the education of children and other modern expenses have altered the economic advantages, encouraging alternative ways of converting wealth to prestige. The point is well taken. Here I am concerned with 87 samples, 35 from pastoral and 52 from non-pastoral societies in sub-Saharan Africa, selected because their rates of polygyny have been sufficiently noteworthy to record. However, this is not to deny that in other areas a comparable distribution of prestige may manifest itself in other ways.

As an initial step towards analysis, we may consider the two most obvious indices (or parameters) of any distribution of data: the average and the spread around that average.

For the 87 samples in this exercise, the average (or 'mean') rate of polygyny ranges widely from 1.06 to 2.54 wives/elder. Some societies higher on this scale exploit neighbouring peoples and boost their averages by taking wives, only occasionally giving any in return. This is true of the Parakuyo Maasai, for instance, who head the list of pastoralists, benefiting from their close proximity to agriculturalists, whom they dominate culturally. It is also true of the Yako, who at the time of the survey still had wives that had been purchased as girls from foreign traders.[3] However, a one-way flow of women is comparatively rare, and the clear majority of wives are inbred rather than imported.

This raises the problem of the availability of surplus women necessary to sustain any level of polygyny. A succession of ethnographers have noted that polygyny does not imply fewer males as such, but rather a delay in their first marriage as compared with women.[4] Thus, while there are generally about equal numbers of each sex, the excess of married women in a highly polygynous society is associated demographically with a queue of unmarried men who must wait as bachelors for some years, an underprivileged sector biding their time. Here I shall refer to the married men as 'elders'. Thus the average polygyny rate of a society is often an indirect measure of this delay in the age of marriage of young men and hence a measure of the extent to which the elders can maintain a monopoly over marriage and over the privileges associated with this.

In this sense, the mean rate of polygyny, *m*, may be generally regarded as a measure of the distribution of power and prestige between old and young. It is

---

[2] Phillips (1953: p. xiv).

[3] Hurskainen (1984: 21); Forde (1941: 81).

[4] Wilson (1950: 112); Mair (1953: 56); Gibson (1958: 18); Dorjahn (1959: 109); Lienhardt (1961: 26); Spencer (1965: 96); Bohannan (1966: 158); Clignet (1970: 27–8); Brain (1972: 143).

broadly a measure of *gerontocracy*, both in terms of the younger men who have to wait and more poignantly in terms of the extent to which women are subordinated to husbands much older than themselves, and sometimes very much older. There are some clear exceptions. Among the Hima, as noted in Chapter 1, gerontocracy does not manifest itself in high polygyny rates, but in older men actually denying themselves further wives in order to tie their own sons down with early marriage and family responsibilities.[5] Conversely, there are societies in which a high rate of polygyny is not associated with gerontocracy, but rather with the virility and economic drive of younger men; the Gonja and Yako are in this category but appear to be atypical.[6] 'Gerontocracy', then, is a useful though occasionally misleading label for this variable. The development of this model, however, hinges primarily on the other parameter.

The second parameter is a measure of the spread of wives among elders—that is, the extent to which the available surplus of women is widely shared among elders or is monopolized by a few. The interpretation of this spread has been well expressed in relation to different communities among the Nupe by Nadel. 'In Nupe as in most polygamous societies in which marriage is by bride-price (and a high bride-price at that) the number of wives a man possesses becomes an infallible index of wealth and status. In the peasant districts, where we find comparatively little inequality of wealth, the range of polygamy also varies within narrow limits.' But in Bida, the royal capital,

the great inequality of wealth and status is reflected in the widely varying range of polygamy. In the houses of the *talakaz*, the 'poor ones,' monogamy is the rule: in the 'middle class' the conditions are much the same as in the peasant districts, but as regards the men of substance and rank, though it would be correct to say that they have rarely less than four wives, the upper limits of their polygamy are very fluid, and cannot even be ascertained with any accuracy. Popular notions attribute to certain royal princes and, above all, to the kings of Nupe, numbers of wives varying between 100 and 200.[7]

One may note the contrast between remote areas, where a mild degree of polygyny was the privilege of many, and the royal capital, where monogamy was the lot of many and excessive polygyny the prerogative of a few.

The spread of a distribution for statistical purposes is often expressed in terms of its 'variance' (s^2), which indicates the extent to which the data are broadly scattered or are narrowly concentrated around the mean. For present purposes, a more sensitive gauge is obtained by defining the spread of polygyny as the ratio of variance to mean (s^2/m), and this is referred to here as 'variability'

---

[5] If one regards resident daughters-in-law as further wives attached to the households of the older Hima men, then the effective polygyny rate would increase from 1.12 to 1.50 wives per elder. (Abstracted from Elam 1973: 24, 37, 187–8. Cf. also Spencer 1965: 15).

[6] E. Goody (1973: 82–3); Forde (1941: 77–80).

[7] Nadel (1942: 151).

(*d*). Consistent with the interpretation of the mean polygyny rate as a measure of social differentiation between elders and younger unmarried men, one may interpret 'variability' in the distribution of wives as a second measure of inequality, but this time *among* the married men: it expresses *social differentiation among elders*. Those who possess several wives are assumed also to have associated privileges at the expense of others who are less fortunate. Once again, this is only a first approximation and a modified interpretation is suggested later in this chapter.

The rate of polygyny is normally represented in terms of the number of wives per elder, but alternatively it may be expressed as the number of further wives after the first marriage. The Nupe village of Mokwa, for instance, had an average of 1.55 wives per elder, which is equivalent to 0.55 further wives. For reasons that are elaborated in a later section, the second measure is adopted here. However, one may also note a consistency with the present argument. On this scale, a completely monogamous society would register an average of no further wives ($m = 0$), implying no delay in the age of marriage of young men and no gerontocratic restrictions on first marriage; in this sense a nil rating is logical. So far as variability is concerned, the alternative measure focuses on the distribution of *further* wives—surplus women—and again in a sense this is the more relevant figure for analysis. To express this in a slightly different way, we are considering societies in which every adult man normally expects to marry, and a mature bachelor is regarded as somewhat anomalous. Monogamy is a man's inherent right, whereas polygyny is a measure of his ability to achieve an ideal. For the development of independence from senior kin and the founding of a family, a man's first marriage is of course extremely significant. However, in the tacit competition for prestige, aiming towards a larger and polygynous family, the first marriage may be regarded as his point of entry into a new game.

In Fig. 2.1*a–b* the 87 samples are plotted according to the estimated values of their parameters *m* and *d*, for the pastoralist and non-pastoralist societies respectively. If one accepts the above interpretations of these parameters, this then raises new issues when comparing neighbouring societies. For example, among the pastoralists:

(i) Asmarom Legesse has suggested that the 'extreme disparity of wealth' among the Booran is difficult to measure, but at least it is revealed indirectly in their polygyny rate. Yet, the Booran and also other Oromo groups appear to have a strikingly low position in Fig. 2.1*a*.[8]

(ii) Philip Gulliver's comparison of the Turkana and Jie in 1948 suggested more gerontocratic control among the Jie, but this appears to be contradicted by the higher polygyny rate among the Turkana in Fig. 2.1*a*.

---

[8] Legesse (1973: 174). The Uaso Booran have a higher polygyny rate, but the adoption of Islam is just one aspect of their social distance from the Booran proper.

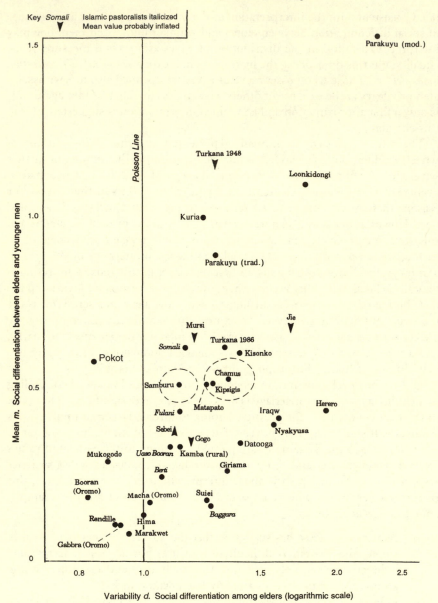

(a) 35 Pastoralist samples

FIG. 2.1. *Social differentiation and the distribution of further wives*

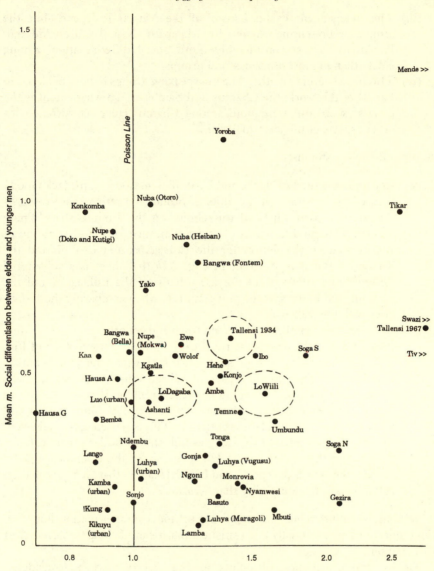

Variability *d.* Social differentiation among elders (logarithmic scale)

(*b*) 52 Non-pastoralist samples

FIG. 2.1. *Continued*

(iii) The independent egalitarianism of the Maasai is legend, but the samples representing them (the Matapato, Kisonko, Loonkidongi, Parakuyu) suggest considerably more 'social differentiation' among elders than in most other pastoral groups.

(iv) This has a bearing on other Maasai-speaking groups to be considered in Part II of this work: the Chamus and Samburu. To what extent is the greater 'social differentiation' among Chamus elders consistent with other aspects of the later analysis?

Among the non-pastoralists:

(v) In comparing the LoDagaba and LoWiili domestic groups, Jack Goody focused his attention on the units of production rather than of reproduction and partly justified this choice on the grounds that: 'There seemed to be no differences of any significance [in the distribution of wives] between the figures for the LoDagaba, and LoWiili and the Tallensi.'[9] But it is apparent in Fig. 2.1*b* that there is a substantial difference in variability of polygyny between the LoDagaba and the LoWiili, and in the average polygyny rate when comparing these societies with the Tallensi.

(vi) In his notional continuum between town and country among the Nupe, Nadel would have placed the royal capital to the extreme right of Fig. 2.1*b*, and the remoter villages such as Mokwa, where the 'chief's rank is merely the highest in the order of village ranks', towards the left. Somewhere in the middle would be the less remote villages of Doko and Kutigi, where commoners are a class apart from the ruling dynasty and there is a degree of social differentiation. This is reflected, he suggested, in the polygyny rates (Table 2.1), which show a wider range in Doko and Kutigi than in Mokwa.[10] However, as in the example cited by Goody, the table is deceptive, and Fig. 2.1*b* shows that Doko and Kutigi actually have less variability than Mokwa.

Whether such differences are significant or not is another matter, however. Such questions are essentially of a statistical nature and belong to *Section B* of this chapter.

Finally, the distribution of points in Fig. 2.1*a–b* may be considered in relation to a proposition concerning traditional African societies. This is Jack Goody's suggestion that there is an association between high polygyny rates and lack of social differentiation, since any accumulated wealth is systematically dispersed through polygyny by paying for more wives and having

[9] J. R. Goody (1958: 57, 89).
[10] Nadel (1942: 50–1, 54, 55, 63, 151). In Table 2.1, I have assumed that the numerical errors are in Nadel's totals and not in his recorded frequencies for polygyny.

TABLE 2.1. *Polygyny rates among the Nupe*

Village	Number of further wives							Parameters	
	0	1	2	3	4	5+	Total	*m*	*d*
Mokwa	44	28	3	3			78	0.55	1.02
Doko and Kutigi	68	96	20	11	1	1	197	0.91	0.92

more inheriting children.[11] While this argument appears to hold for particular African societies, if it is generally true then it should be reflected in Fig. 2.1*a–b* by a certain clustering of points along a diagonal from upper left to lower right: the higher the average polygyny rate, the less the differentiation among elders.

By way of contrast, one may consider an alternative hypothesis. If 'gerontocracy' is a theme that is pervasive in some societies and less marked in others, then one could expect to find a high rate of polygyny (emphasizing the differentiation between elders and bachelors) associated with a high 'social differentiation' between senior men, who have been stockpiling wives for many years, and younger husbands, who find considerable difficulty in acquiring a second wife: even as elders they still face gerontocratic restrictions. This would tend to produce a clustering along the other diagonal, from upper right to lower left.

Visually, the second pattern—'persistent gerontocracy'—is very positively reflected in Fig. 2.1*a*, and this is confirmed by the very strong correlation indicated in Table 2.2. The correlation is even more marked if one focuses on the pastoral continuum within eastern Africa as defined here, excluding the five Islamic samples and also the Herero, who belong to a quite separate milieu in southern Africa. The alignment suggests that pastoral societies are ranged along a scale of increasing 'persistent gerontocracy'.

Neither pattern appears to predominate among the broader scatter of non-pastoralist samples in Fig. 2.1*b*. However, closer analysis does reveal a certain trend in the array of points towards 'persistent gerontocracy' even here. The alignment along this diagonal is visually more obscure than in Fig. 2.1*a*; but Table 2.2 shows that there is a certain correlation nevertheless which is statistically significant at 5 per cent, indicating that we can be 95 per cent confident

[11] J. R. Goody (1973: 10–11, 13, 17–18); cf. N. Dyson-Hudson (1966: 50–1); Dahl and Hjort (1976: 256); Parkin (1991: 69). There are, as Goody notes, exceptions in which high polgyny rates are associated with low bride-wealth payments (e.g. the Samburu), but this overlooks the burden of later marriage payments noted in Chapter 1. One might add that there are others in which the emphasis on primogeniture inhibited the dispersal of the family estate (e.g. the Rendille, the Oromo and also the Luhya; see Wagner 1940: 231).

TABLE 2.2. *'Persistent gerontocracy': tests for the underlying trends in Fig. 2.1*

Section of Fig. 2.1 tested for the alignment of points	Correlation coefficient	Level of significance
	0.00	(random scatter)
Fig. 2.1b: 52 non-pastoral samples	+0.29	5% (diffuse alignment)
Fig. 2.1a: 35 pastoral samples	+0.65	<<0.1% (close alignment)
Fig. 2.1a: 29 pastoral samples, excluding		
the five Islamic samples and Herero	+0.71	<<0.1% (even closer alignment)
	+1.00	(complete alignment)

that this is not a fluke result.[12] Among these societies, there appears to be a more variable pattern of inequality, probably associated with a variety of factors, but above all reflecting the range of cultural variables to be expected over a wider geographical area. If the difference between the two figures demonstrates anything, it is perhaps the degree of homogeneity within the pastoral continuum in eastern Africa, accounting for the eccentric position of the Herero in Fig. 2.1a and a broader scatter in Fig. 2.1b.

SECTION B. THE STATISTICAL INTERPRETATION OF POLYGYNY PROFILES

This statistical morsel brings us to the main course of the present chapter, and it is at this point that readers who wish to avoid the technicalities may move directly to *Section C*. They will, however, have to take on trust the resolution of questions concerning significance, and above all the thrust of the argument here. This accepts the claim that statistics has no ultimate claim to truth. In attempting to understand phenomena through hypothetical models, these may be compared with Weber's ideal types that elaborate specific characteristics of society and distort reality up to a point in order to analyse it. If a mathematical model may be regarded as an ideal type among ideal types and a supreme distortion, it nevertheless provides a powerful tool in the extent to which it may succeed in illuminating our anthropological understanding through its own logical critique.

Consistency and the Limits of Confidence

The arrays in Fig. 2.1a–b suggest a wide range of comparative issues that could be explored. However, any analysis of these would be no more valid than the

---

[12] The correlation was tested using the product moment method. Student's *t* tests for significance of the successive correlation coefficients in Table 2.2 indicated $t = 2.1$, 5.2, and 5.6, with 50, 32 and 26 degrees of freedom respectively.

accuracy of the data available and the form in which they are presented. Where, for instance, there is a grouping of 'more than five further wives', as in Table 2.1, this obscures the profile of the upper tail and some form of guesswork is necessary, redistributing this grouping plausibly among five, six, seven . . . further wives in order to calculate estimates for the mean and variability.

One also has to rely on the context in which each survey was conducted and accept the possibility that the sample may not be representative of the wider society because of shortcomings in the survey techniques. Larger samples may be statistically preferable, but they may also have been collected with less concern for accuracy.[13] Terminal polygyny rates derived from genealogies of ancestors would be higher than current polygyny rates derived from an existing community where many men will still take on further wives.[14] In societies where the wives of one man may be widely dispersed, polygynists are more likely to be included in a local survey than monogamists.[15] Again, it is not always clear whether concubines or inherited widows or separated wives have been counted as wives for the purpose of sampling.[16] A major weakness of the current exercise rests with these reservations. Apart from those samples that clearly fall short of the ideal, there is no clear statement of sampling procedure for most of the remainder. For the sake of the present argument, the samples have to be accepted as they stand, but with a certain caution in the final analysis.

If some convention had to be proposed for collecting data relevant to this exercise, I would suggest that a sample should cover the current wives of each elder in a defined area together with those partners and inherited widows who *de facto* (if not *de jure*) are comparable to full wives. It should exclude any wife who is separated or living elsewhere, unless it is quite clear that the husband maintains control over her household. In such a case (following Barnes 1949) the elder's presence would be notionally divided between his various wives for purposes of the survey. Thus, if an elder has two wives within the survey area

[13] Where the census is thought to be related to tax liability, there would be a tendency to understate the number of wives (Culwick and Culwick 1938: 377; Wagner 1949: 50; Mair 1953: 25; Dorjahn 1959: 90). Conversely, if a claim to be polygynous is also a display of prestige, then the tendency could be to exaggerate.

[14] Rates recorded for the Kgatla, Otoro, Heiban, and Gogo are inflated for this reason, and also for the Jie and Turkana (1948), which included dead wives.

[15] Barnes (1949: 42–3) discussed this point and suggested that polygynists should be notionally divided between their homesteads. See also Spencer (1965: 318) and the appendix to this chapter for the adjustment to the available Ashanti data.

[16] Among the Nupe, for instance, because of Islamic limitations on polygyny, concubines appear to be wives in all but name (Nadel 1942: 151–2). Among the Jie and Turkana, P.H. Gulliver (1955: 114, 243) was uncertain how far he was successful in omitting inherited widows from his data. However, one may plausibly argue that widows who were so absorbed into other men's households as to be perceived as wives can also be regarded as wives for present purposes. The simple expedient of ignoring separated wives in surveys of this kind may also be the most appropriate. One would be less concerned with problems of precise marital status, and one could seriously question whether a man's inability to retain his wife would reflect a higher prestige. Similarly, surveys that relate to cumulative marital experience (serial polygyny) have not been included in the present exercise.

and a third wife who maintains a separate household for him elsewhere, then he should be counted as two-thirds of an elder with two wives; his remaining one-third and his absent household are not relevant to the survey.

Quite apart from the care with which each survey has been conducted, there is also the question of the statistical confidence that can be placed in the results because of the element of chance that distorts small samples. Each point in Fig. 2.1*a–b* merely represents the most reliable estimate that can be made for the two parameters of the parent population from which the sample has been taken. Had the calculation been based on an altogether larger survey that minimized chance (ideally the *total* population), then the 'true' value for the parameters might have been anywhere in the vicinity of this point. This reservation, at least, can be translated into more precise statistical terms in response to the issues (i–vi) raised in the previous section. The ovals drawn around a selection of points in Fig. 2.1*a–b* represent a boundary of confidence: there is a 50 per cent probability that the 'true' point for the parent population in each instance lies somewhere inside the relevant oval.[17] Let us consider point (iv) 'social differentiation' among the Chamus and Samburu, for instance, because of the relevance of these two peoples for Part II of this work. As a probability estimate for the true values of each parameter for, say, the Chamus or for the Samburu considered separately, a 50 per cent chance is not particularly impressive. Taken together, however, there are grounds for confidence. Of the remaining 50 per cent chance that the 'true' Chamus point lies outside the oval, the 'true' value for *variability* is just as likely to be further away from the Samburu oval (25%) as it is to be closer (25%). Similarly, the 'true' value for Samburu *variability* is as likely to be further away from the Chamus oval (25%) as it is to be closer (25%). Thus the chances that the 'true' values for *variability* for the Chamus and Samburu broadly correspond—that the 'true' Chamus point lies outside its oval towards the Samburu *and* that the 'true, Samburu point lies outside *its* oval towards the Chamus—are less than 1 in 16 or 6.25 per cent (i.e. 25% × 25%). This is strong evidence that the Samburu are a more egalitarian society than the Chamus, at least so far as the distribution of further wives is concerned. *If two ovals do not overlap, there is at least a reasonable probability (93.75%) that the societies they represent are dissimilar.* As the distance between ovals increases, so do the chances of a real difference. Thus the Samburu and Chamus samples, with a clear gap between the ovals, are *very* likely to represent different types of society as measured on the scale of *variability*.

A further set of ovals drawn in Fig. 2.1*b* indicates that, despite Goody's comments (v), the LoDagaba appear to be significantly more egalitarian than the LoWiili, and both appear to be significantly less gerontocratic than the Tallensi. The basic dimensions for the ovals relating to all 87 samples are listed

---

[17] For fuller details of the calculation of confidence limits, see Spencer (1980: 157 n. 11). Here these 50% limits were obtained by multiplying the earlier (68%) formulae by 0.6745.

in the appendix to this chapter ('50% limits of confidence'), and more ovals could be superimposed on the figures by the reader. These would reveal that (ii) the Turkana (1948) appear to be significantly more gerontocratic than the Jie; and that (vi) among the Nupe, while there is no basis for Nadel's inference that Doko and Kutigi are more differentiated than Mokwa, they appear very significantly more gerontocratic. Clearly, if one accepts the present interpretation of the parameters, these examples pose further questions regarding the data and the societies in which they were collected that were not considered by the authors. At a 93.75 per cent level of probability, these conclusions cannot be dismissed on the grounds of chance and the smallness of the sample sizes alone. In betting terms, the odds against pure chance are greater than 15 to 1.

Characteristics of the Negative Binomial Distribution

Polygyny data bear on what is popularly known as Pareto's Law, referring to the unequal distribution of wealth within any society whereby a minority of the population control the major share of resources. This kind of distribution may be represented graphically as an asymmetrical humped curve with a relatively low maximum value (the less affluent bulk of the population) and a trailing upper tail (the privileged rich and excessively rich). The degree of skew of each sample may vary, providing, in effect, a third dimension for analysis in addition to the mean and spread which are associated with more routine statistical analyses based on symmetrical bell-shaped distributions.

A distinctive feature of polygyny frequencies as an index of wealth is that they are discontinuous and form a stepped series rather then a continuous curve. Thus a landowner may have 2.5 hectares of land; but he cannot have 2.5 wives. For heuristic purposes, the distinction my be of little importance: a continuous distribution may be presented in the form of a stepped histogram or bar chart; alternatively, a stepped distribution (or *series*) may be perceived as approximating to a curve. Mathematically, however, continuous and stepped distributions are quite different, and this distinction is a basic feature of the argument put forward here. In statistical terms, curves and bar charts are ways of modelling the spread of quite different kinds of phenomena.

Among the various skewed and stepped distributions is a theoretical class that can be referred to as *binomial series*. Any member of this class can be defined in terms of the parameters m and d, which together determine the shape of its profile. Thus, corresponding to each point in Fig. 2.1a–b, which plot m against d, there is a binomial profile that matches the recorded polygyny data in terms of mean and variability, and can be compared with these data to see how closely it matches also in terms of shape.

For a true binomial profile, the value of d is invariably less than 1.0. In the context of sampling theory, such a profile could be relevant to the frequency of chance events over a period of time: the number of days over a period on which (*a*) no cattle stray from the herd, (*b*) one cow strays, (*c*) two . . . , etc., or that herdboys truant, or that diviners cast certain combinations of objects at random. If the size of the herd is increased while the *average* number that stray over a period remains constant, then this implies that the chances of any particular cow straying are reduced and would be associated with an increase in the value of d. Extending this to the limiting instance of an extremely low chance of this cow straying from an extremely large herd, then the profile is known as a Poisson distribution, and the variability d attains the value of 1.0 at this point. Here, in a quite different context, the Poisson may be regarded as the midpoint in a spectrum that stretches beyond to a range of distributions in which d is greater than 1.0. The profiles at this end of the spectrum are known as *negative binomial distributions*. Mathematically, the true binomial, the Poisson, and the negative binomial distributions comprise a family. They are logically linked in a continuum, and in Fig. 2.1*a*–*b*, a vertical line with the value of $d = 1.0$ is labelled 'Poisson Line'. To the left of this line is the area associated with true binomial distributions; to the right is the area associated with negative binomial distributions. The latter are relatively unknown among social scientists and yet seem to have an especially wide range of application to social phenomena, and polygyny in Africa is no exception. As such, the negative binomial provides us with a working tool with which to examine further the data considered earlier.[18]

The historical development of negative binomial distributions from the Poisson has a relevance for the present argument. The Poisson concerns the recurrence of chance events when the probability of each recurrence remains constant. Thus, given the average daily rate of accidents within a large population (cf. the number of cattle lost while herding per day), one can predict with considerable accuracy the number of days in the year on which there will be 0, 1, 2, 3 . . . accidents (or lost cattle). Poisson distributions of this kind have been widely observed in natural phenomena, and this was seen to have a relevance for insurance purposes in calculating risk.

However, a different pattern emerged when early attempts were made to apply this type of distribution to predict the profile of accident rates over a period for individuals within a population: that is accidents per person rather than accidents per day (cf. cattle lost per herdsman). The variability, d, was found to be altogether greater than 1.0 when applied to people rather than to acts of God. This suggested that the probability of having an accident was not uniform throughout the population, and that a minority were altogether more prone to accidents than the remainder. It was therefore necessary to infer a range of proneness so as to develop a new distribution that had the observed parameters m and d. Mathematically a skewed and *continuous* array of proneness

---

[18] For fuller details summarizing the properties of the binomial continuum in relation to a graphical model, see Spencer (1980: 152–6).

within the population had to be assumed upon which could be superimposed the random possibility of having an accident. This continuous array was the *gamma curve*, which was both flexible and ideally adapted to the problem. By in effect combining a gamma spread of pronenesses with a Poisson distribution of chance recurrences, a new hypothetical distribution was generated, which was found to correspond well with the observed profile of accident rates when the recorded parameters m and d were used for the curve. Because this new distribution could be shown mathematically to have an inverted relationship with the already established (true) binomial distribution, it was dubbed the 'negative binomial'.[19]

Fig. 2.2*a*–*c* shows some typical negative binomial profiles and the corresponding gamma curves indicating the hypothetical array of proneness that would give rise to this distribution. For each profile, the horizontal axis refers to the frequency of events, such as accidents during a fixed period of time ($r =$ 0, 1, 2, 3, etc.), and the vertical axis refers to the population associated with these frequencies. In the three successive diagrams, the value for m is kept constant while the value for d is reduced, thereby increasing the compactness of both the negative binomial and especially the gamma curve. If d were reduced further to 1.0, then the profile would become a Poisson distribution and the gamma curve would reduce to a single vertical line at a value of m, indicating no variation in proneness within the population.

Thus the statisticians inferred an underlying property of proneness distributed among the population to account for the observed profile of accident rates. Clearly, however, similar reasoning could apply to a range of social phenomena. Among pastoralists, the distribution of cattle lost per herdsman would indicate an underlying array of skill/ineptness. Similarly, the frequency of visits to consult a diviner could indicate an underlying proneness to become ill (or anxious); variations in the rate of nomadic migration could indicate an underlying array of mobility; the distribution of visits between age mates could indicate an array of sociability. Research into comparable Western phenomena has, in fact, revealed negative binomial profiles, lending credibility to the assumption of an underlying array of morbidity, mobility, and sociability which show similarities to proneness.[20]

With regard to the analysis of polygyny rates, this has a parallel relevance, since it has already been noted that the distribution of further wives reflects an underlying array of prestige. Unlike the wives, however, the array of prestige would be continuous, and an underlying gamma curve could be very appropriate (and certainly convenient) to describe this. The three profiles shown in Fig. 2.2*a*–*c* are, in fact, closely similar to those recorded respectively for polygyny

[19] Greenwood and Yule (1929).
[20] Froggatt, Dudgeon, and Merrett (1969), doctor consultations; Spencer and Wright (1971), mobility and consultations with colleagues.

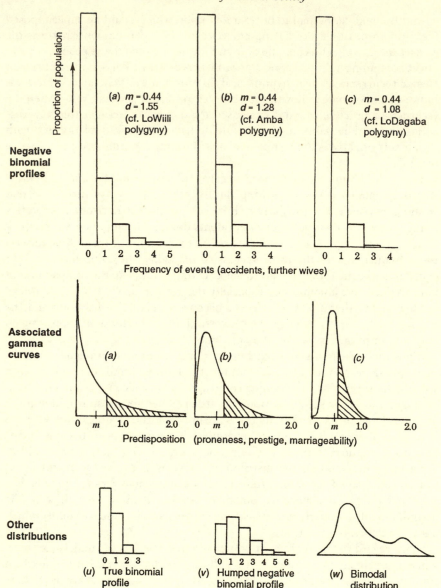

FIG. 2.2. *Negative binomial profiles and associated gamma curves*

among the LoWiili, Amba, and LoDagaba, and the associated gamma curves in each case would be the inferred arrays of prestige.

A possible objection to this argument is that wives are not only the culmination of prestige as accidents are of proneness: they can also be a source of prestige and ultimately perhaps of further wives. A partial answer to this is that the available data refer to polygyny rates at a point in time, a snapshot view, whereas the objection extends beyond this to a more dynamic view for which data are generally not available. An attempt is made later in this chapter, however, to extend the model over time to meet this point.

A second objection is that the hypothesis would apply only to those samples whose variability d is greater than 1.0. It could not account for a possible Poisson or a true binomial profile among the remainder. While this problem concerns only a minority of the samples, it will be shown to provide a vital clue in developing the model.

Inferring the sociological relevance of a gamma curve and the associated negative binomial distribution echoes the insights of Durkheim and Pareto. Durkheim (1951) recognized the chance events that precipitate individual suicides but sought the underlying social causes that could be inferred from comparing suicide rates. His 'predispositions' that run through any society may be equated with a collectively induced array of proneness. It would not be wholly inappropriate to discuss prestige and polygyny in terms of a collectively induced predisposition to have wives. It is the predisposition rather than the wives that one wishes to measure, but this can only be inferred.[21]

Again one may cite Pareto's Law, noted earlier: the popular notion that 20 per cent of a population (or thereabouts) control 80 per cent of the resources. In relation to the possession of wives as resources, it is possible to be more precise than this. In the three examples of Fig. 2.2*a–c*, the most polygynous 20 per cent of the elders have 78, 72, and 67 per cent of the further wives, respectively. If, however, one wishes to infer the hypothetical array of prestige that underlie the possession of wives, then one must turn to the corresponding gamma curves, and this suggests a greater contrast between the three examples: the most prestigious 20 per cent of the elders are inferred to possess 52, 43, and 33 per cent of the available prestige, respectively; this 20 per cent is shown as the shaded areas in each curve. Clearly, the gamma curve provides a more sensitive and in some ways more meaningful indication of social differentiation. However, it can only be inferred as an assumed social characteristic that could explain the observed distribution of wives.

Pastoralists also have comparable concepts. They may be impressed with the size of a man's herd, but they are also aware of a combination of factors that have contributed to this. On the one hand, they all have experience of the

---

[21] Mitchell (1970: 32–3) makes a similar point in relation to labour migration.

element of chance and may interpret this in a variety of metaphysical ways: this is the 'Poisson' element. On the other hand, they are also aware of the personal qualities of the owner that have enhanced his chances. It is their perception of these underlying qualities rather than of the number of cattle that influence their dealings with him, and their confidence in him is a measure of his credibility. In Fig. 1.2, 'creditworthiness' and 'marriageability' were shown as expressions of prestige that related to polygyny in the sense of expectation rather than to any precise number of cattle or wives.

Thus a gamma curve concerned with an array of predispositions and a negative binomial distribution concerned with chance events are not especially new ways of thinking among ourselves or among remote pastoralists, but they may serve to give mathematical expression to familiar concepts.

Binomial Distributions and the 87 Samples of Polygyny

Having established the general characteristics of the negative binomial distribution in relation to the gamma curve, the profiles of the 87 samples of polygyny can now be examined to assess how closely they approximate to this distribution, and to explore the underlying patterns further.

As a first step, one may note that the earlier decision to consider only the distribution of further wives simplifies the problem. The negative binomial invariably requires some estimate of the population whose frequency is nil—for example, no wives or no accidents. If one is considering only the distribution of further wives among married men, then clearly the population with no further wives are the monogamists. If, on the other hand, one is considering the distribution of *all* wives among *all* men, then the task becomes more complex, since it is not at once apparent whether the class with no wives should include only eligible men, or all males, or some intermediate category. Moreover, various ethnographers have adopted different conventions as to which bachelors, if any, should be included in their samples. Apart from the logical consistency of excluding bachelors, it is also a matter of expediency in order to examine the profiles of the observed distribution for comparison with the negative binomial.

In this exercise, the calculated parameters m and d for each sample (as plotted in Fig. 2.1) were used to generate an initial set of matching negative binomial distributions (or a true binomial where appropriate). These were then compared with the observed profiles of polygyny to observe how closely they compared. However, these were not necessarily the closest matches that could be obtained; by modifying the parameters slightly—in effect moving the point around within each oval—a revised binomial distribution could be generated to obtain an even closer approximation to the observed data. It was then possible to see how far the observed data (O) diverged from the best binomial match (E) as a test of the hypothesis. Table 2.3 shows (*a*) a selection of the results

TABLE 2.3. *Profiles of the polygyny samples and the negative binomial hypothesis*

(*a*) Comparison of selected observed profiles (O) and expected distributions (E)

Group		Number of further wives (%)						Sample base	Parameters		Chi-square significance
		0	1	2	3	4	5+		*m*	*d*	
Konkomba	O	34.4	41.7	16.7	7.3	—	—	96	0.97	0.84	not at 10%
	E	34.2	39.7	19.7	5.4	0.9	0.1				
Nupe (Doko	O	34.5	48.7	10.2	5.6	0.5	0.5	197	0.91	0.92	5%
and Kutigi)	E	37.8	38.1	17.8	5.1	1.0	0.2				
Nupe	O	56.4	35.9	3.8	3.8	—	—	78	0.55	1.02	not at 10%
(Mokwa)	E	55.8	31.6	9.8	2.2	0.4	0.1				
Samburu	O	62.2	26.8	9.3	1.1	0.6	—	186.5	0.51	1.13	not at 10%
	E	61.7	27.6	8.2	2.0	0.4	0.1				
Matapato	O	63.3	26.0	7.7	2.2	0.4	0.3	210.5	0.61	1.27	not at 10%
Maasai	E	63.4	25.7	8.0	2.2	0.6	0.2				
Basuto	O	88.6	9.8	1.2	0.3	0.1	—	64,314	0.14	1.33	0.1%
	E	88.6	9.5	1.6	0.3	0.1	—				
Chamus	O	64.8	23.1	8.3	2.8	0.9	—	108	0.52	1.35	not at 10%
	E	64.6	23.8	8.0	2.6	0.8	0.4				
Jie	O	61.1	22.2	7.6	6.2	2.1	0.7	144	0.68	1.68	not at 10%
	E	60.3	22.5	9.5	4.2	1.9	1.6				
Loonkidongi	O	45.1	26.5	14.7	5.9	5.9	2.0	102	1.10	1.79	not at 10%
	E	44.1	27.1	14.5	7.3	3.6	3.3				
Parakuyo	O	35.4	28.0	17.1	6.1	6.1	7.3	82	1.54	2.30	not at 10%
	E	36.3	24.0	15.2	9.4	5.8	5.6				
Swazi	O	68.5	16.9	9.7	1.6	3.2	—	124	0.65	3.46	not at 10%
	E	66.5	17.0	7.6	3.9	2.1	2.9				

(*b*) Classification of all 87 polygyny profiles

Chi-square fit or misfit at a 10% level of significance	Pastoralist samples	Non-pastoralist samples	Total
Trivial (low *m*, low *d*, chi-square inconclusive)	7	11	18
Observed diverges from a binomial profile	—	8	8
Observed does not diverge significantly from a			
negative binomial profile (*d* > 1.1)	25	22	47
Poisson profile (*d* ~ 1.0)	2	9	11
true binomial profile (*d* < 0.90)	1	2	3
TOTAL	35	52	87

indicating the significance of any divergence in the final column, and (*b*) a summary for all 87 samples. Fuller details are listed in the appendix to this chapter.[22]

[22] The method adopted for calculating the negative binomial distribution corresponding to each set of data is described in Spencer (1980: 152–4). The use of a computer to obtain an even closer fit and to reduce error in the present exercise is a departure from the earlier draft, leading to slight changes in the parameters but no significant shift in the analysis.

For the 87 profiles, the exercise of fitting a negative or true binomial distribution can be summarized as follows.

(a) In 18 instances (7 pastoral and 11 non-pastoral), the task is trivial: the polygyny rates are low, and an almost perfect fit could be obtained without in any way testing the present hypothesis.

(b) In 8 instances (all non-pastoral), the observed data diverges from the hypothetical distribution at a statistically significant level (2 at 10%, 2 at 5%, 1 at 1%, and 3 at 0.1%). In these instances, the 'proneness' hypothesis cannot be accepted as it stands.

(c) In the 61 instances remaining (28 pastoral and 33 non-pastoral), the fit between observed and calculated is close enough for statistical purposes. Of these, 47 have a reasonably clear negative binomial profile (their ovals are entirely to the right of the Poisson Line in Fig. 2.1), 3 (the Pokot, Kaa and Konkomba) have a reasonably clear true binomial profile, and the ovals for the other 11 are intersected by the Poisson Line and could be classified either way.

The initial hypothesis that there is an underlying gamma spread of prestige reflected in a negative binomial distribution of further wives, then, appears to have some substance for 47 of the samples. However, the remainder pose a number of questions.

• What is the interpretation of those polygyny profiles that approximate to a Poisson distribution (where $d = 1.0$)?
• What is the interpretation of those polygyny profiles that approximate to a true binomial distribution (where $d < 1.0$ and no underlying distribution of prestige can be inferred)?
• Can one discern alternative patterns among those profiles that diverge significantly from a negative or true binomial distribution?

In the course of answering these, a further question is considered.

• Can one relate the model to the accruing of prestige and wives with age?

Profiles that Approximate to a Poisson Distribution

A negative binomial profile of further wives is taken here to imply a (gamma) spread of prestige, and the Poisson profile is a limiting case in this model, implying no variation in prestige throughout the entire population of married men. Up to 11 of the polygyny samples have distributions that approximate to a Poisson profile. This would imply at first sight that the laws of chance play a stronger role in the acquisition of further wives than any other law. Certainly, there are early reports of West African peoples who gambled with their wealth, and then with their wives as a higher stake, and ultimately with their freedom.

Fortunes were determined by chance in this way, and this might logically have generated a Poisson distribution of further wives.[23] For more fully and recently described societies in this region, however, gambling and social mobility do not appear to reach such proportions. Some skill, some quality, or some other attribute that is not uniformly distributed could be expected to be relevant to the acquisition of further wives.

Nevertheless, one may note that there are undoubtedly random factors affecting polygyny in any of these societies: barrenness or illness in one wife will induce the husband to take on another; some eligible elders have unexpected difficulty in obtaining further wives; some, idiosyncratically perhaps, do not want them; other relatively inconspicuous elders may accrue several wives, possibly as a result of the luck of inheritance or of having a number of marriageable sisters for direct or indirect exchange. Then, of course, there are always the idiosyncratic choices of ethnographers in devising schemes for data collection, and of their informants in providing information. Any of these will introduce additional random factors in the data available for analysis.

Moreover, a Poisson distribution is not inconsistent with a complex system in which the interplay of different forces obscures any obvious pattern and gives the appearance of random behaviour. Thus polygyny profiles that approximate to a Poisson distribution do not deny the possibility of differences in prestige within the society. However, they do imply that there is little evidence in the samples as they stand of social differentiation between elders, and one must analyse the data further or consider other explanations. For the Yako, at least, whose profile is close to a Poisson ($d = 1.04 \pm 0.09$) this is consistent with the remark that 'there is little emphasis on the number of wives as a direct impression of a man's importance and prestige'.[24] But the other ten exceptions also diverge uncomfortably from the model as it stands.

Profiles that Approximate to a True Binomial Distribution

Beyond the Poisson distribution lies the even more anomalous true binomial, associated with 17 samples in Fig. 2.1. Of these, 3 were close to a Poisson; and 11 others may be regarded as trivial in the sense that the exercise of matching a true binomial distribution was undemanding where m and d were both low, and a good fit did not seriously test the hypothesis. Trivial or otherwise, however, this profile cannot be derived logically from some underlying gamma spread of prestige or predisposition, and some alternative interpretation is necessary.

A possible explanation is that random sampling error could conceivably have distorted what might otherwise be a negative binomial profile. However, this is

---

[23] Siegel (1940: 16–20); Chapple and Coon (1947: 624–5).
[24] Forde (1941: 77).

rather unlikely in the instances of the Pokot, Hausa G, Bemba, Kaa, and Konkomba shown in Fig. 2.1, and to argue that the other 12 samples are *all* biased in the same manner is to stretch a weak point further. One may argue with equal logic that the samples that approximate to a weak negative binomial distribution are in fact distorted true binomials. The argument can work both ways.

In order to seek an alternative explanation, it is necessary to revise the basic model and to reinterpret the horizontal dimension of variability in a quite different way. Given some tendency for societies to diversify, the interpretation of the spread of 47 'non-trivial' points to the right of the Poisson Line in Fig. 2.1*a–b* seemed feasible in terms of a negative binomial hypothesis. The approximation of further points to a Poisson distribution could be grasped with some difficulty and even incredulity. Beyond that we are confronted with a residue of samples that appear to reflect an underlying 'negative proneness', and at first sight such a concept is elusive or even meaningless. It is as if, despite the laws of chance, which would tend to distribute further wives somewhat unevenly, and the existence of inequality, which would make the distribution still more uneven, there are certain forces acting in the opposite direction to ensure a more even distribution. The Islamic restriction on a maximum of four concurrent wives could produce this effect among the Hausa, for instance, but in the two Hausa samples only one man has so many wives, and it is as if there is some prescribed limit below this number.

The apparent switch in emphasis is away from a measure of social differentiation implying a tacit competition for prestige and towards a certain conformity with a norm. Thus, instead of portraying this dimension simply in terms of 'social differentiation among elders', one is now tempted to substitute a scale representing some balance between *competition* (to the right) and *conformity* (to the left). Questions that were previously couched in terms of the evidence for greater social differentiation among the LoWiili and Maasai than among their neighbours may alternatively be couched in terms of greater opportunity for successful competition and lower pressures towards conformity.

Seen from this point of view, the Poisson Line becomes the point along the scale of variability where the contrary pressures towards competition and conformity exactly balance. Neither predominates. It represents an interplay of forces, as suggested in the previous section, and the observed profile has the appearance of a random process of selection.

This revised model, however, raises new problems regarding societies in which a high degree of differentiation is ascribed and not the product of unbridled competition; this is considered later. Here, the point to emphasize is that nothing succeeds like success in an unbridled free-for-all, increasing the wide difference in achievement between the successful and the unsuccessful (d is high); whereas in the opposite situation, differences will be inhibited and the successful individual will be under greater constraint to conform (d is low).

Logically, although the gamma curve no longer has the same meaning when d is less than 1.0, one could expect some 'negative' gamma to be related to a true binomial profile in a way that parallels the relationship between the true gamma curve and the negative binomial profile. Intuitively, the whole argument has to be inverted, and the inverse of a distribution of prestige that encourages diversity—if it has any meaning at all—would seem to imply a distribution of pressures that penalize those who deviate from a norm. In terms of polygyny, this would restrict the distribution of further wives, and the restrictiveness would increase as the value of d decreased.

This exercise pointed initially towards a model based on the notion of proneness in relation to the negative binomial distribution. However, the total array of available polygyny data has forced us to extend the explanation from the negative binomial sector of the spectrum, through the Poisson distribution, to the true binomial sector. An underlying gamma spread of prestige is still tenable, but now it is seen as more applicable to situations in which the element of competition predominates: prestige has to be achieved at the expense of other players. At the true binomial end, any association between prestige and plural marriage achieved in a free-market situation is inhibited: the emphasis is on restraint. At points along this spectrum there is a changing balance between these two countervailing forces.

This twist in the argument is fundamental. At the risk of belabouring the point, it may be reiterated in a different context. Suppose one were examining the distribution of success in finding wild beehives. As an initial hypothesis, one might assume that this is a matter of luck determined solely by chance. If so, then the distribution of finds over a period of time among the local population would be a Poisson distribution. Indeed, knowing the average number of finds per person over a period, one could predict the numbers of people within a population who could be expected to have found 0, 1, 2, 3 . . . beehives respectively. However, skill may also be relevant, and one might assume that this skill could be distributed in some gamma curve as an alternative hypothesis, in which case the distribution of finds would conform to some negative binomial. By searching for the best negative binomial fit, one would be in a position to infer the underlying gamma spread of skill in the human population. The more closely the profile of finds approximates to a Poisson distribution, the less important the element of skill and the greater the element of chance.

Among the Bemba, however, we are told that there is a certain resentment towards undue success: for a man to be much better off than his fellows is dangerous, and he may be considered to have achieved his good fortune by some form of sorcery. In Bemba terms, to find one beehive in the bush is luck, to find two is very good luck, and to find three is witchcraft.[25] In such

---

[25] Richards (1939: 188, 215, 232; cited by Gluckman 1965: 59).

circumstances one would not expect a man to push his luck (or skill) too far; he would feel under a wider restraint. This would inhibit the degree of variation between the most and the least successful collectors of honey, and one could hypothesize a true binomial distribution of finds, indicating the strength of the social pressures towards conformity. Switching from beehives to marriage, one may note that the distribution of further wives among Bemba commoners is indeed a true binomial.

Samples that Diverge from a Negative (or True) Binomial Profile

All the 35 pastoralist samples in Fig. 2.1*a* are plausibly distributed along a negative (or true) binomial profile. Among the non-pastoralists in Fig. 2.1*b*, however, 8 samples diverge significantly from such a profile. They are the *Tonga* and *Mende* (diverging with a significance at 10%); *Nupe (Doko and Kutigi)* and *Gezira* (5%); *Hehe* (1.0%); *Luhya (Maragoli)*, *Nyamwesi*, and, most notably, *Basuto* (0.1%).

It is the larger samples especially that tend to diverge from the theoretical profile. Of the 8 samples that diverge with a significance of 10 per cent or less, 6 extend to more than 800 married elders, and these include the Basuto, which is more than ten times larger and diverges more strikingly than any other sample. Only 2 samples with more than 800 married elders conform plausibly to the theoretical profile.

One reason for this is that the statistical tests for significance are more critical for the larger samples and reveal more clearly a departure from any theoretical profile. As this calls into question the validity of this exercise, I prefer not to stress the probability that the actual data in the larger samples, often derived from official sources, reflect less concern for accuracy than most of the smaller samples. Rather than dismiss the larger samples as possibly misleading, the aim here is to discern some regularity in the patterns of divergence.

One point should be stressed at the outset: the fact that a number of samples diverge significantly from a negative binomial profile does not imply that such a profile is a bad first approximation, but it does emphasize that it is only a first approximation. A consideration of the individual instances that diverge and of the more general pattern of divergence can point towards a more refined model.

Islamic restrictions on the upper tail

The restriction imposing a maximum of four wives among Muslims has an obvious relevance for the profile of polygyny, abruptly truncating the upper tail. This is fully consistent with the sharp cut-off point in the (Islamic) *Gezira* sample, but it is not a characteristic of any of the other divergent cases. Among the five pastoral Islamic societies in Fig. 2.1*a*, only the Somali achieved four wives to any notable degree, and even there the numbers were too small to register any significant divergence from a negative binomial profile. As noted in

Chapter 1, levels of polygyny in Islamic societies are generally moderate as compared with some other African societies.

Bimodal distributions of marriageability

An underlying assumption of this model is that the population is homogeneous in character, with the spread of prestige/marriageability approximating to a gamma curve. It could well be that a shortcoming of this exercise is not the assumption that there is such a gamma spread within any homogeneous population, but rather the assumption that each sample represents a homogeneous population in the first place.

This is clearly questionable where a sample spans an established division between (say) commoners with a low incidence of polygyny and an élite with a high incidence. With two contrasting populations within one sample, one would not expect a regular gamma spread of prestige/marriageability, but rather a bimodal distribution with a second smaller hump at the high prestige end of the scale, as indicated in Fig. 2.2*w*. The negative binomial hypothesis assumes a homogeneous population which does not exist in such societies.

A bimodal distribution of this kind is explicitly indicated or broadly implied for 3 of the 8 diverging samples: the *Mende, Nupe (Doko and Kutigi)*, and *Basuto*.[26] In these instances, the evidence does not simply point to a wide range in the distribution of wives between rich and poor which is allowed for in the model of homogeneity, but it also indicates a cleavage: a separate set of rules and a higher polygyny rate that apply to a privileged élite and not to the remainder of the population.

A similar explanation is possible where the sample mixes two sharply separated sectors: traditional and modern. The (divergent) *Tonga* sample, for instance, was deliberately selected by Colson to contrast conservative with progressive regions, and combining these together would create a heterogeneous sample. Similarly, the *Luhya (Maragoli)* sample was cited by Wagner as an example of an area where polygyny been suppressed by missionary activity and this could have led to a heterogeneous mixture of monogamous Christians and unrestrained non-Christians who were confined to different communities.

The hidden truths in large samples

Of the 5 largest samples, 4 were also the most divergent (the *Hehe, Luhya (Maragoli), Nyamwesi*, and *Basuto*), and 3 of these—quite possibly all 4—were derived from tax registers that had originally been compiled to impose a poll tax

---

[26] Crosby (1937: 254); Nadel (1942: 51, 63); Ashton (1952: 80). There was similar evidence for the (non-pastoralist) Swazi and Soga samples (Kuper 1947: 137; Fallers 1956: 163), although these did not actually diverge at a 10% level of significance. In four other non-pastoralist instances, the combination of commoners with an élite was avoided here by separating out one highly polygynous chief from the remainder of the sample (the Ashanti, Gonja, Bangwa Bella, and Bangwa Fontem). By focusing solely on the commoners, a reasonable negative binomial fit was achieved in each instance; whereas incorporating the chief led to no easy fit.

on wives.[27] The pattern of divergence among these samples is striking. One would expect the official records to reveal a restricted range of polygyny as tax dodgers under-report their wives, and this indeed is a source of inaccuracy noted by various authors.[28] This would lower the mean and presumably diminish the upper tail. But, in fact, it is precisely these 4 examples that have a more pronounced upper tail than the negative binomial would lead one to predict. To reinforce the point, among the non-divergent samples, the *Luhya (Vugosi)* also has a pronounced upper tail, and this too was compiled from a poll-tax register of polygyny: it is a fifth large sample. If one *assumes* a negative binomial distribution of polygyny in the actual population, it is as if a small section have grossly over-reported their wives, which seems an oddly unnecessary expense, or that the more polygynous sector have under-reported their wives, with a few notable exceptions, which is more plausible. The exceptions could have been notable elders whose prominence made it harder for them to conceal their polygyny from the authorities. In other words, this seems to be an alternative form of bimodal distribution between a modest majority who conceal their wives and those who feel obliged to reveal them.

The bigamist's dilemma

A recurring feature in these divergencies is that there are more polygynists with one further wife and fewer polygynists with two further wives than expected. This is especially marked among the profiles for 7 of the 8 diverging samples. In these samples, it is as if there is a tacit barrier through which an elder must pass before he can obtain his second further wife.

　　Seen from a purely male point of view—and these are characteristically male-oriented societies—this theme could reflect the drawback of polygyny in relation to the management of resentful co-wives. The problem was identified by Georg Simmel in the transition from a twosome to a threesome, and was also vividly expressed by a highly polygynous Bangwa: 'A compound of wives is like a handful of poisonous snakes. The tighter you hold them the more they squirm: the more they escape; the more they bite. I say two wives are one too many. But we go on marrying them just the same.'[29] It could be argued that three wives are very much worse than two. In sociometric terms, two wives have only one communication link through which to quarrel or form an alliance against the husband, whereas three wives have three such links. The prospect of a threefold increase in their problems of domestic management could deter a number of bigamists from further marriage regardless of prestige. Thereafter, with successive wives, the problem may not increase so steeply: four wives

---

[27] A hut tax operated in Basuto, and this would have been the most likely source of information for the census.

[28] Culwick and Culwick (1938: 377); Wagner (1949: 50 n.). But see also Brown and Hutt (1935: 107 n.), who suggest that the official tax records in Hehe are broadly accurate.

[29] Wolff (1950: 139); Brain (1972: 148). See also Parkin (1991: 74).

(with six links) lead to a twofold increase, and five (with ten links) to an increase of 67 per cent. As he accumulates more wives, the deterrent for the elder who can cope, thrive, and even triumph would diminish. With his tenth wife, his problems only increase by 25 per cent, and this is reduced to 10 per cent by his 22nd wife, and to 1 per cent by his 202nd wife. Long before this point is reached, however, some internal organization of his harem will be necessary, and it will be possible to separate wives who are jealous of each other or who collude against him, and to delegate responsibilities for internal management to certain senior co-wives as an enticement for their collaboration. Indeed, when he has passed the critical point of three wives, it becomes possible to divide them into two independent pairs, each internally ranked, as among the Maasai, and the problems of a shrewd elder are simplified. This is to suggest that, in societies such as these, a man can expect to cope with two wives on an *ad hoc* basis. More than this, however, demands a certain flair for management, and a pause for second thoughts.

Two themes recur in the analysis of these divergences. The first is that there are more elders with a large number of wives than any feasible negative (or true) binomial distribution would lead one to expect: the upper tail is unduly pronounced. At first sight, this might reflect a cleavage between commoners and the more polygynous élite, as noted above, yielding a bimodal distribution in prestige. However, the recurrence of the poll-tax anomaly suggests that official policies may also have distorted the true profile of polygyny, encouraging a certain concealment of wealth. The second divergent theme is the apparent dilemma of bigamists faced with the disturbing prospect of a third wife.

It is possible to measure the recurrence of the two themes by reorganizing the results summarized in Table 2.3*a*. This compared the observed distributions of wives (O) with the corresponding negative (or true) binomial expectation (E) for a selection of samples. The degree of divergence between the observed and the expected data for 0, 1, 2, 3 . . . further wives can be assessed to provide a series of component parts for a chi-square test, indicating the level of significance of this divergence. This is shown for the *Basuto* in the top two rows of Table 2.4, where these components are listed horizontally and may be added to give the chi-square value of 226.5. The remainder of the table has been compiled by grouping the samples as shown and repeating this exercise within each grouping, row by row, and then in effect adding the columns vertically rather than the rows horizontally. The values in italic type in Table 2.4 represent the degree of divergence from the theoretical negative (or true) binomial so as to highlight the recurrence of the two themes in each of the four groupings.[30]

---

[30] Table 2.4 excludes 18 samples for which the exercise of fitting a binomial distribution was trivial (see p. 70).

The Dimensions of Pastoral Society

TABLE 2.4. *The pattern of divergence from a (negative) binomial profile among 69 non-trivial samples*

Samples grouped according to degree of divergence from a (negative) binomial profile	Reaggregated component parts of chi-square for successive wives					
	0	1	2	3	4	5+
Basuto: significant misfit at below 0.1% (chi-square = 226.5)						
underestimates (E < 0)	0.0	*20.0*	—	—	—	*84.2*
overestimates (E > 0)	—	—	*112.7*	9.0	0.0	0.5
Other significant misfits at 10% or less (7 samples, all non-pastoralist average chi-square = 15.9)						
underestimates (E < 0)	—	14.9	6.2	1.9	0.5	26.3
overestimates (E > 0)	0.5	2.7	*51.2*	5.1	1.9	—
Other non-pastoralists that were not significant at 10% (33 samples, average chi-square = 2.7)						
underestimates (E < 0)	0.4	*8.1*	5.0	5.6	0.7	*11.5*
overestimates (E > 0)	0.3	1.1	*17.1*	18.8	16.1	3.0
Pastoralists, none significant at 10% (28 samples, average chi-square = 1.6)						
underestimates (E < 0)	0.1	*3.9*	2.7	5.7	4.3	*1.2*
overestimates (E > 0)	0.1	0.4	*12.6*	8.1	1.3	4.0
			2nd theme			*1st theme*

The top half of this table, representing the Basuto and other diverging samples, merely confirms the points that have already been noted, expressing the general pattern of divergence in numerical terms. The other non-pastoralist samples, shown as the third grouping in the table, are those that do not diverge significantly from a negative (or true) binomial profile. But a similar pattern nevertheless is revealed. There is a shift towards both themes; and this suggests that, in any refinement of this exercise, one would look for an alternative theoretical distribution that could give more emphasis to these characteristic themes in order to arrive at a closer fit.

For the present work, the most striking feature of this table is the contrast between this pattern which is repeated among non-pastoralists in the first three groupings and the pastoralist samples, which are shown as the fourth. Among the pastoralists, the first theme is distinctly absent, and the second theme (the bigamist's dilemma) is arguably less pronounced. Not only are there no divergent samples among the pastoralists, but there is generally a closer approximation to the negative (or true) binomial profile. This is surely cogent evidence that the pastoralist samples are drawn from more homogeneous populations in general. To this extent, despite the very considerable inequalities and differences in wealth that can exist, there is an underlying continuity among the pastoralists that is less evident among the non-pastoralists. It indicates a continuum with fewer major cleavages in terms of the distribution of power.

SECTION C. INEQUALITIES AND CONSTRAINT

The discussion so far has identified a general pattern in which polygyny profiles among the non-pastoral samples tend to reveal a discontinuity between the more polygynous élite and the less polygynous bulk of the population, implying a certain class formation. Among the pastoralist samples, it is not so much that the distribution of wives is invariably egalitarian as that there is no evidence of a sharp rift between more and less successful sectors of the population. In this respect, each pastoral sample appears to display a continuum and a certain equality of opportunity in the long term, consistent with the volatile conditions in which they live. The statistical model assumed homogeneity and this fitted the pastoral samples well; whereas among the non-pastoralists there was a range of bad fits, implying more discontinuity of status and opportunity.

The discussion has also reinterpreted the horizontal scale of variability in Fig. 2.1*a–b* as one of competition towards the right and conformity towards the left, with the Poisson Line (where $d = 1.0$) representing a neutral balance between these tendencies. With this in mind, we are in a position to examine changes in the balance of pressure towards conformity and competition in relation to the careers of adult males.

The Growth of Prestige and the Family Developmental Cycle

In polygynous societies, there is a general tendency for the number of wives to increase with the age and prestige of each elder, and with the development of his family. Among the pastoralist samples especially, the advantages accruing to older men in the market for further wives may be regarded in terms of both gerontocracy *and* social differentiation among elders: younger men cross their first hurdle on their initial marriage, only to find themselves still in a relatively junior position among elders (Table 2.2).

It is possible to explore this developmental process graphically for 36 of the 87 samples of polygyny where the profiles are broken down by age. In order to simplify analysis, the samples are regrouped in Fig. 2.3 according to the slopes of the profiles, since these imply different patterns of development. Inevitably, this refinement involves smaller sub-samples for each age group and lower limits of confidence. Those in Fig. 2.3*a–b* appear to be the most significant statistically: following the earlier argument, for any of these there is less than a 6.25 per cent probability (1 : 16) that the true slope lies in the opposite direction. To this extent, the grouping of samples between the two figures is relatively certain and the implications for family development remain valid. The profiles

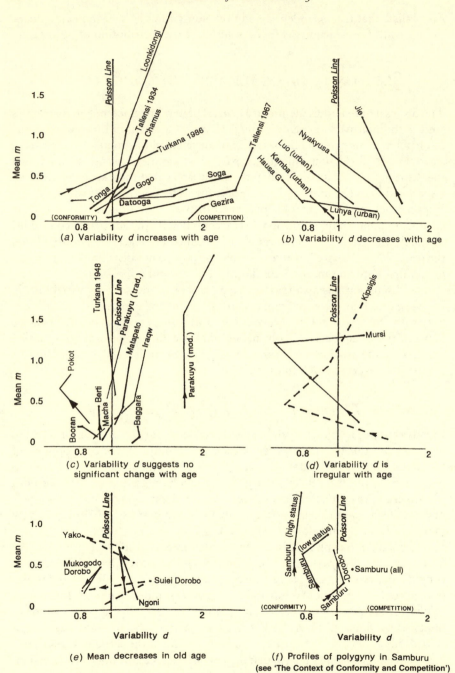

FIG. 2.3. *Patterns of development of polygyny with age*

in Fig. 2.3*c* also point upwards as polygyny increases with age, but they form an intermediate category whose lie of points could tilt either way: at this level of probability, they could belong to either of the first two figures, but not with any pronounced slope.

In Fig. 2.3*a*, the positive slope of these profiles gives a clear impression of a pressure towards conformity upon younger men which relaxes with age as they become increasingly self-reliant elders and are able to assert themselves. One may regard the Poisson Line as a stage that each age group transcends at some point as the pressures towards conformity are outmatched by tendencies to-wards individualism and assertiveness in the pursuit of prestige and wives. The Tallensi exemplify such a pattern well: they have a concept of *Yin* or personal destiny which is weak among young men, but grows more powerful as they grow older and wish to assert some independence from their fathers. The process is more dramatically illustrated by Hart's 1967 sample than by Fortes's 1934 sample in the same community, and suggests that under modern condi-tions the older men are increasingly free of restraint.[31] A similar difference occurs between the earlier and the more recent Turkana samples.

To the extent that the profiles in Fig. 2.3*a* appear to radiate from the foot of the Poisson Line, this has a special significance as natural paths of develop-ment. Logarithmic or compound growth is normally associated with economic and natural phenomena in an unrestraining environment where the absolute growth of an enterprise or species increases with its size. Pursuing the negative binomial hypothesis, if there is an underlying gamma spread of prestige that tends to increase logarithmically with age, then it can be shown that the polygyny points for successive age groups would radiate in this way.[32] In this respect, the Tallensi profiles are again the most striking. Hart's 1967 data suggest a process not unlike the development of a game such as Monopoly, where all the players begin on equal terms, but cumulative variations in success occur between the 'haves' and the 'have-nots'. The slow starters are left behind, their *Yin* perhaps predestining them for a mediocre future, while the front runners bound from success to success in ever-increasing polygyny.

Fig. 2.3*b* appears to reflect the opposite trend, with competition among younger men giving way to increasing restraint as they grow older. It is as if they are competing in an obstacle race in which the obstacles get harder the further they go, inhibiting the front runners. Among the Nyakyusa, for in-stance, there is evidence of considerable differences in wealth that contradicts the egalitarian thrust of their age villages, and this wealth is ultimately a means

---

[31] Fortes (1949: 227). Fortes (p. 72) also notes the newly won riches of chiefs and headmen—an innovation that would seem to have gathered momentum by 1967.

[32] For a mathematical explanation of this radiation from the foot of the Poisson Line, see Spencer (1980: 155–6). In that earlier version of this chapter, the horizontal scale demonstrated this point on a linear scale. Here, as in Fig. 2.1, a logarithmic scale has been used for easier comprehension, and the corresponding radiation would no longer be represented by straight lines.

towards polygyny. The backward slope of the Nyakyusa profile implies that the competitiveness is more closely associated with younger men, whereas older men (who traditionally detached themselves from matters of government) are more egalitarian. As they grow older, elders appear subject to restraint, investing perhaps in the marriages of their sons.[33] This backward slope appears also to typify the urban samples.

Of the remaining profiles, Fig. 2.3c shows some intermediate profiles in which there is no consistent change in the balance between conformity and competition with age. The two profiles in Fig. 2.3d suggest maximum conformity in mid-life and raise questions concerning patterns of career development among men at the time of the survey. In Fig. 2.3e, this pattern is repeated among the Yako, whereas the Suiei show the exact opposite, with least restraint in mid-life. The consistent feature of the four profiles in this figure, however, is the decline in the average number of wives among the oldest age group. In polygynous societies generally, this is not unusual among the very oldest men as they begin to lose wives without taking on new ones to replace them; but they tend to be a handful of survivors, and they are normally grouped with middle-aged men in polygyny surveys to provide a viable sample of older men. The unusual feature of Fig. 2.3e is that this decline in polygyny appears to start early enough in elderhood to be explicitly revealed in these four samples.

The broad impression from these various studies is that the analysis of polygyny data can provide different models of growth in relation to the family developmental cycle, indicating the changing balance of pressures between conformity and competition with age. As a tool for comparative analysis, this would seem to offer considerable opportunities. It bears out a point raised by Meyer Fortes when stressing that

numerical data are essential for the analysis of the developmental cycle of the domestic group. Each phase of the cycle can be thought of as the outcome of a set of 'pushes' and 'pulls', antecedent and contemporaneous. They come in part from within the domestic domain and in part from the external structure of society. Numerical data provide a means of assessing the relative strength of these forces and of describing their configuration at a given phase.[34]

The Context of Conformity and Competition

A notional scale ranging from conformity to competition is hardly new. The idea has been toyed with by a number of writers since Margaret Mead proposed

---

[33] M. Wilson (1950: 128; 1951: 15, 22; 1977: 17, 86, 106, 117). The relation between generations among the Nyakyusa is discussed in more detail on (pp. 31 and 120–3). There appears to be a similar diminution of wealth with old age among the pastoral Giriama, but this is not revealed in Parkin's sample because the data do not extend to age groupings (Parkin 1991: 61, 69, 80).

[34] Fortes (1958: 13).

a typology of societies along these lines in 1939. One point that Mead emphasized was that 'no society is exclusively competitive or exclusively cooperative'. The very existence of highly competitive groups implies cooperation within groups, and again there may be a lively rivalry within a cooperative activity.[35] It should be stressed, therefore, that any interpretation of conformity or competition among the various societies considered here refers specifically to the context of acquiring further wives; it does *not* assume that these societies are inherently conformist or competitive in every respect. To emphasize the relevance of this point, I consider three instances in which it can be illustrated: the urban samples in Fig. 2.3*b*, the Samburu profiles in Fig. 2.3*f*, and earlier discussions on bride-wealth, which bear on points raised in Chapter 1.

Turning first to David Parkin's three Nairobi samples (urban Luhya, Luo, and Kamba), these are close to the Poisson Line in Fig. 2.3*b* and therefore appear to be less competitive than the majority of rural samples, including those collected in an earlier era for the Luhya and more recently for the Kamba. The striking feature is not just the consistency between these three urban samples on the horizontal scale of variability, but also the apparent contradiction with the general notion that life in urban areas tends to be less restrictive and more achievement-oriented than life in many rural societies. In relation to urbanization in Africa, Banton has noted that 'in the city an individual has to compete for place and promotion . . . In the new social order of the city, roles and status are more and more being assigned in accordance with individual achievements and this trend will doubtless continue.' One might therefore expect the urban samples to lie towards the competitive end of the scale, assuming that urban competitiveness is reflected in marriage patterns. Parkin, however, emphizises the extent to which the main focus of competition in Nairobi—especially for jobs and housing—was between the major ethnic groups, and this entailed a very strict control over marriage and maintaining strong rural links. Far from there being a free market for wives in an unrestrained urban competition, there were virtually no inter-ethnic marriages in his samples, and among the Luo and Luhya the freedom of women in the urban situation was firmly held in check by their close kin.[36]

With regard to the Samburu, successive refinements of polygyny data are traced in Fig. 2.3*f*. Here, the point to the right of the Poisson Line corresponds to that in Fig. 2.1*a*. The displacement of the three Samburu profiles to the left of this point indicates less 'variability' when the aggregate data are refined, distinguishing between different categories of clan as well as separating the higher polygyny rates for older men from the lower rates for younger men. From the left, Samburu (high status) is the profile of two very worthy clans. They achieve a relatively high polygyny rate for each age group (*m* high), which

[35] Mead (1937: 460); Gluckman (1965: 77).
[36] Banton (1957: 80); Parkin (1974: 126, 129, 132).

is a clear indication of their popularity as husbands: their reputation for worthiness as eligible suitors is revealed in their polygynous success. At the same time, this reputation brings with it high standards of constraint to conform with Samburu ideals, and this appears to be reflected in the lack of variety in the polygyny rates of these worthier clans (*d* low). Worthiness is upheld by concerted effort, supporting the suits of weaker members, on the one hand, and restraining the more ambitious and irascible members, on the other. Reverting to the idiom of Chapter 1, such clans maintain a high level of confidence in their 'marriageability' by being seen to act as a united and responsible group.[37] Samburu (low status) represents two less worthy clans who adopt a similar stance, but their claims have less credibility, their marriage suits are less welcome, and their polygynous achievement is lower. The extent to which they do not succeed in supporting their less desirable members' marriage suits or in restraining their more ambitious members appears to be reflected in the higher degree of variability for each age group: they are judged more on individual merit (*m* low, *d* high). Samburu-Dorobo represents a further step towards unworthiness and is taken from a sample of those living by Mount Ngiro who are undoubtedly Samburu pastoralists, but they also cultivate bees and do not conceal that they were once foragers or Dorobo. At the time of fieldwork, there was in this area a certain relaxation of the restrictions of the Samburu age system and of exogamy, allowing boys an earlier circumcision and *moran* (warriors) an earlier marriage. Because of their ritual precedence in the changeover of age-sets, the Samburu of Mount Ngiro have a mixed reputation, but certainly in their polygyny pattern they appear less marriageable even than the low-status clans (*m* lower and *d* higher). However, one may also note that the polygyny rate continues to increase into old age, and to this extent there is a greater respect for older men even among the Samburu-Dorobo than among the true Dorobo samples noted in Fig. 2.3*e*. Among Dorobo, marriages are still more a matter of individual merit and even the premiss of gerontocracy is upturned. Thus conformity is present up to a point *within* all Samburu clans, and there is competition *between* them; but within the less worthy clans (and especially among the Samburu-Dorobo), there is an element of competition that tempers their reputation and success.[38] The Samburu and the urban

---

[37] See p. 17 above.

[38] Data for the Suiei Dorobo were collected at the same time and with the same age categories as among their Samburu neighbours, and to this extent the corresponding profiles are directly comparable. Suiei men were seen by the Samburu to reach an early independence, breaking free of family constraint and exhibiting a greater degree of competitiveness, which earned them a local reputation for sorcery (Spencer 1965: 285, 286). Lee Cronk's more recent data for the Mukogodo Dorobo have a similar profile to the Suiei in Fig. 2.3*e*, but the variability is consistently lower, suggesting a pronounced tendency towards conformity. The variety in polygyny rates between Samburu clans (or phratries) was linked to a previous attempt to devise a competitive-conformist scale (Spencer 1965: 290). Here I have drawn on the same data: the high-status clans were Lngwesi and Lorogushu, and the low-status clans were Loimusi and Masula (Maralal and Wamba only in order to exclude the Samburu-Dorobo of Mt Ngiro who are entirely Masula). The age groups in the graphs were the Merisho, Kiliako, and Mekuri/Kimaniki (combined).

examples illustrate ways in which competition at one level may entail a degree of restraint at a lower level in the context of marriage practices.

The context of conformity and competition is again relevant when one considers the topic of marriage payments. The argument in Chapter 1 was that these payments contain an element of economic calculation within a broadly accepted strategy that varies between pastoralist societies.[39] This has been expressed by those writers who have argued that bride-wealth should be viewed primarily in terms of a competitive free market. Thus Max Gluckman has suggested that 'the types and quantities of property available, and the proportions of the sexes and their relative marriage-ages, may by the laws of supply and demand affect the marriage payment and the divorce rate'. Similarly, Jack Goody has noted that 'there is an interesting link between economic calculation and the prevalence of plural marriage. . . . Bridewealth and polygyny play into each other's hands [and] standard payments seem to fluctuate in relation to the cattle population, so that an increase in the herds does not lead to cheap marriages.' However, bride-wealth expectations are often structured by local convention that requires a degree of conformity. Even in the open-ended system of Samburu marriage payments, we have already noted the element of self-discipline against exploiting this loophole in order to maintain the clan's reputation for marriageability. In relation to Fig. 2.3*f*, bride-wealth and polygyny play into each other's hands in a different sense. This suggests an alternative approach focusing on constraint rather than market competition. Mary Douglas, for instance, has portrayed bride-wealth in the hands of privileged elders as coupons whose acquisition and restricted use controls the rationing of wives; and Goody has also suggested that in certain instances 'bridewealth acts in favour of the equal distribution of women; it is a substitute for sister exchange, a form of sexual rationing'.[40] The notion of rationing neatly conveys restraint in the distribution of wives rather than free competition. Each approach accepts that women are in short supply, but focuses on diverging ways in which they may be distributed, and each approach may be illustrated with reference to selected societies. It is tempting here to envisage the differences in terms of the scale of variability, and to explore the extent to which bride-wealth is comparable with coupons in societies at the lower conformist end of the scale and with a less restricted currency at the upper competitive end. The trend in Fig. 2.3*a* in particular would suggest younger men bound by moral commitments when they acquire their earlier wives and then entering a freer market for wives as they mature. The pattern for the Nyakyusa and others in Fig. 2.3*b* suggests rather the reverse. The two aspects of the argument were noted in Chapter 1, reiterating the importance of defining the contexts within which bride-wealth and women are exchanged in any attempt to arrive at generalizations. Unfortunately, unlike polygyny, data on different systems of

---

[39] See pp. 12–13.
[40] Gluckman (1950: 192); J.R. Goody (1973: 10–12, 18); Douglas (1967: 127–9).

bride-wealth cannot so easily be reduced to a standard format and this detracts from a more systematic search on this aspect.

Conclusion: The Hidden Implications of Polygyny Profiles

A considerable number of ethnographers have collected material on the incidence of polygyny in sub-Saharan societies, illustrating the importance and extensiveness of this practice. However, analysis does not normally proceed beyond this point, whereas the accumulation of data conceals a wealth of further information and may provide indices for comparison that bear on a variety of issues. Those raised here include: profiles of prestige that lie concealed within the distributions of wives; the nature of inequality among pastoral societies that contrast with their less egalitarian non-pastoral neighbours; the changing balance of pressures towards conformity or competition in the life course of adult males; and ways of testing the claims of certain authors, providing a critique for further analysis. Polygyny data provide a tool for comparative analysis, and as such lie well within the normal ambit of anthropological enquiry.

In this exercise, the attempt to fit a statistical model to such data has been to explore the inner logic of the system. This has involved comparing polygyny profiles with just one type of mathematical distribution of probability, known as binomial. Quite apart from the binomial theorem, the little known literature on the statistical nuances of the negative binomial distribution has been matched by a wide range of social phenomena that approximate to a negative binomial profile. The initial temptation was therefore to follow the lead of others who have considered the social relevance of this distribution and to posit some form of 'proneness'—in this case, an underlying distribution of propensity within each population to take on further wives. While this seemed plausible, it did not explain those few samples that appeared to approximate to a Poisson and even less those that approximated to a true binomial, for which there was no ready hypothesis.

The development of the argument follows quite closely the successive stages in my own understanding of the problem. As the number of societies considered was increased, the distributions of recorded polygyny rates invited comparisons, tested the generalizations and comments of various authors, and led eventually to a transformation of the initial model. The problem was comparable to that of a child learning to subtract (in fact my son at that time): at first he found it easy to take 3 away from 5 but difficult to take 5 away from 3 because he had not yet grasped the concept of negative numbers. At this stage in his reasoning, zero was seen as the limiting case in a range of positive numbers rather than as a transitional point that led on to a new and inverted range of numbers that required an intuitive leap of imagination. Similarly, taking the proneness hypothesis, one had a wide range of possible distributions, with the

Poisson as a (highly unlikely) limiting case. However, according to the data, the Poisson appeared to be a transitional point in a continuum, and one therefore required a modified hypothesis that inverted the argument in order to account for the samples that approximated to a true binomial. Intuitively, this seemed to reflect a scale between the extremes of competition and conformity in the acquisition of further wives, with the Poisson representing a midway point where the two forces exactly balance. As one moves from this neutral midpoint towards the competitive extreme, one increasingly encounters a situation in which success breeds further success and failure breeds failure. As one moves towards the conformist extreme, success brings a handicap and failure brings encouragement, reflected in a more compact distribution of wives. The notion of proneness at one end of the scale has to be complemented by the notion of immunization at the other.

The samples of polygyny considered here appeared to conform quite closely to a negative (or true) binomial distribution as a first approximation; but there were clear exceptions among non-pastoralist samples where the parent populations were often more heterogeneous (Tables 2.3 and 2.4). There was also clearer evidence of a scale of 'gerontocracy' persisting into elderhood among the pastoralist samples (Table 2.2): higher polygyny rates tended to coincide with greater variability in the distribution of wives. Both patterns were significantly present among the non-pastoralists, but they were even more pronounced among the pastoralists. To this extent, polygyny in Africa appears to exhibit some clear characteristics among the pastoralists that are blurred elsewhere. It is not that they are invariably more polygynous, but the samples appear to show fewer discontinuities in the distribution of wives and prestige and in this sense the pastoralists are more homogeneous. This is not to claim greater equality for them, except in the sense of the distribution of risks and opportunities in the long term, with power more broadly shared. For further insight into the dynamics of this power, we turn now to the analysis of age systems, which also characterize the pastoralist societies of East Africa.

APPENDIX

Details of the 87 Polygyny Samples

Tables 2.5*a*–*b* summarize the findings of this exercise for the pastoralist and non-pastoralist samples respectively.

Further comments on the pastoralist samples

Chamus. Peter Little, personal communication. Polygyny rates for 0, 1, 2, etc. further wives, respectively: men aged 60+ years: 5, 4, 1, 1, 1; 47–59 years: 9, 5, 4, 2; 34–46

TABLE 2.5. *Parameters of the 86 polygyny samples*

(a) 34 pastoralist samples

Society, location, and source	Sample size	Mean and 50% limits of confidence	Variability and 50% limits of confidence	Chi-square test for (negative) binomial misfit	Divergence significant at 10%?
CHAMUS, Kenya, 1980–1. P. Little (p.c.)	108	0.52 +/−0.05	1.35 +0.13/−0.12	0.12, df. 4	no
DATOOGA, Tanzania, 1994. A. Blystad (p.c.)	98	0.33 +/−0.05	1.42 +0.14/−0.13	1.22, df. 4	no
DOROBO, Kenya					
Suiei, 1959. P. Spencer (unpublished)	139	0.17 +/−0.03	1.25 +/−0.10	0.44, df. 3	no
Mukogodo, 1986. L. Cronk (p.c.)	93	0.28 +/−0.03	0.88 +0.09/−0.08		trivial
GIRIAMA (pastoral), Kenya, 1985. D. Parkin (p.c.)	200	0.25 +/−0.03	1.33 +/−0.12	0.05, df. 3	no
GOGO, Tanzania, 1961–3. Rigby (1969: 181) (unrep.)	195	0.35 +/−0.03	1.19 +/−0.08	1.55, df. 3	no
HERERO, Botswana, 1953. Gibson (1958: 14)	45	0.44 +/−0.09	1.90 +0.28/−0.26	1.25, df. 4	no
HIMA, Uganda, 1965–7. Elam (1973: 24)	154	0.12 +/−0.02	1.00 +0.08/−0.07		trivial
IRAQW, Tanzania, 1994. A. Blystad (p.c.)	115	0.42 +/−0.05	1.58 +0.15/−0.14	0.92, df. 4	no
JIE, Uganda, 1950–1, P. H. Gulliver (1955: 242) (unrep.)	144	0.68 +/−0.06	1.68 +0.14/−0.13	2.75, df. 5	no
KAMBA (rural), Kenya, 1976, O'Leary (1984: 55)	72	0.32 +/−0.05	1.13 +0.13/−0.12	1.85, df. 3	no
KIPSIGIS, Kenya, 1982–3. Borgerhoff-Mulder (p.c.)	670	0.51 +/−0.03	1.28 +0.07/−0.06	2.35, df. 4	no
KURIA, Kenya, 1988, Alsaker-Kjerland (p.c.)	77	1.00 +/−0.09	1.25 +0.14/−0.13	2.89, df. 4	no
MAASAI, Kenya and Tanzania					
Kisonko, 1939. Fosbrooke (1948: 44) (extrap.)	558	0.61 +/−0.03	1.41 +/−0.06	2.82, df. 6	no
Matapato, 1977. Spencer (1988: 26)	210.5	0.51 +/−0.04	1.27 +0.09/−0.08	0.02, df. 4	no
Loonkidongi, 1977. P. Spencer (unpublished)	102	1.10 +/−0.09	1.79 +0.18/−0.16	2.37, df. 5	no
Parakuyu (mod.), 1983. Hurskainen (1984: 19)	82	1.54 +/−0.14	2.30 +0.25/−0.23	4.36, df. 7	no
Parakuyu (trad.), 1982–5. Von Mitzlaff (1988: 139)	171	0.89 +/−0.06	1.29 +0.10/−0.09	1.35, df. 4	no
MARAKWET, Kenya, 1980–1. H. L. Moore (1986: 32–5) (abstr.)	45	0.07 +/−0.03	0.95 +0.14/−0.13		trivial
MURSI, Ethiopia, 1970. Turton (1973: 146) (unrep.)	389	0.66 +/−0.03	1.20 +/−0.06	2.10, df. 5	no
NYAKYUSA, Tanzania, 1965–9. Konter (1974: 15) (extrap.)	387	0.39 +/−0.03	1.54 +0.08/−0.07	0.01, df. 3	no
OROMO, Ethiopia and Kenya					
Booran, 1962–3, Legesse (1973: 297–315)	119	0.18 +/−0.02	0.82 +/−0.07		trivial
Gabbra, c.1970. Torry (1976: 277–9) (abstr.)	50	0.10 +/−0.03	0.92 +0.13/−0.12		trivial
Macha, 1968. J. Hultin (p.c.)	126	0.17 +/−0.03	1.02 +0.09/−0.08	0.17, df. 3	no
POKOT, Kenya, 1985. F. Zaal (p.c.)	171	0.58 +/−0.04	0.87 +/−0.06	1.27, df. 4	no
RENDILLE, Kenya, 1960. P. Spencer (unpublished)	86	0.10 +/−0.02	0.91 +0.10/−0.09		trivial
SAMBURU, Kenya, 1958. Spencer (1965: 319–20)	186.5	0.51 +/−0.04	1.13 +/−0.08	1.16, df. 4	no
SEBEI, Uganda, 1961–2. Goldschmidt (1976: 82) (unrep.)	99	0.36 +/−0.04	1.12 +0.12/−0.11		trivial
TURKANA, Kenya					
1948–50. P. H. Gulliver (1955: 243) (unrep.)	92	1.16 +/−0.09	1.29 +0.13/−0.12	2.10, df. 5	no
1986–7. H. Muller-Kempf (p.c.)	94	0.62 +/−0.06	1.33 +0.14/−0.13	2.53, df. 4	no
ISLAMIC PASTORALISTS					
Baggara, Sudan, 1961–2. Henin (1969: 259)	779	0.15 +/−0.01	1.26 +/−0.04	1.90, df. 3	no
Berti, Sudan, 1961, 1965. Holy (1974: 12–13)	247	0.23 +/−0.02	1.06 +0.07/−0.06	0.38, df. 4	no
Fulani, Nigeria, 1952–5. Hopen (1958: 144)	194	0.43 +/−0.03	1.14 +/−0.08	5.10, df. 4	no
Somali, Somalia, 1955–7. I. M. Lewis (1961: 142)	127	0.62 +/−0.05	1.15 +0.10/−0.09	0.12, df. 3	no
Uaso Booran, Kenya, 1978–9. Hogg (1981: 113)	160	0.32 +/−0.03	1.10 +0.09/−0.08	0.86, df. 3	no

Notes

p.c.: personal communication. See further comments.

abstr.: abstracted from diagrams.

excl. chief: excluding a chief: the exercise assumes a homogeneous population, and a highly polygynous chief included in a sample of commoners has been omitted from the calculations.

unrep.: unrepresentative: the data included dead or divorced wives or those living outside the survey area, increasing the mean polygyny rate. These samples are represented by down-pointing arrows in Fig. 2.1a–b.

interp./extrap.: the data were presented in a condensed form and required interpolation or extrapolation. In such instances, the chi-square test could not be applied more rigorously.

trivial: the exercise of fitting a negative (or true) binomial series to the sample was trivial because the low mean and variability ensured a perfect fit. A chi-square test was therefore superfluous.

years: 19, 6, 3; 21–33 years: 38, 9, 1. Little's data are used here in preference to my own, which were based on a sample that was barely large enough for the present exercise and altogether too small to divide into age groupings for Fig. 2.3.

Datooga. Astrid Blystad, personal communication. Polygyny rates for 0, 1, 2, etc. further wives, respectively: men aged 46+ years: 22, 6, 1, 0, 1; 35–45 years: 27, 4, 2, 1; below 35 years: 25, 9. These rates were collected simultaneously with those on the more progressive Iraqw (below) in a combined study.

(*b*) 52 non-pastoralist samples

Society, location, and source	Sample size	Mean and 50% limits of confidence	Variability and 50% limits of confidence	Chi-square test for (negative) binomial misfit	Divergence significant at 10%?
AMBA, Uganda, 1950–2, Winter (1956: 37)	143	0.47 +/−0.04	1.29 +0.11/−0.10	2.66, df. 4	no
ASHANTI, Ghana, 1945. Fortes (1954: 286) (commoners, excluding chief)	502	0.41 +/−0.02	1.04 +/−0.04	0.44, df. 5	no
BANGWA, Western Cameroons, 1965. Brain (1972: 147)					
(Bella commoners, excluding chief)	41	0.56 +/−0.08	0.98 +0.15/−0.14	0.24, df. 3	no
(Fontem commoners, excluding chief)	83	0.82 +/−0.08	1.25 +0.14/−0.13	0.48, df. 3	no
BASUTO, Lesotho, 1936. Basutoland (1937: 19)	64,314	0.14 +/−0.00	1.33 +0.01/−0.00	226.46, df. 8	yes, @ 0.1%
BEMBA, Zambia, 1939. Richards (1940: 119)	209	0.36 +/−0.03	0.87 +/−0.06		trivial
BOTSWANA (Kaa), 1850. Cited Schapera (1940: 99) (unrep.)	278	0.54 +/−0.03	0.88 +/−0.05	0.42, df. 3	no
(Kgatla), 1929–34. Schapera (1940: 99)	74	0.50 +/−0.06	1.05 +/−0.12	0.47, df. 3	no
EWE (Anlo), Ghana, 1962–3. Nukunya (1969: 158)	222	0.59 +/−0.04	1.18 +0.08/−0.07	1.42, df. 4	no
GEZIRA, Sudan, 1961–2. Henin (1969: 259)	875	0.12 +/−0.01	2.06 +/−0.07	8.92, df. 3	yes, @ 5%
GONJA, Ghana, 1956–7. E. Goody (1973: 82) (commoners, excluding chief)	171	0.26 +/−0.03	1.28 +0.10/−0.09	0.01, df. 3	no
HAUSA, Northern Nigeria, 1949–50. M. G. Smith (1955: 23)					
(G: traditional craft area)	198	0.38 +/−0.02	0.70 +/−0.05		trivial
(A: affluent area with owners and slaves)	81	0.48 +/−0.05	0.94 +/−0.10	0.16, df. 3	no
HEHE, Tanzania, 1933. Brown and Hutt (1935: 107)	3,028	0.53 +/−0.01	1.36 +/−0.02	21.42, df. 6	yes, @ 1%
IBO (Aglo), Nigeria, 1911. Thomas (1913: 18)	554	0.54 +/−0.03	1.52 +/−0.06	1.45, df. 6	no
KAMBA (urban), Nairobi, 1968. D. Parkin (p.c.)	123	0.17 +/−0.02	0.93 +/−0.08		trivial
KIKUYU (urban), Nairobi, 1968. D. Parkin (p.c.)	102	0.07 +/−0.02	0.93 +/−0.08		trivial
KONJO, Uganda, 1952. Taylor (1969: 91) (interp.)	1,677	0.48 +/−0.01	1.34 +/−0.03	3.27, df. 3	no
KONKOMBA, Ghana, c.1951. Tait (1961: 166)	96	0.97 +/−0.06	0.84 +/−0.08	2.11, df. 4	no
!KUNG, Soweto, 1952–3. L. Marshall (1976: 252)	88	0.10 +/−0.02	0.91 +0.10/−0.09		trivial
LAMBA, Zaire, 1946. Mitchell and Barnes (1950: 46)	125	0.06 +/−0.02	1.24 +0.11/−0.10		trivial
LANGO, Uganda, 1966. Curley (1973: 29)	96	0.23 +/−0.03	0.87 +0.09/−0.08		trivial
LODAGABA, Ghana, 1950–2. J. R. Goody (1958: 89)	67	0.42 +/−0.06	1.10 +0.13/−0.12	0.00, df. 3	no
LOWIILI, Ghana, 1950–2. J. R. Goody (1958: 66, 89)	87	0.43 +/−0.06	1.57 +0.17/−0.15	2.43, df. 4	no
LUHYA, Kenya, 1934–8. Wagner (1949: 50)					
(Vugusu)	5,339	0.22 +/−0.00	1.32 +/−0.02	6.95, df. 6	no
(Maragoli)	5,700	0.07 +/−0.00	1.27 +/−0.02	20.25, df. 5	yes, @ 0.1%
LUHYA (urban), Nairobi, 1968. D. Parkin (p.c.)	210	0.19 +/−0.02	1.02 +/−0.07		trivial
LUO (urban), Nairobi, 1968. D. Parkin (p.c.)	309	0.41 +/−0.02	0.99 +/−0.05	0.38, df. 3	no
MBUTI, Zaire, 1957. Turnbull (1965: table 4) (abstr.)	31	0.10 +/−0.05	1.62 +0.30/−0.26		trivial
MENDE, S. Leone, c.1934. Crosby (1937: 259) (extrap.)	842	1.40 +/−0.05	3.27 +/−0.11	7.11, df. 3	yes, @ 10%
MONROVIA, Liberia, 1959. Fraenkel (1964: 14)	446	0.18 +/−0.2	1.43 +0.07/−0.06	2.49, df. 3	no
NDEMBU, Zambia, c.1953. Turner (1957: 282)	158	0.28 +/−0.03	1.00 +0.08/−0.07	1.18, df. 3	no
NGONI, Zambia and Malawi, 1948–9. Barnes (1951: 24)	98	0.19 +/−0.03	1.24 +/−0.12		trivial
NUBA, Sudan, 1938–40. Nadel (1947: 116–17)					
(Heiban) (unrep.)	103	0.87 +/−0.07	1.20 +0.12/−0.11	1.82, df. 4	no
(Otoro) (unrep.)	92	0.99 +/−0.07	1.06 +0.11/−0.10	6.83, df. 5	no
NUPE, Nigeria, 1934–6. Nadel (1942: 151)					
(Doko and Kutigi) (interp.)	197	0.91 +/−0.04	0.92 +/−0.06	11.96, df. 4	yes, @ 5%
(Mokwa)	78	0.55 +/−0.06	1.02 +/−0.11	3.66, df. 3	no
NYAMWESI, Tanzania, c.1936. Culwick and Culwick (1938: 377)	10,784	0.17 +/−0.00	1.46 +/−0.01	34.13, df. 6	yes, @ 0.1%
SOGA, Uganda, 1950–2. Fallers (1956: 75)					
(northern villages)	250	0.28 +/−0.03	2.07 +0.13/−0.12	4.72, df. 5	no
(southern villages)	205	0.54 +/−0.05	1.82 +/−0.12	10.31, df. 6	nearly @ 10%
SONJO, Tanzania, 1950s? Cited R. F. Gray (1960: 39)	164	0.12 +/−0.02	1.00 +0.08/−0.07		trivial
SWAZI, Swaziland, 1934–7. Kuper (1947: 37) (extrap.)	124	0.65 +/−0.09	3.46 +0.31/−0.29	2.46, df. 4	no
TALLENSI (Tongo), Ghana.					
1934. Fortes (1949: 65)	111	0.60 +/−0.06	1.39 +0.13/−0.12	5.23, df. 4	no
1967. K. Hart (p.c.)	220	0.64 +/−0.06	2.78 +0.18/−0.17	12.26, df. 8	no
TEMNE, S. Leone, 1954. Cited in Banton (1957: 198) (interp.)	61	0.38 +/−0.06	1.43 +0.18/−0.17	0.01, df. 3	no
TIKAR, Cameroons, 1938. McCulloch et al. (1954: 46) (interp. and excluding chief)	472	0.98 +/−0.05	2.56 +/−0.11	3.21, df. 4	no
TIV, Nigeria, c.1950. Bohannan (1954: 64–6) (abstr.)	48.8	0.55 +/−0.14	3.56 +0.51/−0.46	5.54, df. 7	no
TONGA (Plateau), Zambia, 1946–50. Colson (1958: 96) (extrap.)	309	0.30 +/−0.02	1.34 +/−0.07	7.74, df. 3	yes, @ 10%
UMBUNDU, Angola, c.1933. Childs (1949: 30–1)	37	0.35 +/−0.08	1.62 +0.27/−0.24	2.39, df. 3	no
WOLOF, Senegambia, c.1954. cited Gamble (1957: 53)	c. 300	0.54 +/−0.03	1.16 +0.07/−0.06	0.23, df. 4	no
YAKO, Nigeria, 1939. Forde (1941: 78)	121	0.74 +/−0.05	1.04 +/−0.09	1.91, df. 4	no
YORUBA, Nigeria, 1951–3. Galletti et al. (1956: 70–4) (extrap.)	757	1.18 +/−0.03	1.37 +/−0.05	0.36, df. 3	no

Notes
As for Table 2.5a.

Dorobo (Suiei). Data were collected from tax books. For further information regarding the Suiei Dorobo, their pattern of marriage, and the tax book census, see Spencer (1965: 283–5, 319; 1973: 206–8).

Dorobo (Mukogodo). Lee Cronk, personal communication. Polygyny rates for 0, 1, 2 further wives, respectively: men aged 70–81 years (Tiyeki): 5, 2; 57–69 years (Mekuri): 9, 3; 43–56 years (Kimaniki): 11, 6, 2; 30–42 years (Kishille): 26, 7; 20–29 years (Kiroro) 18, 4.

Giriama (pastoral). Data collated with permission from David Parkin's field note-books. Polygyny rates for 0, 1, 2, etc. further wives, respectively: 162, 30, 6, 0, 0, 2. See also Parkin (1991: 91).

Gogo. In Fig. 2.3*a*, the two points determining the graph are homestead heads and dependent elders respectively.

Iraqw. Astrid Blystad, personal communication. Polygyny rates for 0, 1, 2, etc. further wives, respectively: men aged 46+ years: 7, 9, 3, 2, 0, 1; 35–45 years: 17, 7, 2, 1; below 35 years: 58, 7; age not known: 0, 1. See Datooga above.

Kipsigis. Monique Borgerhoff-Mulder, personal communication. With males circumcised at about the age of 14 years, polygyny rates for 0, 1, 2, etc. further wives, respectively: men circumcised before 1931 (Nyongi and Maima): 10, 11, 10, 7, 0, 0, 0, 1, 0, 1, 0, 1; before 1946 (Chuma): 49, 66, 21, 7, 2, 1; before 1962 (Sawe): 106, 85, 10; before 1979 (Korongoro): 262, 16, 2, 2.

Kuria. Kirsten Alsaker-Kjerland (1995 and also personal communication). Polygyny rates for 0, 1, 2, etc. further wives, respectively: circumcised 1907–24: 5, 6, 1, 2; 1927–42: 19, 18, 6, 4, 1, 1; 1945–56: 6, 6, 1, 0, 1. The oldest and youngest samples were too small to provide reliable data for Fig. 2.3.

Maasai (Matapato). Data for the older age-sets have been scaled down to offset the bias caused by stratifying the sample by age.

Maasai (Loonkidongi). A subclan of Prophets and diviners who tend to be highly polygynous.

Maasai (Parakuyu). Of two surveys undertaken about the same time, one (trad.) was in a more remote area (von Mitzlaff 1988: 140). The other (mod.) was closer to urban development, more strongly affected by the market, and with easier access to non-Parakuyu wives, which could account for the particularly high degree of polygyny in this sample (Hurskainen 1984: 21, 73).

Oromo (Booran). In collating data from Legesse's survey, no correlation was found between polygyny rates and *gada* (age-set) status. In other words, any prestige that might be gained through polygyny appears to be quite independent of the political system in which *gada* status is especially important.

Oromo (Macha). Jan Hultin, personal communication. Polygyny rates for 0, 1, 2 further wives, respectively: men aged 50+ years: 33, 7, 2; 40–9 years: 18, 6; 30–9 years: 35, 5; below 30 years: 20.

Pokot (W. District, Segor Division). Fred Zaal, personal communication. Polygyny rates for 0, 1, 2, etc. further wives, respectively: men aged 60+ years: 10, 16, 4, 2; 40–59 years: 26, 30, 8, 1; 20–39 years: 55, 18, 1.

Samburu. The settlement census was used for Fig. 2.1*a* and for the Samburu-Dorobo (Mt Ngiro) in Fig. 2.3*f*. The tax-book census was used for the other profiles of Fig. 2.3*f*, where a larger population of selected clans was necessary.

Sebei. Goldschmidt indicates that this sample discounts wives resident elsewhere, implying that the true m is higher and possibly d also—whence the chi-square test on existing figures would be misleading.

Turkana 1986. Harald Muller-Kempf, personal communication. Polygyny rates for 0, 1, 2, etc. further wives, respectively: men over 50 years of age: 27, 13, 6, 5, 1; younger men: 28, 14. The data were collected by research assistants and may have included leviratic widows.

Uaso Booran. I am grateful to Richard Hogg for permission to collate these data from his unpublished Ph.D. thesis.

Further comments on the non-pastoralist samples

Ashanti (Agogo commoners). The total is inferred from the published data. Each woman in the survey was asked how many wives her husband had. Following Barnes (1949: 42–3), the actual polygyny rate has been calculated by weighting the different replies. Thus 81 women replied that their husbands had three wives, which is taken as equivalent to a sample of 27 polygynists with three wives. With the chief, the mean would increase to 0.40, and the variability to 1.50, and no satisfactory binomial fit would be possible.

Bangwa (Bella commoners). With the chief, the mean would increase to 0.93, the variability to 6.69, and no satisfactory binomial fit would be possible.

Bangwa (Fontem commoners). This sample excluded a considerable number of monogamists who had moved elsewhere. With the chief, the mean would increase to 1.33, and the variability to 17.41, and no satisfactory binomial fit would be possible.

Basuto. Significant divergence from a negative binomial profile at $<<0.1\%$. The extent of this divergence is due to the sample size, which makes the test altogether more demanding. As a first approximation, the negative binomial provides a useful fit; see Table 2.2.

Gezira. Described by Henin as a population of ex-Blue Nile nomads who had been settled in the 1920s.

Gonja (commoners). With the chief, the mean would increase to 0.33, and the variability to 3.43, and no satisfactory binomial fit would be possible.

Hehe. The divergence from a negative binomial is significant at 0.5%. Same comment applies as to Basuto (see above).

Ibo. Aglo was the only one of three surveys that was personally checked by Thomas (1913: 10).

Kamba (urban). David Parkin, personal communication. Polygyny rates of 0, 1, or 2 further wives, respectively: men over 40 years of age: 37, 15, 1; younger men: 66, 4, 0. The sample is of household heads, and excludes married lodgers, whose wives would normally live in the rural areas. See also Parkin (1974: tables 2 and 3; 1978: 45).

Kikuyu (urban). David Parkin, personal communication. Polygyny rates for 0, 1 further wives, respectively: men over 40 years of age: 43, 4; younger men: 52, 3. Regarding lodgers in this survey, see note above on urban Kamba. See also Parkin (1978: 45).

Konkomba. At first sight this sample would appear to be of a Muslim area, with a sharp cut-off at four wives, producing a low variability. However, Tait (1961: 11) notes that he knew of no Muslims in the area.

Luhya (Maragoli). An area where missionary activity has depressed polygyny.

Luhya (urban). David Parkin, personal communication. Polygyny rates of 0, 1, 2, or 3 further wives, respectively: men over 40 years of age: 64, 22; younger men: 110, 12, 1, 1. Regarding lodgers in this survey see note above on urban Kamba. See also Parkin (1978: 45).

Luo (urban). David Parkin, personal communication. Polygyny rates of 0, 1, 2, or 3 further wives, respectively: men over 40 years of age: 72, 54, 15, 1; younger men: 134, 28, 4, 1. Regarding lodgers in this survey, see note above on urban Kamba. See also Parkin (1978: 45).

Nupe (Doko and Kutigi). Significant divergence from a true binomial profile at 2.5%

Nyamwesi (Ulanga). Same comment applies as on Basuto (see above).

Tallensi 1967. Keith Hart, personal communication. Polygyny rates for 0, 1, 2, etc. further wives, respectively: men over 45 years of age: 51, 33, 13, 4, 0, 1, 1, 1, 0, 1, 0, 1; men between 31 and 45 years of age: 53, 17, 6, 1; younger men: 36, 2.

3

The Dynamics of Age Systems in East Africa

Within any society, some overarching premiss may be characteristic of a much wider region. Studies of rural Mediterranean societies, for instance, emphasize the concept of *honour* associated with the integrity of the family. Studies of Hindu society stress the concept of *purity* which defines status within the caste hierarchy. Correspondingly, in studies of traditional Africa, a theme that recurs is the association of *respect* with age. It is hardly surprising that the terms 'elder' and 'elderhood' are so well established as translations of vernacular terms. They convey a sense of status and respect.

There are, of course, variations on this theme, and it persists only to the extent that it has not been undermined by recent change. But typically in rural areas, older people are expected to have cultivated a sense of respect, and they claim a right to the respect of others based on their accumulated experience and seniority. Explicitly or implicitly, older people foster an ethos of gerontocracy—an assumption of privilege—and their juniors acquire a stake in this way of thinking, ensuring their own future even before middle age.

However, the premiss of respect in old age is also ambiguous. It has the appearance of a clear-cut notion, but it does not quite match up to relations between young and old. If older people are characterized as having achieved a sense of respect—a state where they are both respected and respecting—then this implies that younger people have not yet achieved this ideal. To this extent, the young do not invariably show respect for elders, and elders do not have respect in every sense of the term: they have a sense of respect, but are not altogether respected, and they cannot altogether respect the disrespecting young. Again, this emphasis on respect for old age may be tinged with fear; and a grotesque caracature of self-indulgence among older people may be one of greed and envy, associated even with witchcraft or sorcery. This appears as a perversion of the norm, but it hints at an unscrupulous streak in the power of older people. In these ways, the premiss of respect is relevant to the rhetoric between different ages, but ultimately it is flawed. One is therefore led to look more closely at ways in which the ambiguities of ageing are contained within the institutions that legitimize the claim to authority among elders.

This authority is commonly expressed through the extended family dominated by the senior generation with control over property and marriage, both in giving away daughters and in restricting sons. This may be elaborated through ancestor cults, manipulated by those closest to the ancestors. In West Africa especially, it is elaborated through *secret societies*, in which careers are marked by paying for successive initiations into the secrets of more exclusive senior grades. Secret societies provide a useful model against which to view societies with age organization. Thus in the Kalenjin age system, the notion of esoteric knowledge and ultimately power is paraded by initiated men as a device to overawe their juniors. However, secret societies are not age systems in any strict sense, because promotion to successive grades depends on the ability of individuals to foster patronage, whereas among the Kalenjin, for instance, initiation is explicitly linked to age and not to patronage or wealth. It is as members of an age cohort that they are initiated and not as privileged individuals; and it is in systems of age organization that respect for seniority by age in its own right becomes a key issue.

While systems based on age have been widely recorded, the best-known concentration is among East African pastoralists. Here, they are often highly elaborate, and it is fruitful to examine this career pattern in the contexts of family development and community life: this is the stuff of ethnography. In order to explore age organization, however, it is necessary in the first instance to grasp the tangled logic of the rules which focus almost exclusively on ageing among males.

Among anthropologists, a consequence of this complexity and localized concentration is that the topic of age systems tends to be esoteric and is popularly regarded as primarily a regional speciality.[1] To this extent, the broader sociological problems have hardly been explored. The topic is richly covered in the individual ethnographies, but with little attempt at comparison. A clear exception is Frank Stewart's *Fundamentals of Age-Group Systems* (1977). This provides a pioneering and unsurpassed attempt to place a world-wide range of these systems within a logical framework, devising a method of analysis and identifying the implications of the rules that characterize them. Yet the very breadth of his work inhibits detailed consideration of the wider settings against which the workings of such systems can be judged. It is Stewart's insights and the limitations of his work that have largely inspired the present chapter.

The Age Ladder and Ambivalence towards Ageing: The Maasai Case

In the analysis of age systems, the term *age grade* refers to some level of status or rank associated with age. This has to be distinguished from an *age-set*, which identifies a group of peers and is not concerned with status as such. Youths are assigned to the most junior age-set following initiation, and with their peers they pass as an age-set from one age grade to the next, rather as a class in school is promoted from form to form. Switching analogy, it is as if they are climbing a ladder, with successive rungs representing the sequence of age grades. Climb-

---

[1] Cf. Stewart (1977: 15–16); Kertzer and Keith (1984: 22).

ing onto the bottom rung of the ladder involves initiation for youths as they form their age-set, and thereafter they climb together as an age-set, rung by rung, from one age grade to the next. The rate of promotion up the age ladder is geared to a set of rules that prescribe the order of events in an extended ritual cycle. The formation of a new age-set occurs at one point in this cycle, and subsequent events may trigger off a series of promotions higher up the ladder. At the head of the queue on the uppermost rung is the oldest surviving age-set.

An age system provides a culturally defined sense of time, encompassing the life courses of men and extending backwards to oral traditions associated with earlier age-sets in the distant past. Figuratively speaking, with each ceremonial upgrading from rung to rung, time is ticking away, and the continuous process of men's ageing is publicly demarcated into discrete stages. These are very age-conscious peoples, and there is a premiss of inequality based on age differences and built into their concept of ageing and of time itself. To become a full member of society—that is, to acquire a sense of being—is to enter into this premiss of age inequality at the bottom rung and to have a role in perpetuating it as one climbs upward.

Age systems vary in complexity, and normally they are complicated by a variety of factors besides age; even age itself may become less relevant once younger men settle down to elderhood. Yet, a form of organization based essentially on age and persisting to old age does occur among the southern pastoralists of East Africa. Here it is useful to consider the age system of the Maasai-speaking (Maa) peoples as a model in this respect, and especially as this system has a direct bearing on Part II of this volume.

Among the Maasai, age-sets are typically spaced apart by about fifteen years, with a focus on the ritual cycle of warriorhood that spans this period, and also on the link between the age-set of *moran* (warriors) and elders who are two age-sets their senior and act as their ritual *firestick patrons*. Differences of interpretation alter the thrust of this age system between north and south. The northern variation is typified by the Samburu and focuses on the major groupings by age grade and sex, drawing attention to the power that is retained in the hands of the elders by controlling the marriages of women and the rate at which young men mature.[2] It is through the age system that the firestick patrons maintain this control, and the depressed status of the *moran* is reinforced by denying them access to deliberations on public matters. With the delayed marriage of *moran*, the high polygyny rate among elders is maintained, and the *moran* are trapped in a state of social suspension: they are not allowed to acquire the knowledge and wisdom of elderhood because they are held to lack respect, and they are not held in respect because they lack the knowledge and wisdom of elderhood. Cast out into a political limbo, they adopt a delinquent life style

[2] See p. 29.

and become involved in a form of gang warfare among themselves, confirming their lack of respect in an extended adolescence throughout their twenties. The monopoly of concealed wisdom maintained by the elders resembles a secret society in some ways with a delayed admission of *moran* to the company of the elders around the time they settle down to marry. The emphasis on ultimate ritual authority concentrated towards the upper end of the age ladder creates a power vacuum lower down, and the price that the elders pay for their heavy-handed dominance is a certain loss of control over the younger men.

Whereas the northern age system focuses on the distinctions between the *age grades* of boyhood, *moranhood*, and elderhood, the southern Maasai model is altogether more dynamic and focuses on the *age-sets* themselves. This has been well described by Philip Gulliver for the Arusha, but clearly extends to their pastoral neighbours, the Kisonko Maasai.[3] From their respective positions on the age ladder, there is a jostling between adjacent age-sets for possession of particular rungs, and there are unoccupied rungs elsewhere as age-sets pass fitfully up the ladder. These apparent anomalies are aspects of the cyclical pattern: about fifteen years later, when a new age-set has entered the queue from the bottom, jostling and unoccupied rungs occur at the same positions of the ladder as before, while the age-sets have moved on. In this southern version, the rivalry between neighbouring age-sets (e.g. *A* and *B*, *B* and *C*, etc.) creates an alliance between alternate age-sets (between *A* and *C* in opposition to *B*). Typically, this involves an age-set of *moran* (*C*) in their *physical* prime and their firestick patrons (*A*), who are thirty years older and in their *political* prime. Together these two age-sets (*A* and *C*) dominate from the two most powerful rungs of the age ladder and for a time form a commanding alliance against any rival claims from the intervening age-set of inexperienced elders (*B*) or from the incipient age-set of novice *moran* (*D*). However, as they age during the next fifteen years—over one age-set cycle—their rivals (*B* and *D*) will step into the prime positions as the ruling alliance, nudging their predecessors into retirement, which is transitional for the younger men (*C*), who now have to adjust to elderhood, but permanent for the older men (*A*).

These two interpretations of the Maasai age system highlight different aspects of the process of ageing. Apart from the differences in emphasis between north and south, both are applicable to all Maa, focusing on various tensions that tend to surface at different stages of the development of *moran* and hence at different points of the fifteen-year cycle.[4] Taking the two models together, one becomes aware of the ambivalence of the relationship between *moran* and their firestick patrons: they are ideologically opposed in the first model and political allies in the second. Again, there is the ambiguity of old age: in the first

[3] P. H. Gulliver (1963: 25–47); Spencer (1976; 1989: 297–9).
[4] Spencer (1989: 315–16).

model, antipathy between the *moran* and the elders focuses on their middle-aged patrons, and there is great respect for the oldest men, underscoring the premiss of gerontocracy; in the second model, as they age, older men are nudged from political power by their successors and the system is not strictly speaking a gerontocracy. This parallels the pattern implied in Fig. 2.3*e*, where polygyny rates actually declined in later life and older men appeared to slip from a dominant position as they ceased to accrue wives. Ambiguities and contradictions of this sort are inherent in any age system, and the relatively simple form of organization associated with the Maasai is no exception.

A further point that has a bearing on the present chapter is the demographic underpinning of age systems. In the southern Maasai model, it is the structure of alternating alliances that seems to account for the fifteen-year cycle between successive age-sets: over a period of forty-five years, from the age of about 20 until perhaps 65, adult males pass through the prime of youth and then, after a period of adjustment, through the prime of middle age. Before this period they are mere boys and afterwards they are a dwindling array of ageing men. If men aged more slowly, then the periodic cycle of age-sets would extend beyond fifteen years. Each age system has its own characteristics, and the system of alliances with a fifteen-year cycle is peculiar to the Maasai. However, in approaching other age systems, the Maasai instance prompts one to note that it may be useful to examine the demographic implications for some clue to their inner working.

Although women are not normally ascribed to age-sets in this area, their status may still be defined with reference to the age system of men. Among the Maasai, for instance, a girl may be closely associated with the age-set of her *moran* lover; but it is her father's age-set with whom she is identified when her marriage is arranged, as she is 'their' daughter; and subsequently it is her husband's age-set who share certain privileges with respect to her, as she is 'their' wife. Once her first son is circumcized and she becomes a 'mother of *moran*', she may accompany him to the warrior village (*manyata*), where she is closely identified with his age-set for a period of about five years. Subsequently, she may repeat this role for her younger sons, attending the warrior villages of as many as three successive age-sets, and returning to her husband between each *manyata* episode. As a widow, she may be identified with any of these roles in her dealings with men: she remains a 'daughter', 'wife', and 'mother' of different age-sets, and may even draw on earlier friendships formed with the age-set of *moran* before her marriage. The emphasis of each encounter varies with context. Women are attached to male age-sets by association only and do not form age-sets in their own right. Thus, even at times when they dance together and are collectively poised to assert their rights, seizing the central arena as married women opposed to elders at large, they do not act as an age-set, but as a peer group in a much broader sense.

Age and Generation Systems

The Maasai age system is associated with a complex cycle of ritual detail and is open to a variety of interpretations and regional variation, but the basic rules that govern this process are essentially unambiguous. In other systems, the process of recruitment may be complicated by rules relating to generation in addition to age and this raises the complexity to a new level. In extreme cases, the rules may seem contradictory and perverse, and the system takes on the appearance of some archaic machine. At first sight it seems as though it cannot possibly work and perhaps does not work in quite that way. However, to be cynical and disbelieving is to follow the path of the proverbial mathematician who proved that bumble-bees cannot fly. If these improbable systems are supported by firm ethnographic evidence, then one has to accept that perhaps they *do* work in some fashion, and this may offer an insight into their role within the wider workings of society.

It is precisely this aspect of age systems that was considered briefly in Chapter 1, for the issue that is often dismissed in the ethnographies is not the question of whether age systems work, but whether they have a wider relevance. Yet arguments that try to account for unwieldy generation systems as self-contained modes of action or thought have an inconclusive ring. Thus Gulliver's claim that the Jie generation system is almost exclusively concerned with ritual affairs misses the political dimension that is explored in Lamphear's work as a historian. Similarly, Paul Baxter explains the rules of *gada* generation-sets among the Booran as an engaging philosphical system that is communicated by speech and symbol. This in turn relegates the political dimension explored by Legesse to a matter of rhetoric rather than power.[5] To disclaim the wider relevance of esoteric ritual knowledge and privilege in the hands of older men is to overlook the pervasive trappings of power and the relevance of secret societies as a model for understanding age systems.

The central topic of this chapter is an attempt to unravel just one of these generational systems. This is shared among the Karimojong-speaking peoples, represented in Figs. 2.1*a* and 2.3*a–c* by the Jie and Turkana. Among these, the version of the Jie is particularly interesting, not because it is unique in its generational complexity, but because the problem appears to be especially intractable and the literature is unusually rich in providing enough clues to explore possibilities.

In this analysis, various points that emerged from the outline of the Maasai age organization have to be borne in mind. The system should make demographic sense. Attitudes towards younger men and towards ageing are frequently ambivalent: the premiss of gerontocracy does not automatically lead to respect for old age nor to the willing compliance of younger men. The system

[5] P. H. Gulliver (1953: 164; 1955: 11); Lamphear (1976: 153–4); Baxter (1978: 152–3); Legesse (1973: ch. 3).

is likely to be concerned with the dynamics of power relations with age, and this may become transformed in the cyclical process of development where first one model and then another may be more appropriate: young men who are pinned down or elders who are respected at one point may be in a quite different position later in the cycle. As with the dynamics of family development, so with age systems, it is useful to envisage a developmental cycle, or better a spiral, as the age-sets or generation-sets process up the ladder, rather as bands on a revolving barber's pole appear to progress upwards. The addition of generation to age complicates the analysis, but it does not alter the fact that these are still primarily systems of age organization.

The Jie Generation Paradox

The Karimojong-speaking peoples share a tradition of common patrilineal descent and the close similarities between them extend to their age/generation systems. In the ethnographic literature on these, it is the system of the Jie of Uganda that poses the clearest problem for analysis, highlighting the divergence between generation and age. Within any lineage, the age span of each successive generation increases, so that any grouping based on both generation *and* age is liable to break down at the margins where the most junior members are increasingly young and the most senior are increasingly old. The paradox of the Jie system is that they hold firmly to the criterion of generation for recruitment into an extended age-set, and the ethnographies of Gulliver as an anthropologist and Lamphear as a historian both insist that this system is stable.

Referring to the grouping based on a single generation stretching across all lineages as a 'generation-set', the four principles for the Jie are listed by Gulliver as follows.[6]

1. *All* the members of one generation must have been initiated before *any* members of the next generation can be initiated. Corollary: only one generation-set at a time can be open to recruitment.
2. A man *must* belong to the generation-set immediately following that of his father. Corollary: the youngest members of a generation at its tail-end cannot slip down to join the succeeding generation-set destined for their sons: there is no slippage.
3. When a new generation-set is formed and its first initiations take place, at least some members of the grandfather's generation-set should (if possible) still be alive. Corollary: there is ultimately a time limit to the period that the father's generation can remain open to recruit its most junior members.
4. Within each generation-set, there is a grouping of men of broadly the same age into a series of named age-sets.

[6] P. H. Gulliver (1953: 147–8).

This exercise is primarily concerned with the anomalies that arise from the first two rules. As Gulliver points out: 'It will be appreciated that when a new generation begins to form sets there will be a large waiting list of men, some of whom will be middle-aged or more.' At the same time, the youngest members of the previous generation will probably have to be initiated well before the usual age of about 20 years because of the pressures towards the formation of the next generation-set.[7] Neither Gulliver nor Lamphear seriously consider the extent to which this problem might increase with each generation if these rules are followed systematically. In their fine and detailed ethnographies, it is as if the anomaly is fully contained within each generation.

The problem is aggravated by the practice of polygyny, whereby some rather elderly men continue to take on young wives, and by the rule that widows cannot remarry but should continue to bear children on behalf of their late husbands. Thus, even though a man's first marriage tends to be relatively late when he is perhaps 30 years or more, it is quite possible for there to be an age difference of fifty years between the first son of his first wife and the last son of his most junior widow.[8] In the next generation this gap between oldest and youngest grandsons could conceivably increase to 100 years, and to 150 years in the next, and so on.

A possible solution to the problem of cumulative mismatch between age and generation is simply that the system is comparatively new and short-lived: it cannot persist, but must break down as the spread of ages increases with successive generations. This, after all, is the impression given by the simplified age/generation system reported among the Turkana, who have a myth of earlier descent from the Jie. Again, the Karimojong are another neighbour of the Jie with a similar generation-set system, and Dyson-Hudson noted that their system came close to breaking down before the formation of a new generation-set in 1956, when they experienced an 'aberration . . . beyond the tolerance of the system'. However, from Lamphear's account, the Jie system is clearly not new, nor is it said to be breaking down. Abandoning the ritual restrictions in Turkana has been ascribed to their entering a more demanding environment, and not to any inherent defect in the system itself. And among the Karimojong, the initiation of a new generation-set did not accompany a breakdown of the whole system, but displayed a return to traditional order instead.[9]

An alternative solution is that the system may have certain slip mechanisms which allow those men who are too young to drop a generation unobtrusively

---

[7] P. H. Gulliver (1953: 152, 154; 1958: 920); Gulliver and Gulliver (1953: 44); cf. Lamphear (1976: 38–40).

[8] These figures are based on demographic data for the Samburu. It is later argued that the Samburu and Jie are comparable in this respect.

[9] Gulliver and Gulliver (1953: 53); P. H. Gulliver (1958: 920); N. Dyson-Hudson (1966: 199); Lamphear (1976: 35).

(or those who are too old to climb up). One of the major differences between the Karimojong and Jie systems is that the Karimojong admit to having such a mechanism for the most junior members of a generation, whereas this is denied for the Jie. In this respect, the Karimojong pose less of a dilemma and are more flexible. In another respect, however, the Karimojong have the more rigid system: no uninitiated man among the Karimojong may marry or raid or claim adult status, whereas these restrictions do not apply to the Jie.[10]

A further possible solution is suggested where the ethnographies imply an escape route available for individuals or even whole subtribes. At a subtribal level, Dyson-Hudson notes the possibility of secession if unity within a tribe is strained. The generation-set system alone provides the setting for tribal gatherings and unity, and, if the strains of mismatch between age and generation vary between regions, then fission is always possible. Thus, the premature dwindling of the senior generation-set in one remote region of Karimojong in 1956 appears to have been a major factor that increased pressure for new initiations. With mounting delays, this led to a unilateral changeover within this region and it was poised to become a newly independent tribe within the cluster with its own autonomous generation-set system, following the example of other territorial segments that had previously seceded from Karimojong, such as the Jie and Dodos.[11] At a more intimate level, John Lamphear has noted the extent to which the oral traditions of Jie clans cut across the tribes within this cluster and indicate paths of migration at times of crisis.[12] Lamphear does not consider the anomaly of men who are too old or too young for their generation-set, but it is evident that a man who appears to be trapped by his age does have the alternative of emigrating out of the system that has trapped him to his clansmen elsewhere. The myths of origin of the Turkana especially echo this type of movement by uninitiated men who seceded from their fathers. However, secession by whole segments or by individuals appear as possibilities for escape only as a last resort. They are presented as anomalies rather than the norm, and this leaves unexplored the nature of the forces that perpetuate the generation-set system within the tribe and the accommodation of those that remain within it, despite the age discrepancies.

Frank Stewart has proposed a solution to this generation paradox, suggesting hidden slip mechanisms *within* the system. He points out that the Karimojong permit the youngest members of a generation to slip down to the next set, taking care of the problem of underageing: those who are rather young for one generation-set are of a suitable age for the next. This flexibility does not apply to the oldest members who are overaged in relation to their generation-sets, and

[10] N. Dyson-Hudson (1966: 202–4); P. H. Gulliver (1953: 158); Lamphear (1976: 36 n.).

[11] N. Dyson-Hudson (1966: 258–70) does not make the generational mismatch in this region wholly explicit (but see also 1966: 198).

[12] Lamphear (1976: 26–8).

they have to wait until their generation peers have caught up with them, avoiding any problem of cumulative overageing.[13]

This neat explanation cannot be applied to the Jie since they do not permit slipping by the underaged nor do they delay marriage among the overaged; hence the age span between senior and junior lines would seem to increase with each generation. To resolve this, Stewart suggests that the Jie slip unintentionally, and he invokes the principle of 'structural amnesia' which Gulliver discusses elsewhere in the context of Jie descent groups.[14] Structural amnesia describes a process in which the spread of a growing lineage is tacitly narrowed down as less-remembered ancestors are forgotten and their descendants transfer their claims of descent to better-remembered men; in this fiction, former cousins become 'brothers', and distantly related lineages are drawn together. It relates to a way of handling the second-generation crisis among the Jie that was considered in Chapter 1. All Gulliver's illustrations that refer to processes of this kind respect the generation principle (Rule 2), and nowhere does he suggest that an ancestor may actually slip a generation. Stewart, however, suggests that this is precisely what does happen, and in effect it is the memory of ancestors that slips the odd generation, allowing a whole lineage of descendants who are grossly underaged to assume a generation for which they are better fitted. Thus, while Gulliver suggests a certain lateral movement in the context of discussing the dynamics of Jie descent groups, Stewart shifts the context to the dynamics of the age/generation system and proposes a certain vertical movement also.

Clearly Stewart has a point. Yet one may note that 'the Jie are adamant that the basic principle of their system can never be broken' (Lamphear); and that 'the Jie make conscious efforts to prevent a mixing of successive generations in order to prevent a breakdown of the formal structure' (Gulliver). Stewart's invoking the notion of structural amnesia implies that this is a rather shallow consciousness of generational details, whereas Gulliver conveys structural amnesia as a process in which generational propriety is a more important principle for organization than the precise details of descent. Consistent with Gulliver, Lamphear's study of Jie history is based on the strongly corporate nature of their clans and descent groups, coupled with strict adherence to generational principles.[15]

Later in this exercise, an alternative solution to the problem of over- and underageing based on Lamphear's historical material is considered. First, however, this search for hypothetical slip-mechanisms is surely skirting round the central issue. Without demographic data indicating the span and profile of age in successive generations, one just does not know the extent of the problem.

---

[13] Stewart (1977: 42–66, 214–23).
[14] Stewart (1977: 220–2); P. H. Gulliver (1955: 113–17).
[15] Lamphear (1976: 23–4, 35); P. H. Gulliver (1958: 920).

Societies with age organizations are ideally suited for providing an indication of true age in relation to demographic problems of this kind. Unfortunately, the Jie age system with its generational constraints is almost the worst conceivable, and to describe the subgroups within each generation-set as 'age-sets' is up to a point a misnomer: men of the same age can belong to different generations. But, in any case, these authors provide no suitable census data and none found the apparent anomaly worth exploring. It is conformity to the rules that is stressed. Even among the Karimojong at a time of changeover and maximum strain, the slip mechanisms are treated by Dyson-Hudson as a minor issue: the underaged are apparently borderline cases that can be dealt with as they occur without posing a major anomaly.[16]

The problem in demographic terms is an issue that Stewart considers closely with reference to data collected in the USA. He is fully aware of the pitfalls of using such data from an affluent sector of Western civilization and applying it to remote societies such as the Jie, and his discussion on this topic is therefore somewhat inconclusive. He does, however, make a further tentative suggestion to which I must pay tribute, since the present attempt to resolve the paradox stems from this. Stewart suggests: 'We do not have all the demographic information necessary in order to form a clear idea of these generational processes among the Jie (though *I imagine that one could combine what we do know about the Jie with data on more or less similar peoples and produce a hypothetical projection*).'[17]

This is to suggest a mock-up, a simulation of the Jie system to explore it further. In fact, the right conditions do appear to exist among the Samburu, for whom the relevant data are at least available. The Samburu are neighbours of the Turkana, and share many features in common with the Jie, including a pastoral basis to their economy, similar rules regarding the continued fertility of young widows on behalf of their late husbands, and first marriage for men normally after the age of 30. This age of first marriage is generally a useful indicator of the range of polygyny, which would therefore probably be similar among the Samburu and the Jie. Above all, with their non-generational type of age organization, the Samburu lend themselves readily to age censuses, and this lends itself in turn to a simulation of the Jie system.[18]

This is a demographic problem, and leads us to search for some demographic solution. The following argument is therefore once again mathematical, and again I would invite those who are uninterested in such nuances to pass over the next section. At the same time, I would reassure others that the method is straightforward and the resolution of the problem is unexpectedly simple.

---

[16] P. H. Gulliver (1953: 154); N. Dyson-Hudson (1966: 204).

[17] Stewart (1977: 55; emphasis added).

[18] P. H. Gulliver (1955: 242); Gulliver and Gulliver (1953: 43); Lamphear (1976: 33); cf. Spencer (1965: 86, 96, 219). The fact that the Jie appear to have a higher polygyny rate than the Samburu (Fig. 2.1*a*) may stem from the inclusion of dead wives in the sample collected by Gulliver (1955: 243).

Simulating the Jie Generation-Set System: The Demographic Implications

The basic assumption in this exercise is that the Samburu are similar to the Jie in terms of life expectations, age at first marriage, distribution of wives, and fertility rates. This is a useful step towards exploring the problem, taking the cue from Stewart's earlier attempt. However, it is necessary to depart from Stewart in one respect: he bases his approach on data concerning fertility and life expectation among Americans, and American women at that. In his model, it is the women who have babies, and 'generation' is calculated down the female line. From a Jie point of view, however, it is the generations of men—alive or dead—and of sons born in their name that count. Thus, somewhat perversely, one is concerned with the 'fertility' of men—even dead men—and calculations should be based on the male line.

With these points in mind, Table 3.1 is derived from genealogical data for 646 males of a Samburu clan concerning their age-sets and those of their fathers. In this table, all fathers are notionally assigned to age-set *J* as the first generation and the corresponding age-sets of their sons as the second generation are assigned accordingly (*K, L, M* . . .). Over the relevant period, Samburu age-sets were spaced apart by an average of about 14.5 years, and this provides a base for estimating the range of age differences between fathers and sons—that is, between successive generations in the Jie model.[19]

From this table, it is possible to infer the age spread of successive generations on the assumption that the third generation will bear a similar relation to the second as the second does to the first, and so on. That is, each generation is assumed to have the same 'fertility' rate as its predecessor and to differ only in its age profile. Figure 3.1 indicates the spread of successive generations. The curve for the second generation is taken directly from the table, and subsequent curves are derived from it by repeating the calculation for each age-set.[20] To simplify presentation, the figure assumes no population growth, and hence the areas bounded by successive curves are identical and the populations they represent for successive generation are constant.

It may readily be seen in Figure 3.1 that there is an increasing overlap between generations so that, while there is a distinct gap between the first and second generations, there is no gap between the second and third, and by the 150th year there is even a discernible overlap between the third generation and the fifth. This is a clear indication of the extent to which the Jie system would get out of hand if the rules were applied systematically: the extent of overlap

---

[19] Source: Samburu clan census (Spencer 1965: 318–21). My earlier estimates of the period of the Samburu age-set cycle varied from thirteen years (1965: 154) to fourteen years (1973: 149), giving an average of 13.5 years. Coupled with this is the lowering of the age of initiation by about one year per age-set since about 1900, suggesting that age-sets have been effectively spaced apart by about 14.5 years.

[20] This extrapolation has been obtained by multiplying the final column of Table 3.1 by itself over successive generations.

TABLE 3.1. *Age differences between fathers and sons among the Samburu*

Age-set	Average span of time between age-set *J* and subsequent age-sets (years)	Recorded proportion of sons of *J* in each age-set (age-set profile of second generation) (%)
J	0	
K	14.5	
L	29.0	0.9
M	43.5	52.6
N	58.0	33.6
O	72.5	10.5
P	87.0	2.2
Q	101.5	0.2
TOTAL		100.0

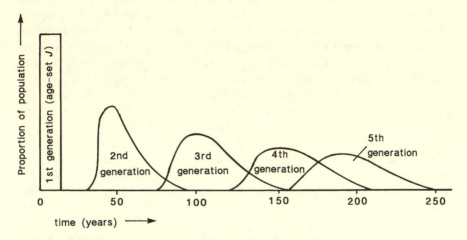

FIG. 3.1. *The age spread of successive generations among the Samburu*

increases to a point where the notion of contemporary generation-sets becomes unworkable. One therefore has to look more closely at the problem in its early stages to explore how this runaway threat to the system might be contained.

An uncertain feature of the Jie ethnography concerns the interval between successive generation-sets. Gulliver estimates this to have been between twenty and thirty years, a figure that Lamphear and Stewart both question.[21] However, Lamphear's suggestion of a forty-year interval is itself questionable, and appears to stem from his estimate of a mean span of 35–40 years between a Jie elder and his oldest surviving son. This would imply that the interval between

[21] P. H. Gulliver (1953: 148); Gulliver and Gulliver (1953: 44); Lamphear (1976: 45); Stewart (1977: 76).

generation-sets is geared to the senior line of older sons, while junior lines stemming from younger sons would become progressively underaged.[22]

Table 3.1 summarizes the extent of the problem. On the one hand, it indicates that an interval of forty years between generation-sets would imply very serious underageing (among younger sons). On the other hand, a more leisurely interval of eighty years would lead to even more serious overageing (among older sons). A crude and in some ways the safest assumption would be that the system is most likely to run with minimum difficulty if the span between successive generation-sets is identical to the average age differences between generations. Table 3.1 suggests a span of about fifty-two years for the Samburu, and this appears a plausible midpoint for the Jie in the present model.

This leads to three further graphs that are derived from this table and Fig. 3.1 with particular reference to the second generation. They explore the implications for changeover at either end of this generation as the notional span between successive generation-sets increases.[23] Fig. 3.2 concerns the problem of overageing among mature 'boys'. Initiation occurs ideally at about the age of 20, and the line marked 'A' indicates the proportion of older sons who would be above this age before their generation-set is open for recruitment. The more extended the period during which their fathers' generation-set continues to initiate its own members, the longer the delay for the sons and the larger the proportion who become overaged. Whence the graph shows an increase over time.

Fig. 3.3 concerns the corresponding problem of underageing at the tail-end of the same generation: those who are still too young for initiation. Below the line marked 'A', the proportion who are underaged diminishes as the span of their generation-set extends from thirty up to ninety years. The problem resolves itself over time, and hence the longer the delay before a changeover, the less serious the problem.

In these two graphs, the curves labelled 'A' mark the lower limit of those who are appropriately placed in the system, reaching the age of 20 while their generation-set is recruiting members. The areas below these curves represent the misfits who have been born too soon in the first graph or too late in the second. Beyond these limits, the ethnographies indicate a range of tolerance of about ten years on either side of the ideal age for initiation: some boys as young as 10 can be initiated early if necessary to facilitate a changeover; conversely, those men who have to wait until the age of 30 before initiation are unlikely to be married at that point or to have left the cattle camp where young men spend most of their time.[24] The curves marked 'B' in the two figures indicate the upper limit of 'gross misfits' who are beyond this range of tolerance and are

[22] Lamphear (1976: 39 n., 45–6); cf. Stewart (1977: 48).
[23] This again involved extrapolation from Table 3.1, assuming that the first generation were equally divided between age-sets *J*, *K*, *L*, and *M*.
[24] P. H. Gulliver (1953: 154; 1955: 18–20, 242); Lamphear (1976: 33, 38, 40).

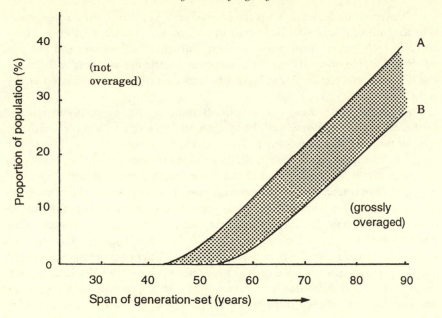

FIG. 3.2. *Proportion of overaged older sons prior to a new generation-set*

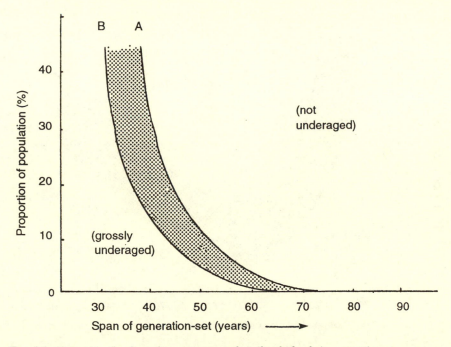

FIG. 3.3. *Proportion of underaged younger sons at the tail-end of a closing generation-set*

grossly over- or underaged. Thus the shaded areas between these curves represent the 'mild misfits' who lie within the range of tolerance. In Fig. 3.2 they
are rather old 'boys' who must wait for initiation but not beyond the age
when they would normally expect to marry and settle in the elders' villages. In
Fig. 3.3 they are rather young boys who can nevertheless be initiated at the
right time.

Fig. 3.4 combines these two graphs. It indicates the extent to which the
misfits pose a major anomaly in the system, and how this would vary with the
span of time between the formation of successive generation-sets. The upper
curve 'A–A' suggests that, with a span of about fifty-one years, the proportion
of misfits would be 15 per cent and at a minimum (8.5 per cent underaged and
6.5 per cent overaged). If the system were run so as to minimize the proportion
of misfits, then this would be the ideal span. However, given that the system
tolerates a mild degree of misfit, the lower curve 'B–B' is more pertinent. This
indicates that the proportion of gross misfits is at a minimum after fifty-five
years, representing only 2.5 per cent of the total (1.9 per cent grossly underaged
and 0.6 per cent grossly overaged). This is not perhaps a wholly insignificant
proportion, but it compares very favourably with a figure of 12 per cent for
gross misfits if one takes Lamphear's estimate of a span of forty years, and with

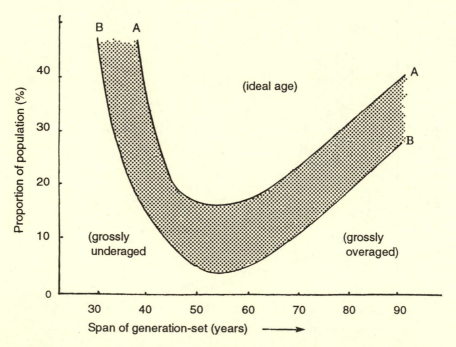

FIG. 3.4. *Proportion of misfits as the span of a generation-set increases*

41 per cent if one takes Gulliver's upper estimate of thirty years. For the changeovers affecting the second generation-set at least, the problem does not after all appear intractable.

These estimates assume that overageing and underageing are equally undesirable for the Jie. However, Rule 1 prohibiting recruitment into more than one generation-set at a time could be taken to imply that the system tolerates overageing and delay more readily than it tolerates underageing and an early changeover. Underageing concerns a generation-set that has been in place for a long time, whereas overageing concerns a generation-set that does not yet exist. If, for instance, the Jie rate *two* grossly overaged 'boys' as no worse than *one* grossly underaged youth at a time of changeover, then Figs. 3.2 and 3.3 could be weighted accordingly to construct a revised Fig. 3.4. This would indicate that the optimum span between generation-sets would be fifty-six years. If *three* grossly overaged 'boys' are no worse than *one* grossly underaged youth, then the optimum span would be fifty-seven years; and so no. In other words, the optimum is not especially sensitive to assumptions regarding the balance of undesirability.

Altogether, whatever the assumptions, there is a reasonably consistent estimate for an ideal generation-set span of about fifty-five years, and the solution is 'robust' in this sense. With this span, 84.3 per cent of the second generation-set would reach the age of 20 years for initiation during the period of formal recruitment. There would be 10 per cent overaged before their set formally opened (9.4 per cent between 21 and 30 years and 0.6 per cent between 31 and 36 years), and at its close there would still be 5.7 per cent who are underaged (3.8 per cent between 10 and 19 years, 1.5 per cent between 0 and 9 years, and 0.4 per cent as yet unborn).

It is possible also to comment on Rule 3: that at the time of changeover, some members of the most senior generation-set should still be alive. If one accepts a generation-set span of about fifty-five years, then this would imply that 'grandfathers' who were 20 years old at the time of their initiation would all be over 75 years. This would reduce to 65 years if one were to include also the tail-end who were initiated young (the mildly underaged). In the Samburu sample, there were enough survivors even into their eighties to satisfy this rule.

In this exercise, a simple demographic model has been used without resort to a computer. The problem is quite simple, the calculations are very straightforward, and the solution is 'robust'. A more sophisticated model did not seem necessary, and it is questionable whether any elaboration of the basic assumptions would have affected the shape of the solution in any significant way. As it stands, the exercise would seem to provide a useful perspective against which to resolve the problem, and it could plausibly simulate the true Jie situation. Taking just two successive generation-sets, the Jie system does appear more feasible than it suggested at first sight. This is at least an important step towards a solution of the Jie generation paradox. However, if there is no slip mechanism to accommodate the gross misfits amounting to 2.5 per cent in the second generation-set, then this problem would be magnified in the third and progressively get out of hand.

This is useful evidence, then, that the Jie system *can* work, but one still has to consider *how* it works and to bear in mind the problem of non-slippage which could build up to a runaway threat to the system.

The Changeover Crisis and the Karimojong: The Politics of Age Relations

The resolution of the Jie paradox, then, lies in Fig. 3.4, which shows that the generation-set rules laid down by Gulliver can be sustained *if* the generation span is of the order of fifty or sixty years, rather than twenty or thirty years, as he suggested. With such a span, an overwhelming majority of boys are of the right age for initiation at the right time, especially if one allows for the permissible leeway of ten years either way for the mildly over- and underaged (the shaded area in the figure), with an accumulation of rather old youths initiated at the inauguration of a generation-set and a tail-end of rather young youths hurried through before it closes.

To understand the dynamics of the generation-set system in this area, it is useful to compare the Jie with their Karimojong neighbours, who are very similar in many respects. Neville Dyson-Hudson's account of the Karimojong suggests that their system is more flexible than the Jie in relaxing Rules 1 and 2 at the time of changeover: they allow the underaged a brief spell of initiation *after* changeover, and the remainder slip into the new generation-set among their age peers when all 'grandfathers' have died. Yet the Karimojong are also more rigid in restricting overaged 'boys', who may not marry or fight as warriors until they have been initiated into the system. Each of these devices resolves the problem of cumulative misfit. The grossly underaged slip down out of sight. The grossly overaged can only begin to have sons at the same time as younger members of their generation. Given the low incidence of these grosser anomalies (1.9 per cent underaged and 0.6 per cent overaged in the simulation), it is understable why Dyson-Hudson barely discusses the problem.

A further difference reported for the Karimojong concerns the fate of the most senior generation-set after changeover. It is not simply that some members should still be alive when their 'sons' are promoted and their 'grandsons' are initiated (Rule 3), but that this step precipitates the retirement of these survivors to a senile political limbo. They are considered as 'children' with no further influence in public matters. Lamphear firmly denies such a situation among the Jie, whereas the reluctance of the Karimojong grandfathers to relinquish all responsibility becomes a major cause for delay in the changeover. It is only when they have dwindled to a handful of survivors and have lost the will to persist as a political force that changeover to a new generation-set becomes possible.[25]

The value of Dyson-Hudson's study is that he undertook his research at a critical time when a new generation-set was being formed. The study provides a vital description of how the system did on one occasion work, rather than how it might be made to work by some experimentally minded Samburu. Like Gulliver, Dyson-Hudson envisaged an ideal generation-set span of between twenty-five and thirty years, and he then had to account for the fact that at the time of changeover, the junior generation-set had actually been recruiting for about fifty-seven years. This, he suggested, was partly because of recurrent drought and partly because the system itself was breaking down under modern conditions. Approaching the time of changeover, he noted increasing unrest as more and more youths of the uninitiated generation took the law into their own hands, raiding when as 'boys' they had no right to raid, assuming personal ornaments to which they had no right, and even marrying prematurely. The fact that the situation was getting out of hand precipitated the changeover ceremony and the formation of a new generation-set. This in turn led to a re-emergence of the traditional order, as the 'fathers' of the newly formed generation-set succeeded in reasserting their authority over their 'sons'. The deviants were now fully within the generation-set system and more directly under the control of the elders.[26]

A striking feature in this account is the closeness of the reported span of perhaps fifty-seven years to the simulated span of about fifty-five years. This prompts one to suggest that the disorder, delay, and innovation are not merely symptoms of the imminent breakdown of the traditional system under modern pressures, as suggested by Dyson-Hudson. They might actually reflect the way in which this system works and has always worked. This is to infer that there may always be an explosive situation during the period leading to a changeover, with a growing number of mature 'boys' who find the restrictions of the system increasingly irksome. Ranged against them are a dwindling number of ageing men of the senior generation-set (their 'grandfathers'). This oldest generation is defunct in some areas, but is still resilient enough in others to resist retirement. As the number of uninitiated 'boys' swells, the physical restraints that have governed them so far are no longer effective. So long as they are kept outside the generation-set system, they are not morally bound by the rules of respect for the more senior men, and to this extent they are outlaws—and behave as such. Moral authority can only be exerted by permitting a changeover and bringing them onto the bottom rung of the ladder and hence into the system. As the situation escalates out of control, it forces the hand of surviving members of the senior generation-set. Through their wilful stub-

---

[25] N. Dyson-Hudson (1966: 159, 175, 193, 198, 202–3); Lamphear (1976: 153–4).
[26] N. Dyson-Hudson (1966: 146–7, 156, 187, 191, 198–9).

bornness, clinging to the illusion of power, they lose esteem and all authority. They now have no option other than to agree to retire, promoting their 'sons' to the senior position of authority, and making room for a new generation-set of 'grandsons'.[27]

Turning once again to the simulation, Figs. 3.2–3.4 were presented previously in static terms to examine the implications of different generation-set spans for the problems of over- and underageing. If the horizontal axis of these diagrams is now redefined as 'years lapsed since the previous changeover', then a more dynamic interpretation of these graphs becomes possible. The vertical axis now represents pressure *for* changeover in Fig. 3.2, and resistance *against* changeover in Fig. 3.3. Taken together, the left-hand portion of Fig. 3.4, indicates how there is a decreasing resistance against changeover during the first fifty-five years, as the underaged increasingly come of age and the oldest generation-set dwindle. After that point, the pressures for a changeover increase very sharply as the number of overaged 'boys' grows. During the years fifty-five to sixty-one, gross underageing would decrease by two-thirds (from 1.9 per cent to 0.6 per cent), but over the same period there would be an eightfold increase in gross overageing (from 0.6 per cent to 4.7 per cent). Thus, while the problems of underageing at the tail-end of the closing generation-set slowly dwindle and continue to delay the changeover, the overageing of the unformed generation-set rapidly builds up and threatens the system. This is to suggest that it is this build-up that sounds the warning to the elders and triggers off a changeover. In this way, the events observed by Dyson-Hudson may be interpreted to fit the simulated model with no bearing on changing times.

A similar process could occur among the Jie, except for Gulliver's insistence that the generation-set system and its associated ritual have little or no economic or political importance. Yet, it was noted earlier that the system appears to be more closely related to social control and the rules of respect for age than Gulliver concedes.[28] From his own material, for instance, this system does appear to play an important role in controlling the queue of bachelors for wives, and ultimately in determining status within the wider community. Lamphear confirms this impression, noting the great respect that Jie should have even for younger members of a more senior generation-set, and the control that members of the senior generation-set have over the movement of cattle, with authority that extends to economic, judicial, and political affairs. 'To the Jie, seniority can be achieved only within the context of the generation-set system' and

---

[27] P. H. Gulliver (1953: 148, 150) noted that the grandfathers' generation-set quickly fall away after changeover, and were defunct by the time of his visit. N. Dyson-Hudson (1966: 197, 202) noted that the most senior generation-set were dwindling at the changeover of 1956, but a score still survived and their sons would continue to be initiated into their correct generation-set until all had died, when the remainder would slip into the succeeding generation-set. The fact that Lamphear noted parallel recruiting into two generation-sets by the Jie around 1970 when many 'grandfathers' survived would be compatible with the Karimojong practice.

[28] See p. 33.

TABLE 3.2. *Interpretations of the Jie and Karimojong generation-set systems*

Ethnographer	Dyson-Hudson	Gulliver	Lamphear
Discipline	Social anthropologist	Social anthropologist	Historian
Fieldwork	Karimojong (1956–8)	Jie (1950–1)	Jie (1960–71)
Date of most recent changeover	1956	1920–3	1963
Assessment of the generation-set system			
Estimated span of generation-sets	25–30 years	20–30 years	40 years
Marriage before initiation?	Not allowed	Allowed	Implicit in text
Slippage among the underaged?	Allowed to facilitate changeover	Not allowed: Rule 2	Not allowed
Retiring generation-set at changeover	Forced into a political limbo	Must still be alive: Rule 3	Remain active afterwards
Two generation-sets allowed to recruit simultaneously?	Briefly, while retired generation-set still survive	Not allowed: Rule 1	Allowed, as retired generation-set remain numerous
Perceived stability (but see p. 116)	'Breaking down'	'Stable'	'Stable'

through it men move closer to God.[29] Taking all this evidence together, one has a clear impression that the emphasis on generation-set ritual is a key feature in the moral order of Jie society and that any anomaly that challenges the rules of precedence at a time of changeover would be a challenge to the moral order itself. The Jie and Karimojong may differ in their precise handling of the misfits, but the dynamics of the generation-set systems seem logically very similar in essence, especially over a period of changeover.

Jie and Karimojong: Breakdown or Steady State?

While the Karimojong generation-set system in 1956 may not have been as anomalous as Dyson-Hudson supposed, there still remain anomalies in the Jie ethnography. The uncompromising rules listed by Gulliver concerning generation-sets appear to have been partially relaxed by the time of Lamphear's study. Was this a symptom of breakdown under modern conditions? Or might it be seen as an aspect of the cyclical system in which rules are ideals that bend under the strain of a changeover, as among the Karimojong? The second argument again is attractive, bearing in mind the phases in the generation-set cycle when the different studies were made. Both Dyson-Hudson's Karimojong at a time of changeover and Lamphear's Jie following a changeover permitted parallel recruitment ('fathers' and 'sons') for as long as the most

[29] Lamphear (1976: 34–5, 36 n., 153, 155, 157); cf. P. H. Gulliver (1953: 164; 1955: 11 n.).

senior generation-set ('grandfathers') survived, whereas Gulliver's Jie were at a different point in the cycle, when none of these older men survived and Rule 1 was upheld, forbidding parallel recruitment.[30] The notion that rules are negotiable in this way appears convincing for the Karimojong, and was in fact a central tenet in Gulliver's later writings (on the Arusha (1963)). However, while rules may be negotiable and the Karimojong system may have been stable, here I wish to argue that the Jie system is actually breaking down after all. As a first step, it is useful to summarize the points of difference between the three ethnographers. These are shown in Table 3.2.[31]

Each of the authors stresses the close links between the Jie and Karimojong: Gulliver in environmental and ethnographic terms, Dyson-Hudson in terms of an evolutionary model, and Lamphear in terms of their oral histories.[32] Originally, they formed a single group, and Lamphear estimates that an initial split had occurred by the early years of the eighteenth century, leading to the emergence of distinct Jie and Karimojong communities by about 1770 and 1840 respectively.[33] It follows that any significant differences between them today should have evolved since (say) 1700. In Lamphear's account, the Jie prior to 1880 were a relatively small disorganized group whose warfare was based on the prowess of independent companies of adventurers underpinned by the generation-set system. Among their principal enemies were the Karimojong to the south and the Dodos to the north, each similarly organized to the Jie, but altogether superior in numbers. At this time, the Jie were clearly overshadowed by these more powerful neighbours, and also by the Acholi to the west. Their survival as a group was threatened. The climax of Lamphear's account occurred between 1880 and 1910 with the emergence of a Jie leader, Loriang, who reversed their fortunes through his military and diplomatic skills. Loriang's initial step was to reorganize the principles on which the Jie army was based with the full connivance of senior elders and backed by their ritual collaboration. He 'substituted an organization based on . . . territorial divisions in place of the more unwieldy traditional organization based on generation and age-sets'. With this reorganization, he led the Jie to take the offensive against their enemies and maintained their superiority until peace was imposed by the British. Lamphear does not suggest that Loriang's innovations modified the generation-set rules, but this is the clear inference. Biological age rather than generation as such now played an important part in the newly organized army, with clear roles for the older veterans and younger warriors, and even for uninitiated 'boys' to gain their first battle experience. The inclusion of boys was consistent with the incorpo-

---

[30] N. Dyson-Hudson (1966: 160, 202); Lamphear (1976: 45); P. H. Gulliver (1953: 147–8).

[31] P. H. Gulliver (1953: 148) suggested that the previous changeover occurred around 1935. In Table 3.2, I have deferred to the historian, Lamphear (1976: 37, 46–8), who suggests 1920–3.

[32] P. H. Gulliver (1952); Gulliver and Gulliver (1953: 28–52); N. Dyson-Hudson (1966: 258–70); Lamphear (1976: ch. 4).

[33] Lamphear (1976: 107, 140, 200).

ration of other non-traditional elements to swell his small army. This reorganization for survival appears to have been more profound than any other change
that Lamphear reports and was specifically not matched by any corresponding
reorganization among the Karimojong or the Dodos.[34]

This suggests that the Jie had a system that was similar to that of the
Karimojong prior to 1880. If so, then slippage from one generation-set to the
next would have been permitted to combat gross underageing, and marriages of
the uninitiated would have been delayed, as among the Karimojong, avoiding
cumulative overageing. There is no indication that Loriang's reorganization
directly affected these earlier rules, but the basic premiss of generational stratification was clearly compromised. The innovations identified true age rather
than generation as the key to effective warfare. Uninitiated men were incorporated into the Jie army to serve with those of a senior generation but similar age.
In this way, constraints on overaged 'boys' were first loosened. It is a short step
from this to suggest that, once these 'boys' had been given the right to participate as full adults in this critical aspect of Jie survival, then the prior restrictions
on their marriage might well have been lifted from this point.[35] This would be
to acknowledge the increasing irrelevance of generation and to take a significant
step towards Gulliver's model which views generation-set organization in 1950
as pure ritual, with no restrictions on marriage, warriorhood, or access to
power.

Removing the restriction on marriage among the uninitiated would precipitate a chain reaction. It would first remove a vital constraint on cumulative
overageing: an overaged oldest son could now marry sooner, and his oldest son
in due course could be even more overaged and marry sooner still. This would
bring forward the pressures of overageing which could only be resolved by
bringing forward the formation of a new generation-set also. However, this
expedient would serve to replace endemic overageing with a new situation
of cumulative underageing, increasing the pressure to keep the promoted
generation-set open for recruitment after the new generation-set had also
been formed, thus modifying Rule 1, and it would progressively increase the
number of survivors in the retired generation-set who would still be physically
robust.

In fact one would have a situation denied by Gulliver in 1950 and unantici-
pated at this phase of the generation-set cycle, but very similar to that recorded
by Lamphear in 1970 following a changeover. The fact that Lamphear noted
that the Jie did not insist that the 'grandfathers' should actually retire could be

---

[34] Lamphear (1976: 230, 231, 233, 238, 239, 247).
[35] Lamphear (1976: 33) quotes the Jie as complaining: 'Young people are growing up faster nowadays
than in the past. Even children are marrying these days.' He interprests this as an allusion to the
occasional marriage of men in their late twenties. Given the emphasis that the Jie also place on
generation as well as age, however, it could quite conceivably be an allusion to the recent marriages and
social recognition of mature uninitiated men who in Jie terms would also be 'children'.

that, by the time of his visit and with the shortened span of generation-sets, there was an accumulation of middle-aged 'grandfathers' who were in a position to demand respect and dismiss any suggestion that they had retired in any political sense.

An important clue to the transformation of the traditional system is the Karimojong practice of permitting continued initiation of the underaged until all members of the generation-set of their fathers have died. Among the Karimojong, this involved a very few aged men who could be expected to die within a few years of changeover. With the modified Jie system witnessed by Lamphear, however, membership of this senior generation continued to thrive and meanwhile there was parallel recruitment into the two younger generation-sets eight years after a changeover. This is to repeat the earlier suggestion that Rule 1 was always marginally relaxed at a time of changeover, as among the Karimojong. However, with the changes to the system, what had previously been marginal was now mainstream, and the rule was suspended. The promoted generation-set seemed poised to remain open for recruitment for an indefinite period.

Once this point has been reached, the problem of underageing resolves itself. With the breakdown of Rule 1, the underaged can be accommodated as they mature. In this way, the Jie can maintain Rule 2, which forbids slippage, unlike the Karimojong, who with traditional pressures permit the underaged to slip as a final resort.

Thus ironically, while Gulliver and Lamphear have given a clear impression that the Jie system persists intact and Dyson-Hudson has suggested that the Karimojong system is breaking down, here I am suggesting that the two situations are reversed. Dyson-Hudson's evidence for breakdown appears quite normal in the situation of changeover and the span of about fifty-seven years which he regarded as quite anomalous is not necessarily abnormal. In fact it is so close to the simulated figure that this adds to the impression of 'robustness' in the system. The Jie evidence is equally far-reaching: it suggests serious overageing before the changeover of 1963, which occurred at a time when there was still serious underageing. The period since the previous changeover of only forty years or so cited by Lamphear may have influenced his general assumption of a forty-year cycle but appears surprisingly short unless it is the consequence of cumulative pressures that will continue into future generations-sets.

This interpretation is to suggest that the successive columns of Table 3.2 form a logical historical sequence: from Dyson-Hudson's Karimojong, to Gulliver's Jie, to Lamphear's Jie, but it is also to question the final row of this table regarding the stability of the system. Instead of reading 'Breaking-down . . . Stable . . . Stable', it should now read 'Stable . . . Poised to break down . . . Breaking down'.

Gulliver's study of the Turkana would logically form a further column to the right of Table 3.2, with the overlapping of generation-sets having developed to a point where there is no longer any stratification between 'fathers' and 'sons', but only two alliances of alternate generations running in parallel (cf. the southern Maasai model of alternating age-sets). The element of generational stratification in the system has by this point broken down altogether.

The scope for reinterpreting the data highlights the problem of ritual cycles that extend beyond the fieldwork experience of any one ethnographer. For conventional age systems with a compact cycle as found among the Maasai, elders at least have a direct experience of the recurring process. However, when approaching a system based on the succession of generations with a natural cycle of fifty years or more, as among the Jie and Karimojong, this goes well beyond the adult experience of the most politically active elders. At the Karimojong changeover of 1956, only a few surviving elders had been involved in the previous changeover as the youngest members of their generation-set when it was promoted. Some of them had lost any memory and others their credibility, and they were all expected to die within the next few years. Recurring patterns of the total generation-set cycle lie beyond individual experience and this is reflected in the contradictions between the various ethnographies. There is no traditional wisdom for viewing the critical transitions of the cycle or for disentangling recent historical trends from characteristics of the ebb and flow of the cycle itself. It is this that appears to account for the problem of assessing the stability of such systems, and the confusion of the final row in Table 3.2.

A remarkable aspect of John Lamphear's study of the Jie is the historical depth he was able to achieve by piecing together clan histories, which enabled him to date events back as far as the late seventeenth century. If one accepts the present understanding of their system, then this achievement is even more remarkable. By assuming that the Jie cycle extended to a span of forty years only since Loriang's time, but to perhaps fifty-five years before then, as in the simulation, this takes the earliest events even into the sixteenth century. The revised chronology is shown in Table 3.3.

The Jie–Karimojong Cluster and the Maasai: A Comparison

In approaching the Jie and Karimojong generation-set systems, once the contradiction between generation and age and the uncertainties concerning historical change have been resolved, there remains the problem of identifying some mainspring that feeds the recurring cycle of development from one generation-set to the next. Here, it has been suggested that the Jie and Karimojong data should be viewed as evidence of a system that effectively pins down the younger generation for a prolonged period. It works in favour of established elders in terms of privileges and access to marriage. Ultimately, because of the extended and inconclusive span of each generation, this provokes a critical point in the

TABLE 3.3. *Revision of Jie and Karimojong chronologies*

Generation-set	Year of formation (changeover)		Comments
	Original estimate	Revised estimate	
Jie			Original estimates in Lamphear (1976: 36–7)
Ngisir	1680	1590	Ancestral group of Jie, Karimojong, and Dodos.
Nigpalajam	1720	1645	
Ngikok	1760	1700	Jie community emerges after this date, but no initial change of the generation-set system.
Ngisiroi	1800	1755	
Ngikikol	1840	1810	
Ngikosowa	1880–5	1865	Jie generation-set rules modified after this date by Loriang. Overaged 'boys' were enrolled into the army from around 1880 and then (it is suggested here) those who had served as warriors were allowed to marry prematurely.
Ngimugeto	1920–3		Followed by Gulliver's study in 1950–1. He noted considerable signs of overageing but reported strict adherence to Rule 1.
Ngitome	1963		Formed after an interval of only forty years because (it is suggested here) of the pressure from overageing due to the innovations of Loriang. However, the tail end of Ngimugeto were still underaged, and they continued to recruit. When Lamphear left in 1971, this divergence from Rule 1 was expected to continue.
?		2003?	Predicted date of the next changeover.
Karimojong			
Ngimoru	1899?		N. Dyson-Hudson (1966: 146–7, 191)
Ngegete	1956		N. Dyson-Hudson (1966: 147, 197)
Ngingatunyo?		2013?	Predicted date of the next changeover (N. Dyson-Hudson 1966: 156–8; but see also Lamphear 1976: 43 n.)

cycle. Overaged members of an unacknowledged generation become increasingly restless and begin to take the law—and marriage—into their own hands, and the members of the most senior generation-set have to accept the inevitability of their own retirement. The apparent unworkability of the system lies in adamant claims that there is *no* premature marriage (Karimojong), or *no* slippage and no new generation-set until the members of the previous set have *all* been inititated (Jie). If such claims are viewed as the rhetoric of elders with an interest in pinning down the junior generation, however, then this allows for a more pragmatic resolution of the problem when the situation threatens to escalate out of control. The rules can be invoked to dominate and delay but they may be more malleable when the status quo becomes untenable. The adaptability of the rules then becomes an aspect of the system alongside the warning bleep in the cycle. Hence, some premature marriage *does* occur in Karimojong and an overlapping between generation-sets *has* developed among the Jie. It is the way in which the system works that resolves the paradox.

There are obviously some far-reaching differences between generational systems and conventional age systems where members of an age-set really *are* peers. Yet, once the problems of generations and misfits have been resolved, there are also some telling similarities. Comparing the *generation* system of the Karimojong–Jie with the *age* system of the Maasai, both control the flow of young unmarried men to elderhood, relieving the family of potential strain in the competition for wives.[36] Each has a recurring developmental cycle of ritual as the sets spiral towards old age. The basic systems in each case are gerontocracies up to a point, with elders in their prime manipulating rules to their own advantage, buying time and wives against the inevitability of their own ageing. This poses the problem of persuading the oldest men that they should retire to promote movement up the ladder and allow a new age-set onto the bottom rung. This appears to be highlighted among the Karimojong, but occurs also in the southern Maasai model, building up to a crisis for ageing men on the top rung, when they in effect are forced to step upwards into space. Indeed, the account of the Karimojong changeover in 1956 appears closely paralleled by Gulliver's account of the Arusha Maasai changeover in 1959, where there was also a tendency towards breakdown under modern conditions beforehand and then a reassertion of the traditional system afterwards.[37] In the Maasai models, keeping control over younger men is a matter of special concern in the north, and reluctance over retirement as old age approaches is a characteristic of the south. Both appear to be features of the Jie–Karimojong generation system at the time of changeover.

If these are not quite gerontocracies in the strictest sense, then this is because the premiss of gerontocracy has its contradictions, as does any other absolute theory of government. Stratification by age highlights the problems of the oldest men who can no longer compete with elders in their prime, and of elders in their prime who cannot quite control the virile excesses of younger men. It highlights the extent to which uninitiated young men can only be controlled by allowing them a stake in the system. In due course there is a characteristic build-up of pressures leading to a crisis point and the formation of a new set. Jie, Karimojong, Maasai, and Samburu each have their own distinctive features, but the evidence points to similar inner workings.

---

[36] See pp. 29 and 33.

[37] N. Dyson-Hudson (1966: 198–9); P. H. Gulliver (1962: 447); Spencer (1988: 216–19). See also Baxter (1954: 315, 336), who was told of bands of unruly young *raba* men among the Ethiopian Booran prior to their circumicision into the *gada* system at the head of their generation.

The Oddity of the Nyakyusa Age-Village System

Given the general gerontocratic premiss throughout this region, however flawed, there appears to be one celebrated exception. This is Monica Wilson's account of the precocious age villages of young men among the Nyakyusa chiefdoms in southern Tanzania. Geographically, the Nyakyusa are the most southern society considered here, but they are (or were) within the pastoral continuum of East Africa, and their age system had elements in common with other age systems in the area. It is necessary here to distinguish between Wilson's first and best-known work on Nyakyusa age villages (1951) and her later volumes that elaborated other aspects of Nyakyusa society.

The first account outlines the traditional process whereby a whole generation of elders would 'retire' every thirty years or so, moving to one side and handing over the government of their country to the next generation, who at this point celebrated their 'coming out'. Before this transition, control would be in the hands of men aged between 35 and 65 years. Afterwards, it would pass down to younger men below 35 years, led by their own village headmen and chief within each area. Then the retiring chief of the senior generation was expected to die, and the village headmen of this generation would tend his shrine in a priestly role.[38]

This account seems to provide a clear exception to the premiss of gerontocracy, and raises the question: in the final analysis, what sort of power was actually handed down to the younger men? How far, for instance, did their control over their own affairs extend to control over the affairs of the senior generation? To what extent was their role in governing the country superior to the priestly role of the older men? Above all, what kind of a generational system might this have been in the past, given that it had been radically modified by the time of the Wilsons' fieldwork in the 1930s, when older men were clearly in control? The evidence is based on the testimony of older men who would have experienced it only as youths and seen it still perhaps through the eyes of young men, distorting their vision.

The subsequent volumes clarify this uncertainty. It becomes clear that senior elders retained substantial authority over their juniors, and they were feared for the misfortune that could result from their anger. They continued to control the flow of marriage cattle, to take on further wives at the expense of their sons, and to retain mystical power in relation to all forms of fertility.[39] Meanwhile, the chief of the *junior* generation had to depend especially on the experience and ritual expertise of the village headmen of the *senior* generation as 'priests', and these retained their position of influence until they became old. Apart from some raiding by younger men on their seniors after coming out, the senior generation were clearly well respected, and their headmen placed themselves

[38] M. Wilson (1951: 22–32).
[39] M. Wilson (1957: 1, 3, 8, 179, 215, 223, 226; 1977: 1, 6, 63, 85–6, 94, 98, 106).

strategically between the rival chiefdoms of young men, holding them in check.[40] This again raises the problem of historical inference in understanding the dynamics of age systems. The first account presents a model of radical change in the relations between young and old—from juventocracy to gerontocracy—whereas the evidence of the later writings points to the persistence of tradition involving a deep-seated ambivalence in the relations between generations.

Similarities between the Nyakyusa and Maasai are striking, with regard to the rift between old and young following a changeover within the age cycle. Rather as young Nyakyusa controlled their own age villages, so the Maasai *moran* controlled their *manyat* or warrior villages. In both societies, these young men were responsible for the defence of their country and raided for cattle, displaying their physical prowess and claiming 'to rule'. This autonomy was an ambiguous claim in both societies where the older men maintained a ritual pre-eminence: these were the headman-priests in Nyakyusa, and the firestick patrons in Maasai. The latter discounted the claims to rule of young men as the 'play of children' in times of peace, but needed their warrior prowess in less certain times. In both societies, it was the elders who controlled cattle and marriage, practising extensive polygyny at the expense of the younger men. Rather as the Nyakyusa stressed that their age-village system served to maintain a proper sexual avoidance between the generations, so the Maasai stressed that the *manyata* system cultivated respect in young people. But in both instances at a more strategic level, this segregation clearly kept the younger men away from the wives of highly polygynous and patriarchal elders. It served the elders well.[41]

There are also some clear differences. Maasai *moran* returned from their *manyat* to their fathers' villages on reaching elderhood, whereas the Nyakyusa tended to remain with their peers in their age villages. Moreover, the Nyakyusa had a generation system absent among the Maasai. That this was a system with two politically active generation-sets within each chiefdom needs to be stressed. It was less problematic than among the Karimojong (or Jie), as it was only the chief who was strictly bound to remain with his generation, which was named after him. He *was* the generation. Commoners might slip a generation if they were too young, or climb to inherit their fathers' position, moving to his village. To this extent the Nyakyusa had 'generation-sets' only in a notional sense. Prominent among the commoners who climbed were those who inherited their fathers' position as village headmen where they inherited also the priestly role. This ensured a continuing virility within the senior generation, whose numbers did not dwindle with age. Because a chief of the junior generation could not

[40] M. Wilson (1959: 4–5, 91–3, 96).
[41] M. Wilson (1950: 128; 1951: 78, 81, 159, 162; 1977: 17, 63, 65, 86, 94); Spencer (1988: 84–6, 107–11, 272–7).

climb, the span of between thirty and thirty-five years from one generation-set to the next appears to have adjusted itself to the process of ageing of successive chiefs alone. In other words, in Nyakyusa, a junior generation-set broadly comprised a chief and his younger peers, and the factors of over- and underageing that increased the generation-set span to between fifty and sixty years among the Karimojong were absent.[42]

In another respect, there appears to have been a clear parallel between the Nyakyusa and the generation-set system of the Karimojong (and earlier Jie). Table 3.4 summarizes the similarities and differences, highlighting the process of changeover between successive generations. As with the Karimojong, the period of changeover in Nyakyusa involved a crisis of ageing. The Karimojong crisis concerned the few survivors at the tail-end of the senior generation; among the Nyakyusa, it was a crisis for the ageing chief, who was in the forefront of the junior ('ruling') generation. Both were under pressure to concede to a changeover that held no future for themselves. It led to social oblivion for the Karimojong survivors; and it foreshadowed death for the Nyakyusa chief. Both were reluctant to agree until their hand was virtually forced by the succeeding generation-set poised to step up to take a central position. In both societies, there was unrest among the newly formed incoming generation-set around this time. In the Karimojong case this was a factor that precipitated the changeover. Among the Nyakyusa it followed 'coming out', when there was a popular upsurge in confidence as young men increased the raiding against their immediate rivals and seized cattle for marriage from their fathers of the senior generation, as their right. A period in the age cycle that has been described as a ritual of rebellion among the Maasai verged on rebellion itself among the Nyakyusa and Karimojong, where the cycle extended to the span of a whole generation and the upheaval was more dramatic.[43]

The anomalies of the Nyakyusa system have led to various reinterpretations of Wilson's data. On a less promising level, Frank Stewart has described the Nyakyusa in his pioneering study as the 'most idiosyncratic of all systems of age organization' with 'too many gaps to make extended analysis worth while'.[44] Yet the data are unusually rich and extensive. The underlying problem seems to be that, like the ethnographers on the Karimojong–Jie, Monica Wilson did not at first anticipate the logical questions that inquisitive readers of her writings might wish to raise. It was sufficient that the system appeared to have worked, at least in retrospect and according to her informants. As a result, the ethnography never quite resolved the apparent contradiction between handing over power to younger men as a matter of principle and retaining it in the final

---

[42] M. Wilson (1951: 31–2; 1959: 49, 92, 94–5, 97; 1977: 9).
[43] M. Wilson (1951: 23; 1959: 50–1, 54, 159–60, 217; 1977: 87, 98); Spencer (1988).
[44] M. Wilson (1975); Charsley (1969); McKenny (1973); Stewart (1977: 8, 19); de Jonge (1985); Hartmann (1991). The earlier writers would not have had access to Wilson (1977).

TABLE 3.4. *The Karimojong and Nyakyusa generation systems compared*

1. KARIMOJONG (cf. Jie before 1880)

	Before inauguration of a new generation		After inauguration	
Defunct generation	(A)	All dead	(B)	Dying off & marginalized
Senior 'ruling' generation	(B)	Survivors politically feeble	(C)	Promoted
Junior generation	(C)	Becoming politically virile	(D)	Promoted
		Inauguration Ceremony ↗		
'Boys'	(Future D)	Becoming physically virile		

2. NYAKYUSA

	Before 'Coming-Out' of a new generation	Chiefly line	Commoners	After 'Coming-Out'	Commoners
Defunct generation	(A)	Previous ancestral chief	Probably all dead	(B)	Ageing survivors
Senior generation 'retired' commoners	(B)	Immediate ancestral chief	Ageing survivors	(C)	Promoted ('retired')
Junior 'ruling' generation	(C)	Ageing chief	Becoming politically virile	(D)	Promoted
			'Coming-Out' Ceremony ↗		
'Boys'	(D)	Chief elect	Becoming physically virile	(E)	Recognized
Sons of 'Boys'	(Future E)		Immature		

analysis among elders, notably in relation to control over ritual. It was this contradiction that offered a challenge to those who have found Wilson's ethnography compelling but incomplete. Here, however, the essential point is that her writings do reveal a system that was both workable and unambiguous. Above all this fits relatively well within the general range of East African age systems, with power transferred uneasily and reluctantly from one generation to the next. It is the structuring of generation and age that highlights the problem and makes the transfer of power a major issue.

The Gada 'Puzzle' and the Cushitic Fringe

The most complex generation system on record is surely that of the Booran of southern Ethiopia. This has been analysed in detail in the complementary ethnographies of Asmarom Legesse (1973), focusing more on political aspects of the *gada* system, and Paul Baxter (1954, 1978), who provides a broader overview. *Gada* is based on an elaborate developmental spiral from youth to old age through a series of twelve grades before final retirement. In comparison with the age systems considered so far, the cycle appears over-defined and rigid, with a narrow band of elders in their prime assuming the task of governing the country for an eight-year period of office: *gada*. The allocation of responsibility is determined by birth. A man follows his father's career path exactly a generation later, but the sequence for different families is staggered. This is achieved by linking each patrilineage to one of five descent groupings (*luba*). Within a *luba*, generations are strictly coeval and form generation-sets. Between *luba*, generation-sets are formally synchronized to trail one another at intervals of eight years. The role of *gada* passes in relay from one descent grouping to the next over a cycle of forty years ($= 5 \times 8$), returning to the first descent grouping in its next generation and so on, rather like the staggered succession of firing in the cylinders of a combustion engine.[45]

The rules of *gada* seem geared less towards enhancing the power of elderly men, who are honoured but under stringent ritual constraint, and more towards the succession of those older sons who are just the right age for their generation. It is they who assume executive responsibility in *gada*, tempered by the sheer expense of holding office. To the extent that the system is governed by a strictly regulated chronology, it does not respond to demographic pressures that might hasten any changeover. In fact, it seems adapted rather towards restricting population growth. The possibility of overageing is eliminated by disposing of infants born before their allotted time, either by infanticide or by handing them over for adoption among non-Oromo. Underageing, on the other hand, is common but disadvantageous. Underaged younger sons are allowed to participate with peers of their own age as warriors. However, they lag behind their generation, and they do not have the status attached to their older brothers as they progress to elderhood. By being born late, they are passengers at the tail-end. Only the lines of more senior sons have a reasonable chance of being born at a time that brings them into their prime to become eligible for office within *gada*.[46]

The intricacies of this system have prompted Baxter to claim that *gada* is a symbolic exercise, a ritual maze with no political or economic significance, and

---

[45] Baxter (1954: 284; 1978: 156–9); Legesse (1973: 8, 51–2, 81, 130–1).

[46] Legesse (1973: 70, 99, 173); Baxter (1954: 280, 307; 1978: 159, 172, 176–7). For a useful assessment of the Booran *gada* system, highlighting the problems raised by contradictions in the literature, see Stewart (1977: 159–74).

Legesse to label it a puzzle, minimizing the relevance of kinship. Instead, Legesse considers the possible origins of *gada* as a system that is logically in the process of breaking down because of progressive underageing. By computing this process backwards in time, his model suggests that each generation would have been fully contained within the system with no underageing around AD 1623. This suggests a date for the pristine inception of *gada* and for Booran expansion leading to the incorporation of other peoples into the Oromo federation, as peripheral 'younger brothers' of *gada*.[47]

Legesse's is a neatly contrived exercise; however, one may note that his assumption of breakdown echoes Dyson-Hudson's view of the Karimojong generation system, and Legesse too overlooks the possibility that the system he has observed may in fact be stable and that the element of underageing may be an aspect of this stability, structuring power relations within the family.[48] Similarly, Baxter's argument that *gada* is primarily a symbolic exercise echoes Gulliver's claim that the Jie generation system is concerned solely with ritual. This overlooks the extent to which control within *gada*, as in Jie ritual, is concerned with the hidden power of esoteric knowledge. It is those of the right age and with the longest pedigree of ancestors, in step with *gada*, who are close to the seat of influence, especially if they also have the necessary wealth to fulfil the responsibilities of office. Eligibility for office is of the essence here and not necessarily marriageability.

Clearly, kinship *does* have a role. Outside *gada*, patrilineages are ideologically slanted towards senior sons and the principle of primogeniture. The rules of inheritance and of the *gada* system conspire to marginalize younger brothers at the tail-end of their generation. They have certain minimum rights, but may find themselves in conflict with their older brothers; and as they mature they tend to leave the cattle economy, migrating to establish a livelihood elsewhere and effectively dropping out of the system. With the emphasis on strict primogenture, it is oldest brothers who inherit wealth and status within the family and it is also they who are more likely to arrive at the right age into *gada*. In accounts of the earlier period of Booran expansion also, it was younger brothers who tended to settle as migrants in areas peripheral to *gada*, while their older brothers returned to their homelands to take up their inheritances. Thus the Booran *gada* is certainly complex, but at least it appears workable at first sight in a way that the Jie system did not, and it tallies neatly with the rules governing succession within the family. It consolidates power within the extended family, although towards the senior lines of descent rather than towards birth order or the senior generation as among the Jie. Primogeniture rather than age as such seems to be the central feature, and limiting family size is more important than growth. There is no suggestion that impoverished younger sons

---

[47] Legesse (1973: 129–78 (esp. 159–60); 221, 224); Baxter (1954: 280; 1978: 152–3, 156).
[48] Cf. Baxter (1978: 177).

can build up their own fortunes, as the Maasai or Samburu do. The spirit of enterprise is constrained; or, rather, it leads the more enterprising younger sons to leave their parental homes to pursue their fortunes elsewhere.[49]

Consistent with this restraint on growth, Fig. 2.1*a* shows the three Oromo samples (the Booran, Macha, and Gabbra) grouped towards the lower end of the polygyny scale. Nearby in the diagram are the camel-owning Rendille, who are identified politically with the Samburu (Fig. 1.1) and historically with the Somali in opposition to the Oromo.[50] In terms of their social organization, however, the Rendille appear closer to the Oromo, with low polygyny, strict primogeniture, population limitation, the intermittent emigration of younger brothers (to Samburu), and an age system that is geared to these practices with a cycle of forty-two years (= 3 descent groupings × 14 years). Whatever links the Rendille may have with the Somali or Samburu, their age system and social organization more generally bear an unmistakable affinity with other Cushitic-speaking peoples in north-eastern Kenya, notably the Gabbra and Sakuye, but extending also to the Oromo federation.[51]

Another approach to this group, that has been systematically pioneered by Gunther Schlee, concerns oral traditions of intermigration between different peoples that link clans and lineages across the region. One aspect of this is the dispersal of younger brothers impoverished by the rule of primogeniture which is associated with *quasi-gada* types of age organization, a feature that again extends to the Rendille. Elsewhere, migration between tribal groups is a common feature of oral tradition, for instance among the Jie. *Gada* and the Jie-Karimojong generation systems are of quite different orders, but the problem of generational spread haunts each system and emigration offers the possibility of an escape route. This appears institutionalized among those with *gada* affinities, and was perhaps a last resort among the Karimojong and Jie formerly. The spread of generations leads to the spread of families and clans throughout the region, and it provides a measure of insurance in the longer term as intermigration routes are established and maintained, rather as herds are dispersed among a network of stock associates to secure the future.[52]

---

[49] Legesse (1973: 19, 25, 35, 66); Baxter (1954: 50, 65–6, 320); Hultin (1979: 285–6). Cf. Spencer (1976: 179); Dahl (1996: 172).

[50] Spencer (1973: 147); Schlee (1989: 5–6).

[51] Schlee (1989: 9–25). Three Rendille customs appear especially close to Booran practice: (*a*) the 'sharing camels' noted in Fig. 1.1, cf. *dabarre* among Booran (Spencer 1973: 37–40; Schlee 1989: 56–8, 213); (*b*) the system of staggered descent groupings (*teeria*) over a cycle of 42 years, cf. the *gada* cycle of 40 years (Spencer 1973: 35); (*c*) the practice of allowing older sons especially to climb up to an age-set three below their fathers', cf. five age-sets in *gada* (Spencer 1973: 33–5; Stewart 1977: 112–13; Sato 1980: 6; Schlee 1989: 73–92).

[52] Schlee (1989); Baxter (1954: 65–6, 317); Legesse (1973: 35, 66); Bartels (1970: 139 (cited by Hultin 1979: 285–6)); Bulcha (1996: 52); Spencer (1973: 130–40); Lamphear (1976: 24–31). See also pp. 18–19 and 24.

Conclusion: Age Systems and the Problem of Historical Change

Age systems associated with East African pastoralists pose a double anomaly: the extent to which ethnographers have denied them any wider relevance is matched by the persistence of these systems even into the post-colonial era when so much else has changed. The very fact that they concern relations between the young and old bears on a variety of perennial topics in social anthropology generally: rituals of transition, the life course of individuals, the developmental process of families, and problems of generational succession. Age systems and families are the public and private sectors respectively; and if they are not popularly seen to prop each other up, then this may reflect the unpopularity of functionalist assumptions in anthropology. In contemporary terms, age systems may be seen as anachronisms, but their persistence suggests that the functionalist argument has a peculiarly resilient ring, and the search for links with kinship systems here has been rewarding.

Nevertheless, there has clearly been change, and this raises the problem of disentangling historical shifts from the recurrent phases of development within the age/generation-set cycles, especially when direct observation by the visiting anthropologist amounts to little more than a passing glimpse. It is arguably possible to distinguish between these two types of change where the age-set cycle has a duration of about fifteen years, as among the Maasai: mature informants have enough experience of the spiral of ageing to separate the two aspects. Even among the Booran, where the *gada* cycle extends over forty years, the repetition of events every eight years provides a cumulative experience that is widely shared. However, when the span is a generation-set that extends to fifty years or more, as among the Jie or Karimojong, then there may be no conventional wisdom on phases of development or the strains of changeover. Evidence of strain can then be interpreted either as a unique historical event or as a phase of the cycle, and the balance between these is a matter of personal judgement. Dyson-Hudson for the Karimojong and Legesse for the *gada* system have both argued the case for historical change to explain the incongruities. However, this chapter has attempted to reverse both arguments, suggesting that the strains provide clues to the workings of each system with no direct bearing on history as such. This is again to argue in favour of the stability of these systems, at least in the remoter areas that have been less affected by modern change.

On the other hand, age systems have clearly evolved in response to circumstance, guided by elders responsible for their upkeep. The Booran provide perhaps the most striking example of this in relation to their *gada* cycle. This culminates every eighth year in a massive assembly of delegates from all parts with an open remit to revise any aspect of customary law and binding powers.[53]

---

[53] Legesse (1973: 86, 93, 97–8). Cf. Baxter (1978: 177).

In a similar vein, the Jie radically altered their generation system in response to the pressure of events. Among the Maasai also, elders were the repositors of the wisdom underlying their system, intimately involved in its operation, and they sought to uphold tradition at each stage of their age cycle. But they also assumed a licence to reinterpret the rules in response to new circumstances as *they* saw necessary. Each age system has the appearance of a richly cultivated tradition, rather like a well-established garden that needs upkeep and renewal. In this way, the traditions were not lost but were subject to creeping reinterpretation, and the age systems modified over time. Often these changes appear to have been a mild form of tinkering, but the modification of tradition to ensure survival was far-reaching in the case of the Jie, apparently leading towards irreversible change. Generally, the evidence points towards a creeping change, and the resilience of the age systems may have been precisely their ability to adapt rather than persist unchanged. The age systems in the remoter areas may have survived, not despite colonial and post-colonial interventions, but rather because they adapted at each stage.

Over substantial parts of the pastoral region, probably no change has been more far-reaching than the colonial intervention, fixing boundaries and imposing a measure of peace. To the extent that this restricted young men, the new regime affected the distribution of power with age; and this has a bearing on the remainder of this work. Part II provides an evolutionary slant on the development of pastoralism, adapting over successive age-sets to new pressures and opportunities as recent economic forces have permeated even to areas where the population remains sparse and nomadic. This is to switch attention from the dynamics of traditional pastoral systems to the impact of irreversible change.

PART II

Opportunism and Adaptation to the Pastoral
Niche: The Case of the Chamus of Lake Baringo

4

The Chamus Tradition of Pre-Pastoral Origins

The emphasis on tradition in pastoral societies of East Africa may be viewed up to a point as a denial of historical change. The Maasai, for instance, portray their past largely as a projection of the recent present and tend to assume that earlier communities were not radically different from their own at the time of post-colonial Independence in the 1960s, apart from being more exposed to the uncertainties of warfare and shifting borders. There is little sense of earlier historical development, and even the sequence of past age-sets, which provides an ideal scale for a chronology of events, is perceived less in terms of social change than as a demonstration of the persistence of tradition, replicating the ahistorical process of ageing.

In Part II, a single case study serves to extend this discussion to the topic of change among the Chamus, a community who have adopted a pastoral way of life and now share the problem of accommodating this to post-colonial trends. The Chamus claim a long history of association with their Maa-speaking neighbours, the Samburu and Maasai, but hold an altogether more dynamic view of their past.[1] Their oral traditions concern changing interaction, and the sequence of earlier age-sets is associated with innovations as they developed a mixed economy and adapted their social organization appropriately. To this extent, the reconstruction of the Chamus past is not simply a historical exercise, but reflects their awareness of their own accommodation to change while remaining firmly entrenched in the vicinity of Lake Baringo. Through this extended ethnographic illustration, the study reaches beyond persisting traditions to a view of pastoralism as a historical phenomenon, adopted and modified over time.

The Foraging Niche in a Pastoral Region

Lake Baringo lies in a barren region of the Rift Valley in Kenya just north of the equator, relieved by rivers fed from the escarpments on either side. According to their oral traditions, the Chamus were originally a Maa-speaking community of hunters and gatherers who were established in the valley around the lake. Here, the term foragers is used to express the very feature that has led

---

[1] The (Il-) Chamus are also known as (Il-) Camus, (Il-) Tiamus, and in the early literature as Njemps or Njamus. Njemps is still the formal name of their location. 'Tiamus' is the least likely to be mispronounced (Tucker and Mpaayei 1955: 311); however, 'Chamus' seems to have become established usage in recent literature.

pastoralists such as the Maasai to hold them in contempt: the fact that they had no wealth of their own and were forced to forage in order to subsist. Small communities of this kind were scattered throughout the Maa area and their earlier relationship with their pastoral neighbours provides a backdrop for the present chapter.[2]

The boundary separating the two forms of livelihood was permeable. The foragers exploited an ecological niche that the pastoralists regarded as inferior but also complementary to their own. In times of hardship, pastoralists who had lost their herds were reduced to whatever opportunity presented itself for survival. As individuals or as families, refugees could join the foragers, some temporarily until the crisis had passed and others for an indefinite period. At other times, individuals from a foraging community might ally themselves to a pastoral household, young men as herders or young women as casual wives, and either would acquire a certain acceptance if they could establish themselves within the pastoral niche, and even considerable respect if they surpassed expectations. The numbers involved either way would never have been substantial, but at times of crisis when many pastoralists perished, some at least could survive among foragers; and in easier times there would be a net flow in the opposite direction, from foraging to herding.

Among the foragers, an aspect of the symbiotic relationship with their pastoral neighbours was to trade products of their hunting for small stock, or to serve as trackers or spies in times of war, even allying themselves at different times to rival groups of pastoralists. These were aspects of their subsistence strategy. A new product from whatever source offered a new opportunity to extend their niche; when Swahili traders and then Europeans appeared on the scene, foragers were often among the first to trade as middlemen and to offer themselves for employment, while the pastoralists were (and still are) among the last. The pastoral niche was defined through stock ownership, whereas the foraging niche would spread pragmatically to any new opportunity for livelihood within their territory.

In this interplay, there was never any doubt that the foragers had a lower status than the pastoralists. They avoided owning herds of their own that would restrict their freedom and attract raiders. Their strategy was to maintain a lower profile, typically adopting the superficial aspects of the culture of their closest pastoral neighbours: their dress, adornments, clan and age-set names, and even their language. But the refinements associated with these were lacking among the foragers, and in the presence of pastoralists their uninhibited lack of finesse and crude display of self-interest merely reaffirmed their low status. Those who wished to become accepted among the pastoralists had to adapt themselves to higher ideals.

---

[2] Spencer (1973: 199–209; 1974: 419–20). This pattern has been elaborated further by John Berntsen (1976: 3–5; 1979: 110–14).

Tides of fortune also affected the major pastoral communities in their relations with one another and their claims to territory. Depending on their ability to dominate, they would expand into better grazing areas, displacing other pastoralists, or they would contract and be displaced, or even be eliminated as a corporate community. The vagaries of population growth, epidemic, and the random spread of tsetse infestation or drought also altered the balance. The territorial claims of pastoral communities had shifting boundaries, responding to pressures and opportunities. Foragers, on the other hand, appear to have held aloof from competitive striving for territorial gain and to have remained fast in their territorial niche during periods of adversity. The inference is that their detailed knowledge of the local terrain was an essential part of their foraging, and that this limited the rivalry between neighbouring foraging communities. The changing pattern of pastoral dominance led to a certain chameleonlike response among the foragers. When their pastoral neighbours changed, so did the prevailing fashion among the foragers, who would if necessary switch to a new language, new forms of dress, new clans, new age-sets. They merged into their new surroundings, rather as cautious hunters, and were then poised to form new alliances. In my earlier survey, five out of seventeen Maa-speaking foraging groups in northern Kenya had either changed their language comparatively recently, or appeared in the process of doing so. In this way, groups recorded as (Kalenjin-speaking) 'Okiek' or (Oromo-speaking) 'Warta' at one stage could become (Maa-speaking) 'Dorobo' at another, and vice versa. These are all terms applied to foragers. The identity of these groups did not change, but only their outward trappings in a strategy for retaining their territorial niche as their circumstances changed.

According to Chamus traditions, they were once 'Dorobo' who have since developed a mixed economy extending to irrigation agriculture and pastoralism. They are no longer simply foragers, but in their oral traditions there are aspects of their society that are reminiscent of the pragmatic opportunism associated with foragers in the above model. The Lake Baringo basin has always remained their niche. In the earliest writings on the area, the Chamus are reported as living in two villages that served as a strategic trading post where ivory hunters and early explorers from the coast could replenish their diminishing supplies of food. Correspondingly, the Chamus provided a niche for refugees from pastoralist communities during periods of drought and famine. Serious drought was, however, an erratic hazard that they too had to contend with, adding an element of uncertainty to their own subsistence and making them at best an unreliable source of surplus for others when they themselves were periodically reduced to foraging once again for survival.[3] An intriguing aspect of their oral history, as it unfolds, concerns successive adjustments in the balance of their mixed economy. It is as if they have retained a foraging strategy

---

[3] e.g. Thomson (1885: 312); von Hohnel (1894: 4).

and outlook, extending their range of subsistence activities as the opportunities arose. One is presented with a dynamic flexibility beside which Maasai or Samburu accounts of their own histories have the somewhat flat quality already noted—a concern solely with the pastoral dimension as their herds have increased and diminished over time. In pre-colonial as well as post-colonial times, the Chamus economy has been involved in a somewhat erratic economic development to an extent that has been shunned by pastoralists. Correspondingly, Chamus institutions and practices have adapted pragmatically to these changes. As they themselves see it, their foraging is ancient, their irrigation long established, and their pastoralism relatively new, and each of these is associated with different institutional arrangements that have modified over time. The resistance to innovation widely reported among the pastoralists is not just a prejudice among ethnographers whose static models do not extend to the concept of change. When viewed beside the successive adaptations of the Chamus, the Maasai and Samburu have been quite strikingly resistant to the pace of change.

Age-Sets and Clanship in Chamus History

An important aspect of the Chamus sense of history is their age system, with named age-sets reaching back well over a century. This provides a useful chronology for events, but only up to a point, given the uncertainties of oral tradition. The memory of Chamus age-sets lies somewhere between an account of true history and an expression of the way in which they structured their traditions at the time of my fieldwork in 1977. Table 4.1 lists the sequence of age-sets with some indication of the year in which each might have been initiated from available evidence.[4]

---

[4] The initiation dates 1889–1959 had been independently assessed in the records available in Marigat during my first visit in 1959. David Anderson (1984: 113–15) has suggested an age-set interval of fourteen years in extrapolating dates back into the nineteenth century as against my own assumption here of twelve years. Two pieces of evidence he cites are inconclusive. The first is to link the defeat of the Laikipiak with the *moranhood* of the Laimer, Tarigirik, and Peles age-sets among the Maasai, Samburu, and Chamus respectively. However, from the chronologies Anderson cites, this could fit either scheme: an interval of twelve *or* fourteen years. Secondly, the earliest migrations of the Samburu (Toiyo) to Baringo are cited by Anderson as occurring when the Samburu age-set of Kipeko were *moran* (*c*.1837–51) and Nyangusi in the Chamus, and this is indeed compatible with a fourteen-year interval (placing Nyankusi *moranhood* at 1846–60 as against 1853–65 in the twelve-year scheme). However, these migrations were from the Kerio Valley area, and, in the Samburu chronology cited by Anderson, it was noted that the Turkana only reached the northern end of the valley and menaced the Samburu when the Kiteku were *moran* (*c*.1851–65); and this would again be consistent with an interval of either twelve or fourteen years. The existence of identically named age-sets among the Chamus and Maasai (Table 4.1) coupled with the Maasai chronologies calculated by Fosbrooke (1956: 194) and Jacobs (1968: 16) provides altogether firmer evidence for an average span of twelve years for Chamus age-sets in earlier times (see p. 135). Anderson also records separate age-set names for the two Chamus villages from the Peles age-set onwards. My own material suggests that his Down-River names refer to all Chamus corresponding to Table 4.1 and the Up-River names express a local identity within the wider community, a subgroup within the whole, as occurs among other Maa (Spencer 1965: 88; 1988: 189).

TABLE 4.1. *Chronology of Chamus age-sets*

Age-set	Notional year of initiation	Comment on chronology
Karankuti		
Twaati	1841	In 1977, elders of Kiliako age-set recalled seeing some very old Twaati elders in their youth. (Maasai Twaati (I) were initiated in *c.*1836–9.)
Nyankusi	1853	Two elders of this age-set reported to be still alive in 1928. (Maasai Nyankusi (I) were initiated in *c.*1851–3.)
Peles	1865	Prominent in Chamus oral history (see below)
Kideni	1877	
Kinyamal	1889	Said to have been *moran* when the Europeans raised their flag at Baringo. Presumably this referred to the initiative in 1890 by Carl Peters (1891: 273). No living survivors in 1977.
Kiliako	1901	A few survivors were still alive in 1977.
Irimpot	1913	Year estimated in the administrative records.
Napunye	1927	Year recorded in the administrative records.
Parimo	1939	Year recorded in the administrative records.
Merisho	1948	Year estimated in the administrative records.
Meduti	1959	Year recorded during first field trip.
Bikisho	1970	*Moran* during second field trip. Also known as Kiaapo.
Mopoiye	1982	*Moran* until 1994.

This chronology gives an approximate age-set span of twelve years, based on three pieces of evidence. First, during the period for which there are independent records of initiation (1913–59), four age-sets elapsed giving an average span of 11.5 years. Secondly, a somewhat blunt piece of evidence is the survival of the oldest men. The fact that a few Kiliako were still living in 1977 and that two Nyankusi had been reported still alive forty-nine years earlier suggests an interval of about twelve years (49/4) in pre-colonial times.[5] Thirdly, the names for Twaati and Nyankusi were identical to successive Maasai age-sets and it is likely that these terms were coined by the Chamus for age-sets that were contemporary with their Maasai namesakes, especially if as boys they were initiated around the same time. The Chamus saw themselves as within the Maa cultural milieu, and this extended to identifying with their age peers across tribal boundaries when they paraded themselves in celebration around this time of changeover. In casual conversation, the name of one age-set is even substituted for the other.[6]

Another feature of Chamus society that has relevance to their perception of history is the clan system. Very broadly, different clans are seen as having immigrated to the area at different times and from different neighbouring communities (Map 2). These accounts can be deceptive, since immigrants came

[5] Baringo District Annual Report, 1928, AR/727.
[6] Spencer (1988: 70). A casual substitution of this kind seems to have occurred, for instance, when Dundas (1910: 54) cited two Samburu age-sets, Terito and Merisho, as authentic Chamus names. Cf. Anderson (1984: 115).

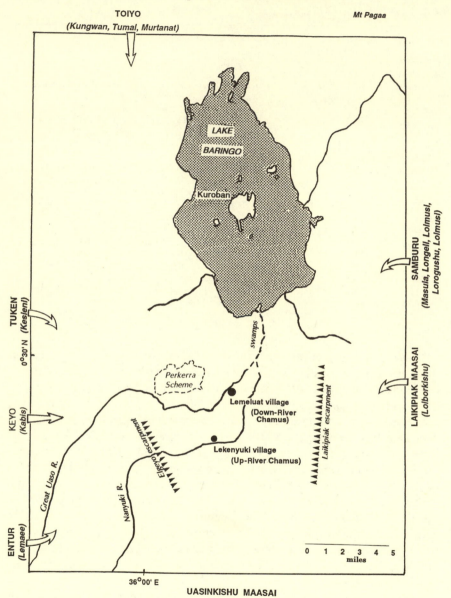

TOIYO
(Kungwan, Tumal, Murtanat)

Mt Pagaa

LAKE
BARINGO

Kuroban

SAMBURU
(Masula, Longeli, Lolmusi,
Lorogushu, Lolmusi)

TUKEN
(Keslenl)

0°30' N

swamps

LAIKIPIAK MAASAI
(Lolborkishu)

*Perkerra
Scheme*

Lemeluat village
(Down-River
Chamus)

KEYO
(Kabis)

Laikipiak escarpment

Elkeyo escarpment

Lekenyuki village
(Up-River Chamus)

Great Uaso R.

Nanyuki R.

ENTUR
(Lemaee)

0 1 2 3 4 5
miles

36°00' E

UASINKISHU MAASAI

MAP 2. *The Baringo region and clan traditions of migration*

as individuals rather than as established clans, which probably only emerged subsequently. Thus, immigrants from the Keyo (Elgeyo) are said to have arrived as individuals before they became recognized as a distinct clan known as the Kabis. Again, certain subclans may claim a separate origin from their parent clan, or a new clan failed to emerge. Thus, a number of Uasinkishu Maasai families have settled down among the Chamus, but, instead of grouping together, they have been absorbed by other clans. It is the clans with their established traditions that have significance for the Chamus, while the more intimate traditions claimed by individual families are seen as incidental, distinguishing them from one another but with less relevance for Chamus affairs.[7]

With this dual framework—successive age-sets and emergent clans—it is possible to trace in greater detail the oral traditions of the Chamus, although with certain reservation. My two visits to the Chamus (in 1959 and 1977) were relatively brief, and the thrust of my information was supplied by elders who were associated with the dominant Chamus section (previously the larger of their two villages). To this extent, any alternative interpretation among the smaller section is absent here. My earlier visit had posed problems concerning the mix of familiar Samburu and unfamiliar Maasai elements. On my second visit, having now worked among Maasai also, I wished to clarify this Chamus mosaic. This led naturally to questions concerning their earlier contacts. From this starting point, it was *their* enthusiasm for their history and the richness of their accounts that shaped the course of my enquiry. This is related here from the perspective of 1977, when my information came mainly from elders of the Irimpot, Napunye, and Parimo age-sets.

The Keroi and the 'Karankuti' Transformation

Among the Chamus, the Parsaina clan (also known as Sakaam) claim to be the true descendents of the Keroi, the aboriginal community associated with Lake Banrigo. Age-sets of this early period are essentially disembodied names— eventless terms that older Chamus remember having heard. Some perhaps have more recently been borrowed from the Samburu (Meishopo, Kipayang, Kipeku), while others, with no obvious parellels elsewhere, may have been genuine Chamus age-set names (Leponguai, Kisaiti, Ratanya).[8] Generally,

---

[7] Details of dispersal among the Chamus include: the Uasingishu lineages of Lenguesena, Lesoiti, and Leparsupore which were dispersed among the Loimusi, Tumal, and Murtanat clans respectively; refugees from the Laikipiak Maasai and the Sakutet of Meru descent, who together formed the new Loiborkishu clan; and the Murtanat, who seem to have been a Toiyo subclan at one time before becoming more closely affiliated with the Lorogushu.

[8] Spencer (1973: 150–3). Anderson (1984: 113) also notes two other earlier age-sets: *Kupai* is identical to an early right-hand Maasai age-group noted by Hollis (1905: 262), suggesting a further Maa link; *Kinyany* could just conceivably be the same as Salganya recorded in the Baringo District Annual Report (1928) and corresponding to the notable Samburu Salkanya age-set dating back to the eighteenth century (Spencer 1973: 150). The same administrative record also notes Ichinnoyu and Likibaiyam among earlier age-sets.

information on these is lacking, but the Chamus insist that they did have age-sets at this time, with ritual leaders, circumcisions, and warriors (*moran*) who observed certain food avoidances in common with other Maa-speaking peoples.

This aboriginal situation changed, they say, 'when Karankuti were *moran*'. Karankuti may well have been a momentous age-set, but so much is claimed for this period that the term 'Karankuti' suggests much more besides. It appears to be used as a label for a fundamental transformation that is likely to have extended well beyond a single twelve-year period of *moranhood*. It borders on the timelessness of mythical events, long, long ago. For this reason no date is suggested for the Karankuti initiations in Table 4.1.

The first event associated with 'Karankuti' times was the immigration of Leparsaraash, an elder from the Kalenjin-speaking Keyo, who were also foragers (i.e. 'Okiek') some distance to the west of Baringo. This elder settled among the Keroi and became wealthy (presumably in wives). Other Keyo then followed and would seek out his homestead and settle beside him. Soon a community of Keyo built up and became established as the Kabis clan. Meanwhile, an older brother of Leparsaraash remained in Keyo and he too became wealthy and the founder of the Kabis clan there.[9] This clan, in other words, cut across tribal boundaries, a feature that typifies later migrations. According to the myth, the Kabis in Baringo grew to a point where they wanted to take over the whole of Keroi territory. Pretending to go out hunting with their bows, they killed ten leading Keroi men ('bulls') and contrived to pass this off as an accident. The Keroi scattered, many fled south to Ongata Nanyukie and settled among the Uasinkishu Maasai. Only a handful remained at Baringo and the Kabis then became the most powerful clan there. This oral tradition has its ceremonial expression in the age system. Since that time, the Chamus ritual leader for each age-set was always a Kabis clansman, installed by Kabis *moran*. There was also a deputy ritual leader who could be of any clan, but it was *moran* of the Parsaina clan who installed him in recognition of their status as direct descendants from the aboriginal Keroi.

The next clan to arrive is said to have been the *Lamaee*, who came from Entur in the Kamasia (Tuken) Hills to the south-west of Baringo. They were also traditionally foragers and had their own language that was neither Maasai nor Kalenjin. Among the Lamaee that remained at Entur were some who had already discovered how to cultivate crops. Entur was occupied by Tuken subsequently, and the Lamaee there were absorbed as a clan and adopted the Tuken (Kalenjin) language, while the Chamus Lamaee adopted Maa.

After a considerable lapse, but still in 'Karankuti' times, more migrants

[9] H. L. Moore (1986: 27–8) records a clan named Kabisioi (cf. Kabis) who have constructed one of several furrows in Marakwet and claim to have migrated from Baringo.

arrived from the west, this time true Tuken, and it was these who formed the Kesieni clan. While the Kesieni do not figure prominently in this account, they were to have some pronounced ties of respect (bond brotherhoods) with later clans and also with their former Tuken kinsmen. The Tuken today are very close to the Chamus geographically, although culturally they are still distinctly Kalenjin. With the arrival of the Kisieni, a group of clans comprising the traditional core of Chamus society had emerged. Among these, only the Parsaina as direct descendants of the Keroi had any claims to earlier Maa links.[10] Yet at no time is it suggested that the Chamus established close links with the Kalenjin peoples (such as Keyo or Tuken) or that their language was other than Maa, and this despite the early dominance of those Keyo who became the Kabis clan. There is, for instance, no tradition that the Chamus ever held 'white' Kalenjin forms of bush circumcision. They identify themselves firmly with the 'black' Maa style of village circumcision. Again, none of the earlier age-set names remembered before Karankuti bear any resemblance to Kalenjin age-sets, even those that are neither Maasai nor Samburu names. In other words, if there was historically a closer link with these non-Maa peoples, then this appears to have been expunged from the oral traditions. Their tradition is that their earliest links were with the Samburu. They speak a form of Maa that is close to Samburu and see themselves as having remained culturally within the Maa milieu throughout their remembered history. A continuous link with the Samburu is maintained in this oral tradition, and it was from the Samburu that the next spate of immigrations was to come.

But first, even possibly before the arrival of the Kesieni, the Chamus are said to have acquired irrigation agriculture by serendipity. The precise timing of this transition is particularly vague and associated loosely with age-sets ranging from 'Karankuti' and 'Meishopo', to the relatively recent 'Peles', according to different informants. Again, the gist of their information is that it all happened 'a very long time ago'.

---

[10] Given the location of Baringo, the earliest link with Maa culture could logically have been with the Uasinkishu Maasai, who in the nineteenth century dominated the area to the south. The myth of the Keroi seeking refuge from the Kabis among the Uasinkishu is represented as an isolated incident, but other evidence seems to suggest a more established relationship. Dundas (1910: 53) appears to reverse the myth: the Parsaina clan (Keroi) was said by some to have been Uasinkishu before taking refuge among the Chamus (see Thomson 1885: 242–3; Powell-Cotton 1904: 162). Apparently independently, Huntingford (1950: 11) lists seven Uasinkishu clans, one of which is named as Parsaina. None of these is listed by Sankan (1971: 3), whose clan names correspond almost exactly to a list that I collected among the Uasinkishu (although I recorded Ilmalatime as a further clan). In other words, Dundas and Huntingford, whatever the sources of their information, may point to some earlier link between the Keroi and the Maa through an earlier branch of Uasinkishu. (However, according to my 1977 field notes (vi. 20f), a Uasinkishu elder told me: 'None of the Chamus families are known of here—even *Parsaina*.' This would have been unprompted information, since at that point of my fieldwork I would not have known of the possible significance of the term 'Parsaina' in this context. It may have been an innocuous remark, or might it have referred obliquely to some earlier link?)

The Traditional System of Irrigation

The first crop cultivated by the Chamus was *ndapa*, or *mbeke*, probably the African variety of finger millet that is well adapted to semi-arid areas and ideal for long-term storage against the possibility of drought. As a second traditional staple cereal, the Chamus later acquired *mosiong*, which seems to have been red-grained sorghum, a bitter variety again well suited to semi-arid areas. According to myth, a bird flew from the hills where the Lamaee had lived, carrying a sprig of *ndapa* in its beak. As it followed the course of the Great Uaso River, it dropped this sprig, and a Kabis clansman picked it up. Wondering what to do, he planted it, and from this the Chamus acquired their first crop. Following this incident, members of the Kabis clan are held to have the power to curse any crop because they were the first to cultivate, and the Lamaee have a similar power over the irrigation water because the bird came down the course of the river from their ancestral home. Stemming from this belief, members of both clans had a central role in a variety of rituals associated with the irrigation calendar. After new water channels had been dug in the dry season, for instance, the members of the Lamaee clan were the principal performers in a blessing to ensure the flow of water following rain.[11] It was also a Lamaee or Kabis elder who would bless any formal decision governing the irrigation system. On other occasions, one of these elders would be asked to bless the crops four days before harvest or sooner if the growth was stunted. This practice has been abandoned since the Parimo age-set were *moran*, but even in 1977 elders with Lamaee or Kabis wives would ask these women to bless their crop if it had any disease.

It is at this early period, when myth merges into oral history, that the Chamus maintain they lived in two fortified villages, as they were later found by the first European travellers.[12] The larger village was Lemeluat or 'Down-River Chamus' (*Ltiamus-leabori*), situated by the Great Uaso River (Perkerra). It was described as nearly a mile in circumference (1897) and with an estimated population of perhaps 750 people (1902).[13] The smaller village was Lekenyuki

---

[11] Dundas (1910: 54) gives details of such a ceremony: a Lamaee elder accompanied by ten others—and no one else—ritually killed a sheep and sprinkled its fat, dung, and blood at the mouth of the furrow which was then opened. The meat was then consumed and the Lamaee wore the skin bound round his head for two days. All these elders then had to avoid sexual intercourse until harvest.

[12] For a brief description of these villages, see von Hohnel (1894: 1); Thomson (1885: 263); Peters (1891: 268). For photographs that indicate the close clustering of huts, see Johnston (1902: 812–13).

[13] Austin (1899: 307). The estimate of 750 people in the larger village is derived from Powell-Cotton (1904: 162), who counted some 250 huts in the larger village in 1902. This figure, coupled with an official estimate of about 3.0 people per hut in 1936, would imply 750 people in this village. Evidence for the size of the smaller village appears ambiguous: von Hohnel (1894: 5) suggests that it contained 1,500–2,000 people in 1887–8, which is far larger than the above estimate of 750 people in the larger village in 1902. For a possible explanation of this disparity, see p. 158. The terms 'greater' and 'lesser' applied to these villages appear to have been Swahili traders' labels that were adopted by subsequent European travellers, but with no indication of their relative sizes (Thomson 1885: 232; Peters 1891: 268; Gregory 1896: 120; Johnston 1902: 18; Dundas 1910: 49–50). With the continuing trend towards pastoralism, an

or 'Up-River Chamus' (*Ltiamus-lekeper*), situated on higher ground by the Nanyuki River (Molo) several miles further south. These rivers fed their irrigation systems and then merged into the mosquito-infested swamps to the south of the lake. All clans were represented in each village, with the huts of Lamaee situated in the south-western sector, closer to the river sources that they ritually protected.

From Chamus accounts, a key feature of control over each irrigation system was the village council of elders known as *olamal*, and it was they who decided on the allocation of land and water for irrigation. Among the Maasai proper, the term *olamal* refers to a ritual delegation with coercive powers and a propitious aura so long as the authority of their combined will meets with total and unquestioning respect. Where the integrity of an *olamal* is violated, however minor the infringement, misfortune is expected to follow.[14] The use of this term among the Chamus suggests the gravity attached to the deliberations of the irrigation council. They consisted of a variable number of worthy elders; while it is not clear how these were selected, others could be co-opted, and any elder could attend their deliberations and offer an opinion. Any elder whose crops were wilting could ask to be allowed extra water. Any reasonable request would be considered, but the *olamal* insisted on complete discipline and resisted the emergence of any factions or cliques. They were particularly active during the period of preparation towards the end of the dry season, involving repairs to the irrigation channels and digging individuals plots. They also met regularly in the growing season, except when the ground was so well watered with rain that the irrigation system became superfluous, literally. No one could sow or harvest his crop until the *olamal* had given their permission, and this would be finally ratified with a blessing by an elder of Kabis or of Lamaee.

The repeated emphasis in these descriptions is on the authority of the *olamal*. Any man who wanted a plot within the irrigation system had to seek their permission and obey their decision on sowing, harvesting, the use of water, and keeping his plot in order. If he disobeyed, he might be warned once; if he persisted, then he would be expelled from the system. The rules *had* to be obeyed. If an elder from one village wanted to migrate to the other, he would normally be given an irrigation plot without question. If he had been expelled

---

increasing proportion of the Chamus dispersed with their herds, notably from the smaller village. This is implied in successive administrative records, which give a diminishing ratio of population between larger and smaller villages from about 3 : 1 (1914–15), to about 4 : 1 (1927–8), to over 5 : 1 (1933–7). My own informants in 1977 suggested that circumcisions in the two dispersed parts descended from these earlier villages involve about 100 initiates in one as against 30 in the other. Estimates for the Chamus population have increased from 1,500 at most (Dundas 1910: 49), to 2,065 in 1927 (Baringo District Annual Report), to 4,000 in the 1948 census. Most recently, figures of the order of 9,000 have been suggested (Little 1992: 21). Taken together, these would imply an annual growth rate of about 2% (cf. Little 1987*a*: 200).

[14] Spencer (1988: 213).

for disobeying the rules, but pleaded in the other village that he had been young and ill-advised and now wanted a second chance, he might be given a plot conditional on his good behaviour. However, if his expulsion was underpinned by a generally bad reputation, then he would be refused. The traditional response refusing an elder irrigation rights was one of expulsion from the society: 'Go back to your own country.' This emphasized that all Chamus (except the Keroi) were ultimately immigrants and had no absolute right to remain in the area. No one could expect tolerance in matters that bore on the discipline required within the irrigation system, especially in the use of water.

This aura of strictness that surrounds the reputation of the *olamal* in the past may well have been largely rhetorical and couched in somewhat extreme terms to impress newcomers that their welcome was conditional on their good behaviour. In practice, the accommodation of wrongdoers appears to have gone to considerable lengths.

> *Case 1.* Olodaru was a Uasinkishu Maasai who had lost all his cattle before settling as a pauper in Lekenyuki village, where he had brothers. There, he quarrelled with a *moran* who had filched his irrigation water. As a Chamus, he should have complained to the *olamal*. As a Maasai (according to the Chamus), he wanted to settle the matter himself, and he shot the *moran* with an arrow. The *olamal* told him to leave their village. He then moved to Lemeluat village, where the elders agreed to accept him, provided he complied absolutely with their regime. He successfully settled down there.

This is a tale that reveals both the Chamus view of Maasai of all ages as headstrong warriors, and also their own partiality for expulsion as an effective form of punishment. It also suggests that there was an element of accommodation alongside the rivalry that clearly existed between the villages providing a second and final chance for serious offenders. To this extent, each *olamal* could afford to maintain a tough stance on discipline in the knowledge that the two villages together provided a softer, more humane regime.

Consistent with the gravity attached to the task of the *olamal* council, various early writers refer to restrictions on social life during the period of irrigation. Dundas (1910) noted that Lamaee elders who had blessed a new water channel could not cohabit with their wives until after the harvest; that water would cease to flow in the channel if anyone were to quarrel with the Lamaee during this period; and that, if any member of the Lamaee clan became angry for more than ten days, the channel would dry up for the season. Various writers have also noted limitations on their foraging during the irrigation season. Elephant, buffalo, and fish could be eaten, but not antelope, waterbuck, eland, oryx, zebra, rhinoceros, or hippopotamus. Anyone who killed or ate a forbidden species between sowing and harvest would be expelled from the village.[15]

---

[15] Thomson (1885: 318); Powell-Cotton (1904: 163); Dundas (1910: 54); cf. Gregory (1896: 355).

The banning of such foods at this season takes on a further significance when one bears in mind that the peak of irrigation activity was also one of general food shortage prior to the harvest. Generally, one senses a period of restraint when the need for conformity associated with the operation of the system pervaded community life, overseen by the vigilant and ritually powerful *olamal* council. In this respect, the Chamus clearly rose above any reputation as self-seeking foragers.

Within the irrigation system, the main canal fed from the river could be controlled by bungs of wood, stones, and mud and led to secondary and tertiary channels, also controlled by bungs, that fed in turn into individual plots. Each of these plots was divided into a fallow half and a cultivated half, alternating every other year, with no notion of rotating crops. There was also a major division of tenancies between the two sides of the main canal, with tenants of alternate age-sets sharing the same side, although both sides were still under one joint *olamal*. It was held that this resolved the most likely source of dispute over water—between adjacent age-sets. Within each side, there was no further division relating to age-set or clan, they claim, for none was needed with such an effective control over the water.

In the traditional system, no one actually owned the land, nor the river or channels; and these did not belong to any clan, not even the Lamaee. They were owned by the whole village. A man would enter the system and start cultivating only after he had married. If all available land had been allocated at that point, he could be offered spare land that lay just beyond the system, downstream of the water channels, to make use of any residual water that reached this far. Ironically, there was a revival of this practice after the colonial administration had re-established the run-down irrigation system of the larger village in the 1950s (the Perkerra Scheme). The majority of tenancies were offered to outsiders from Tuken because they were prepared to pay for these. The excluded Chamus then developed their own *risaab* (reserve) scheme using the surplus water that ran in the channels leading from the official scheme, and administered it after their own fashion, downstream of their own earlier irrigation system.

If an irrigator left the village, then his plot reverted to the community. If he died, then his wives and sons could continue to cultivate the plot, maintaining usufructuary rights. Any elder who lived in the irrigation area retained full tenure to his plot so long as he cultivated it and obeyed the *olamal*. If, for instance, he had been allocated a large holding to feed a large family, he could retain it even if his family became depleted. However, he also had to maintain it, digging the channels, preserving the boundaries, and accepting more responsibility for the upkeep of the irrigation system. With a smaller family and labour force, sooner or later he was expected to negotiate for a smaller plot.

Within each household, the elder's power over his wives in relation to their food production and consumption appears to have been far-reaching. He was the principal tenant and only he could operate the water system, opening or closing the channels as necessary. When the *olamal* had given permission for harvesting, wives still had to wait until their husband had given his permission also. Women had the tasks of digging and weeding, planting and harvesting the crops, and grinding the grain and cooking for each meal. The household plot was divided into patches for each of the wives, with the husband retaining a strategic patch for his own use. He could order any wife to plant his own as well as her own patch and she should not refuse, but he could also choose to help her in busier times. Each wife had her own grain store for her harvest; and the husband's store was located in the upper sleeping area of his own hut. After the harvest, with his sleeping area full of grain, a rich elder would sleep in the hut of one of his wives, leaving his vacated hut for his *moran* sons to sleep on the floor, guarding the grain store above. Wives had a certain autonomy in what they cultivated, but only within the overall regime administered by their husband, who in turn was accountable for his whole family to the *olamal* in irrigation matters.

Rather as the *olamal* had responsibility for maintaining the irrigation system as a cooperative venture in an uncertain climate, so the elder had a similar responsibility towards all his dependants. This involved controlling the supply of grain from the family reserves. John Gregory, as one of the earliest visitors to the area, entrusted his own reserves to be guarded by his Chamus hosts, and seems to provide a clue on a method for securing the granaries from pilfering. 'I had to wait for a short time until the boys had collected some spiders, and these had spun lines of web across the cracks around the door. I was then asked to take particular notice of the arrangement of these, so that on my return I could be sure that no one had been into the hut to steal my goods.'[16]

It was each elder's responsibility to devise a strategy for making the food last and ensuring that his family never went hungry. After the harvest, his store was closed at first, and the family shared grain from the wives' stores. If the grain in one wife's store was finished before the others, then she still had a right to her share of grain. When all the wives' stores were empty, the elder could decide that some alternative food should be used (such as fish or game), holding his own store in reserve. At a time of his own choosing, he would give permission for this store to be opened. Only his senior wife could do this, giving each of the other wives a heap of grain on a hide. The senior wife shared some of the responsibility for rationing the food as it became scarce, on the grounds that, if junior wives were allowed access to the elder's store, then the food would be quickly finished. If the elder happened to be away at a critical time of hunger, the senior wife could open his store to take just sufficient food for the family needs to tide them over until his return. If an elder was guardian over his

---

[16] Gregory (1896: 125).

brother's widow, then she effectively became part of his household so far as food was concerned. She had to have his permission to harvest, she had to share her own grain with his wives in a similar way, she too had her share from his grain store, and he could warn her too if she was depleting her grain store too quickly. In managing his whole household of wives and dependants, a Chamus elder assumed a responsibility and a control that was closely comparable to the power of elders among the pastoral Maa.[17]

The Toiyo–Samburu Immigration and the Patronage of Fishing

It seems probable that fishing would have been a source of livelihood for as long as people were settled close to Lake Baringo, and this would imply the aboriginal times of Keroi. However, the part played by fishing in the earlier foraging economy of the Chamus and the manner of fishing was generally absent from the oral traditions I collected. Similarly, there was a general vagueness concerning the acquisition of small stock (sheep and goats). Both fish and small stock were seen as having a supplementary role in the early irrigation economy, but with no pronounced practices or associated myths. These foods were, however, a central feature of livelihood for those Chamus who lived on the small islands of Lake Baringo, more than ten miles north of the two villages. These islanders were known as *Kuroban* and they consisted of Chamus of all clans. The islands were too rocky for cultivation, but they provided browse for small stock and a sanctuary from marauders. Those living on the islands are said to have had a crude form of boat which could be used for communication and to ferry loads, such as grain, small stock, or personal possessions, and they maintained close and possibly seasonal contact with the mainland.[18]

Fishing acquired an importance in the Chamus oral tradition from an unexpected quarter. It was after they had begun to obtain small stock that more immigrations are said to have occurred, this time of Samburu from the north. The first wave of newcomers was associated with a branch of the Samburu known as Toiyo (Toijo). At this time, the Toiyo are said to have been established further north, bordering on the south-western region of Lake Turkana. They maintained a friendly but distant contact with the Chamus, possibly moving south to graze their herds towards Baringo in good wet seasons when it was safe to do so. The Toiyo were the first acknowledged body of immigrants to the Chamus who were pastoralists and shared with them the Maa language. The intrusion of the pastoral tradition was to have a decisive impact on Chamus society and this is discussed in Chapter 5. When the Toiyo immigrated,

---

[17] Cf. Spencer (1988: 14).

[18] Cf. Powell-Cotton (1904: 88–90); Dundas (1910: 53), who both describe Chamus boats as small canoes made of basketwork. Gregory (1896: 134) describes them as skin coracles. See also photographs in Fedders and Salvadori (1980: 88–9). Powell-Cotton (1904: 92) also notes some fourteen families on one of the islands, subsisting chiefly on fish and their flocks.

however, they had lost nearly all their stock and were driven by hunger, settling among the Chamus as refugees.

In several other respects, the newcomers had a very relevant expertise. They brought with them a family of blacksmiths, a craft that was absent among the Chamus and despised also, although it clearly had a very practical value.[19] Less tangibly, one of their subclans, the Kise, claimed a special ritual power to bless or curse on behalf of the community, deterring their enemies and increasing the chances of rain.[20] Another Toiyo lineage, the Lepisia, had been associated with special ritual powers on the shores of Lake Turkana, where they had a blessing that could bring success in fishing and a curse that could spoil the fishing or cause fish bones to lodge in their victims' throats.[21] The Lepisia now claimed a ritual patronage over fishing in Lake Baringo that was comparable with Lamaee claims over irrigation water and Kabis claims over cultivation. The Toiyo ability to establish these claims is perhaps a measure of the mounting strength of the Samburu newcomers among their hosts as further immigrants flowed in. Once established, the Lepisia patronage over fishing was assumed by others of the same Toiyo clan (Tumal). The Tumal insisted that the only proper way to catch fish was by clubbing them and only after a Lepisia elder had given permission. If the Tumal learned that someone had speared a fish or even tried to do so, they would want to spear him in retaliation, as though they themselves had been attacked.

Among the mainland Chamus, fishing was a riverine diversion, I was told. No one tried to catch fish in Lake Baringo; it was too difficult and too danger-ous.[22] They therefore would wait until the rains came and the rivers flowed, for then the fish would swim up the rivers from the lake and could be clubbed easily. The fishing season started in March or April with the spring rains, but it was with the heavy rains from June to August that the conditions were ideal. Then, with the rivers in full flow, a Tumal elder from the Lepisia lineage would be asked to open the season. He would catch a small fish, bless it, and let it go. Next day, swarms of fish, some even as long as a man's arm, are said to have swum up the rivers from the lake. At any convenient spot, two or three men would collect to club the fish, who at this time would continually break the surface and offer an easy target so long as there were only a limited number of fishers, for they would quickly swim away from any crowd. Further parties coming to fish would therefore form small groups elsewhere. As each elder

[19] Tumaal is a general term for blacksmiths in Somali and Rendille (I. M. Lewis 1955: 51; Spencer 1973: 63). Cf. photograph in Johnston (1902: 835).

[20] These were known by the Samburu term *laisi*. Spencer (1973: 116–17).

[21] It was suggested among the Samburu that the Lepisia had been Elmolo, who fished on the south-western shores of Lake Turkana (cf. Spencer 1973: 213–18), and that the Sirukua subclan had close connections with the Chamus. However, Toyio subclans generally were thought to have derived from the Booran (cf. n. 19 above, which also is consistent with some Custhitic origin).

[22] Powell-Cotton (1904: 109–10) describes a more refined method of fly-fishing on the edge of the lake (cf. South Baringo District Annual Report, 1947: 2).

TABLE 4.2. *Rainfall and the Chamus seasonal calendar*

Season and month	Upland rainfall feeding Baringo (mms)[a]	Corresponding month in Chamus (approx.)	Activity and comments
Light rains			
Mar.	30–126	*Laingok*	'First month'. Begin irrigating fields. Some fishing.
Apr.	86–243	*Purkula*	All crops are planted. Boys are circumcised. Fishing.
May	121–247	*Loonkukwa*	Fewer fishing opportunities. Gregory's visit in 1893.
Continuing rains (*Lorikine*)			
June	55–145	*Kuluwa*	Hunger, but ideal for fishing. Gregory's visit in 1893.
July	131–234	*Ladakun*	Early crops are harvested. Ideal for fishing.
Aug.	34–114	*Lorikine-lesiedi*	Crops are harvested. Ideal for fishing.
Lighter rains (*Lorujuruj*)			
Sept.	16–130	*Lorujuruj-lekwe*	No further fishing, but granaries are full.
Oct.	36–69	*Lorujuruj-lekeji*	No fishing. Austin's visit in 1897.
Nov.	32–99	*Lorujuruj-lesiedi*	No fishing. Thomson's visit in 1883.
Dry season			
Dec.	13–54	*Looraatambo*	No fishing. Von Hohnel's visit in 1887.
Jan.	6–34	*Impala*	No fishing. Thomson's revisit in 1884; Peters's visit in 1890.
Feb.	6–97	*Aarat*	Irrigation furrows and plots are dug. No fishing.

[a] Interquartile range at Kabarnet, 1915–1938.

stunned a fish, he threaded it through the mouth on a line, building up his own pile. If he accumulated a large catch, he would give his surplus to others, especially to those that had caught rather few. When he had finished, he would send for his wife to collect his catch.

Fishing was an important supplement to Chamus irrigation; and this is well illustrated in Table 4.2, which outlines the seasonal balance of their diet before the pastoral dimension of their economy had been developed.[23] In their calendar of activities, the fishing season is seen to coincide neatly with the hungriest period of the irrigation cycle, which ended after the harvest. In noting this point, it is also necessary to stress the extent to which the vagaries of the climate distorted what might appear to have been a neat and predictable arrangement. The rainfall pattern is also shown for Kabarnet in the Kamasia Hills, which are the major source of water feeding into the irrigation system. This pattern equates up to a point with the Chamus view of their seasonal calendar, but it also shows a high incidence of monthly variation making prediction in the irrigation cycle from one month to the next a dubious exercise, corresponding to the arbitrary fluctuation of good and bad years. Rainfall in the Baringo Valley

[23] As set out in Table 4.2, *Laingok* ('the bulls') is recognized as the first month of the Chamus year, when the irrigation waters are first used. I was not given a specific name for the sixth month, apart from *Lorikine le sidei*. (However, cf. Dundas 1910: 55.)

is typically less than half that at Kabarnet, with no rain for four or five successive months during the winter period.[24]

Conclusion: The Hazards of the Oasis Economy

There is considerable archaeological evidence of systems of irrigation in various
parts of East Africa. However, unlike pastoralism, those that have operated
within historical times are scattered with little suggestion of interaction. The
Chamus, for instance, have no oral tradition of earlier links with any of
the elaborate systems of irrigation elsewhere in north-western Kenya, just as
the Sonjo in northern Tanzania appear to have no shared traditions with the
Chagga.[25] In terms of scale, the Chamus political system could not compare
with the Chagga network of alliances and chiefdoms up the slopes of Kilimanjaro that were linked to the harnessing of irrigation water. The Chagga had
a vibrant system of exchange that stemmed from sporadic famines and the
seasonal and ecological variation at different altitudes up the mountain,
whereas the Chamus had no developed markets or external trading prior to
their first contact with Islamic ivory traders around 1840. In this respect
at least, the Chamus were similar to the Sonjo, with irrigation systems that
were organized at village level through ritually strong councils associated
with an age organization, although there is no trace of any monumental
religion among the Chamus comparable to the messianic beliefs that
towered over the Sonjo annual cycle of irrigation.[26] Robert Gray's analysis of
Sonjo shows some Maasai features in their age system, and his account
of warriorhood emphasizes the military aspects of an increasingly outmoded
and irrelevant institution. Yet this is to overlook the extent to which the
policing role and ritual subservience of the Sonjo warriors to the village council
may have had a contemporary relevance also, instilling in them a respect for
water discipline that would be essential when they were 'jostled into position'
on entering the irrigation system as elders. Among the Chamus too, it seems
more than likely that the period spent as warriors in a peaceful community was
also one of induction to the principle of compliance. The importance of communal discipline is well brought out by one feature shared by the Chamus,
Chagga, and Sonjo alike—the deterrent of exclusion from the system of water
rights for those who defied authority and refused to collaborate in the irrigation
regime.[27]

    Knowledge of the Chamus irrigation system reached the coast in the nine-

---

[24] Cf. Little (1983: 93; 1985*b*: 134) for an assessment of the sparser rainfall at Marigat, which would
be especially relevant to the grazing available in the Baringo basin. Again it is the high variability that
Little stresses.
[25] Adams and Anderson (1988: 523–7); Gray (1963: 17, 21).
[26] S. F. Moore (1986: 23); Anderson (1988: 245); R. F. Gray (1962: 491; 1963: ch. 7).
[27] R. F. Gray (1963: 61, 94, 96, 148–9); S. F. Moore (1986: 88–9).

teenth century through ivory-hunting caravans who used it as an inland provisioning point, and gave the Chamus their first opportunity to trade grain for products from the coast. The caravans were followed by the first European visitors who recorded their impressions. This outline of pre-pastoral Chamus society refers to a period that ended shortly after this. There seems little doubt that the irrigation system at its height depended on a high level of community organization that was more than a mere extension of Chamus foraging. The earliest writers described it as 'a wonderfully ingenious system of irrigation by artificial canals of (for them) great magnitude' (Thomson 1885). 'Large tracts of ground are divided, like a chess-board, into plots from three to four miles square' (von Hohnel 1894).[28] However, although the early writers had mostly visited the area during the winter period when the granaries should have been at least half-full, they all reported widespread famine, with no surplus for visitors. Their descriptions make it clear that the irrigation system was stretched to its limit in a very uncertain environment. Famine in the area was clearly the obverse of the reputation of Chamus as a surplus economy that could feed all-comers.[29] Their population at times appears to have reached a critical level, possibly as a result of successive migrations. Irrigation as an alternative niche to foraging had its limits. In better years, it provided a layer of surplus provisions sufficient to attract refugees from neighbouring tribes and hungry ivory traders from the coast. In the worst years, this layer was stripped bare and the Chamus were reduced once more to foraging and so were their coastal visitors: while the Chamus foraged even for rats, the visitors shot larger game to feed their entourage.[30]

It is in the context of this Malthusian trap that the pastoral expertise of the recent Samburu immigrants promised new hope. The question was: in what ways would Chamus society have to adapt to cattle, and how far would the pastoral influence of Samburu immigrants transform their way of life, as the Kabis are said to have done in 'Karankuti' times?

[28] Thomson (1885: 264) and von Hohnel (1894: 5); cf. Peters (1891: 271). In contrast to these, among the second-hand accounts of even earlier visits to the area by traders, one clearly coincided with the peak of their fishing season and another refers to Toiyo agriculturalists and fishers living on islands at the southern end of the lake (Wakefield 1870: 326–7; New 1873: 465; cf. Gregory 1896: 133).

[29] Thomson (1885: 312); Peters (1891: 271); von Hohnel (1894: 5, 7); Gregory (1896: 119, 120, 140, 312); Austin (1899: 307). For a perceptive reconstruction of this aspect of the Chamus irrigation economy at this time, see Anderson (1984: 116–20; 1989).

[30] Thomson (1885: 264, 312); von Hohnel (1894: 6).

5

The Thrust of Pastoral Innovations

The general absence of cattle among the Chamus up to this point reflects their vulnerable position. The nomadic livelihood of their pastoral neighbours was ideally suited for flexible grazing in a region where rainfall was unpredictable and raiding was a constant threat. Because they were not tied down by cultivation, the pastoralists could expand, contract, or shift their ground as they jostled strategically for control over the best grazing areas and in defence of their herds. The region was dominated by nomadic pastoralists, and the Chamus could minimize the risk of harassment by avoiding cattle and limiting their flocks of sheep and goats. Originally as foragers, they appear to have relied on their intricate knowledge of their area and then irrigation farming placed an added restriction on their movement. Having no cattle avoided the problems of grazing away from the villages and tempting their pastoral neighbours to raid. But there could be no final guarantee of security, and there are early reports of former Chamus settlements that had been deserted because of marauding pastoralists. However, the two substantial villages, Lemeluat (Down-River Chamus) and Lekenyuki (Up-River Chamus), still survived, and each was protected by a sturdy double ring of thorn fence.[1] Other Chamus living on the islands of the lake needed less protection, but they also had little to protect.

At this point in their history, it is useful to identify the earlier clans associated with their pre-pastoral origins as 'proto-Chamus'. The aboriginal Keroi were assumed always to have spoken Maa, and each of the immigrant clans had apparently adopted this language. This gave the Chamus a special relationship with neighbouring Maa-speaking pastoralists: the Uasinkishu Maasai in the south and south-west, the Laikipiak in the east, and the Samburu in the north and north-east. The Samburu in particular share the tradition of close contact with the Chamus from their earliest oral traditions, and the Toiyo immigrants from the north were able to invoke this distant bond.[2] At this time in the mid-nineteenth century, the Toiyo had became isolated from the main body of other Samburu clans and were steadily driven southwards by the Turkana, who invaded the area from the north-west, extending their southern boundary as their numbers built up. These Toiyo then found themselves forced into the bleak area to the north of Baringo that was too waterless for their cattle for most

[1] Thomson (1885: 263–4); Peters (1891: 268); von Hohnel (1894: 1, 4).
[2] Spencer (1973: 150–2).

of the year, and this depleted the remnants of their herds, forcing them into the vicinity of Baringo itself. At first, as with earlier immigrations to the Chamus, it was just individual families that drifted into the area as refugees, and they became absorbed by existing Chamus clans. As more Toiyo arrived, so their earlier groupings re-emerged as new clans, notably the Tumal and Kunguan, and possibly Murtanat. Of these, it was the Tumal who appear to have thrust themselves into the Chamus ritual cycles, as Kabis had done previously among the proto-Chamus. The importance of the Tumal may well have been estab-lished through their initiative in adding a pastoral dimension to the Chamus economy once they had regained their strength. However, their ritual claim to status was couched in at least two traditions of origin.

One of these has already been noted concerning the ritual expertise in fishing claimed by the Lepisia lineage on the shores of Lake Turkana, which they now transferred to the vicinity of Lake Baringo. The other was an ancestral link with the Mount Pagaa area just to the north of Baringo, which has relevance to the inauguration of each age-set for various Samburu clans.[3] The two locations are over one hundred miles apart, but both claims are reasonably tenable, given the seasonal nature of grazing in the Pagaa area and the sheer pressure to migrate over long distances in this arid zone.

The claim to have migrated from the Lake Turkana area has an intriguing relevance to a problem posed by Neal Sobania. He has noted an incongruity between the historical claims of the Turkana to have displaced a Maa-speaking population called 'Ngikor' from the region to the west of the lake and the complete absence of any Samburu tradition concerning this region or contact with the Turkana at that time: who could the Ngikor be if not Samburu? But the Toiyo suggest that they at least *were* harried by the Turkana in this region, and a tradition that is absent among the Samburu interviewed by Sobania appears to be alive among the Chamus.[4] It suggests that the Toiyo who became separated from the main body of Samburu could have been Sobania's 'Ngikor' with, as I shall argue, a body of tradition that differed slightly from other Samburu.

The Peles Age-Set (c.1865–1877) and the Impact of the Pastoral Culture

The Chamus sequence of age-sets provides a useful scale for the chronology of events, at least as perceived in 1977. In this scheme, the warriorhood of the PELES age-set is associated with the immigration of Toiyo, or at least it repre-sented a period when the presence of earlier Toiyo immigrants came to be felt. The same age-set are also held to have begun to acquire cattle and to have

---

[3] Cf. Dundas (1910: 50); Spencer (1973: 86).
[4] Sobania (1980: 62, 77); cf. Lamphear (1992: 5–6, 27–8; 1993: 93, 98).

devoted themselves to their care. In the developing mixed economy, cattle and cattle management are seen to have entered Chamus society at this period, even if they were at first only the possession of a privileged few who had the necessary skills. The establishment of the Toiyo clans as a corporate presence among the Chamus, in other words, appears to coincide with their re-establishment as pastoralists and with the reputation of the Peles.

A variety of evidence points towards a clash of life styles between those in the irrigation economy and the pastoral newcomers. This is reflected in the very early literature contrasting Chamus and Maasai behaviour. Charles New (1873) reported that the Chamus 'receive strangers kindly', whereas the Maasai were 'cruel and remorseless to the last degree'. Joseph Thomson (1885) found the Chamus 'singularly honest and reliable', 'most pleasing natives' whose 'unassuming ways and their charming unsophisticated manners' contrasted with 'the ferocious and arrogant warriors of the Masai country'. Carl Peters (1891) described the Chamus as 'a colony of peaceable and friendly Massais', 'more modest than their insolent cousins on the plateaus', who like other pastoral nomads had developed 'a propensity for plunder and a thirst for blood'. Again, K. R. Dundas (1910) recorded an alternative version of the massacre of the Keroi, which was attributed to (pastoral) Laikipiak and Toiyo and not to (proto-Chamus) Kabis.[5]

Various episodes recalled by Chamus—whether viewed as myth or historical events—provide a flavour of the strains of this period, contrasting two ways of life. One of these episodes has already been noted as Case 1, in which a Uasinkishu Maasai immigrant was obliged to move to the other Chamus village for shooting a thief with his bow instead of seeking redress through the village council. In its recounting, it is a tale that seems to express the Chamus view of all Maasai—even their elders—as headstrong and violent in contrast to their own more peaceful ways of resolving disputes, by expelling those that would not comply. Another episode, with certain similarities, is set within the developing pastoral side of the economy.

> *Case 2.* It is said that, when the Peles were *moran*, rivalry built up between the two villages. The climax of this occurred when four *moran* from Up-River Chamus stole a goat belonging to the other village. *Moran* of Down-River Chamus were alerted and, following the tracks, they found three of the thieves roasting the meat and killed them on the spot. The fourth thief had gone to fetch a pot to make soup for their meal, and he returned with it only to find his partners dead while he himself had been spared by luck.

A widespread Maa convention is that, if stock thieves are caught, then the one who first claims a rear leg should be spared punishment; in this story in a

---

[5] New (1873: 463, 469); Thomson (1885: 234, 264); Peters (1891: 224, 272); Dundas (1910: 52). Cf. Edgerton (1971: 176–83).

comparable way, one of the four *moran* is spared. The story ends on a note of reprieve for the surviving thief, as with the reprieve for the Uasinkishu elder in Case 1. But the story also reveals excessive retribution on the other three *moran*. This incident is remembered as the climax of antipathy between the two villages, with *moran* on both sides taking the law into their own hands. One may also note that this story does not touch on any tension between the proto-Chamus clans and the newcomers but refers to the prior division into two villages with the smaller (and ritually inferior) village cast as victims of their own wrongdoing. The accommodation between the two villages in Case 1 gives a certain gloss to the apparent rivalry between them in Case 2. However, both episodes are recounted in a tone of censure that implies a keen tension between two ways of life. Theft and the violence it provoked in each instance seem associated with pastoral newcomers to the area. In the second episode, the *moran* involved on either side were not specifically Toiyo. The emphasis is that they were Peles, the age-set who through Toiyo immigrations had given a pastoral thrust to the economy, leading to trouble over stock. Among the Chamus, Samburu (and hence Toiyo) *moran* are notorious as casual stock-thieves who readily pilfer small stock to satisfy their hunger. Whoever these Peles *moran* were, whether they were Toiyo or ex-Maasai or even proto-Chamus, they behaved like Samburu and their headstrong (Samburu) offence led to a headstrong (Samburu) response. The thrust of the story concerns an abhorrence of lawlessness and violence caught up in a vicious circle. It seems to express a culture clash in Peles times. In relating these episodes of their past, it is as if the Chamus are portraying themselves as moderate in their behaviour and the pastoralists as immoderate; and yet the outcomes conform to a broad Chamus pattern of accommodation. The pastoralists, in other words, are seen as having brought a rougher side to Chamus existence that had to be contained as long as they remained predominantly an irrigation people.

The ritual status claimed by the Tumal clan may also be viewed in this light. It was they who are said to have usurped the Parsaina role of hosting the festival that inaugurated each new age-set in Down-River Chamus, rather as Kabis *moran* had previously usurped the Parsaina role of ritual leader. The Tumal claim was to an equally ancient link with the area, but the fact that they were ex-pastoralists with thrusting ways is likely to have been relevant. Altogether more recently, within living memory, a further step was taken in the same direction. The ritual leader for each age-set is presented with a herd of cattle in the course of his installation, and this became an issue when the Parimo were *moran*. On this occasion, ex-Samburu clans of Up-River Chamus refused to give any cattle due to the new ritual leader, on the grounds that the Kabis clan had been irrigators and not pastoralists. They chose their own ritual leader from the Tumal clan and performed their own separate festivals. The issue was hotly debated among subsequent age-sets, highlighting the rivalry between the two factions of Chamus society rather than clan origins as such. But from this point, as a result of an initiative associated with pastoral ideals, the installation of two ritual leaders became established—provided by the Kabis in Down-River Chamus as before, and by the Tumal in Up-River Chamus.

The Kideni Age-Set (c.1877–1889) and Adaptations to Pastoralism

The Peles age-set were followed by the KIDENI. It is the Kideni *moran* who are remembered as consolidating the thrust to build up Chamus herds. This also involved establishing their role as warriors to defend these herds, and hence, it was argued, the need for (Samburu) *ilmugit* festivals to consolidate this role. From a Chamus point of view, this suggests a striking transition of their economy at this time, as it spread out from the irrigated environs of their villages to grazing further afield. A Samburu interpretation of the revival of *ilmugit* festivals would go one step further. In Samburu, these ceremonies are seen as a necessary means for the elders to retain control over the *moran*, which in the Chamus context would imply retaining control in the irrigation villages over *moran* dispersed further afield with the herds and perhaps dangerously out of reach. Away from the constraining influence of the elders, the *moran* were in a position to pilfer small stock and even to stir up trouble by raiding friendly neighbours of the Chamus. The revival of the *ilmugit* festivals at this time therefore suggests a certain independence among younger men that was new to the Chamus irrigators but a familiar problem to the Toiyo–Samburu elders now settled among them. It is again indicative of a source of strain that the pastoralists may have brought to the irrigation culture.

It is no longer possible to identify the precise nature of the transformation from the proto-Chamus age system due to the influence of the Toiyo immigrations. However, the system, as it was outlined to me in 1977, has a variety of Maasai as well as Samburu and other features. According to my oldest informants, the most significant Maasai features were added more recently. This then leads one tentatively to reconstruct the age system as it might have developed in Kideni times. With this in mind, Table 5.1 outlines a feasible 'Kideni' age system, deliberately omitting the Maasai elements that were (arguably) added later. The timescale on the left of the table estimates the typical age of older members of the age-set of *moran*, assuming an age cycle of twelve years. It is useful to list in separate columns those features that were the concern of the age-set as a whole and organized by the firestick patrons of the *moran*, two age-sets senior to them and responsible for their moral development, and those that were primarily family matters and organized by the father in his own village.

A feature of this reconstruction may be noted at once. Generally, the restrictions of pastoral age systems were more loosely observed among those that had come under their influence, whether as foragers or cultivators. The Chamus had been both, and correspondingly each age-set of *moran* were allowed to

TABLE 5.1. *The sequence of* moranhood *among the Chamus, excluding Maasai features: a Kideni reconstruction*

Age of moran	Firestick patrons' concern and performed by age-set	Fathers' concern and performed at home	Comments on stages (and Samburu features)
19	*Boys' ox* provided by Tumal clan in Lemeluat village (Down-River Chamus)		Previously claimed by the proto-Chamus (comparable to Samburu ceremony held at Mt Ngiro)
		Boys are initiated	(Follows Maa pattern, but, unlike Samburu, there is no collective village)
		Sheep of the arrows	Firestick patrons take over responsibility for new *moran* from fathers (An *ilmugit* festival in Samburu with oxen slaughtered and not sheep)
22	*Ilmugit of the birds*		(An alternative name for the {earlier} *Ilmugit of the arrows* in Samburu)
24	*Ilmugit of the ritual leader*		Installation of a ritual leader from Kabis clan. (Corresponds to Samburu *Ilmugit of the name*)
		Ritual leader's marriage	A marriage by coercion (as in Samburu, but arranged by his father and not his age-set)
		Goat of the roasting sticks	Marks the father's permission that his *moran* son may marry. (Also the name of an earlier *ilmugit* in Samburu that follows the *Ilmugit of the arrows/birds*)
		Moran begin to marry	(Samburu moran begin to marry much later)
30	Ritual leader's *Ox with which the moran go to their homes*		Ends restrictions on the *moran* and their association with the bush. (A Toiyo feature?) Prerequisite for the *Boys' ox* of the next age-set
31	Ritual leader's *Fire ceremony*		Ritual leader's hair is shaved. (a Toiyo feature?) Boys' initiations about now
	Other *moran* perform the *Fire ceremony* individually		Performed by each *moran* after his household is well established with several children. (Cf. Samburu elders' blessing on a *moran* and his wife)

marry sooner than their contemporaries among the Samburu, and celebrated only two *ilmugit* festivals as compared with five or more. This seems to illustrate a derivative form of age organization in a mixed economy.

According to oral tradition, at least two features had been proto-Chamus. It has already been noted that the role of ritual leader for each age-set is said to have been usurped by the Kabis in Karankuti times from the aboriginal Parsaina, although the Parsaina are still responsible for installing his deputy. A similar belief concerns the feast of the *Boys' ox*, which establishes a new age-set and is held to be altogether more ancient than the Toiyo immigrations. In this tradition, the feast had always taken place in Lemeluat as the ritually senior village, and the Parsaina were the hosts, as the most ancient of the proto-Chamus clans. Such a claim is consistent with the general assumption that the Chamus had always been a part of Maa culture, although it also contradicts the notion that they had no cattle and hence no ox to slaughter. Whatever the form of this feast in the pre-pastoral period, it is held that the Tumal clan of Toiyo usurped the role of host from the Parsaina. In deference to the Parsaina tradition, it is they who still act as hosts and provide the *Boys' ox* whenever a suitable Tumal family cannot be found.

Another feature of the 'Kideni' age system appears to be a historical curiosity. In the transition to elderhood, the *Fire ceremony* in particular, and also the *Ox with which the moran go to their homes*, seem to have no exact Samburu or Maasai equivalent and yet they have a familiar pastoral-Maa ring. These differences may of course simply reflect the extent to which the Chamus and Samburu systems have evolved independently over the past century; or they may even reflect certain elements of a Chamus age system that pre-dated the Toiyo immigrations. However, this also raises a further possibility: that they might have derived from some specifically Toiyo practice. The argument would run as follows. While the Toiyo were well established as one clan among the Samburu in 1977, they also had a tradition of having been slightly apart to the south-west of Lake Turkana. They were seen as Samburu but also with their own independent traditions and distinct identity. In Peles times, Toiyo refugees had migrated to Baringo, and then recovered their herds by Kideni times when they introduced the *ilmugit* ceremonies. The principal influx of other Samburu clans only occurred later, and they came as stockless refugees. It seems conceivable, therefore, that these peculiar features of the Chamus age system, as *moran* anticipate elderhood, could be derived from some Toiyo variant of the basic Samburu system, introduced to the Chamus in Kideni times.[6]

Exactly how the proto-Chamus were affected by the growing success of pastoralism is not clear. The two sectors of the economy were concurrent for some time. On the one hand, this would imply a pastoral involvement based on independent family initiative that bound a son to his father in cattle matters but also introduced an element of competitiveness, especially among younger men.

---

[6] Unfortunately, I was not aware of the possible significance of Toiyo separateness during my earlier fieldwork among the Samburu and did not explore this issue (but for a hint of this, see Spencer 1973: 88).

On the other hand, the irrigation sector involved a collectively controlled economy within which young men were expected to settle down sooner as independent cultivators, and this implies an earlier marriage, less polygyny, and a less pervasive age system.

Some 'pastoral' aspects of the age system may at first have been confined to the Toiyo and then other Samburu clans, but they were certainly more widely adopted as the proto-Chamus clans began to acquire a stake in pastoralism through intermarriage and exchanging bride-wealth with the newcomers, and perhaps even joining in cattle-raiding as *moran*. To the extent that the Chamus as a whole came to accept what was essentially a Samburu age system, this would have estranged young men as a collectivity, delaying their marriages and enhancing the prospects of their fathers and other older men for taking on further wives. The development of pastoralism among the proto-Chamus clans, in other words, appears to have had a relevance for a new distribution of power between old and young, within and beyond the family.

'The Disaster'

It was later in the *moranhood* of the Kideni in the 1880s that a further wave of migrations occurred. This was a period remembered as 'the Disaster' (*emutai*), when a combination of cattle and human epidemics and an escalation of warfare swept through East Africa, threatening the very survival of pastoralism and shifting the initiative towards non-pastoralists. At this time, the Laikipiak Maasai were wholly annihilated as an entity by their enemies. Those that arrived in the Baringo area as fugitives became the Loiborkishu clan. They included the only family of diviners to settle among the Chamus, where their skills were regarded as wholly benign and unrelated to the more sinister reputation of Maasai diviners further south. This was a period when the surplus capacity within the Chamus economy seemed to soak up refugees like a sponge, and it is evident that the accommodation of Samburu practices was not matched in relation to other peoples. There are no features of the Chamus age system that are held to derive in any way from the Laikipiak, nor even any Laikipiak customs that are knowingly maintained by Loiborkishu families, other than their family of diviners. The whole Laikipiak system appears to have been obliterated with their defeat. Refugees from the Uasinkishu Maasai at this time left even less trace. Some were absorbed into existing Chamus clans as they settled down, while others returned to their former homes as times improved and no new clan representing the Uasinkishu survivors emerged. The Laikipiak had nowhere to return to, and they remained and formed a new clan. Despite the earlier proximity of the Laikipiak on the western fringes of the Leroghi Plateau to the east of Baringo and of Uasinkishu to the south probably throughout the nineteenth century, these peoples simply do not feature in the Chamus oral traditions I collected until the disasters at the end of the century.

The principal impact of the Disaster came from the Samburu. Situated to the north-east of Baringo, they had become dispersed over a wide area, and fugitives from various clans arrived in Baringo, where they invoked distant ties of friendship both from the past and more recently through the Toiyo. Some stayed for only a brief respite before returning to rejoin the main body of Samburu. However, a substantial number settled among the Chamus, and they became established as a new group of clans, retaining their Samburu clan identities, although with minor modifications. There appears to have been an intermittent migration between the two peoples ever since, notably among families who migrated at this time and retained a dual affiliation.

It is at this time that the evidence of another contemporary writer has a bearing on the situation. Ludwig von Hohnel visited Baringo with Count Teleki in 1887 and his account of the region is among the most informative of these early reports, with a keen eye for practical detail. In this account, he estimated that there were 1,500–2,000 people in Up-River Chamus, the smaller village. This is a strikingly high estimate compared with any official census figure subsequently. It suggests a temporary inflation of the local population due to the Disaster among pastoralists, as does a subsequent encounter von Hohnel described with dispossessed Samburu fishing beside Lake Turkana. A second strand in his account commented on trading with the Chamus. In contrast to the other writers, who had noted the politeness with which they received strangers, he reported an almost aggressive commercial stance, reminiscent of the Maasai.

The people of [Chamus] are quite spoiled by constant and long visits they receive from caravans, and are very exacting about what they will take in payment for their wares. They will have nothing to do with glass beads; the very smallest quantity of grain must be paid for with stuffs, and for ivory they must have cattle. A considerable tribute was also demanded.

Whether or not it was ex-pastoralists rather than proto-Chamus who dominated the terms of exchange, it suggests that the proto-Chamus charm noted in other encounters may have been edged out by the drive among recent ex-pastoral immigrants to rebuild their herds.[7]

---

[7] Von Hohnel (1894: 5, 111). Cf. Spencer (1973: 217). In David Anderson's reconstruction of the expansion of the Chamus economy at this time, he has argued that the ex-pastoralist refugees were incorporated as clients to meet the opportunities offered by traders from the coast (Anderson 1984: 119; 1989: 88). Here, I am suggesting that the ex-pastoralists were soon seeking to build up their own independence and played a major part in dictating the terms of trade, especially for ivory. Either way, the shift towards pastoralism as the dominant aspect of Chamus economy following this period implies that the ex-pastoralists acquired the initiative at some point, and any difference amounts to a matter of sooner, as I suggest, or later, as in Anderson's interpretation.

The Kinyamal Age-Set (c.1889–1901) and the Evolving Clan System

With the incorporation of Samburu and Laikipiak refugees into Chamus society following the Disaster, an elaborate clan system was emerging and this is summarized in Fig. 5.1.[8]

A significant aspect of the incorporation of Samburu clans is associated with the KINYAMAL age-set, which followed Kideni. As noted in Chapter 1, clanship among the Samburu involves an intense network of bonds beyond the immediate family that provide a measure of insurance and support, but correspondingly a strong element of constraint. In sharing a common identity, clansmen also share a reputation which is important especially in conducting marriage negotiations with other exogamous clans. If, for instance, they are demanding as affines, then their daughters will not be popularly sought as wives. Conversely, if they maltreat their wives or exploit the vulnerable widows of clansmen, then other clans will be reluctant to give them daughters in marriage, for they too could be abused. Clanship gives security, but it also implies constraint to maintain the reputation of the clan and ultimately its marriageability.[9] The Toiyo and then other Samburu came to Baringo as impoverished individuals rather than as established clans. They were in no position to offer one another moral support—or constraint—and the checks and balances of their clan system simply lapsed. Corresponding to the apparent switch towards assertive self-interest inferred from von Hohnel's account of the Chamus at this time, there appears to have been a similar switch among the Samburu immigrants whose numbers swelled the Chamus villages, and this may not be a coincidence. As they started to regain their strength, certain unprincipled Samburu elders are said to have exploited their position as guardians over the families and herds of their dead brothers, by expropriating cattle to which they were not entitled. In popular belief, the oldest sons of the dead men were entitled to seize back these cattle by force when they became *moran*, but few if any ever did so, for this would have risked the guardian uncle's curse. Meanwhile, other Samburu immigrant elders are said to have connived with this

---

[8] David Anderson (1984: 110) has provided an alternative listing of Chamus clans, focusing less on the dominant myths of origin and more on the diversity of origin claimed by individual families within each clan. Our different listings seem to reveal the difference between a historian's concern for tracing the network of origins and an anthropologist's concern for identifying contemporary groupings.

[9] Cf. pp. 17 and 84. A rather different example of a clan that failed to build up its status concerns the Leleboo family, whose ancestor immigrated from Tuken when the Peles were *moran* without becoming absored into any Chamus clan. (From about this time (according to Anderson 1984: 119–20), other Tuken were engaged as casual labourers during the peak periods of the irrigation cycle.) By the 1920s, some had settled permanently as associates of the Leleboo family, and together they formed a clan, the Kapisan (rather as the Kabis had done in Karankuti times (see p. 138)). They cultivated Chamus habits, subscribing to their age system and forming a bond-brotherhood with the Kesieni, who also claimed Tuken ancestry. However, in popular esteem they were still regarded as clients and despised because they were felt to be vying with other Chamus for scarce resources. They offered their daughters to Chamus in marriage, but were not given daughters in return: they were not considered 'marriageable'.

Tradition of origin	Clan	Subclan	Comments

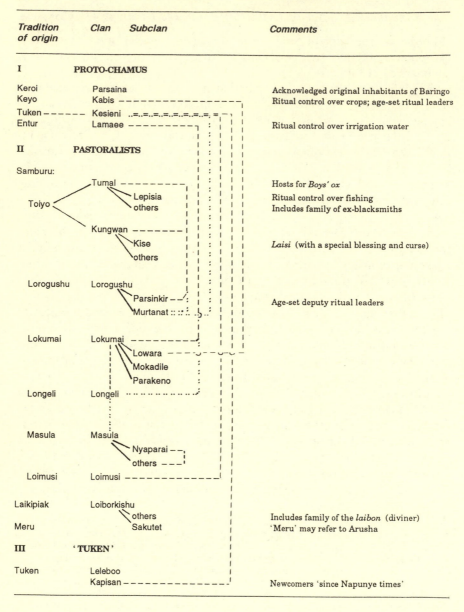

I	**PROTO-CHAMUS**		
Keroi	Parsaina		Acknowledged original inhabitants of Baringo
Keyo	Kabis		Ritual control over crops; age-set ritual leaders
Tuken	Kesieni		
Entur	Lamaee		Ritual control over irrigation water
II	**PASTORALISTS**		
Samburu:			
		Tumal	Hosts for *Boys' ox*
Toiyo		Lepisia	Ritual control over fishing
		others	Includes family of ex-blacksmiths
		Kungwan	
		Kise	*Laisi* (with a special blessing and curse)
		others	
Lorogushu	Lorogushu		
		Parsinkir	Age-set deputy ritual leaders
		Murtanat	
Lokumai	Lokumai		
		Lowara	
		Mokadile	
		Parakeno	
Longeli	Longeli		
Masula	Masula		
		Nyaparai	
		others	
Loimusi	Loimusi		
Laikipiak	Loiborkishu		
		others	Includes family of the *laibon* (diviner)
Meru	Sakutet		'Meru' may refer to Arusha
III	**'TUKEN'**		
Tuken	Leleboo		
	Kapisan		Newcomers 'since Napunye times'

Key

– – – –   Recognized bond-brotherhoods in 1977
· · · · · · ·   Uncertain or lapsed bond-brotherhoods

FIG. 5.1. *The Chamus system of clanship and bond-brotherhood*

malpractice, since they all stood to gain in an arrangement that favoured older men.

Among their Chamus hosts, such misdoings confirmed the pastoral image of the Samburu as unprincipled opportunists. For ex-Samburu, their longer-term interest in building up a sound reputation from which to negotiate for wives was undermined by their own selfish behaviour; the greed of some men reflected also on those who should have restrained them. To improve their standing and become more fully integrated into Chamus life, these ex-Samburu had to recover the self-respect they had lost, and this implied respect for others. This was not an alien concept to them, but one that had been mislaid among so much else in the turmoil of the Disaster. With the initiation of Kinyamal age-set, there was a resurgence of concern for clan reputation among ex-Samburu. This led close clansmen to impose greater responsibility on those who were guardians, emphasizing their accountability on behalf of their dead kinsmen. The full implications of clanship, in other words, which appear to have been forgotten among fugitive pastoralists who had arrived among the Chamus as individuals, were revived as they settled down to consolidate their position. They had to establish that pastoralists too had a sense of self-respect and a strong streak of conformism. In the Chamus setting, they were aware that the long-term interests of many could be undermined by the short-term greed of a few.

Fig. 5.1 also reveals a network of cross-cutting links of 'bond-brotherhood', which involved Samburu clans especially, both among themselves and in their relationship with certain proto-Chamus clans. Bond-brotherhood is a characteristic feature of the Samburu clan system, and one that is absent among the Maasai, for instance, where clanship is less important. The concept of 'brotherhood' in these linkages is a contrived fiction that places a ritual constraint on any casual encounter because of a risk of mystical misfortune. Tempers must be guarded, and therefore conversation is restrained. Requests must not be refused, and therefore should always be reasonable. No intermarriage can take place between them. It is a solemn relationship that borders on avoidance, but is also an ultimate guarantee of security. In migrating to the Chamus, it seems evident that the Samburu carried some of their bond-brotherhoods with them, such as those between the Lorogushu and Toiyo and between the Nyaparai and certain Masula.[10] However, there are also novel bond-brotherhoods between the Lokumai and Longeli, and notably between ex-Samburu clans and three of

[10] The Samburu clan system appears to have been modified among the Chamus by incorporating the Nyaparai into Masula clan and extending their bond-brotherhood with Parasoro to all other Masula. The Murtanat appear to have been a Toiyo clan who previously shared the bond-brotherhood with all Lorogushu. They then became increasingly separate from other Toiyo, intermarrying with them and with the Lorogushu. A localized realignment of clanship ties occurs also in the region of Mount Ngiro, where again the Samburu claimed to have been foragers at one time (Spencer 1965: 72–3, 287–91). In an earlier chart (Spencer 1973: 136), the bond-brotherhoods shown linking the Toiyo of Chamus with the Loimusi of Samburu was a printer's error and should have been with the Lorogushu.

the four proto-Chamus clans. In the absence of any myth concerning the adoption of these new bond-brotherhoods, one is led to suggest that they were progressively formed as the ex-Samburu consolidated their position and an accommodation was reached with proto-Chamus clans. In the context of Samburu culture, the bond-brotherhoods are most readily understood as deriving from some initial hostility that was resolved through a solemn pact pledging the newcomers to peace and support in return for peace and support. It introduced to the Chamus a convention that was extensive in their own ex-Samburu background and above all paraded their capacity to show extreme respect. In the context of Chamus society, one may recall that ultimate authority lay with the village councils that invoked the Maa term *olamal*, implying excessive ritual constraint with mystical overtones. Given the reputation of the pastoral newcomers for opportunism, disrespect, and even belligerence in their affairs, illustrated by Cases 1 and 2, the constraining element in these ritual bondings could be very significant. They were more than a casual or introductory linkage between families. The scale of the total pattern in Fig. 5.1 takes on the complexion of a bridge between cultures, constraining the assertive individualism of the pastoralists to merge into the more collectivist irrigation economy. The adoption of the institution of bond-brotherhood alongside the elders' *olamal* council would have fitted well into the pattern of a constrained economy.

The Kiliako Age-Set (c.1901–1913) and the Maasai Innovations

Following the Disaster in Kideni times, the scenario among the Kinyamal and then the KILIAKO age-sets is of increasing herds of cattle. The vulnerability of the inhabitants of the Baringo basin to raids from their more powerful neighbours had been noted by the early visitors to the area, and among the Chamus there is little doubt that the security offered by the spreading colonial presence facilitated the transition to pastoralism from the turn of the century. Chamus *moran* of the Kiliako age-set were employed by the British as levies in a massive raid against encroachments by the Turkana, returning with cattle to add to their herds. This was followed one age-set later by a lesser raid employing *moran* of the Irimpot age-set.[11]

However, there was a limit to the growth of Chamus herds so long as they remained tied to their two villages. The advantages of a more nomadic form of

---

[11] References to the threat of raiding by the Maasai, Pokot, Laikipiak, and Turkana are given by Thomson (1985: 264); von Hohnel (1894: 4); Peters (1891: 271, 273); Dundas (1910: 52). Anderson (1988: 253–4) suggests that the first Chamus age-set to be employed as levies were the Kinyamal (in 1901, and consistent with his chronology). My own informants suggested that this episode involved the Kiliako *moran* and not the Kinyamal, and this is consistent with the subsequent adoption of *manyat* by the Kiliako to defend their own gains.

pastoralism would have been within the experience of the older ex-Samburu, and the guarantee of security encouraged dispersal. They needed to be free to seek out the best areas of grazing and lessen the risks of epidemics spreading among their herds. These pressures mounted during the *moranhood* of Kiliako, and families began to disperse into smaller settlements that typically numbered only three or four homesteads. Here the elders established new *ad hoc* irrigation systems in small patches along the seasonal streams that fed into the lake, while the *moran* extended their cattle management over a broader area of grazing.

It was this sustained increase in the importance of cattle that led to the adoption at this time of the Maasai system of defence. About twenty *moran* of the Kiliako age-set paid a courtesy visit to the Uasinkishu Maasai, who at that time were just to the south of Baringo, and also to the Purko Maasai on the Leroghi Plateau to the east. There, they stayed as guests among their age peers and encountered their system of warrior villages, known as *manyat* (s. *manyata*). Through this system, Maasai *moran* asserted themselves as a disciplined force in defence of their herds and the supreme agents of Maasai success. The Chamus *moran* were deeply impressed and decided to adopt this system on their return to Baringo.

The establishment of *manyat* villages in Baringo was the principal innovation attributed to the Kiliako *moran*. There are, however, other features of their *moranhood* that show a clear Maasai influence. In the absence of any earlier link with the Maasai, it seems most likely that these were adopted at this point. By the time of the next initiations, the Purko and Uasinkishu Maasai had been formally moved more than one hundred miles southwards; while a residue remained, the thrust of their influence had waned.

Details of the Chamus age system, summarized above in Table 5.1 have aspects consistent with the earlier migrations from Samburu. Table 5.2 provides an elaboration of this, outlining the Chamus age system in its most developed form and incorporating details that have a Maasai resonance. This is further elaborated in the Appendix to this chapter.

A characteristic feature of Chamus *moranhood* is the blend of both Samburu *and* Maasai elements. Thus, in the food avoidances that Chamus *moran* shared with all Maa, they used the general Samburu term *menong* for the obligation to take milk (and cereal foods) only in each other's company, and the general Maasai term *enturud* for the avoidance of meat (and fish) once it had been seen by married women. Again, like the Maasai (but not Samburu), a Chamus *moran* was allowed more than one girl as his lover, but, like the Samburu (and not Maasai), he was expected to avoid sexual relations with the lovers of other *moran*. Yet again, Maasai *moran* hairstyles were preferred, but customs associated with shaving off this hair were very close to Samburu practice. And yet again, the renamed *Ilmugit of eunoto* festival in

TABLE 5.2. *The sequence of* moranhood *among the Chamus, incorporating Maasai features*

Age of *moran*	Firestick patrons' concern and performed by age-set	Fathers' concern and performed at home	Comments on stages (and Maasai features)
19	*Boy's ox* provided by Tumal clan in Lemeluat village (Down-River Chamus)		(Competition for seizing the ox's horn as in Maasai)
		Boys are initiated	(A cluster of Maasai features not shared by the Samburu)
		Sheep of the arrows	
20	*Moran* build their *warrior* villages (*manyat*)		(*Manyat* copied from Maasai)
22	*Ilmugit of the birds*		
24	*Ilmugit of eunoto*		More usual name for the *Ilmugit of the ritual leader*. (Corresponds exactly to the Maasai *Eunoto*, 'the planting')
		Ritual leader's marriage	
		Goat of the roasting sticks	
	Manyat begin to disperse	*Moran* begin to marry	(These two transitions are broadly associated events in Maasai also) Chamus *moran* are allocated the bulk of their herd on marriage
25	*Moran Drink Milk* (alone)		(A Maasai feature, but, unlike Maasai, this is an age-set ceremony and not the father's concern)
26	*Moran Eat Meat* (seen by married women)		(A Maasai feature and similarly an age-set cermony)
30	Ritual leader's *Ox with which the moran go to their homes*		
31	Ritual leader's *Fire ceremony*		
		Each father blesses a stool for his *moran* son, who may now move away to live independently	(Cf. the *Stools ceremony* in northern Maasai, although unlike Maasai this is an age-set festival. Formal separation from the father is rare in Maasai)
	Other *moran* perform the *Fire ceremony* individually		

effect switched from a Maasai *eunoto* to a Samburu *ilmugit* in mid-course of its performance.[12]

There are two aspects of Chamus practice shown in Table 5.2 that diverge from both Samburu and Maasai versions. The first concerns a shift in authority

[12] Spencer (1965: 74, 112; 1988: 112–13). See also n. 27 below. Dundas (1910: 53) refers to the 'celebration of [e]unoto' among the Chamus, providing independent evidence of the incorporation of a striking Maasai element by this time.

away from the firestick patrons and towards the father in Chamus age-set matters. Expressing this slightly differently, in all three societies a father retained ultimate control over his herds until he died.[13] However, Samburu and Maasai age systems each represented a separate domain from the paternal family (cf. Fig. 1.2), whereas this separation was less marked among the Chamus. The age system can be seen as a development from within the family rather than a separation from it. This difference raises questions of historical explanation, as we shall see.

A second feature concerns the ideal of an earlier marriage than among the Maasai or Samburu. This bears the stamp of the irrigation sector where a youth would marry at a relatively young age and form his own wholly independent household with his own plot and food store, even if he still chose to live in his father's homestead. There appears to be a reflection of this in the pastoral sector, where (unlike Samburu or Maasai) a Chamus would be allocated the bulk of his future herd at marriage, even up to twenty cattle. This signalled a significant shift in his domestic circumstances, as in the irrigation sector at this time.[14]

However, the father clearly retained considerable power over his son's herd that he lacked in matters of irrigation. The separation of domains in Chamus society did not concern family versus age-set spheres of interest so much as the two sectors of the economy, derived from separate traditions and sets of constraint. Irrigation and pastoralism independently had good and bad years, but over this period these were generally better for pastoralism, and increasingly erratic for irrigation. It was pastoralism that came to assume a dominant position, and the development of *moranhood* around the pastoral ideals of the *manyata* system reflects this trend.

The Manyata System

The Maasai model of the *manyata* system involved a ritualized rebellion of *moran* against their fathers, in which they snatched away their mothers and some cattle to form their own semi-autonomous warrior village. After this, the fathers were powerless to recall these mothers—their own wives—and even had to obtain permission from the *manyata moran* to visit them.[15] There is no means of knowing the precise nuances of the Chamus *manyata* system set up by

[13] The power of the Chamus father in pastoral matters broadly follows the Maasai pattern (Spencer 1988: 232–4). Among the Samburu with a more stringent delay for the marriage of *moran*, an elder is likely to be well over 65 years old when his first son marries (cf. Table 3.1). He retains ultimate authority, but the competitive edge of their relationship is blunted.

[14] Spencer (1965: 89; 1988: 172). Unlike the Samburu or Maasai, a Chamus is given no stock as a herdboy and only one heifer at initiation; and he cannot expect more until his marriage. Among the Samburu and Maasai, marriage is the point at which a man allocates his bride a portion of his herd, but he receives no cattle from his father at this point.

[15] Spencer (1988: 86–119).

the Kiliako age-set. Elders of subsequent age-sets in 1977, however, indicated a shift in emphasis from the Maasai model, with altogether less autonomy for the *manyata*, less tension between *moran* and elders, and more authority remaining with the father. There was no outburst by *moran* when they formed their *manyat*, and the inauguration of these warrior villages was almost a casual matter by comparison. Groups of *moran* would parade to build up their numbers and then decide on the location of the various *manyat* in a spirit of concensus rather than of ritualized confrontation. The firestick patrons would then light the inaugural fire and lecture the *moran* on their duties, and then leave. There was no demonstration of power directed against fathers or the elders at large, and no attempt at intimidation by the patrons. It was each father of *moran* who decided which of his wives if any should become a *manyata* mother. She was not snatched away, and the father could visit her in the *manyata* at will.

The father would also decide how many of his uninitiated children and cattle should accompany his wife and *moran* sons to the *manyata*. Generally, elders were expected to keep their best milch cattle for their own use at home and to lodge the remainder of their herds for protection at the *manyata*, even up to 100 head. A father could recall any of his possessions without explanation at any time—his wives, children, or cattle—if he felt the *moran* were neglecting their duties. He retained the initiative in these matters in contrast to the Maasai father, notably among the Purko. In this way, Chamus fathers collectively had the power to starve a *manyata* out of existence, leaving the *moran* to go their own way 'like poor men' (*ilaisinak*).

If the Chamus *manyata* system was in some respects a pale reflection of the Maasai phenomenon, it was still an impressive institution in its own right, and one that was wholly absent among the Samburu. The Chamus regarded the *manyata* as a place where there was work to be done. It had its ritualized aspects that followed Maasai practice up to a point, but these were regarded as elaborations on what essentially served as a cattle camp where the *moran* were expected to look after their fathers' herds and oversee the herdboys. In the dry season, the *manyata* might move to a better area, but it kept together as a single village, instead of dispersing as other villages might do; and it was always expected to maintain a vigilance in defence of the herds. Raiding by this time was infrequent, but a façade of alertness was necessary to deter any would-be raiders, and there were other predators beside.

At first, there were just four *manyat* in different parts of Baringo, increasing later to six.[16] Each had its own spokesman and typically between thirty and fifty *moran*. There was no notion of a catchment boundary between *manyat* terri-

---

[16] Two *manyat* were sited at Mokotan to the north, two at Ngambo in the south-east, one at Mesuri in the west, and one at Lekeper beyond Ngambo. The *moran* of the islands had no *manyat* of their own and went to the most convenient *manyata* on the mainland.

tories for recruitment; any *moran* could choose which *manyata* to join, and full brothers could even elect to join different *manyat*, taking with them separate portions of their father's herd. However, their initial choice had to be final: having chosen, they could not move to join another *manyata*. Correspondingly, a girl living at one *manyata* would not be allowed to choose a lover from another, or the two *manyat* might fight over her.

Generally, milk and meat were plentiful at the *manyata*, and only a few mothers cultivated their own vegetable patches nearby to add to the variety of food. Small stock were not allowed there, however, and this discouraged some widows from accompanying their *moran* sons. They preferred to remain in the elders' villages to tend their flocks, while their sons could bring some cattle from the family herd and attach themselves to the huts of close friends, like other motherless *moran*. All *moran* were expected to switch their attention between the *manyata* and the fathers' villages according to the seasonal demand. On the whole, they were not too far from the elders' villages, and each day parties of *moran* would go to these villages to drink milk together. It was not difficult for a *moran* to visit his father, go out herding, and return to the *manyata* on the same day. Gratuitous visits to the elders' villages were discouraged, and the encouragement given by Chamus elders for maintaining the *manyata* system may well have reflected their concern for segregating their younger wives from bachelor *moran*. A *moran* who went to an elders' village to drink milk by himself was suspected of adulterous intent and was despised by the elders. The *moran* at the *manyata* too would feel that their reputation as a disciplined force dedicated to the herds was threatened by philanderers and wastrels (*ilshankili*). They would want an explanation from any of their number who could not account for his absence from the *manyata* for more than one or two nights.

In one aspect of *manyata* life, there was a feature that is closely identifiable with Chamus culture and the irrigation economy. Among Maasai or Samburu *moran*, age-set punishment would involve the confiscation of an ox for slaughter, or in the final resort a beating or even a curse. Among the Chamus, any *moran* who did not respond to the wishes of his age-set would be expelled from the *manyata*. Sanctioning offenders by extrusion was a Chamus way of handling offenders, consistent with the pivotal need for total compliance with the rules laid down for irrigation. Discipline was maintained simply by excluding those who would not comply. Wastrels, thieves, and even *moran* who neglected their appearance were first warned and then told to leave the *manyata*. They were allowed to keep the trappings of *moranhood* but condemned to their own company. Once expelled, no other *manyat* would accept them.

As the *moran* married individually, the *manyat* began to disperse. Sometimes a married *moran* might leave his bride at his father's home and return for a time to the *manyata*; but he would never bring her with him. One by one, *moran* drifted away from the *manyata* back to their fathers' villages, some even before their marriages had been arranged. When the *manyata* had diminished to an unrealistic size, those that remained would agree to dissolve it, brewing beer for their firestick patrons to pronounce their blessing before they all dispersed.

Conclusion: Pastoralism and the Changing Balance of Power with Age

An impressive aspect of the Chamus account of the shift towards pastoralism is the ready response in the development of their age system. Chapter 3 drew attention to ways in which other age systems appear to have broken down under modern conditions as among the Jie and Nyakyusa, whereas the present chapter has examined an age system that actually appears to have built up over the same period to an institution comparable to other pastoral Maa, although with its own distinctive features.

The attempt to identify Samburu and then Maasai influences on the Chamus is only possible with the benefit of hindsight, and this may overlook some less obvious nuances in the historical process of change. This is particularly problematic in approaching relations between young and old—the very stuff of age systems—where a changing balance in these relations over a period of time can become enmeshed with the uniquely personal experiences of informants and notably their disgruntled encounter with old age and the fragile upper rungs of the age ladder. Their awareness of some irreversible trend in their relations with younger people—their successors—may be an indeterminate mix of social change, on the one hand, and the age-old experience of growing older, on the other. Analysis then becomes confused because each new age cohort has a uniquely different view, even of recurrent dilemmas. What informants perceive as change at one level may coexist with persistence at another. Historical reconstruction then becomes problematic: whence the Jie and Karimojong paradoxes and the Nyakyusa oddity that were considered in Chapter 3.

This raises the question of change in the balance of power between warrior assertiveness and elder authority among the Chamus. The irrigation system of the proto-Chamus appears to have been firmly in the hands of elders through their *olamal*, with no coherent role for younger men and no suggestion of a delayed marriage. The transition towards pastoralism, on the other hand, is directly associated with the *moran*. In the first wave, it was immigrant Samburu of the Peles age-set who started to build up their herds. Then, in a second wave of expansion after the Disaster, it was again younger men who recovered cattle as levies in punitive expeditions when the British colonial presence in the area was being established. In this second phase, it was *moran* of the Kiliako and Irimpot age-sets who held the initiative in setting up their *manyat* to defend their gains.

Yet this was in a climate of increasing peace, and any military role of these warrior villages seems to have been superfluous. *Manyat* were absent among the Samburu, who remained beyond British colonial protection for some time yet; and even among the Chamus *manyat* provided only discontinuous cover, with an extended gap between the disbanding of the *manyat* of one age-set and the inauguration of their successors. While the evidence is impressionistic, this suggests that the notion of adopting *manyat* could have been a deliberate attempt by the *moran* to defend their cattle, not so much against their predatory neighbours as against the claims of their own fathers and of elders at large. It was, I suggest, a matter of segregating the herds that they themselves had acquired as *moran* rather than of fighting to defend them. This would be fully in accord with the spirit of independent assertiveness of *manyat* among the Maasai, who impressed them so much at this time. Moreover, to argue here that the Chamus *manyat* were a façade that concealed an underlying motive would be the counterpart to the elders' willingness to retain the obsolete notion of *moranhood* as a means towards delaying marriage and retaining their own monopoly over polygyny.[17]

If one accepts this interpretation, then there must have been a considerable shift in power *back* towards the Chamus elders subsequently. This follows from the general features listed in Table 5.2 and the account of the *manyata* system, which represents the age system from the perspective of 1977. The thrust of control over the system would therefore seem to include further innovations introduced by the same pioneering young men after they had become established as elders, seeking to retain the claim to herds that they themselves had built up. This is to suggest that it was perhaps the Kiliako and Irimpot age-sets, the principal benefactors of Chamus herds and initiators of the *manyata* system, who subsequently as fathers and firestick patrons laid down the conditions under which later age-sets of *moran* were allowed to continue building *manyat*. In this way, they would have retained the initiative as they settled to elderhood and took a step towards establishing a more gerontocratic balance of power. This was no chance development. Throughout the pastoral areas of Kenya at this time, the new administration was seeking to establish indirect rule through the elders, and such a shift towards elder-power in Baringo had the administration's full support and was just one further example of a more general trend.[18]

In Chapter 6, a more recent trend still will be examined in which the initiative in Chamus affairs began to shift back towards younger men as the era of colonial isolation came to an end.

[17] Cf. p. 29.
[18] Baringo District Annual Report 1927; cf. Waller (1976: 550), and p. 48 above.

APPENDIX

Notes on the Ritual Sequence of *Moranhood*

The *manyata* organization of the Chamus appears to have held over four successive age-sets until the 1960s, when it was progressively abandoned, continuing in an attenuated form among those who held to pastoral ideals. The ritual sequence of *moranhood* outlined in Table 5.2 seems broadly to have followed a similar course.

A new age-set was established by killing the *Boys' ox* in the larger and ritually senior Down-River Chamus village.[19] The boys from all over Chamus would gather to display their strength to their firestick patrons, two age-sets above their own. If these elders were satisfied that the boys were mature enough for circumcision, some were first sent off to gather sticks for arrows from Mount Loloroi, while another delegation of nine boys accompanied by one patron was sent north to the area where the Toiyo claimed to have originated, Mount Pagaa, to collect *silalei* resin to tip these arrows and chalk for use in the ceremony itself.

The *Boys' ox* ceremony involved two similarities with Maasai practice that had not been recorded among the Samburu. These were:

(*a*) For their *enkipaata* dance, boys borrowed warrior gear from their older *moran* brothers, with spears, shields, thigh bells, and lion headdresses.

(*b*) Before the slaughter, there was a tussle between the two rival groups of boys from Down-River and Up-River Chamus to seize the ox's horn. The competition was said to be fixed so that Down-River Chamus always won.

After the ox had been killed and shared among the boys, they returned to their homes for circumcision. Chamus initiations were broadly typical of Maa 'black' circumcisions, held in the village and emphasizing that the initiates must not flinch during the operation. At circumcision, one elder held the initiate's back and another his leg. It was these two elders who then made the arrows that he used to shoot birds for a distinctive headdress while he remained an initiate. Initiation involved further Maasai features:[20]

(*c*) Brothers were circumcised in order of birth, but this did not extend to *all* siblings including sisters, as in Samburu.

(*d*) Boys were circumcised individually at their fathers' homes and *not* collectively in a large ceremonial village, as in Samburu.

(*e*) There was *no* prohibition on initiating the sons of firestick patrons, as in Samburu.

Each father decided when his initiate son had recovered sufficiently to kill his *Sheep of the arrows*, shooting away his remaining arrows into the ground from the doorway of his mother's hut.[21] He would then lay aside his initiate garb and assume the avoidances

[19] The *Boys' ox* is also known as the *Ox with which the boys are divided, Olmongo ongishirieki*: from *a-ngisha*: to be divided. Cf. Spencer (1973: 80).

[20] Spencer (1965: 83, 98; 1973: 75, 85, 87; 1988: 56–8, 71, 77–8 n.).

[21] The *Sheep of the arrows* (*Loolbaa*) corresponds in ritual sequence to the Samburu pattern (Spencer 1965: 86–8; 1973: 90). Normally the animal provided for each *moran* is a sheep, but an ox is provided by two ex-pastoralist families (the Lepartenan of Murtanat and the Lesakutet of Loiborkishu). At this

of *moranhood* shared by all Maa: to avoid drinking milk alone or eating any meat seen by married women. It was at this feast that responsibility was transferred from the father to the firestick patrons, who inducted the initiate as a *moran* into his age-set by kindling a fire, whence their title.

Chamus *moran* performed just two *ilmugit* festivals, supervised by their firestick patrons. At each festival, held over four successive days, every *moran* provided an ox for slaughter outside the village, or a fat sheep or goat if he had no ox. Further from the village, the *moran* had their own enclosure. This was their *ilmugit*, after which the ceremony was named, as in Samburu. It was here that they celebrated among themselves and with girls, dancing and eating their own portions of meat. The first festival to be held was the *Ilmugit of the birds*, which involved a concerted effort by the firestick patrons to establish authority over the high-spirited *moran*. The second festival was the *Ilmugit of the ritual leader*, which was regarded as the principal event of their *moranhood*, establishing the new age-set as fully mature. The age-set was now given a formal name and linked to this, a ritual leader. After the Parimo age-set became *moran*, rivalry between Down-River and Up-River Chamus led to their having separate ritual leaders and *ilmugit* festivals, as occurs among Samburu sections.[22] At no time, however, was it suggested that there should be separate *Boys' ox* festivals inaugurating each new age-set, even though Down-River Chamus refused Up-River Chamus any consultation in its timing or organization. To divide this festival, it was argued, would divide Chamus totally.

As Maasai practices came to be adopted, this second *ilmugit* became known as the *Ilmugit of eunoto*, grafting the Maasai *Eunoto* onto the Samburu festival. *Eunoto* among the Maasai refers to the 'planting' of the *moran*, establishing their age-set, and the term had perhaps a particularly apt connotation in the context of the Chamus irrigation culture. Before the festival, a deputy ritual leader was chosen and presented with a heifer. Then the ritual leader was told of his appointment by a delegation of *moran* driving nine heifers to present to him at his father's home. His *ilmugit/eunoto* ox was then slaughtered on the spot.[23] The ritual leader was chosen without the kind of drama witnessed among the Maasai or any pronounced beliefs in his impending misfortune. However, after brothers of the ritual leaders of both the Kiliako and Irimpot age-sets had died young, it was decided to avoid the possibility of recurrence by choosing only-sons to fill this post in future.

At the spot where the ritual leader's ox had been slaughtered, a large hut, the *esinkira*, was built. The deputy ritual leader's ox was then slaughtered and roasted at a short distance from the village, and this became the site for the *ilmugit* enclosure. Following this, the *enkipaata* dance was performed as *moran* processed to enter the *esinkira* hut. The *moran*, however, refused entry to known adulterers, exposing them publicly, and elders in addition would forbid entry to any other *moran* who had offended them in any way.[24]

---

festival, the brisket fat is shared by the new *moran* and his partner in the bush. The hip bone is broken and shared with other *moran* (and not with the mother, as in Samburu, and there is no horseplay between the sexes, as occurs in the Maasai *Loolbaa*). The stomach, neck, head, and hide are given to the mother.

[22] Cf. Spencer (1965: 87–8; 1973: 89–91).

[23] The hide of the ritual leader's ox is slit in the middle and placed round his neck by the deputy ritual leader, whence the deputy's title (*ilboruenkeene*). Cf. Spencer (1988: 145, 158).

[24] Unlike the Maasai, the Chamus elders do not place a curse on the *esinkira* hut against *moran* adulterers (*ilkerekenyi*), and if no other *moran* know of an adulterer's secret affairs, he might bluff his way into the hut. Cf. Spencer (1988: 160–1).

After this episode, all *moran* dispersed to their own *manyat*, to build their own *ilmugit* enclosures and slaughter their oxen there; and in effect this provided a transition from Maasai features associated with their *Eunoto* to a routine Samburu *Ilmugit*. There is a clear resemblance between the village *esinkira* hut in those Maasai sections where it is the possession of *moran* (such as the Kisonko and Loita), and the bush *ilmugit* enclosure in Samburu. The Chamus had both, one after the other in sequence.

A *moran* had to obtain his father's permission to kill his *Goat of the roasting-sticks* before he could marry. In this ceremony, a group of perhaps five *moran* performed together, each providing a goat to be cooked on roasting sticks, and then hurled these sticks into the bush like spears.[25] Ideally, the ritual leader should be the first of his age-set to perform this and then to marry, and others who followed each gave him a female kid or lamb. Those who had been given special permission to marry earlier had then to give him a heifer for his blessing.

There was a general belief that wives of *moran* would bring misfortune if they came to the *manyata*. This was reversed at the time of *Eunoto*, when any wives of *moran* would run with their infants to their own fathers' homes, for it was held that the *moran* would stamp their children (born and unborn) into the ground as they performed their *enkipaata* dance. Similarly in the past, if a married Chamus *moran* went to war, then his wife would run away to her father's home until all the *moran* who had killed enemies had undergone ritual cleansing, whether or not her husband had killed.[26]

In order to relax the food restrictions of *moranhood* after the *manyata* had dispersed, the Chamus adopted two successive ceremonies from the Maasai whereby *moran* first 'drank milk' (alone) and then 'ate meat' (seen by women).[27] At first, they resisted the initiation of a new age-set that would switch popular attention from their arena. They would allow boys to have relations with rather small girls, but refused them their own bigger girls, and only relaxed their guard when all these girls had married.[28] They were then ready to end their coveted role and ritual association with the bush.

Once this point had been reached, the ritual leader provided a large ox for slaughter at his homestead. This was the *Ox with which the moran go to their homes*.[29] The firestick patrons organized this feast, and shared the meat with *moran* from all over Chamus. The *moran* had now taken a significant step towards elderhood, and the age system was ready to receive a new age-set of young *moran*, starting with the next *Boys' ox* ceremony.

Shaving their braided hairstyle was the final act of *moranhood*; and it was the ritual leader who was first to do this, at his *Fire ceremony* when his herd was inside the village. First his father had to provide him with a stool which he had blessed. The ritual leader's

[25] The roasting-sticks are known as *watenata*. Cf. Spencer (1973: 90, 93; 1988: 183).

[26] These beliefs in misfortune affecting the wives of *moran* appear to be peculiar to the Chamus. In other respects, customs associated with warfare followed Samburu practices that were absent among the Maasai. These included the ceremonial cleansing of a killer in war, and the absence of customs associated with loosening the hair or removing the ornaments of a *moran* killed in war. As among the Samburu, the hair of *moran* could be shaved prematurely when they were seriously ill and likely to die or when another *moran* of the same sub-lineage had just died (Spencer 1965: 74; 1973: 96–7, 108; 1988: 27).

[27] Spencer (1988: 174–5, 179–82).

[28] Chamus *moran* have full intercourse with their girls until their breasts develop. From that point, they practise coitus interruptus. When she first menstruates, the girl's mother will tell the father, who will then arrange for her circumcision and marriage as soon as practicable.

[29] For the *Ox with which the moran go to their homes* (*Olmongo opuoieki enkangitie*), cf. the Maasai *Olkiteng loolbaa* (Spencer 1988: 252).

wife then shaved off his hair and extinguished her fire. Then some firstick patrons lit a fire in the yard and carried a flame into the hut to rekindle her fire, putting some tobacco into it and pronouncing their blessing.[30] If any *moran* were to have his own hair shaved before this point, it was held that the ritual leader could weaken and die, and the offender would have to pay him a cow to annul his curse. Following the ritual leader, his deputy performed his *Fire ceremony*, and then any other *moran* could follow an identical procedure, but only after he had married and again only with his father's permission. A father was unlikely to delay this to the point that bad feeling developed between them, and he might even encourage his son to take on further responsibility by giving permission sooner rather than later.

Generally, by the time he had two or three children, a mature *moran* was expected to have a wholly independent homestead and to have performed his own *Fire ceremony*, and shaved his hair and become an elder in a full sense. At first, he might move only a short distance from his father, but he was free to move further away at any time. However, the father always retained the right to revoke the son's independence if he abused his freedom by neglecting his family or herd.

[30] The father's blessing a stool when his son retires from *moranhood* has an affinity with a similar blessing by the patron elders of the *moran* in the *Stools* ceremony among the northern Maasai (Spencer 1988: 196 n. 5). Cf. Spencer (1965: 89; 1973: 92–3) for a similar ceremony among the Samburu.

The Emergence of Individualism and New Forms of Inequality

Early accounts of the Chamus seem to indicate that the irrigation systems of the two villages were already failing as they built up their herds of cattle. There are two interpretations of this decline. David Anderson's painstaking reconstruction of their economic history has suggested that, towards the end of the nineteenth century, the Chamus economy was upset by their strategic position as a provisioning centre for Swahili caravans, whom they supplied with grain in exchange for items that could be retraded locally for cattle. Chamus eagerness to build up their herds at this point led them to over-cultivate, he argues, spoiling the fine ecological balance of their irrigation system. They then compounded this further by diverting labour to tend their growing herds, but at the expense of maintaining the irrigation system, bringing about its disrepair and decline.[1] Robert Chambers's alternative interpretation puts the failure of the system on a wider ecological footing and at a later stage. As the herds built up after the Disaster, he notes, there were reports of serious overgrazing, and this would have interfered with the natural drainage that fed the irrigation system. Rain could no longer be retained by the soil, leading to a more spasmodic supply of water.[2] This culminated in a flash flood in 1917, which diverted the Great Uaso River from its normal course and placed the major irrigation system of the Down-River village beyond repair.

Both explanations are carefully argued and point in the same direction in terms of the destructive role of the thrust towards pastoralism. Both could have contributed in successive stages to the final outcome. Anderson's argument that the ex-pastoral refugees were absorbed because they provided extra labour for the intensified irrigation does not consider the possibility that it might have been precisely these newcomers who were most keen to rebuild their herds but less experienced in the limits to which irrigation farming could be stretched.[3] This is to suggest that the aggressive edge that the pastoralists had brought to Chamus existence could have extended to their economic response as impatient

[1] Anderson (1984: 117, 119; 1988: 250–1, 253–4; 1989: 88, 93–5); Adams and Anderson (1988: 528). Cf. von Hohnel (1894: 3, 5), who noted Chamus trading ivory for cattle, and also the unsuitable quality of the soil for cultivation in the Baringo area, compounded by the hazards of the environment and the arduous care needed to produce crops.

[2] Chambers (1973: 346). Cf. Homewood and Rodgers (1987: 120–3).

[3] Anderson (1984: 119).

cultivators and not simply supplementary labourers. How far active proto-Chamus then joined the ex-pastoralists in neglecting the maintenance of the irrigation system as the herds built up is not clear. Early records indicate a general thrust in this direction which would imply both sectors of the population.

With the adoption of Maasai *manyata* practices, the Chamus age system appears to have remained largely unchanged for four successive age-sets after the Irimpot, surviving the years of colonial administration. This is a useful indication of the extent to which pastoralism and the segregation of *moran* had become firmly established. By the late 1920s the Chamus were described as an essentially pastoral people who had ceased to cultivate to any extent. However, the dryness of the area limited opportunities for pastoralism and by the mid-1930s the position was reversed when heavy stock losses caused considerable emigration from the area, especially back to the Samburu, while scattered irrigation had been revived among those that remained.[4] The fortunes of the two sectors of the economy continued to fluctuate over the years, but the age system persisted. Thus, while the commitment to irrigation among the Chamus was questioned by some administrators, population pressures encouraged a mixed economy that combined irrigation and pastoralism. There was a considerable attachment to cultivation among older men, who could for the most part survive and even thrive with their wives and younger children close to their plots, retaining some milch cattle for their needs, notably during the wet season when a good milk supply offset the hungriest period before harvest. Younger unmarried men identified with the pastoral ideal of tending the family herds. As the human and cattle population grew, the herding spread towards remoter areas in search of pasture, following the scattered occurrences of rainfall for much of the year; then, as the dry season built up, the herds converged on the swampland close to the lake and other permanent sources of water. It was in these wetter areas that the two sectors of the economy were in competition. Previously, when the Chamus had been concentrated in two villages, an irrigation discipline was essential. Now, with a dispersed mixed economy and increasing pressure on land that had to be prepared for the irrigation season, an alternative form of discipline was necessary.

The separation of the two sectors of production, coupled with a need to coordinate these, broadly corresponded to the separation of married elders and younger men through the age system, coupled with the ultimate control of the elders. Within living memory, the importance of pastoralism has never been in doubt. Among the *moran*, herding was a means towards accruing capital for their own marriages. However, they also accepted agricultural foods as a routine part of their diet, and any pastoral stoicism towards a degree of hunger during the months of drought was not in their life style.

[4] Baringo District Annual Reports (1927, 1928, 1936).

TABLE 6.1. *Local rates of exchange among the Chamus*

Local exchange equivalents		Comments
1 honey comb (from Tuken)	= 1 standard bag of grain (*mbene*)	A standard bag of grain could feed a family for perhaps three days.
1 small bag of grain (*nksen*)	= 1 kid or lamb	Small stock could also be bought in exchange
2 standard bags of grain	= 1 sheep or goat	for grain from pastoral Tuken and Pokot.
6 sheep or goats	= 1 small ox	Equivalent to the surplus after a good harvest.
15 sheep or goats	= 1 heifer or bull	Cattle could also be bought in exchange for
25 sheep or goats	= 1 milk cow and calf	small stock from neighbouring pastoralists including Samburu and Somali traders.
1–12 cattle	= 1 wife	Increasing over time. See Table 6.2.

The viability of this mixed economy is reflected in established conventions in their internal dealings, exchanging any surplus harvest to build up their herds, and drawing on these herds in exchange for grain in times of hunger. Trade with the external market when cash was needed was dominated by unpredictable and fluctuating prices; and even bride-wealth payments among the Chamus were subject to a steady inflation. In sharp contrast to these patterns, casual trade between Chamus was characterized by relatively fixed rates of exchange, as shown in Table 6.1, and these are held to have remained constant over a considerable period. Apart from exchange among themselves, these rates also provided a notional standard from which they looked for favourable returns in their dealings with neighbouring peoples. The external market and the marriage market reflected changes that were taking place, but the balance of the mixed economy locally appeared at least to remain unaffected by these changes.

Irrigation versus Pastoral Ideals of Marriage

Polygyny in the earlier irrigation society is said to have been infrequent, extending at most to two wives. This is consistent with the claim that men settled down to marry and cultivate while still comparatively young. Again, it is said that there was considerable freedom in choosing a partner, and a young man's *moranhood* girlfriend frequently became his wife. He was expected to take some initiative in this, seeking her consent and then approaching his own father to arrange a meeting with hers in order to arrive at a final agreement. Either father could refuse the match, but would normally only do so with good reason. Once married, the couple were effectively independent of their parents on either side, and their household formed a basic production unit within the regime of the irrigation system.

This essential independence of the married son among the Chamus contrasts in almost every way with the Samburu pattern of marriage, which was essentially in the hands of the senior generation, notably the bride's father and his close kinsmen, but also the groom's father while he was still alive. Controlling the marriages of the younger generation was in the interests of the elders at two levels. Within the family this prevented younger members from rushing into unwise matches that would dent the reputation of the whole family as good marriage partners. Within the community at large, the power of older men to delay marriage facilitated a high polygyny rate. By the time a Samburu *moran* was eligible for marriage, he could have experienced a succession of girlfriends taken away for older men, leaving him to marry a girl of perhaps half his own age. Even *moran* were expected to accept that the element of attachment between lovers in their youth would make a poor foundation for marriage, which was associated with the unquestionable superiority of the husband and a general mistrust between male and female domains.[5]

Corresponding to the two ideals of freely chosen (early) and arranged (late) first marriage, the trend within Chamus families appears to have been from one pattern to the other—towards arranged marriages and increasing polygyny. As pastoralism became a dominant feature of their economy, sons were increasingly tied to the shared fortunes of the family herd and bound to interests that were wider than their own. It was said to be those with larger herds who were the principal polygynists, aiming to settle the senior wife in the irrigation system and to place younger wives with the cattle elsewhere. But the ideal of polygyny remained ambivalent within the irrigation side of the economy. The tendency among established elders with few cattle was to negotiate first wives for their adult sons rather than further wives for themselves. Their preference was for grandchildren at this point rather than further children of their own. For many older men, the problem of keeping a watchful eye on their younger wives and amorous *moran* was also felt to be beyond their capacity. They preferred to let their sons get on with it and they settled for what they already had: a more sedentary existence close to their irrigation plot. This hybrid pattern is reflected in Table 6.2, derived from the marriages of a sample of living men from three lineages.[6]

In this table, column (*a*) shows the increase in age of successive age-sets, and column (*b*) shows the distribution of wives, with polygyny broadly increasing up to middle age, when there appears to be a tendency for elders to stop accumulating wives. The list of age-sets in the table also provides a chronological scale relevant to columns (*c*) and (*d*), and relates to history rather than to age

---

[5] Spencer (1965: 32–7, 216).

[6] Polygyny data collected by Peter Little (1980–1) are altogether more substantial and provided a finer breakdown for Chapter 2 (Figs. 2.1*a* and 2.3*a* and pp. 87–8). Because Little's sample did not extend to the particular details discussed here, Tables 6.2 and 6.4 rely on my own more restricted data (1977). In the earlier sample, the average polygyny rate appears higher and the variability more restricted (m = 0.69 +/−0.10, d = 1.22 +0.20/−0.18). Plotted on Fig. 2.1*a*, the ovals of the two samples would not overlap.

TABLE 6.2. *Distribution of polygyny with age among the Chamus in 1977, and of bride-wealth payments over time*

Age-set	(a) Age range in 1977	(b) Distribution of wives per elder						(c) Proportion who married a *moranhood* girlfriend	(d) Scale of bride-wealth and period when this age-set were *moran*
		0	1	2	3	4	Total		
Kinyamal									1 cow (1889–1901)
Kiliako									2 cattle (1901–13)
Irimpot	72–83		1		1		2	1/2	6 cattle (1913–27)
Napunye	58–71		4	1			5	2/5	4–9 cattle according to wealth
Parimo	49–57		1	3		1	5	2/5	12 cattle (1939–48)
Merisho	38–48		1	2	3	1	7	1/7	12 cattle (1948–59)
Meduti	26–37	2	6	1	1		10	0/8	12 cattle (1959–70)
Bikisho	25 or less	13	7	1			21	0/8	12 cattle (1970–82)
TOTAL		15	20	8	5	2	50	6/35	

as such. Column (*c*) indicates the extent to which the proportion who married a girlfriend of their *moranhood* has dropped: before the Merisho age-set, five out of twelve elders in the sample had married a *moranhood* girlfriend, as compared with just one out of twenty-three since then. To this extent, arranged marriages became more common over time and marriage between lovers more rare.[7]

It was only after the Chamus built up their cattle herds that the rate of polygyny is said to have increased substantially. This has corresponded to a steady increase in the number of cattle given for bride-wealth, as shown in column (*d*), from a token payment of one cow in Kinyamal times to twelve cattle more recently, six of which are delivered at the wedding itself and the remainder as individual gifts within the following year. The variable payment when the Napunye age-set were *moran* (*c*.1927–39), according to the ability of the groom to pay, suggests an increase in competition for wives at this time that would favour the wealthier suitors. The subsequent standardization of the payment to a fixed and limited number of cattle is similar to Maasai and Samburu practice. It indicates a wide consensus to limit direct competition, largely through the age system and again in the interests of maintaining family reputations as good affines, curbing their greed in order to enhance marriage-ability. No one relishes the prospect of a greedy affine.[8]

Within this general trend, one may note an apparent anachronism in column (*c*). Pastoralism had clearly become the dominant sector of the economy by the mid-1920s while irrigation faltered, and yet it was another twenty years (or two age-sets) before arranged marriages appear to have become the established norm. Part of the explanation may have been that some fathers continued to

---

[7] Chi-square = 7.73, which is significant at 1% (df. 1).

[8] See p. 17; Spencer (1965: 134; 1988: 25).

favour their sons' early marriage, evading the restrictions of the age system. However, this was also a period when there was a reaction among certain *moran* against these constraints in several ways. One of these was in forcing their suit to girls of their choice through various forms of coercion, wresting the initiative from their fathers and older men more generally. In this respect, these *moran* conformed less with the Samburu patterns of late arranged marriage and more with the established Chamus pattern of early self-initiated marriage, as their fathers had done a generation earlier, albeit with a novel element of wilfulness.

One of the more extreme forms of coercive marriage and with undertones of sorcery was similar to Maasai malpractice and associated with the attempt by a thwarted *moran* whose girlfriend had been refused him by her father. This required enacting certain irreversible ritual details of a wedding such that the only propitious outcome would be to complete the ceremony and acknowledge the marriage. The following instance was an episode from a more extended case study that is considered in the next section.

Case 3. Leina, as a *moran* of the Irimpot age-set, wanted to marry his girlfriend, but was refused by her father's brothers. With her connivance he entered her hut at night while her mother slept, and placed a leather maternity belt around the girl's waist, a fibre round her forehead, a mud doll on her lap, and a milk flask for the doll, four arrows and a pair of new sandals down by her side. Finally he placed an iron bracelet (*esayet*) on the sleeping mother's right wrist. He and the girl then ran away as the mother woke up and roused the village. The local elders agreed that it would be ritually dangerous not to complete the marriage, but they demanded a heavy payment from Leina as a price for his presumption. He had to placate each of those he had offended with gifts for their blessing on his marriage.

In examining the practice of coercion in Chamus marriage, a certain pattern emerges. It was immigrants from Samburu who had introduced the pastoral dimension to the Chamus economy, and details of custom associated with arranged marriages were altogether closer to the Samburu pattern than to Maasai practice, for instance.[9] The patterns of coercive marriage, on the other hand, had some striking Maasai features, again extending to matters of ceremonial detail.[10] The inference is that these features were borrowed at about the

---

[9] Chamus marriage procedure is altogether closer to Samburu than Maasai (*a*) in combining a girl's circumcision, her removal as a bride, and the completion of her marriage into one occasion, whereas these events are spread out in Maasai; and (*b*) in building up marriage payments after the wedding, and not as a debt before the marriage, which is permissible in Maasai (Spencer 1965: 26–33; 1988: 35, 42–5, 233–54).

[10] The parallel combination of Samburu and Maasai features in the Chamus age system was examined in Chapter 5. Among the Maasai as in Chamus, certain young men from richer families were permitted to marry sooner, and this could be with their *moranhood* girlfriends and was sometimes accomplished through a forced marriage. Chamus marriages by coercion seem closely influenced by Maasai practice. Compare, for instance, Case 3 with Spencer (1988: 30). In Chamus, the most common form of coercive betrothal, annointing a girl's head with butter provided by the suitor at an unexpected moment, was

time that the Chamus were influenced by Maasai ideas in other ways, especially concerning the independence of their *moran*, associated with the *manyata* warrior villages when the Kiliako were *moran*.

It was not simply that the Chamus *moran* followed the Maasai in certain details, but that they seem to have been impressed by the whole subculture of the Maasai *moranhood*, which contained an undertone of wilful disrespect towards the authority of the elders. Among the Maasai, coercive marriage was an example of the flamboyance of *moranhood*, although in practice it was rare, somewhat unpropitious, and the last resort of a desperate *moran*. Among the Chamus, elders did not suggest that it was particularly rare and could cite various cases, although certain families did regard it as unpropitious. The principle of coercive marriages by assertive Maasai *moran* who wanted to marry their girlfriends seems to have appealed to Chamus *moran* just when the established practice of early marriage was increasingly subject to interference by the elders.[11] While Chamus elders at this time retained the initiative in relation to the *manyata* organization, at least some enterprising *moran* appear to have asserted greater autonomy in relation to their marriages.

Generally, those who adopted Maasai or Samburu age systems coined a somewhat simplified and impoverished form. To the extent that younger Chamus reacted against the constraints of *moranhood*, generating loopholes that suited their personal whims, their age system would have been viewed by their Maasai and Samburu contemporaries as a paler and imprecise reflection of the ideal, as might be expected among a people who had been foragers (Dorobo) and were still not pure pastoralists.[12] A critical litmus test concerned attitudes towards fidelity within marriage. Among the Maasai and Samburu, the demand for strong peer-group bonds within the age-set was unremitting and this permitted casual and discreet intercourse with each others' wives. A husband who ostensibly coveted his wives from his age mates was seen as possessive and to this extent less than faithful to the ideals of his age-set, and he would be

---

actually a normal Maasai procedure. In Maasai this act simply registered the suit and could be refused, whereas in Chamus it was a form of coercion that could not be propitiously ignored: what was normal among the Maasai was interpreted as coercive by the Chamus. Another form of coercive marriage among the Chamus more directly comparable with the Maasai was a coercive foetus betrothal, placing a chain round a pregnant woman's neck, and forming a friendship with her child if a boy or a betrothal if a girl. The Samburu also had two forms of coercive marriage, but neither was close to the procedures adopted by the Chamus. (Spencer 1965: 42–5; 1988: 26, 30, 39, 263.)

[11] Unlike the Maasai, the Samburu were rarely in a position to marry their girlfriends because of exogamous constraints, and coercive marriages were therefore rarely with such women (Spencer 1965: 112, 216; 1988: 114). Among the Chamus, a girl was in a weak position to force the issue of her marriage. She would not dare to flout her father's wishes by becoming prematurely pregnant. If this were to happen, she would be circumcised in the bush and not in her mother's hut; there would be no formal celebration for her marriage, and her father would not receive the prestigious elders' blessing, confirming his spiritual protection over her. Her future ritual status would be anomalous, and, if her lover refused to marry her, then her marriage prospects were bleak.

[12] See p. 132.

punished. Among the Chamus, on the other hand, a husband could claim total sexual rights over his wife. There was no sense in which he was obliged to share her with his age mates, even covertly or at any time. Instead of supporting such adulteries as an aspect of solidarity between peers, his age-set would punish any adulterer, supporting fidelity *within* marriage rather than across it. In Chamus terms, the integrity of the basic family appears to have withstood the impact of pastoral innovations but in Maa terms, it was the Chamus age system that lacked the ultimate integrity.

'Climbing' an Age-Set

With increasing polygyny, delayed marriage was achieved by keeping sons as productive herdboys for a prolonged period and then, after their circumcisions, as bachelor *moran* for a further period. In the Chamus age system (unlike the Samburu or Maasai), *all* circumcisions were held in the same wet season. It followed that if a growing boy was refused initiation at the critical time of circumcision, then there would be a delay from one age-set to the next. Typically this would amount to about twelve years, and he would face the prospect of being a very senior *moran* among his peers and no longer a youth by the time they were allowed to marry. In effect, the Chamus age system had a similar role in delaying marriage and enhancing polygyny as in Samburu and Maasai, the shorter age-set span (twelve years as against fourteen or fifteen) being offset by having no tail-end of late circumcisions for younger *moran*. As I understand it, with no tail-end, the pressures for a changeover would have mounted up more quickly among the Chamus, reducing the span of the age cycle. The system was not expressed quite in these terms by Chamus elders, but the inference follows from their accounts.

In order to discuss how certain young Chamus evaded these delays, it is necessary to recall the method of control over the *moran* through the linking of alternate age-sets shared by all Maa.[13] Discipline within the age system hinged on the curse that each age-set of elders could invoke on the *moran* that were two age-sets below their own. Fig. 6.1 indicates that the Kideni age-set were responsible for cultivating respect among Kiliako as *moran*, and also for their progress through *moranhood* from the time of their initiation (*c*.1901). No members could be recruited into the Kiliako until the Kideni had kindled a fire bringing them to life as an age-set. These elders were the 'firestick patrons' of the *moran*, emphasizing their ritual patronage. Similarly, about twelve years later, elders of the Kinyamal age-set were firestick patrons of the Irimpot, two age-sets below their own, with the same responsibilities. There was a keen rivalry between successive age-sets, especially as *moran*, whose prestige and effectiveness depended partly on size and partly on their unity and ritual

[13] See p. 95.

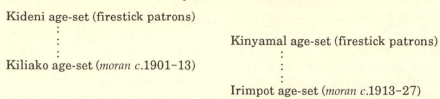

FIG. 6.1. *The alternation of firestick alliances among the Chamus*

panache. This rivalry persisted into elderhood, encouraging a tacit 'firestick' alliance between the *moran* and their patrons: the Kinyamal and Irimpot shared a rivalry with the intervening Kiliako age-set. The Kiliako were not, for instance, allowed near the major age-set sacrifices of the Irimpot, for it was held that they might steal a piece of meat and tamper with it, causing the Irimpot ritual leader to go mad through sorcery. Again, within the irrigation system, alternate age-sets would share the same side of a major irrigation channel to lessen the chances of dispute. On each side within their firestick alliance, men would collaborate more easily with their own age mates and respect their firestick patrons.[14]

It was this neat discipline within the age system that was threatened early in the twentieth century when an unprecedented series of premature circumcisions of boys took place during the closed period between formal initiations, too late for the Kiliako age-set and too early for the Irimpot. These boys faced the possibility of a curse by the Kinyamal age-set as prospective firestick patrons and by their own prospective Irimpot age mates. However, once they were circumcised, they also had a strong if anomalous claim for admission to the intervening Kiliako age-set as a tail-end by *fait accompli*. In the event, the Kiliako welcomed further recruits to their number, and the Kideni as their firestick patrons gave them a blessing to bring them into the regime that was the nub of social order, without undermining the system.

The boys who underwent these illicit circumcisions were known as *il-kailepi*, 'those who climbed'—into the next age-set. The explanation put forward by the Chamus for this irregularity was that the Kiliako and especially Irimpot boys were circumcised very late, so late that some even had grey hairs by the time they performed their *Ilmugit of eunoto*, permitting them to marry. The implication is that it was fathers who delayed the initiation of their sons for one age-set to retain their services as herdboys at a time when their herds were building up very quickly; as the herdboys and herds grew, so did the incidence of polygyny. The illicit circumcisions stemming from these delays seem to have

---

[14] See p. 143. It may be noted that this alliance reflects a 'southern Maasai' model rather than a 'northern' one comparable with the Samburu (p. 96), consistent perhaps with the lower age difference between elders and their senior sons. Cf. Spencer (1988: 140–1).

been of 'boys' well into their twenties who had been held down for too long and were reacting against the trend.

A further explanation is again the increasing contact with the Maasai at this time which stimulated subversive ideas. 'Climbing' an age-set was a recognized slip mechanism in the Maasai system and the Chamus appear to have borrowed the Maasai procedure. There was, however, a radical twist to this Maasai practice. In Maasai, a boy might want an early circumcision, but it was his father (or guardian) who decided and took the risk of subverting the system or negotiated with other elders for their support. In Chamus, it was the boys themselves who took the initiative: they would run away to the Uasinkishu Maasai to seek out an elder who would sponsor their circumcision as a proxi-father. They combined the wilfulness assumed by younger men in Maasai with the Maasai practice of permitting tail-end circumcisions and even the anomaly of defying the closed period.[15]

As with coercive marriages copied from the Maasai, this was an attempt by younger men to counteract the heavy-handed intrusion of an age system that delayed the adulthood of younger men to an unacceptable degree. The thrust of Maasai influence at this time in encouraging young men to react against their elders may be seen as the Chamus counterpart of what I have described elsewhere (1988) as a ritual of rebellion in the Maasai age system: a signal from young men to their elders to allow them more freedom.

Altogether five boys are said to have climbed up to the Kiliako age-set in this way, establishing a precedent for subsequent age-sets. In 1977, little was remembered of the circumstances in which these first climbings took place. Fuller details are available concerning the twenty boys who climbed up to subsequent age-sets and these are summarized in Table 6.3 and discussed below.

Irimpot to Parimo (c.1913–1948) and the Subversive Spread of Climbing

My information on climbing was collected from those who followed the Kiliako, including some who had themselves climbed. Any ambiguity over their rebellious past was resolved by viewing the trend historically, and they did not acknowledge any contradiction between their own frustrations as younger men under a regime that had led to a steady trickle of climbing, as against their current feelings of resentment at the impatience and disrespect of younger men who misunderstood the full responsibilities of elderhood and continued to climb.

---

[15] Cf. Spencer (1988: 67–8, 75). Following the formal removal of the Uasingishu to the Maasai Reserve in 1911, some remained scattered in the area to the south of Baringo, and these would have been at hand for boys who climbed after the Kiliako.

TABLE 6.3. *Boys who climbed an age-set among the Chamus*

Age-sets receiving 'climbers'	Residence		Reason for climbing		
	Lemeluat (Down-River)	Lekenyuki (Up-River)	To become a family head	To marry a girlfriend	To join older brothers
Kiliako	5	—	no details available		
Irimpot	7	3	5	4	1
Napunye	3	2[a]	3	1	2
Parimo	5	—	2	—	2
Merisho	—	—	—	—	—
Meduti	'many'		no details available		

Age-sets receiving 'climbers'	Location of initiation			Origin of clan		
	Uasinkishu	Dorobo	Chamus	Proto-Chamus	Samburu	Other pastoralists
Kiliako	5	—	—	1	3	1
Irimpot	7	—	3[b]	3	5	2
Napunye	—	1	4	—	4	1
Parimo	1	—	4[b]	2	4	1
Merisho	—	—	—	—	—	—
Meduti	?	?	'none'	no details available		

[a] Both families moved from Lekenyuki to Lemeluat before initiation (see Cases 8 and 9).

[b] Initiate's father took the initiative in two of the climbings in this column (a recurrent anomaly in Maasai).

It was the IRIMPOT age-set (*c.*1913–27) who carried the initiative of climbing several stages further before the elders regained partial control over what threatened to become a runaway situation. Each boy who wanted to climb up to the Irimpot had to find some firestick patron—any elder of the Kinyamal age-set—who was willing to kindle his initiation fire. In effect, he was deserting his peers, who would one day form the Napunye age-set, and this risked both their anger which could have the effect of an involuntary curse, and also the anger of the Napunye's future firestick patrons of Kiliako. Following Maasai precedence, a climber's strategy was to be inducted formally by invoking the Irimpot–Kinyamal firestick alliance before the boys or elders of the Napunye–Kiliako alliance had a chance to pronounce a curse that would make it too dangerous to proceed further.

The most common reason for climbing, relevant to one-half of the cases, was a desire to take over management of the family herd. The very first boy to climb up to Irimpot was one of these, and his example illustrates the procedure followed by others.

Case 4. Marime was still a boy when his father died and a paternal uncle was appointed to oversee the family. While other Murtanat clan elders may have regarded the guardian as a reasonable man, Marime and his mother felt that he was exploiting his position, constantly filching cattle from their herd and then opposing Marime's circumcision into Irimpot on the grounds that he was too young. Delaying circumcision also postponed the point at which Marime would be entitled to become fully responsible for the family and herd, and meanwhile the uncle could continue to exploit them. On impulse, Marime ran away without even telling his mother. Following the course of those who had previously climbed up to the Kiliako age-set, he went to Uasinkishu to find an elder to sponsor his circumcision in exchange for promises of future gifts and a lifelong friendship (*osotwa*). When Marime returned circumcised, he had to arrange to perform his *Sheep of the arrows* feast to become a fully established *moran*; and he also had to find a willing elder of Kinyamal age-set to kindle his initiation fire at this feast. A clansman volunteered to do this, and the ceremony was performed promptly and discreetly before other boys could mobilize opposition and threaten to curse Marime as a future age mate. After he had climbed, Marime's mother was told to brew beer for the clan elders to give their blessing to annul the anger of the Kiliako age-set who had been cheated as Marime's prospective firestick patrons. Kiliako elders stayed away from the blessing, for they had no wish to condone any climbing, and Marime remained at risk from their unvoiced curse.

Another recurrent reason for climbing was to join an older brother who was already a *moran*. There was an inherent rivalry between *moran* and boys, as between adjacent age-sets, and this could spoil the friendship expected between brothers. Ideally they should be *moran* within the same age-set to build on this friendship. The following case is also of interest in revealing the extent to which a proto-Chamus family had become fully involved in the growing pastoral economy by this time.

Case 5. Korio was still a boy when his older brother was initiated into the Irimpot age-set. They had always been close friends, but as a *moran* the older brother treated Korio badly, and after the death of their father he even took away stock promised to Korio and shared them with other *moran* at their feasts in the bush. As a mere boy, Korio dared not stand up for himself and provoke other *moran* also. He therefore decided to climb up to his brother's age-set. Without signalling his intentions, he too ran away to Uasinkishu to be circumcised. When he returned, Kinyamal elders collaborated in his *Sheep of the arrows* and lit his initiation fire. Korio then asked elders of his own clan, Kabis, to divide his stock formally from those of his older brother. The brother fully supported him at each stage after his return from Uasinkishu, welcoming him into his age-set, and later as elders they lived amicably in neighbouring huts.

A third reason for impatience for circumcision was once again associated with the extended period of boyhood at that time. Because they were older than usual, uninitiated boys were allowed to have girlfriends. Some of them became very attached to their partners, but had no prospect of marrying them because of the delay in their own progress through the age system. Climbing up to the Irimpot increased their chances of marriage before their girlfriends were married elsewhere.

After the first seven *moran* had climbed up to the Irimpot, it was assumed that the remainder would wait for the formation of the next age-set and the new season of initiations, which was expected very soon. There were, however, three more cases of climbing.

Case 6. As a boy, Leina had no prospect of marrying his girlfriend, and her brother Letema was in a similar position. They therefore decided to run away to climb together up to the Irimpot. Leina obtained his father's permission, but Letema's father was dead and he did not ask his father's brothers, for he knew they would refuse. They stole away with some money to Uasinkishu to be circumcised. When they returned, Leina's father decided to forestall resentment among the Kiliako as firestick patrons to the forthcoming age-set. He brewed beer and called four Kiliako elders of his own clan (the Murtanat) and they agreed to bless the boy. Kiliako elders of any other clan would have been less willing. Similarly, Letema's mother obtained the blessing of four Kiliako elders of her late husband's clan (Loiborkishu), men who were her close friends, cohabiting with her as a widow. (Case 3, concerning Leina's *fait accompli* marriage, was a sequel to this episode, his suit having been blocked by Letema's father's brothers, who as Kiliako elders had resented this double climbing.)

Case 7. Ketere was Letema's half-brother, and when he learned that Letema had climbed, he too wanted to follow this course. He was very close to an older brother who was an Irimpot *moran*, and he encouraged Ketere to become a *moran* too and remain close. By this time, circumcision to the new age-set was imminent. While other boys were on delegations preparing for their circumcisions, his brother arranged to have Ketere circumcised secretly in advance of all the others. Ketere stayed as an initiate for two days only and then killed his *Sheep of the arrows* with the connivance of clansmen of the Kinyamal age-set. If he had waited longer, the legitimate circumcision season for the next age-set would have opened and overtaken his plans. These elders would then have been altogether more reluctant to risk the unpropitiousness of defying the ritual procedure further than anyone else so far. As it was, initiates destined for the next age-set rushed to curse Ketere, but they arrived after his initiation fire had been kindled. His place as an Irimpot *moran* was secure.

A feature of climbing an age-set was the extent to which each instance implanted the idea more firmly, although certain lineages continued to hold themselves strictly aloof from this practice and from those that had climbed.[16] The temptation to climb appears to have spread like a subversive fashion through the social network, within families and clans, between friends, and from one age-set to the next, steadily becoming more widely acceptable and infecting the age system generally. Fig. 6.2 indicates how successive climbers were closely linked.

Following the initiation of the NAPUNYE age-set (*c.*1927–39), the trend towards accepting a limited measure of climbing continued, although there was always opposition from the boys whose age-set would lose a recruit. Moreover, a stigma associated with those that had climbed still lingered, and this cast a shadow over their marriage chances. Cases 8 and 9 also illuminate the relationship between Up-River and Down-River Chamus at this time.

Case 8. Lekoiya's half-brother had previously climbed up to the Irimpot and then died shortly after his marriage, and then their father too died. This left Lekoiya as a boy who had missed the opportunity of being circumcised into the Napunye age-set and was now responsible for a wealthy family with three widows. Because of these successive bereavements, sorcery was suspected and the family moved from Up-River to Down-River Chamus, the larger

---

[16] A further example of the spread of climbing as a fashion is evident in its brief popularity among the Up-River Chamus. At an early date, three instances occurred there in quick succession (the second, third, and fourth climbers to the Irimpot). From that point, this practice appeared to switch to the Down-River community and it became associated with them from that time.

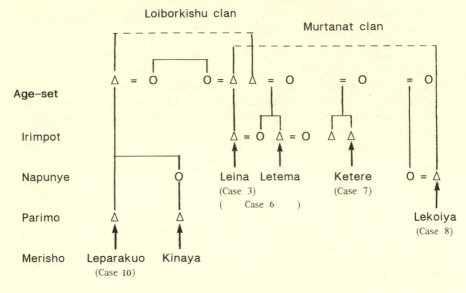

FIG. 6.2. *The infiltration of climbing an age-set through the social network*

community. Once there, Lekoiya wanted to climb in order to settle down to manage his family and obtain a wife. His Down-River clansmen supported this proposal, including Leina, who had himself climbed, but this was still kept as a secret within the Murtanat clan until the climbing was complete. For a wife, his clansmen decided to ask for a girl of Letema's and Ketere's family, since, with a history of having climbed, they would be more sympathetic to his suit than other families that had avoided this practice (Cases 6 and 7). In this incident, Lekoiya's move to Down-River Chamus was regarded as a sensible response and was not taken by either community to imply any difference between them in the incidence of sorcery. The important point was to leave the vicinity as quickly as possible.

Case 9. In another incident that followed this, a widow moved with her younger son from the Up-River Chamus because his older half-brothers kept filching his stock, and she expected more support from their close clansmen in the Down-River community. There, the elders agreed that the boy should be allowed to climb up to the Napunye in order to claim full control over his cattle, but disclaimed any interest in Up-River affairs that did not concern them.

The Napunye age-set was followed by the PARIMO (*c.*1939–48), and further climbings. At least one of these invoked earlier precedents.

Case 10. Leparakuo's father was dead, then his older brother died before marrying, and now as a boy he faced the responsibility of managing the considerable herd he had inherited. He was a first cousin through his mother to Leina and also a member of the Loiborkishu clan (like Letema and Ketere in Cases 6 and 7) and therefore could claim a family precedent of climbing. His circumcision locally was quickly arranged. As word spread round, other boys gathered together and rushed to curse him, but he had already climbed up to the Parimo. When eventually these boys became *moran* of the Merisho age-set, Leparakuo called them and brewed beer for the elders, and asked for their joint blessing to remove any lingering resentment that might serve as a curse.

While it was generally recognized that climbing resolved particular problems of need, there was also an irritation at the increasing number of trivial instances that stemmed more from bravado than real need. Those who climbed to join their older brothers in a senior age-set were not always responding to harassment, and some merely did so to maintain a close friendship with a peer who had climbed, including Leparakuo's close friend Kinaya (see Fig. 6.2). In another instance, a half-brother of Marime (Case 4) not only had no good reason but also bungled his attempt. He ran away to the Dorobo on the Leroghi Plateau to be circumcised, and then stayed there as a *moran* instead of returning to be formally inducted into the next age-set through his *Sheep of the arrows*. He only returned after the circumcisions of the Parimo, and thus he did not actually climb, but remained as a *moran* that much longer. In a third instance, one of the very first climbers, to the Kiliako age-set, argued that his own precedent was now a family custom and that his oldest son should be allowed to climb.

Generally, with the steadily decreasing age of boys at circumcision since the Irimpot, climbing was felt to be increasingly unnecessary and still ritually dangerous. It was the Napunye age-set as future firestick patrons who were the first elders to attempt to stem the trend by placing a curse on further climbing up to the Parimo age-set without permission. This had widespread support and achieved its aim.

Changing Relations between the Down-River and Up-River Communities

Table 6.3 reveals the extent to which the spread of climbing was confined to the Down-River Chamus, apart from three of the earliest cases that had occurred in the Up-River community. This divergence reflects the separateness of these two communities more generally. The villages had been dwindling since the process of dispersal began in Kiliako times, and, as the sites were abandoned, the older names Lemeluat and Lekenyuki were discarded for the more general terms Down-River and Up-River Chamus that applied to the dispersed communities. These two communities were cross-cut by bonds of clanship and intermigration, but they retained their separate identities, associated with different *manyat*, and maintained a sharp distinction between the territories that these *manyat* oversaw. This territorial division became increasingly sensitive as herds grew throughout the region and colonial expansion reduced the area available for Chamus grazing.

Rivalry between the two parts hardened when the Parimo were *moran*, with disputes over the boundaries between exclusive grazing areas now claimed by each side. Among the Up-River Chamus the ex-pastoral clans appear at this time to have been politically dominant, and they claimed to be wealthier in cattle than the proto-Chamus. They therefore objected to the Down-River community hosting their *Ilmugit of eunoto*, where they were expected to bestow cattle on a ritual leader selected from the proto-Chamus Kabis clan. This led them to install their own ritual leader from the ex-pastoralist Tumal clan and to perform their own *Ilmugit of eunoto*.[17] At the time, this was regarded as an anomaly, but the separation was confirmed by successive age-sets and became established as a practice within the age system, constituting a further intrusion by the Tumal clan into the traditional domain of the proto-Chamus. This initiative by the Parimo *moran* follows the pattern of a rebellion among young men against a regime established by the elders. Age-set climbing as a subversive activity was associated with one community, and now promoting the pastoral ideals of *moranhood* subversively was an initiative of the other. This aversion to the ritual seniority of a proto-Chamus clan may also be regarded as an expression of the tension between pastoralism as a growing concern and irrigation as a fading way of life, or indeed the failure of proto-Chamus families to cultivate sufficient pastoral skills despite half a century of exchanging daughters for cattle and generally increasing herds. The persistence of specialized skills within each family, which was discussed in Chapter 1, is the counterpart of the problem of adopting new skills when transferring to a mixed economy. This could have applied as aptly to the proto-Chamus adapting to pastoralism as to the ex-pastoralists turning their hand to irrigation previously when the system faltered.[18]

---

[17] See pp. 153 and 171. Baringo District Handing Over Report, Balfour to Boyle, n.d. HOR/2673, *c*.1957. The administrative account of this friction reads as though it reflects the exaggerated rhetoric of a local dispute at a sensitive time. The Report also confuses the division between the proto-Chamus and expastoralist clans (the Kisieni, Loiborkishu, and Longeli are misplaced), and assumes that these coincide with the two communities. My own informants emphasized that clanship and pastoralism cut across the division between Up-River and Down-River Chamus and migration between them ensured a constant intermixing (but cf. Anderson 1984: 109, 114).

[18] See pp. 26 and 174.

Merisho to Bikisho (c.1948–1982) and the Decline of the Age System

Following the lead of the Napunye age-set, their Parimo successors declared that they would pronounce a similar curse if there was any concerted trend towards climbing up to the MERISHO age-set (*c.*1948–59). But no trend occurred. With the pressure from above and as precedents receded into the past, the incentive to risk climbing also receded. No sons or fathers took the initiative to be the first, and, with no initiative, no others were tempted to follow. No boys climbed up to the Merisho. The fashion, which in retrospect appeared to have spread like a minor epidemic creating a certain subversive momentum of its own, had now lapsed.

A feature of the oral history of colonial rule from the Irimpot age-set to the Merisho, as compared with earlier traditions, is the extent to which the essential elements of Chamus society were perceived as unchanging during the lifetime of my informants. Indirect colonial rule provided a stable setting for the status quo, underpinning the power of the elders and only rarely finding it necessary to give firm support to deal with serious unrest among the *moran*.[19] The *moranhood* of the Merisho age-set was the last period that outwardly displayed an untarnished age system whose constraints and responsibilities extended to all Chamus males. Even the outbreak of climbing over four successive age-sets seemed to have been finally contained.

In one respect there was change, however, and this accelerated with each age-set from the Merisho onwards. Casual wage employment was becoming increasingly available throughout Kenya, and the Chamus needed a supplementary source of income as the population steadily grew while the mixed economy continued to falter. Following the example of a handful of the Merisho, there was widespread approval that the *moran* of subsequent age-sets should now leave the area for limited periods to find work, keeping them away from the villages and the wives of older men, as the *manyat* had done, but with more tangible results. At first, this simply involved the absence of some *moran* who had little to do at home. The ideal of *moranhood* itself, however, was changing, with less call on their services to be seen protecting the herds than in the past. To the extent that labour migration became increasingly popular among the *moran*, the *manyat* had their divided attention and lost the prestige they had enjoyed when the Chamus were building up their herds. The term *manyata* was becoming a synonym for a cattle camp run by younger men and boys, and to this extent it lost sight of the Maasai ideal of a unique experience for instilling an age-set discipline and intensive loyalty among age mates. Only at their *ilmugit* festivals did the *manyata* approach this role. At such occasions,

---

[19] Cf. Baringo Distict Annual Reports 1927 and 1928, AR/726–7; and Handing Over Report by Murphy, HOR/241, 11 Nov. 1936.

moran could identify their unity with ideals of the past. But once they dispersed after such gatherings, those that left the area to return to employment were saving up for their futures as individuals, undermining the sense of identity and sharing within the age-set and increasing the temptation for others to follow this course.

Beyond the economic factors that encouraged this trend among *moran* was the guiding hand of the elders who were trying to distance themselves from Maasai ideals. These had been introduced by the Kiliako and Irimpot age-sets as *moran*, and then modified when they became elders, adopting a more gerontocratic stance in order to retain control over the herds that they themselves had built up. In the present chapter, the initiatives taken by impatient *moran* of subsequent age-sets, the Napunye and Parimo, may be interpreted as a reaction to this regime imposed by their firestick patrons. Then the Napunye and Parimo in their turn became elders and firestick patrons, and they assumed an initiative that aimed at dismantling aspects of their age system associated with outdated notions of warriorhood that they felt had encouraged the spirit of independence among young men when they themselves had been *moran*. The age system survived as the guiding principle of social organization, underpinned by the power of the elders; but *moranhood* as an overarching ideal among young men could not be sustained.

Prominent in this ideal were the privileges of warriorhood claimed by *moran* as the insignia of their status. These had been borrowed from the Maasai as a proclamation of prestige and were a source of bitter rivalry between successive age-sets at the time of changeover when they were claimed by the new age-set of *moran*. Following Maasai practice, a retiring age-set of *moran* were not allowed to attend the festivals of their successors in case their jealousy might incite them to attempt sorcery. In the present climate, the elders regarded these rivalries and ritual avoidances as alien to the Chamus and a relic of Maasai influence. They argued that suspicion of sorcery at this time was invidious. Regardless of what might occur among the Maasai, whose Prophets encouraged sorcery, the possibility of sorcery was discounted among the Chamus where no instances had ever been reported between age-sets.[20] To defuse the rivalries and the pride in the privileges of *moranhood*, elders of the Napunye and Parimo as successive firestick patrons jointly agreed to abolish these particular ritual avoidances and they invited the retiring Merisho *moran* to attend the festivals of their successors of the MEDUTI age-set (*c*.1959–70).

The elders at this time were ostensibly seeking to consolidate bonds within the wider community that cut across age-set rivalries. However, an underlying motive was clearly to consolidate their power over younger men whose status was enhanced by the ambiguities of the age system. It was in this climate, when

---

[20] Cf. Spencer (1988: 140–1, 221).

the Meduti were *moran*, that there was an unexpected spate of age-set climbing. This followed the original pattern of boys running away for circumcision without consulting their fathers. Most of these occurrences were held to be for no good reason, and no climbers were circumcised inside the Chamus. They all ran away to other neighbouring peoples: the Uasinkishu, Tuken, Dorobo, and Samburu. This was no longer seen as an outlet for strain within the age system, but an indication that fathers, elders, and the age system itself had lost control. Taking a broader view, however, these instances of climbing were still *within* the traditions of Chamus society. The climbers were trying to hasten their elderhood for a variety of reasons, but not necessarily to question the dominant premiss of social order associated with respect for age. At this stage, it was *moranhood* that had lost some of its glamour and the elders had lost some of their control, but elderhood itself retained its stature as an ideal among younger men who climbed, at least for a time.

With the transition to post-colonial independence in 1963, the Chamus were more directly exposed to the cash economy of Kenya and to opportunities and pressures for change. Neither these forces nor the new democracy were re-specters of Maasai ideals or of age for its own sake. The status quo under an indirect rule was no longer an option. Those appointed to official positions were now more directly accountable to higher authorities, and they were less accountable to their peers than before. New and irreversible trends were to free young men progressively from age-set restrictions.

Following Meduti, the BIKISHO (*c*.1970–82) were the first age-set to have been significantly affected by the introduction of school education. Up to this time, comparatively few boys had gone to school and fewer still stayed beyond their circumcision. The overwhelming majority went on to the *manyata* as *moran* or off to work. But with the trend towards a lower age of circumcision and the rapid increase in numbers that went to and stayed on at school—boys and girls—the *manyat* became increasingly fragmented except at *ilmugit* ceremonies when the age-set would reconvene. Even the senior ritual leader of Bikisho was a schoolboy. One aspect of the popularity of sending sons to school was that this removed the ambiguity surrounding the *manyat*, where fathers had less control over their *moran* sons than over their other possessions. By sending these sons instead to school, fathers retained control and had an additional investment in their future. If the *manyata* system had faltered when the Meduti were *moran*, it was falling into disarray with the Bikisho. The ideal of *manyat*, originally inspired by some of the oldest men alive when they had been *moran*, could now be seen as another passing and subversive fashion. With its demise, the future of the age system itself was uncertain.

Clanship, however, still retained some of its significance in residential pref-erences. A survey of 48 families in one locality by Kaori Kawai in 1987 revealed three clusters of homesteads in which ex-pastoralist families outnumbered proto–Chamus by 17 to 3, and two further clusters in which it was the proto–Chamus who outnumbered ex-pastoralists by 23 to 5.[21]

Polygyny and New Trends in Social Inequality

In Merisho times, the absence of a few *moran* as labour migrants was no more than a minor innovation. However, with successive age-sets, increasing numbers of *moran* followed this course and a new trend was established once they returned with their savings and the means of setting up their own independent households. Through them, the cash economy was permeating Chamus transactions. Their earnings passed to elders in exchange for cattle and to fathers-in-law along with these cattle as part of the marriage arrangement. The Meduti age–set broadly conformed with Chamus ideals within the limits of these trends. With the Bikisho age–set, coincident with the increasing numbers of younger *moran* at school, an increasing number of older *moran* ignored the formal restrictions of the age system and were marrying early with the connivance of the elders, before their *Ilmugit of eunoto*.[22]

Early marriage for some Bikisho, however, was not a symptom of a general trend towards monogamy, as in some other parts of Africa. Polygyny remained a widespread ideal and this meant a continuing delay in marriage for young men in general. While a minority of Bikisho *moran* had evaded the restrictions and were already married in 1977, the marriage prospects for many others were still distant, and even bleak for some. This contrast in the outlook of young men of the same age-set was an indication of increasing social and economic inequality. It affected the preferences for arranging marriage which had also acquired a new slant. Previously, elders had always been prepared to give their daughters to poor but well-established families. Any young elder who devoted his energies to his herd could surmount his poverty, and no worthy man was thought to have had serious difficulty in marrying after settling down from *moranhood*. In Bikisho times, however, there was now a distinct preference for marrying daughters to richer men or those with good employment prospects. This implied a transition from the traditional stratification by age to an emerging stratification by wealth. Marriage and especially polygyny were increasingly the prerogative of the rich rather than the aged, and to this extent only a privileged sector of younger men could marry early, and notably those that had broken free of the age system by establishing themselves while still technically *moran*. In 1977 older men expressed their sense of alienation from these trends towards the new distribution of privilege; but they too needed to accommodate the cash economy and they gave away their daughters to best advantage and encouraged

---

[21] Loimkumkum locality. Kawai (1988: 18).

[22] The marriages of these *moran* were arranged between families without even seeking dispensation from the *manyata*. However, after the ritual leader had been installed, those that had married *did* pay him a heifer, while he continued to remain at school and unmarried.

the marriages of their sons, conspiring with the irreversible changes that were taking place.

This sharp change in marriage preferences leads one to return again to the hidden patterns of polygyny surveys discussed earlier. In Chapter 2 the profile of Chamus polygyny based on data provided by Peter Little was compared with that of the Samburu.[23] In Fig. 2.3*a* there was a distinct horizontal shift to the right for the Chamus, as compared with the Samburu profiles in Fig. 2.3*f*. This indicated a more egalitarian distribution of wives within any Samburu age-set (in 1958) and a more competitive situation among the Chamus, with greater inequality (in 1980–1). However, Fig. 2.3*a* also suggested that this Chamus inequality increased with age. In other words, it was not just some privileged younger men who were establishing themselves at an early age, but some elders who had achieved an even greater degree of inequality with their peers.

It is possible to take the discussion a stage further by drawing on the alternative polygyny data presented in Table 6.2. This was based on an altogether more limited survey than Peter Little's and statistically it is frankly inadequate. Nevertheless, *if* it can be assumed to provide at least a broad indication of trends, it is also revealing. The advantage of this smaller survey is that it extends to unmarried men and provides a finer breakdown of senior age-sets. It is this smaller sample that is listed in column (*b*) of Table 6.4 as a profile of average polygyny rates according to age. Again, as in earlier discussions here, one is faced with the problem of disentangling unchanging life-career patterns from unique historical trends. With this in mind, column (*b*) can be interpreted in two ways. Viewed synchronically as an ahistorical cross-section of Chamus society, this column suggests delayed marriage for most young men (the Bikisho), a sharp trend towards polygyny among elders as they mature (the Meduti and Merisho), and then a tailing-off of polygyny as they approach old age (the Parimo and Napunye). In 1977 this tailing-off was expressed by some older men as a loss of interest in competing for further wives once their sons had started to marry. Alternatively, the polygyny figures may be viewed in the context of a historical trend. This puts a different gloss on the profile, especially when the Chamus data are compared with an earlier sample of polygyny rates for the Samburu shown in column (*c*). The Samburu profile is for men of the same age ranges as in column (*a*) and is arguably closer to an earlier Chamus pattern, given the influence that the Samburu had had on the development of Chamus society and pastoral ideals.[24] The comparison places a different gloss on the points already noted. Among the Bikisho, it shifts attention from the number that had not yet married to those that had already managed to do so,

---

[23] See pp. 58 and 62.

[24] The Samburu polygyny rates in Table 6.4 are taken from the clan census which provided the finer breakdown by age, facilitating interpolation with the Chamus age spread (Spencer 1965: 320–1). It should be emphasized that the age groupings for individual points in Fig. 2.3*a* and *f* were different for the Samburu and Chamus, and to this extent the polygyny levels (vertically) are incommensurate.

TABLE 6.4   *Age profiles of polygyny and wealth among the Chamus, c.1980*

Age-set	(a) Age range in 1977	(b) Chamus polygyny rates in 1977 (wives/elder)	(c) Corresponding polygyny rates among the Samburu in 1958 (wives/elder)
Napunye	58–71	1.20	2.38
Parimo	49–57	2.20	1.69
Merisho	38–48	2.57	1.46
Meduti	26–37	1.10	0.39
Bikisho	25 or less	0.43	0.003
Base		50	566

Age-set	Age range in 1981	(d) Comparative herd and farm sizes in 1981 (after Little 1985a)		(e) Comparative herd and farm sizes per family member in 1981 (after Little 1985a)	
		herd	farm	herd	farm
Napunye and Parimo	53–75	0.56	0.39	0.70	0.50
Merisho	42–52	1.97	1.17	1.51	0.84
Meduti	30–41	0.75	1.24	0.84	1.42
Bikisho	29 or less	0.78	0.85	1.16	1.26
Adjusted mean		(1.00)	(1.00)	(1.00)	(1.00)
Base		60	60	60	60

disregarding restrictions on marriage among *moran*. Among the Meduti and Merisho age-sets, it accentuates further the rapid build-up of polygyny rates with elderhood. Among the Parimo and Napunye, the decrease of polygyny with age is highlighted.[25] This suggests a striking increase of polygyny in recent years among younger elders, outstripping men of the same age in the earlier Samburu sample. The elders who expressed a loss of interest in acquiring further wives, in other words, were not perhaps simply commenting on their own disengagement, as might be expected among older men, but on their sense of alienation, their inability to compete in a new era that increased the demand for wives among younger men. The Samburu sample is compatible with a model of gerontocratic rule, as men build up their families with age after a delayed start. The Chamus sample suggests an inversion of such a pattern at both ends of the age scale.

Peter Little's more recent study of the emergence of economic stratification among the Chamus provides further evidence of this trend.[26] Column (*d*) of Table 6.4 is derived from his survey of homestead data and shows the variation in comparative wealth between age-sets. The profiles indicate a substantial stake in irrigation as well as in herds among younger married men, and again a sharp decline of wealth among the more senior age-sets, who would have been in their mid-fifties or older by the time of Little's study. Column (*e*) expresses the same findings in relation to household needs expressed as comparative wealth per family member (or adult equivalent). It is clear that the decline of wealth among senior men cannot be explained solely in terms of a general process of adjustment to smaller households as they age: even allowing for household size, they have a lower rating than any other group on each count. To the extent that Little's analysis illustrates the emergence of striking differences in wealth between the successful and the less successful Chamus, the older age-sets appear to be among the more impoverished, whereas among the Samburu previously they would have been easily among the most wealthy. At the younger end of the age scale, columns (*d*) and especially (*e*) show the

---

[25] Two further explanations for the sharp decline in polygyny with ageing seem less likely. First, in 1977, elders did not suggest that marriage to older men had become unstable, leaving them with fewer wives. Secondly, while some wives of older men would have predeceased them, they were normally altogether younger than their husbands and could expect to outlive them.

[26] Little (1985*a*: 253–5). In this adaptation of Little's data for column (*d*), the average wealth is collated from Little's table 5 and the breakdown by age is given in his table 6. For column (*e*), I have assumed that the average number of family members per household is five for the sample as a whole. This assumption is heuristic and affects the actual figures but not the *relative* profiles of column (*e*). Cf. Little (1985*a*: 250 and 258 n.), where the measurements for cattle as 'stock units' and family members as 'adult units' are defined. With regard to the distribution by age, Little (1985*a*: 255) does not distinguish between the Parimo and Napunye age-sets, and his data refer to the holdings of married men only. His table also assumes a 13-year age difference between successive age-sets, whereas elsewhere (1992: 31) his data suggest a figure closer to 11, with recent successive periods of only 11, 9, 10, and 12 years. In Table 6.4 here, I have therefore adjusted the age ranges to my own estimates as in Table 6.2, assuming initiation at about the age of 19 for the oldest members of each age-set.

Bikisho adequately endowed compared with older age-sets. However, these are not averages for all the Bikisho, since the sample excludes those who remained unmarried, with no herds or farms of their own. The unrecorded Bikisho include those with inadequate means for acquiring wealth and poor prospects generally.

The columns of this table, then, provide consistent evidence for a tailing-off of wealth in wives and in property as men age. This reiterates a pattern that was previously considered in Fig. 2.3e in relation to polygyny data in certain societies, and in Chapter 3 in relation to the wobbly upper rungs of certain age ladders.[27] To the extent that the Chamus at one time may have had a form of gerontocracy comparable with that of the Samburu, the new pattern reveals a distinct shift towards an alternative form of stratification in a more competitive milieu.

It is characteristic of Chamus history that the elders adapted pragmatically to the new opportunities that followed Independence, although they had little option. The Chamus economy was fragile and the opportunities of wage labour for their sons provided an access to new sources of income. Inevitably, this undermined the position and ultimate control of the older men, and Table 6.4 confirms that a new form of stratification was emerging, based on wealth rather than age. Traditional values were upturned as prosperity in wives and property became increasingly the prerogative of some younger men. Among the Chamus in 1977, the principles of age organization were formally retained, but the degree of disinvolvement of young men amounted almost to an abandonment of *moranhood* and suggested that the future of their age system itself was in question.

Conclusion: Indigenous Knowledge and the Evolution of Chamus Culture

The analysis in Part II of this work has traced the history of Chamus society as perceived by elders whom I met in 1977. Their account pointed to the elaboration and then subversion of their age system with the development of pastoralism, as pre-colonial, colonial, and then post-colonial encounters changed the nature of their boundaries with the outside world.

This rise and fall of a major institution gives the Chamus view of their history a dynamic quality. There is an awareness of change that is generally lacking in the oral histories of other pastoralist peoples of the area. Among the latter, the legitimacy of tradition is closely associated with the unchanging nature of their age systems, with minor adjustments when necessary to facilitate the persistence of this tradition. The tenacity of tradition in other pastoralist societies is matched by a flexibility among the Chamus as they have

---

[27] See pp. 82, 110, and 122.

responded to changing circumstances. To this extent, the Chamus have a sense of history rather than of tradition.

The prominence of their age system in this account also highlights the role of age in the process of history. Age systems in general are subject to an indeterminate balance of power in the relations between experienced elders and opportunistic younger men, which may vary over time. Each successive age-set is remembered as having been strong in its youth or weak or innovative or whatever the case may be. This variation may seem to follow some cosmic pattern in popular belief, or certain pendulum-like swings may even be a characteristic of the system itself.[28] Beyond these meta-patterns, however, there is variation that responds uniquely to historical circumstance in the shaping of each new age-set. Among the Chamus, virtually every age-set since the Peles appears to have been associated with some shift in the age organization. As pastoralism built up to form the dominant feature of their economy, so the Chamus acquired practices from their Maa-speaking neighbours— the Samburu at one point and then the Maasai at another—to create a hybrid age system that was at the same time distinctively their own. It was younger men who were remembered as the pioneers of these thrusts; and most recently in the post-colonial setting, the innovations of the cash economy were again associated with the initiative of a new generation of younger men for whom the restrictions of the age system became increasingly irrelevant.

However, it would be an exaggeration to attribute the thrust of change to younger men alone. Maturing elders continued to fashion their reputation as an age-set and they had more time and authority to mount a sustained response to circumstance. The adoption of Samburu-style *ilmugit* ceremonies to control the *moran* and subsequently the constraints imposed upon the Maasai-style warrior villages, for instance, were surely the initiatives of age-sets of elders. Switches in initiative between young and old among the Chamus correspond broadly to shifts between predation as a strategy preferred by younger men and peaceful husbandry preferred by the elders. Each new situation modified the collective wisdom of the elders, and this could be challenged at any time by the dubious initiative of younger men. The example of the spread of climbing an age-set as an illicit fashion among Chamus youths, for instance, displays the changing balance of power with age over six successive age-sets. Climbing followed the pattern of a new idea that at first circumvented an established tradition, and was then successfully stemmed by a determined response from the elders, only to reappear with renewed force as the authority of the age system itself was undermined.

---

[28] e.g. the notion of cycles and epicycles underpinning the *gada* system among the Oromo (Legesse 1973: 194–200); of natural cycles in the Dassanetch age system (Almagor 1985); and of certain repetitions in the alternation of Samburu age-sets, which appear also to be a characteristic of the demography of their age system (Spencer 1965: 157, 167–72).

Peter Little's comprehensive analysis of the impact of the latest innovations among the Chamus provides a cue for Part III of this work. In effect, Little has taken over from where my own elderly informants left off in 1977. They looked back to an aspect of Chamus society that endeared itself to them; while they deplored the new trends, at least they were cushioned from them by their wealth and a life style that seemed secure enough in their remaining time. Moreover, despite their reservations, it was the older men who connived with these trends by sending off their sons to school and to work, and by marrying off their daughters opportunistically to young men whose eligibility lay in the new order rather than the old. The elders therefore could not altogether dissociate themselves from changes that undermined their traditional author-ity; nor could they deny that in their time as young men it was avant-garde members of their own age-sets who had subverted the system by climbing and by forcing marriages against the general will of the elders.

There is a further strand in the argument that has a bearing on the final chapter of this work and seeks to look beyond the immediate dilemma facing pastoralists to a broader consideration of the evolutionary pattern underlying pastoralism itself. There is a hint of this where Adams and Anderson have noted with specific reference to the Chamus that: 'Indigenous technologies are not perpetual; they change, evolve, expand, contract and even die out. Identi-fying the dynamics behind these shifts should be of relevance to the planning of modern development in sub-Saharan Africa.'[29] One perceptive African au-thor, Clement Onyemelukwe, takes a harder look at such planning and suggests a process that has an affinity with Darwinian natural selection:

development cannot be planned. One can provide the incentives but many of the activities of men who are at the centre of development elude rational planning. . . . True development is not rationalist in character. It occurs through consistent efforts of individuals and peoples trying, modifying, testing, discarding and replacing. The de-velopment process occurs in the midst of waste and inefficiency, but the trend is always upwards and always finding new levels after each change has worked itself out.[30]

We may put to one side the unbounded faith in ultimate progress revealed here as an elusive ideal: a belief in progress is in any case superfluous to a Darwinian model. However, the notion that indigenous development involves a process of adaptation through trial and error within a wide variety of possibilities has a crucial relevance. It points to similar underlying principles to those of biologi-cal evolution but applied to the development of culture as the aggregate of indigenous knowledge, albeit at an accelerated pace, and in a parallel that has been explored by various writers, notably Karl Popper.[31] This is to acknowl-edge the role of selective pressures and chance encounters in the arena of

---

[29] Cf. Adams and Anderson (1988: 531).
[30] Onyemelukwe (1974: 85), cited by Hyden (1980: 230).
[31] Popper (1963: 216–22); Miller (1983: 78–86, 239–47). Cf. Bray (1973); Darwin (1871: 385).

technological inventiveness and extending to adaptation within any sociocultural system.

Among pastoralist societies throughout the region, a key activity in the continuous process of adaptation was the debating among elders at their formal meetings to resolve immediate problems and keep tradition in good repair. There was a tacit acceptance of creeping change, but above all a premiss that the traditional wisdom of elderhood lay in pooling their collective experiences and insights in order to arrive at a well-considered course of action. In this respect, as noted in Chapter 3, age organization provided a key mechanism for mobilizing a collective opinion backed by firm resolution. Among the Chamus, the elders' *olamal* council played such a role in asserting ultimate authority. As with the Samburu and Maasai, the council was seen to act as a body, selecting from a pool of ideas when faced with a problem, bringing a variety of points of view to bear in a debate that continued until some consensus was reached that was binding on everyone.[32] The wisdom of tradition in coping with the unexpected was seen to lie in this community of knowledge and discourse. Influential men played a central role, generating a consensus enhanced by their imaginative elaboration of this collective wisdom, but their reputation depended on their ability to maintain confidence by responding to popular opinion.[33] Indigenous knowledge, in other words, undergoes an unending process of renewal in response to changing circumstances.

This resilient adaptability of tradition has a bearing on the Chamus economy, which is held to have undergone a series of transformations, from foraging in the Lake Baringo area, to the discovery (or acquisition) of irrigation in proto-Chamus times, to pastoralism introduced by ex-Samburu refugees, and most recently to the fringes of the capitalist economy in post-colonial Kenya. Each innovation presented them with an opportunity that spread as a new and increasingly dominant idea, displacing earlier traditions. In Darwinian terms, each adaptation involved the establishment of a successful 'mutation' within the pool of indigenous knowledge, precipitating a shift in the pattern of dominance. The difference between the spread of a genuinely new idea—from some bird on high, as the Chamus expressed it in their myth of the first cultivation—and the more probable and earthbound diffusion of knowledge, acquired from neighbours, becomes a moot point. Both depend upon the conditions under which the selective adaptation can take place. Like decision-making in the elders' discussions, new ideas are less dependent on the

---

[32] Cf. pp. 127–8. The relation between a variety of opinion and consensus achieved through discussion is expressed in the Samburu saying that an elders' debate resembles a tree, with the various branches of opinion leading towards a single trunk, expressing their consensus. The Maasai have a similar metaphor that refers to the circle of feathers in a warrior's headdress, representing shades of opinion that surround a spokesman who as the 'head' should take account of all these views in debate (Spencer 1965: 176–80; 1988: 105).

[33] P. H. Gulliver (1963: 50–2, 62, 64); N. Dyson-Hudson (1966: 223–4); Spencer (1965: 180–4; 1988: 215); Turton (1975: 170–8).

imagination of any one individual than on the readiness of the community at large to share their knowledge and insights and recognize the opportunity, whatever its source of inspiration.

The Chamus account of a succession of *ad hoc* responses to changing circumstances seems to describe a process of selective adaptation as pertinently as the erratic development of Western scientific understanding in Popper's model and of African development in Onyemelukwe's. In the elders' discussions as much as in the pioneering initiatives of younger men, there is an uncontrolled process of revelation as ideas jostle for attention within the cultural pool of knowledge, and those that are best adapted to the existing circumstances will spread.

In this interpretation of historical development, one is concerned with all 'knowledge' that is perceived to have relevance for the appropriation of resources in the widest sense: ideas, beliefs, and values, extending especially to insights into practical institutional arrangements that underpin this process. Successive shifts in the mix of economic adaptations corresponded broadly to shifts and responses in their institutional superstructure. The development of climbing as a subversive innovation fits this pattern: a mutation within the sociocultural milieu that was regarded as anomalous and yet found a niche and began to spread to successive age-sets. Climbing responded to opportunity and weathered selective pressures until it could eventually be diagnosed as an early symptom of the spread of individualism and a trend that was wholly incompatible with the collectivist traditions of pastoralism.

The point to emphasize is that all forms of social adaptation, extending to the spread of fashions and the diffusion of culture, are aspects of the growth of 'indigenous knowledge', and they involve the evolution and spread of ideas through trial and error. In Chapter 1 the development of Nuer society from some proto-Dinka ancestral group provided a contrasting example to the Chamus, although involving similar principles of the adaptation and spread of a body of developing ideas. In the Nuer instance, this seems to have comprised a form of mutation, a novel mix in their husbandry that emerged and took hold, leading to an elaboration of their superstructure that enveloped their neighbours, like a new dominant species displacing its predecessor. This involved a process of adaptive radiation, and with it spread the notion of Nuer identity.[34] The Chamus, on the other hand, were a receptacle that borrowed ideas and absorbed them in a process that can be viewed either as the adaptive radiation of Maa influence, or, from a Chamus viewpoint, as an adaptive hybridization with neighbouring cultures. The identity of Chamus as a sociocultural system over time appears to have incorporated newcomers, new ideas, the aggressive edge of pastoralism, and steps towards a cash economy, while remaining firmly rooted in one area.

Reaching beyond the Chamus experience of the growth and attenuation of a

---

[34] See p. 36.

tradition as pastoralists, this discussion is now poised to return again to the broader topic of pastoralism in East Africa, examining the impact of capitalism in modern times, not as a further swing of the pendulum in the internal dynamics of age systems, but as a unique force that is in the process of marginalizing pastoralism as a way of life. And Chapter 9 will look beyond the pattern of this development to the evolution of the phenomenon of pastoralism itself.

PART III

The Marginalization of Pastoralism

7

Population Growth, Development, and the Malthusian Dilemma

The final part of this work considers the relevance of three related debates over the future of pastoralism in East Africa. These concern the impact of the growth of population and technology (Chapter 7); dependency theories which bear on the increasing marginalization of pastoralists in the remoter areas (Chapter 8); and the conditions under which pastoralists destroy their own environment (Chapter 9). Uncontrolled population growth, the penetration of world capitalism, and the threat of ecological degradation are the basic premisses of what follows.

The contrast between these themes and the analysis up to this point provides a measure of the impact of recent change, which has acted with the force of a shock wave on traditional systems, irreversibly changing the setting of pastoralism. Yet this concern was anticipated in Chapter 1, which noted the inherent contradiction of the pastoral ideology of family and herd growth, ultimately implying competition for limited resources. In a stable environment, it is possible to envisage a resolution in terms of some dynamic form of equilibrium in which the ideal of growth is only partially achieved, only for a limited period, and only by some of the more successful pastoralists at the expense of others. However, this scenario isolates remoter peoples in a timeless ecological setting. It does not consider the impact of any sustained growth, nor allow for external forces that have edged pastoralists from their niche. In approaching this topic, it is useful to recall the prevailing ecological setting before the shock wave of recent change.

Pastoralism and the Shifting Balance of Advantage

The broad pattern of survival in the more arid regions of East Africa during pre-colonial times appears to have offered considerable room for manœuvre both in the geographic and the economic senses. The pastoral peoples would shift their ground, pushing into new areas and expanding, or being pushed and contracting, as the balance of political advantage changed with the fortunes of warfare, epidemic, and drought. The small hunting groups would tend to remain aloof from these political movements, staying in one area and forming uneasy economic links with their successive neighbours. One also has the impression of periods of relative stability interrupted by critical episodes of political and economic turmoil that spread almost as a chain reaction across wide areas. Given the general preference for large families coupled with the repetition of disasters in oral history, one may again envisage a sawtooth profile of population growth, in which the steady accumulation during periods of relative calm was offset by the sharp reversals at critical times. Those who survived would then turn to foraging in some form, often among their hunter-gatherer neighbours. The profiles of genealogies suggest that many did not survive.[1]

To grasp the essential flexibility of this state of affairs, it is necessary to put aside any notion of immutable tribal groups whose membership was determined solely by birth. Many East African peoples certainly have held to such a model, but there is also evidence of shifting affiliations, especially among the pastoralists, where whole tribes were at times fragmented by disaster, although individuals and families might survive among their neighbours, adapting to new life styles and associations as necessary. This is also reflected in clan traditions that cut across tribal boundaries and provide the notion of remote kinship alliances. Even among the Maasai, where clanship has a narrower significance than among the more northern pastoralists, a stock-owner migrating to an area where he is a stranger should first seek out members of his clan to whom he can turn as kinsmen. The Maasai view expresses the ultimate value of clanship throughout the region. The tribe-centred model of territorial groupings, united in defence of their herds and common pasture, needs to be coupled with a model of family-centred networks of kinship and clanship, capable of cutting across dissolving tribal boundaries as charters for survival and providing the ultimate insurance against catastrophe. Most ethnographies of pastoral societies under an imposed peace tend towards the first model; whereas historical studies of earlier times, and most notably Schlee's reconstruction of shifting identities in north-eastern Kenya (1989), have drawn attention to the relevance of the second. Fig. 1.1, focusing on the Samburu–Rendille boundary, illustrates the ambiguity of any notion of tribe as a discrete entity and can be viewed either way. The interplay of the two models appears to have been characteristic of the process of adaptation within this region, where tribal boundaries could be transient and the claims of kindred or clansmen could be modified through usage.[2]

This implies a degree of underpopulation in the easier times. Periods of relative stability would involve an only partial exploitation of the environment,

---

[1] Spencer (1973: 204–6); see also pp. 41 and 133 above. The census of a well-established Samburu clan, for instance, indicated a large number of descendants from only a handful of recent ancestors, suggesting that the lineages of other ancestors had failed to survive in the course of only 100 years (Samburu clan census: Spencer 1965: 93, 318–19).

[2] See pp. 18–19, 24–5, and 126, Schlee (1989: 145–236); Spencer (1988: 19). Cf. Osogo (1970); Johnson (1991: 109, 114–15); Sobania (1991: 118, 129–39).

leaving considerable room for adaptation as the circumstances changed. In times of drought, for instance, there would be incentive to move outwards into the no man's lands that separated rival groups, to divert energies to alternative foods, and to foster intertribal links that offered alternative possibilities. In this way, the slack in the system would be taken up in hard times, and this offered a longer-term security in an unpredictable and inhospitable environment.

In the less arid areas, where agriculture was possible, the situation was more complicated, but a similar pattern of survival, movement, and changing fortunes appears broadly to have prevailed. The mixed economy of agro-pastoralism offered more leeway, but any land shortage that restricted the mobility of their herds inevitably stunted the opportunities for dodging the worst effects of drought and epidemic, and this limited the size and condition of their herds. Ostensibly, agriculture required a more benign environment and this permitted a more intensive exploitation of the land, but it also attracted a greater concentration of population making heavier demands still, and famine was always a serious hazard as crops faltered through drought (or locusts) and hunger spread. In other words, 'drought' was not simply determined by the random distribution of rainfall, but also by the unfulfilled expectations of those who depended on an unpredictable environment, and the higher concentrations of population in the easier areas tended to spread the risk more evenly. The nomadic pastoralists appeared better able to withstand short periods of drought that could spoil a harvest. However, in periods of prolonged drought their herds could be devastated, and it was then that they would migrate as refugees to any neighbouring agricultural areas, adding to the pressure of population. The accommodation of these pastoralists in times of adversity consolidated the migratory links that afforded agriculturalists an opportunity to take up husbandry in easier times. There was a shifting balance in populations between pastoralists, foragers, and cultivators, depending on circumstance, which consolidated the trading and kinship links fostered over the longer term. For the major groupings, this was regarded as abnormal and marginal, although clearly important in abnormal times. However, for marginal groups such as the Chamus, it was in the mainstream of their experience.[3]

The history of the Chamus, which was examined in Part II, provides just one example of this process, but a particularly useful one, because it reveals the contrast between pre-colonial and post-colonial change. Chamus experience may be taken as a microcosm of what is occurring throughout the region. The transformation of their society and prospects under modern conditions poses the particularly intractable problem of pastoral development that has baffled governments and aid agencies alike, and leaves the pastoralists stranded.

---

[3] Berntsen (1976; 1979). Cf. Salzman (1980: 14–16); Swift (1977*b*: 462–3); Anderson (1984: 107; 1988: 244, 250, 255); Oba (1990: 40–1); H. Kelly (1990: 81).

The Chamus and the Crisis of Modernization

The Chamus are situated on the boundary between pastoralism and agriculture, where the rough edge of this transition is very apparent. Turning to pastoralism did not free them from the problems of famine that had dogged their irrigation system. The population was steadily growing, and reports for the area from the 1920s refer repeatedly to growing herds and overgrazing, and sharp losses in times of drought.[4] It is a view that gives an impression of the sawtooth profile of growth and disaster noted in Chapter 1, but along a downward trend towards permanent drought. The numbers of Chamus stock, it seems, had reached and then overreached their natural limit. Meanwhile, their irrigation faltered from year to year and could not be relied on to tide them over the periods of drought. Many returned to join their clansmen among the Samburu. Significantly, the Baringo area is recorded as among the earliest and most regular recipients of famine relief.[5]

To the extent that the Chamus were cushioned by the protection of the colonial administration, their faltering economy could persist. In official circles, pastoralism was regarded as a self-destructive form of underdevelopment, but policies to encourage an involvement in the cash economy were inevitably flawed. Without outside help, the Lake Baringo area could only produce inferior crops that were unpredictable and unmarketable, and the sale of surplus stock to offset overgrazing was inhibited by prolonged quarantine restrictions. To encourage self-sufficiency in the area, the authorities attempted to reinstate the irrigation system of Down-River Chamus in the 1950s: the Perkerra Scheme. Only a few Chamus agreed to pay as tenants for what they all regarded as rightfully their own. In fact, the subsequent history of this scheme was one of sustained subsidy from the state matching the famine relief that was still needed outside the scheme. While the colonial administrators failed to come to terms with the ecological problems of Baringo, the Chamus under the colonial umbrella were living on borrowed time as the pressures on their environment increased. Young men did not respond to wage-earning opportunities, while the elders were ominously recorded as being 'overfond of beer' (1936) and consuming a 'vast quantity of liquor' (1950). During the same period in the Samburu district, *moran* enlisted in the police and army in considerable numbers as an extension of their tradition, while elders hardly touched alcohol in any form.[6]

---

[4] Annual reports for the Baringo area also reflect an uncertain mix in the Chamus economy with claims that they were now almost entirely a pastoral tribe (1928), although still with a primitive form of irrigation in small areas (1932, 1938) that sometimes at least gave good crops (1937, 1948), and they caught and bartered fish in times of food shortage (1945, 1947).

[5] Anderson (1988: 257–9); Little (1992: 9, 43–4).

[6] Chambers (1973: 347, 352). One Handing Over Report (Boyle to McLean, 1957) refers to 'very few' Chamus left in the scheme, while another report (Annual Report for Baringo District 1958) refers to 45 Chamus out of a total of 151. These would have included outsiders who registered as Chamus. Regarding Chamus drinking habits: Baringo District Handing Over Report 1936, Annual Report 1950: 23. Cf. Spencer (1973: 163–5).

Following Independence for Kenya in 1963, colonial boundaries and protection were lifted and the Chamus were exposed to the full thrust of a growing market economy. They were not immediately affected by the expanding opportunities, but rather by the backwash of expansion nationally. The introduction of the ox-plough in the highland areas to the south and the growing market for maize and then for lucrative export crops displaced subsistence farming in these areas. Poorer farmers were edged into the more marginal areas such as the Baringo basin, increasing the competition for land in a region of diminishing opportunity. With more open frontiers, the Chamus were now faced with the migratory drift of marginalized Tuken peasants from the south-west and also by Pokot pastoralists, pushed by similar pressures from the north-west.

The changes during the *moranhood* of the Meduti and Bikisho age-sets, noted in Chapter 6, have to be viewed in the light of an awareness of new opportunities and a loss of respect for traditional values that could only be sustained while the Chamus remained isolated from the wider forces of change. The infiltration of competition from outside challenged the ideal of *moranhood* as a community of peers that built up its own sense of self-respect, and the moral foundation of the age system dwindled.

It is from this point that Peter Little's research among the Chamus in the 1980s provides a penetrating overview of the impact of change. By the time of his study, young men had grown up in the new economic climate and were taking initiatives that challenged the dominance of older men, not as an age-set of rebellious adolescent *moran*, but as individuals competing for their own interest: the earlier trend towards individualism had become a norm. The diminution of the Chamus age system appears to be due more to their desire to throw aside its restrictions than to any other single factor. The older men predominantly held to traditional values, but at the expense of being marginalized by those who had invested in new opportunities and now emerged as the new élite. Those who had previously chosen to collaborate as irrigation tenants of the Perkerra Scheme now benefited from its subsidies and were relatively wealthy. The more enterprising younger men who had taken up wage employment now invested their capital in irrigation and herding as a business enterprise beyond their own family needs. In the 1960s, because the market for cattle was at best unreliable and also because of the increasing uncertainties of their claim to land, the Chamus showed a renewed interest in irrigation. From the 1970s, with increasing pressure on land, irrigation was no longer an available option, and those who wished to start cultivating had to turn to dry-land farming with a greater risk of failure or at best a mediocre crop.[7]

In Little's analysis of this mixed economy, each family needed to mobilize labour for the seasonal demands of irrigation without jeopardizing the herd. The critical period was during the peak of the irrigation cycle, when the intense

---

[7] Little (1992: 63, 78, 95–6, 103, 116, 166).

preparation of their plots limited mobility and diverted attention from their cattle, which needed care at all times. A further option was to take up wage labour in the irrigation areas, including the Perkerra Scheme, especially during the bottlenecks of the irrigation cycle, when wages were high, but this again diverted attention from their own enterprises at a critical period, overstretching their resources and placing their herds even more at risk. The dilemma facing poorer Chamus was that even unskilled work offered a better immediate return than irrigating their own farms or tending their own herds at these peak times, but it drew them into a downward spiral. The immediate need to feed their families undermined the ultimate need to nurture their capital, and they were forced to deplete their herds, even to the point of selling fertile female stock. Collaborative arrangements between kin and between neighbours could stabilize these pressures up to a point. However, instead of a collective economy, managed by elders and supported by *moran*, Little notes that corporate groups played a minimal role among the Chamus by the 1980s. The older men remained wealthy in cattle, but were losing communal control over the irrigation systems and also over the use of pastures. From a traditional form of social differentiation according to age, there was emerging a new form of differentiation according to success in adapting to new opportunities, and younger men were prominent in this shift.[8]

The problems facing the marginalized poor were the obverse of the opportunities that attracted the more enterprising Chamus, engaged in an upward spiral. Once a man had become moderately wealthy, he could afford to hire causal labour and even tractors to prepare his irrigation plots at the critical point of the agricultural cycle prior to planting. This extended the area he could farm and avoided withdrawing valuable labour from herding. He could not profitably sell his surplus grain for cash, but he could exchange it for cattle or labour from the downwardly mobile poor. In this way, his gains from irrigation farming were reinvested in his farms and his herd, and he could meet his cash needs by selling off less than the natural increase of this herd. Agriculture and pastoralism were complementary for the wealthy, feeding on success. It was they who were best placed to take on further wives and to afford extended schooling for their children, anticipating the possibility of more highly paid opportunities in work and diversifying the household economy still further in the next generation.[9]

Success for the more enterprising was further enhanced by the policy of land registration in Kenya. Those that laid claim to large irrigated farms motivated others to establish larger farms than they could profitably work, and to secure the best dry-season pasture for their stock, fencing their land to establish a claim to exclusive ownership, notably the swampy areas bordering on the lake.

[8] Little (1985*a*: 254; 1992: 13, 61, 78–87, 89, 92, 95–6, 98–100, 114, 117, 142–4, 153–4, 160).
[9] Little (1992: 65, 87, 92, 99–101, 104, 124–5).

As these prime pastures were taken out of communal use, free-range pastoralism was increasingly relegated to waterless tracts.[10]

Beyond the local economy, wealthy Chamus elders found themselves in competition with a new category of influential absentee land- and herd-owners. These were well-connected and salaried non-Chamus who had assimilated capital in the Baringo area, legitimizing their position partly through tenuous links with impoverished Chamus clients who farmed their land and tended their herds, and they were poised to buy the land rights of these clients. To this extent, the ownership of local wealth and labour extended beyond the Chamus and was becoming linked to a system of national patronage.[11]

In this way, the process of increasing individualism was shifting capital and power towards a small emerging élite at the expense of the remaining Chamus population, who were being edged to the dryer margins with diminishing resources. This was not perhaps altogether without precedent among pastoralists, where the successful have tended to consolidate their gains while the unsuccessful have always been edged towards foraging.[12] However, the scale on which it was occurring among the Chamus, with a narrowing élite and a broadening periphery, was a measure of the impact of change. The very fact that Little's survey revealed that about one-half of the Chamus were depleting their herds at a rate that could render them stockless within five years suggests a very radical and accelerating shift in the distribution of power.[13]

When I visited the Chamus three years before Little began his study, the elders were still well established within the pastoral economy and seemed bemused by the full implications of change. They pointed out that younger men had always pioneered the shifts within the system, and elders had always criticized them for their disrespect towards age and tradition. The impact of change had not dislodged their enthusiasm for what they regarded as Chamus ideals, but they did acknowledge that it had interrupted the transmission of these ideals, and that Chamus society could become transformed more radically than at any previous time. A new order of priorities had captivated the younger generation, and, as the elders of the Napunye and Parimo age-sets grew old, so this order was poised to engulf the Chamus way of life.

Drought and the Commitment to Growth

The Chamus experience is by no means unusual.[14] A strikingly similar example has been reported among the Orma, who are the most southern Oromo group

---

[10] Little (1992: 102–3, 143–8).
[11] Little (1992: 139–43).
[12] Little (1992: 115). Cf. Haaland (1977: 184).
[13] Little (1992: 69, 99, 101, 125).
[14] This section and the introductory paragraphs of this chapter are based on an earlier article with the same title (Spencer 1974), providing an initial outline for Chapters 7 and 8 here.

in another part of Kenya, again with an emerging stratification between pastoralists who have been forced into a situation of dependency on the expanding economies of local irrigation farmers, and with absentee owners again impinging at a higher level still.[15] In non-irrigation areas with low rainfall, the opportunities for development are limited, but even here the unmistakable trend is towards the marginalization of pastoralists generally.

There are two fundamental issues in this erosion of the traditional way of life. The first is the impact of population growth. The ideal of growth in sub-Saharan Africa was considered in the first two chapters of this work, where it was seen to be typically associated with polygyny, large families, and a sense of well-being. The widespread concern with fertility and lineage development is an aspect of this ideal, and so too is the commitment towards investment in their herds among pastoralists. A growing herd is a necessary foundation for a growing family and the prospect of further marriages. Expressed in various ways in the religions of these peoples, the accumulation of wealth, the growth of the family, and survival to old age are seen as blessings. Anything short of these is regarded with apprehension. In an uncertain environment where the survival of individuals is always in question, to be stunted is to be vulnerable.

The sheer scale of population growth in the region is illustrated in Table 7.1.[16] Within this sample, Kenya has a remarkable record for population growth, the thirteen other African countries have high rates, and only Ethiopia, dogged by drought and civil war, does not clearly rank above all the Asian and South American countries. Data for population growth in the pastoral areas are harder to assess: the accuracy of official figures varies widely, and they are inflated by the net flow of immigration towards these areas between censuses. An estimate of growth within a Samburu clan exclusive of such migration suggested an annual growth rate of 2.3 per cent, even over a period when they had experienced a reversion to intertribal warfare and two severe droughts accounting for two-thirds of their stock in the first instance, and then after a brief period of recovery leading to further losses estimated at between 50 and 80 per cent. A comparable figure of 2 per cent over the course of the present century has been suggested for the Chamus.[17] The premiss of growth, in other words, is not merely an elusive ideal, but has been widely attained during the present century.

Among the causes of population growth in Kenya have been improvements

---

[15] H. Kelly (1990: 81–2); Ensminger (1992: 134–9).

[16] World Bank (1986: 8).

[17] The estimate of 2.3% growth for the Samburu is from the data opposite, which relate to the clan census in Samburu and suggest an increase of 40% over 15 years for men aged over 32 (Spencer 1965: 318–20; 1974: 421–2). See also Ch. 4 n. 13. Cf. Mbithi and Wisner (1973: 118–19). According to census figures, the Maasai (Kajiado and Narok), Samburu, and Turkana, with 26%, 77%, and 99% of their land classified as of low potential, had annual population growth rates of 4.5%, 3.0%, and 0.2% respectively between 1969 and 1979 (Mbithi and Barnes 1975: 85; Republic of Kenya n.d.: 33–9). The

TABLE 7.1. *Comparison of population growths in the Third World, 1983*

Area	Crude birth rate per thousand	Crude death rate per thousand	Net growth rate (births–deaths per thousand)
Kenya	55	12	43
12 African countries	46–53	15–21	27–40
Ethiopia	41	20	21
Bangladesh	42	16	26
7 Asian/S. American countries	27–34	7–13	19–27
China	19	7	12

in health care. In the second half of the nineteenth century, cholera, smallpox, and bovine pleuropneumonia were major scourges that led to sharp setbacks in any trend towards population growth. In the present century, there have been no comparable epidemics until the advent of AIDS, and this is a useful indication of the effectiveness and popularity of Western medical and veterinary services. While these have been concentrated in the centres of population, they have been complemented by famine relief measures in the remoter parts aimed to save the lives of those most at risk. Demand has been too great to raise standards of health beyond a minimum, but this apparently has been sufficient to sustain the fertility rates even among the destitute.[18]

Beside improvements in health care, other contributions to population growth have been the check on sporadic outbursts of intertribal fighting, and the gradual extinction of the more dangerous animals. For each of these factors, any policy adopted for the more populated settled areas had to apply to the nomadic margins and they were irreversible. A policy of *laissez-faire* to allow remoter areas to achieve some ecological balance was impracticable in a country committed to development. One could not control human and stock epidemics,

implication is that the Maasai area, with growing access to outside cultivators (see below), was a net importer of population during this period, whereas Turkana is widely perceived as a net exporter.

Age-set	Estimated age range in 1958	Recorded alive in 1958	Recorded alive in 1973	Survival rate over 15 years (%)
Marikon	over 82 years	7	—	0
Terito	64–81	23	7	30
Merisho	53–63	70	44	63
Kiliako	39–52	119	99	83
Mekuri	32–38	148	} 177	95
Mekuri	27–31	39		
Kimaniki	17–26	194	185	95
Total aged over 32 years		367	512	

[18] Stiles (1983: 3); Turshen (1987: 198); Dawson (1987: 216–17).

guarantee law and order, and eliminate dangerous animals in the areas for development without extending preventive medical and veterinary measures, curbing intertribal warfare, and endangering the survival of dangerous animals in the remoter areas. Quite apart from any moral or political issues, development in the more populated areas was intrinsically linked to factors that indirectly promoted population growth and pressure on the land in the remoter areas.

This trend displays a sombre parallel to changes in herd growth and structure that resulted from the domestication of stock, as perceived by Tim Ingold and noted in Chapter 1.[19] By protecting the herd from predators, pastoralists ensure that the most vulnerable sector—the young and the sick—have better chances of survival; and this leads to rapid growth of their herds to some critical level of population pressure and then to a sharp downturn: the sawtooth profile of growth and decay. Pursuing the parallel, what pastoralists do for their herds, sophisticated Western innovations have also done for the human population in the area, providing more protection from the predatory forces of nature. Ironically, what pastoralists may regard with fortitude as a necessary strategy for their herds is raised to a tragic level when applied to human beings; and the problems of overbreeding and enhanced life chances extend from the rise and fall of herds to the careers of dependent human populations at large.

Parallel to the problem of population growth has been that of immigrations stemming from development in the more fertile areas. On the one hand, population pressure has led to the fragmentation of holdings and intensification of farming methods; and, on the other hand, the market for export and the introduction of the plough have greatly increased opportunities for extensive cash-cropping, leading to land shortage and problems of underemployment. This has created an agrarian crisis, as displaced peasants have tended to drift towards the barren plains without adapting the crops they grow or their intensive techniques for cultivation to the more infertile soil or the lower and less reliable rainfall. In such areas, even the more robust crops such as maize are unlikely to succeed, and the soil structure breaks down as it is exposed to the elements. Arid land becomes more arid.[20] Nomadic pastoralists in their turn are edged away from their more dependable grasslands—their dry-season grazing—by the immigrant peasants, or they face the choice of turning to subsistence farming themselves or seeking work in the settled areas. Those who do not settle are edging further into semi-desert regions, where they compete with one another and with rival pastoral groups for depleted resources. As cattle husbandry has become more marginal, so the case for turning to camels

[19] See p. 41.

[20] Ominde (1968: 101, 185, 187); Mbithi and Wisner (1973: 114, 119); Baker (1974: 174); Grove (1974: 147); Dahl and Hjort (1979: 8); Carlsen (1980: 74, 221); Njonjo (1981: 37); Bernard (1982: 152); Haugerud (1989: 66–7).

as the final refuge in the driest areas has become stronger. Rather like toppling dominoes, the agrarian crisis has worked its way towards the arid margins.[21]

In this way, the incidence of 'drought' is not just a phenomenon of the remotest areas with low rainfall, but applies to each zone where expectations are too high and maladaptation increases the chances of failure. Population growth is one factor, but another is the degree of success in the more fertile areas which feeds on itself, invading the surrounding areas and increasing the pressure. Parallel to the new opportunities for the successful, there is a cascade of collapsing hopes from just beyond the fertile areas downwards. The sequence of fading hopes leads towards the margins where pastoralists face an even more barren prospect, and the notion of a pastoral continuum disappears into the desert.

The characteristic pattern in population growth and movement in Kenya may be viewed against the uneven distribution of population. This reveals a stark contrast between the arid areas that comprise 54 per cent of the land area and contain 6 per cent of the rural population, and the most fertile areas with a more dependable rainfall where 6 per cent of the land area contain 52 per cent of the rural population. The area between these extremes (40 per cent of the land with 42 per cent of the rural population) is equally divided between areas with an annual rainfall above 300 mm—which seems to be about the minimum for a range of rain-fed crops in favourable circumstances—and areas below this minimum.[22]

The intrusion of cultivators into land used by pastoralists, notably landless subsistence farmers but also including pastoralists who turn to cultivation, has been widely reported in studies that extend from the Sahel to Tanzania.[23] Instances reminiscent of trends among the Chamus are also reported in these accounts, with small-scale irrigation and the fencing of private plots, sometimes on an extensive scale and by influential outsiders. Generally, a progressive loss of land by pastoralists due to the spread of agriculture has been noted in Africa, leaving herders with the option of moving away to areas that are on the whole

[21] Manners (1962: 493); Hjort (1979: 29); Galaty (1980: 158); Gilles and Jamtgaard (1982: 5–6); Wood (1982: 157–60); Gilles (1983: 15); Sperling (1987a: 6–7); Heald (1989: 86–7); Oba (1990: 40–1); Fratkin (1991: 49, 118); Little (1992: 37–8, 50). Cf. Swift (1977a: 175).

[22] Cf. Mbithi and Wisner (1973: 113); Mbithi and Barnes (1975: 84–5); Goldschmidt (1981: 102–3); Njonjo (1981: 31); Bernard (1982: 151); Maro and Mlay (1982: 176–7); Throup (1987: 43); Keya (1991: 73); see also Swift (1977a: 171), who makes a similar point concerning the Sahel.

[23] Oromo: Dahl (1979a: 263); Stiles (1983: 3); H. Kelly (1990: 82); Oba (1990: 40–3); Ensminger (1992: 138–9). Maasai: Hedlund (1979: 30–1); Parkipuny (1979: 137, 154); Galaty (1980: 159–60); Moris (1981: 112); Campbell (1984: 41–3, 58–9); Arhem (1985: 20–2); Kituyi (1990: 91–107); Ndagala (1990: 56–7; 1992: 51, 77–8); Waller (1993: 232–7). Parakuyu: Hurskainen (1990: 80, 86–7); Ndagala (1990: 58–9). Datooga: Kjaerby (1983: 34–5); Ndagala (1990: 60–1). Samburu: Hjort (1981b: 51); Perlov (1983: 128); Fratkin (1991: 7, 13). Turkana: Hogg (1987: 51). Kamba: Wisner (1977: 206). Somali: Konczacki (1978: 102). Baggara: Salih (1993: 25). Sahel: Hoyle (1977); Sorbo (1977); Swift (1977a: 175; 1977b: 474); Dahl and Hjort (1979: 5); Wood (1982: 157–8); Manger (1988: 170–1); Bernus (1990: 167, 171); Salih (1993: 25).

too dry for cattle at the height of the dry season or cultivating in an area too dry and unpredictable for farming.[24]

Corresponding to the population drift towards the remoter areas, there has also been a heavy migration to the centres of employment, predominantly from the areas where populations were highly concentrated, but also with substantial numbers from the pastoral areas. The growth of population in Nairobi has varied throughout the century between 5 and 10 per cent annually, rising to above 11 per cent during the first decade following independence. Comparable rates of growth were experienced by other major towns in Kenya, such as Eldoret, which had more than twice the rate noted for the population as a whole in Table 7.1. With the rapid growth in urban populations, the extent of squatter estates increased along with unemployment and crime, illustrating what Barbara Ward has called the 'pathological acceleration [towards] a terminal crisis of social and economic disintegration'.[25]

Altogether, one has a broad impression of an expanding population with an increasing pressure on resources as the less privileged are thrust into the marginal areas of existence, where their presence creates a local crisis. This may be experienced as the swelling ranks of unemployed and unhoused in the urban areas; as the fragmentation of holdings, with an increase in the number of underemployed dependants and vagrants in the more fertile agricultural areas; as the slow destruction of the soil by attempts to over-exploit it in the more marginal agricultural areas; as recurrent drought, fluctuations in stock, and general deterioration of the land in the remoter arid areas; and these days as increasing numbers relying on famine relief in the scattered refugee camps. As pressure on resources builds up, so flexibility is lost and the hardship caused by drought becomes more certain. Each mode of economic adaptation has less slack and is therefore more prone to unforeseen hazards.

In this way, drought appears at least in part as the longer-term symptom of a social process, a probability derived from the aspirations of economic man, rather than as a short-term arbitrary act of God. Drought describes the situation of those that are pushed out in certain ways, just as urban deprivation, landlessness, and vagrancy describe the situation of others whose problems derive from the same fundamental pressures. Crisis is endemic throughout the region.

Malthusian and Neo-Malthusian Models

Kenya especially appears to exemplify Thomas Malthus's argument that un- checked population growth outflanks the inventiveness of humans to increase

---

[24] Monod (1975: 296–7); Dahl and Hjort (1979: 6); Hjort (1979: 147); Goldschmidt (1981: 102–3; 1982: 19–22); Gilles (1983: 15).
[25] Ominde (1968: 192–4); Ward (1969: 57); Kenya (1970); Ingle (1972: 14); Hjort (1979: 29; 106); Bernard (1982: 153–4); Stiles (1983: 3); Hogg (1986: 325–6); Throup (1987: 56, 71); Nyangira (1987: 23).

food production, leading to a crisis of overpopulation. The falling gross domestic product per head in Kenya is matched by a similar trend in Tanzania. They are the only countries in the region that have not been crippled by civil war, but still the average standards of living have dropped.[26] With an unequal distribution of opportunities, the brunt of the struggle for survival has devolved on those living at the margins: a steady stream of urban immigrants who forage the scraps of civilization, and those in the remoter areas who are caught up in a vicious circle in which large families are regarded as the best security against high mortality rates.

A neo-Malthusian approach takes the argument a stage further. It asserts that economic development compounds the problem of population growth by encouraging unimpeded commercial exploitation. Together these degrade the environment and undermine the world's life-support system. It is not just a problem of uninhibited human sexuality, as Malthus perceived it, but of unrestrained aspirations more generally. If the balanced sawtooth profile of growth and disaster among pastoralists expresses the Malthusian impasse, then the neo-Malthusian emphasis in a number of pastoralist studies depresses this profile along a downward slope towards long-term degradation. The difference between the two models concerns the relative thresholds of resilience of the soil, on the one hand, and of the herds of cattle or the human population, on the other. Gunnar Haaland provides a useful example. Among the Baggara of southern Dafur, for instance, their clayey dry-season grazing land is especially resilient to overgrazing, and during periods of drought it is the survival of the herd that is critical (Malthusian); but their sandy wet-season pastures further north are less resilient to the herds in their prime, and this leads to serious overgrazing and deterioration of the soil in the long term (neo-Malthusian). Or again among pure pastoralists, any increase in the human population beyond the capacity of their herds will lead to the emigration of those who are most vulnerable (Malthusian: e.g. the Rendille); but if they settle to agro-pastoralism, the concentration of population combined with fewer checks on growth can lead to serious pressure on the land (neo-Malthusian: e.g. the Chamus).[27]

It is ironic, and yet wholly within the Malthusian paradigm, that a new epidemic may still alter this situation in ways that cannot be predicted. But it is argued here that neither AIDS nor any other scourge can be expected to resolve the fundamental dilemma of an environment that cannot meet the demands that are made on it. From this point of view, any attempt to increase food production, to develop resources, or to provide any form of famine relief merely serves to buy time without addressing the problem of growing

---

[26] Kenya: Hunt (1984: 298–9); Throup (1987: 70–1); Haugerud (1989: 65). Tanzania: Ingle (1972: 14).

[27] Spencer (1973: 190); Haaland (1977: 184–91); Dyson-Hudson and Dyson-Hudson (1982: 222–3); Hjort (1982: 12–14). See also pp. 25 and 211.

demands. Similarly, arguments that divert the root of the problem from ideologies and expectations to the unequal distribution of resources within the
world at large are appealing in effect for more time rather than resolving the
persisting problem.[28] The neo-Malthusian spectre is ultimately more than a
regional phenomenon and localized famine is nature's response to unrestrained
growth worldwide.

The thrust of the argument in Chapter 1 directly implicated the pastoralists
of East Africa in this dilemma, not just because they are at the critical margins,
but also because their own aspirations also concern the desire for growth, even
if their means are limited and growth is frustrated by recurrent disaster. The
Malthusian approach was expressed in the opening quotation of this work
regarding 'nomadism as a careful pastoral continuum' and 'the least traumatic
of human influences' in the most marginal areas. The more sinister neo-
Malthusian approach is sometimes expressed as the 'Tragedy of the Commons': that each herd-owner has more to gain personally from increasing his
herd than the cost of degrading common pastureland that is shared with others.
This criticism was also raised by the Royal Commission on East Africa, whose
report noted the devastating effect of a 'combination of communal range with
unrestricted individual ownership, because therein neither the community nor
the individual have regard to the effects of their actions on the land'.[29] In the
short term, some individuals may win; in the long term, all individuals ultimately lose. If herds increase to the extent that land is eroded, then the herds
themselves will dwindle. However, this criticism extends to the world continuum of unrestrained capitalism as it intrudes with an equally devastating
effect on the environment: the Commons are worldwide. From the neo-
Malthusian point of view, the pastoralists are caught up in a problem that is
wider than any of their own making.

Pastoralists and the Development Trap

The general assumption that pastoralists are backward, irrational, and represent a form of primitive underdevelopment has prevailed in official circles since
early colonial times. This has accompanied policies encouraging herd-owners
to settle down to agriculture, sell their surplus stock, and adapt to the market
economy.[30] Development schemes as the instruments for pursuing such policies have systematically underestimated the full complexity of the ecological
problem. Regarding the Perkerra Irrigation Scheme in Baringo, for instance,

[28] Hogg (1987: 47); Fratkin (1991: 12, 130–1).
[29] Hardin (1968: 1244); Royal Commission on East Africa (1955: 294); Dyson-Hudson and Dyson-Hudson (1982: 234–5); Livingstone (1977: 210–20).
[30] P. R. Baker (1975: 196, 1977: 157–8, 163); Dahl (1979a: 237); Parkipuny (1979: 154–5); Goldschmidt (1981: 107); Galaty (1984: 16); Gartrell (1988: 206, 211); Ndagala (1990: 54–8); Hurskainen (1990: 80); Fratkin (1991: 112); Little (1992: 164–5).

Little has shown how the planners' concentration on land management has weakened the pastoral sector and the whole balance of the Chamus mixed economy. Chambers has gone further in castigation this scheme as a striking example of misconceived development, which after more than twenty years of planning revealed the extent of the problems of adapting modern technology and the market economy to a marginal area. In this process, difficulties tended to compound one another, leading to an increasingly heavy subsidy from which successive administrations could not extricate themselves. As more money was spent, so it became politically impossible to admit failure and abandon the scheme.[31]

Fully within the pastoral sector, a striking feature of development policies within the region has been their continuity over the transition to Independence. African governments and aid agencies have conspired to disregard the experience of failed policies in colonial times—it is argued that they were failures of colonialism—and yet they have followed a similar approach towards planning, perpetuating earlier assumptions and mistakes. The extent to which such schemes are independent of political ideology is demonstrated by comparing the experience of Maasai group ranches in capitalist Kenya with Maasai ranching associations in socialist Tanzania. Both were designed to improve the quality of Maasai cattle by controlling the use of grazing, restricting the increase in herd sizes, and encouraging herd-owners towards commercial ranching. Neither achieved this. Because the schemes had been introduced in the best grazing areas and for limited numbers of stock, this increased the pressure of cattle and overgrazing elsewhere. Within the schemes, the increase in the numbers of cattle remained unchecked and the restrictions had to be lifted in times of drought to accommodate pressures for immigration over a wider area. Members within the schemes could not refuse their kinsmen seeking refuge for their herds from drought elsewhere, and these members in turn were obliged to migrate elsewhere when the rains failed locally. In other words, with soft boundaries, these schemes failed to prevent local concentrations of cattle which damaged the land, and the schemes effectively ceased to exist in precisely the most critical situations that they had been designed to withstand. Traditional links of kinship and obligation towards *all* Maasai proved stronger than the formal restrictions. Boundaries were drawn and then ignored; plans were bedevilled by drought; marketing arrangements were undermined by quarantine restrictions. To the extent that the schemes claimed a partial success, it was at the expense of the ecological balance in the uncontrolled areas and also of increasing inequalities in wealth. Those who were already well connected were able to enter the schemes, benefiting from the superior resources, while retaining free access to the uncontrolled areas for their surplus herds in easier times. Those inside had the best of both worlds, inside and outside, and those outside

---

[31] Chambers (1973: 361–4); Little (1992: 163, 166–7, 170–1).

had the worst. Both in Kenya, with its policy of land registration with a view to private ownership, and in Tanzania, with the ideal of settled, kin-based *Ujamaa* neighbourhoods, the failures of these ranching schemes have been quite similar.[32]

Clearly, such schemes were designed with important ecological principles in mind, and yet the planners overlooked the erratic nature of rainfall locally, which made necessary a more extensive pattern of nomadic choice to take advantage of the opportunies over a wider region. Rather oddly, the planning of these schemes apparently overlooked the possibility that self-contained arrangements of this kind already existed in the concept of 'tribe', as noted previously in Chapter 1.[33] In contrast to more settled peoples, such as the Gogo, where there is a certain merging with their neighbours, the notion of 'tribe' with hard boundaries is a meaningful concept among the more nomadic pastoralists, and one is led to accept that up to a point 'tribes' evolved naturally because ecologically they made sense, allowing movement over long distance to accommodate unpredictable drought. Within these boundaries in pre-colonial times, there was free movement. The boundaries would shift with shifts in population pressure, but tribes persisted—or they perished and any surviving families were absorbed into neighbouring tribal groups.[34] The problem facing colonial authorities in their attempt to create stable administrative areas was that settled peoples such as the Gogo had no clear boundaries, whereas nomadic pastoralists did have boundaries, but they shifted. Thus the concept of 'tribe' is not a wholly colonial invention, as has sometimes been claimed.[35] Strong group identities did exist, especially among nomadic pastoralists. However, the policy of distinct and firm tribal boundaries has clearly been a recent innovation, and defined grazing schemes for pastoralists took this dogma a stage further.

In a survey of development schemes for pastoralists, Walter Goldschmidt (1981) has listed an unremitting catalogue of ill-conceived planning that showed no evidence of learning from earlier mistakes. Planners seemed to be trapped in an unreflexive mode of thought that did not respond to cumulative experience; and more recent commentators bear this out, reiterating the same points from more recent evidence. As in the Perkerra Scheme or the Maasai ranches, Goldschmidt's list of repeated mistakes reveals a piecemeal approach to a complex ecological balance that shifts the problem rather than resolves it:

---

[32] Hedlund (1979: 29, 31); Parkipuny (1979: 137, 145–7); Galaty (1980: 164); Goldschmidt (1981: 111–12); Arhem (1985: 22–3); Grandin and Lembuya (1987: 1); Graham (1988: 2–3, 5–6); Hurskainen (1990: 80); Kituyi (1990: 137, 201); Ndagala (1990: 54–5; 1992: 70–6); Homewood and Rodgers (1991: 208). The earlier literature on Maasai group ranches in Kenya is also discussed in Galaty (1980; 1994).

[33] See pp. 18–19.

[34] Evans-Pritchard (1940: 118); Dyson-Hudson (1966: 258–70; Rigby (1969: 13–18); Marx (1977: 347). The division of the Maasai into (tribal) sections could well have a similar explanation, since typically each section is associated with a broad ecological zone with a considerable degree of self-containedness.

[35] Asad (1972: 126–8; 1973: 105, 111–12).

encouraging pastoralists to farm in the better areas has pushed the remainder into the more marginal areas; using modern technology to dig water to make these marginal areas more accessible has led to the destruction of the surrounding land through overgrazing; attempts to safeguard the environment by prohibiting burning has led to a decrease in the nutritional value of dry-season grazing and to an increase in tick-born diseases and tsetse fly; introducing veterinary services and cattle dips to offset such health hazards has accelerated the deterioration of the land due to overgrazing. The list extends to the problem of undermining the infrastructure of society itself: when specially advantageous schemes are introduced, they attract the more wealthy and politically aware, increasing social differentiation and again edging the less privileged into more marginal areas; policies to encourage the sale of cattle tend to benefit the middlemen and not the herders, for whom prices remain depressed; enforced programmes to cull stock lead herders to offload old and weak stock and to use their money to restock with younger animals.[36]

In these ways, development projects that aim to ameliorate the position of pastoralists may benefit some, but they serve to marginalize the majority further, adding to the pressures caused by the creep of destitute peasant farmers into these areas. Generally, the severity of recent droughts is blamed on the failure of governments and aid agencies to appreciate the effects of their policies.[37] The whole planning process in this area appears fraught with a dubious logic and a woeful ignorance at each turn.

In fairness to planners, some of their accounts show an awareness of the pitfalls and a concern that the pastoralists should be involved in a mutual learning process.[38] Nevertheless, the accounts of observers reiterate the lack of communication and the stark contrast in life styles that is maintained between the planners and the people, with little attempt by the aid agencies to span the gap. Plans are initiated from above without any awareness of their shortcomings or concerted attempts at local involvement. Plans are oriented towards the market rather than towards overcoming the mistrust that pastoralists have for the market. They benefit the developers and other middlemen in the first instance, leaving little benefit for the pastoralists. They are office-based and leave behind a trail of unfulfilled policies and phantom projects that have overspent their budgets before any tangible results are achieved.[39]

[36] Goldschmidt (1981: 102–10). Cf. Darling and Farver (1972: 681); P. R. Baker (1975: 197–8; 1977: 157–8); Konczacki (1978: 97–8, 112); Parkipuny (1979: 141, 146, 148–9, 155); Oxby (1981: 38); Gilles and Jamtgaard (1982: 6); Perlov (1983: 129–30); Stiles (1983: 47); Hogg (1987: 49, 55–8); Gartrell (1988: 205); Hurskainen (1990: 86); Storas (1990: 145); Fratkin (1991: 95–113); Keya (1991: 79–85); Little (1992: 158).

[37] Darling and Farvar (1972: 679); Baier (1976: 8–9); Swift (1977*b*: 474); Konczacki (1978: 119); Swidler (1980: 31); Gilles and Jamtgaard (1982: 6).

[38] e.g. Moris (1981: 112–13); Moris and Hatfield (1982: 59–61); Sandford (1983: ch. 10).

[39] Ingle (1972: 253–4); Mbithi and Wisner (1973: 140–1); R. Baker (1977: 157–66); Parkipuny (1979: 142–7, 150–1); Hyden (1980: 209–10); Goldschmidt (1981: 112); Arhem (1985: 39); Hurskainen (1990: 80); Ndagala (1990: 60–1; 1992: 50); Fratkin (1991: 102, 111).

To the extent that development plans are funded by loans that have to be repaid, it is the pastoralists who are blamed for non-cooperation, increasing the lack of sympathy for their way of life. The gap between the pastoralists' view of their investment in their herds (Chapter 1) and a capitalist view of reinvesting gains to maximize profits has been well illustrated in David Western's analysis of the seasonal fluctuations of rainfall and cattle sales in Maasai, shown in Fig. 7.1. The pattern, broadly repeated among the Maasai, Samburu, and Chamus, is for these sales to increase according to need in the drier months when the cattle are emaciated and the prices are low. To this extent, they do not take advantage of the more commercial alternative of selling cattle in easier times when they are in peak condition and saving the money for harder times. After all, the Maasai argue, who knows how long the next dry season will last or how

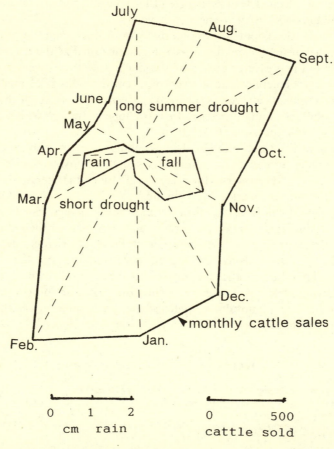

FIG. 7.1. *Cattle sales as a short-term strategy against drought among the Maasai*
Source: Loitokitok District 1970, after Western (1973)

many stock should be sold—if any? The diagram reveals the extent to which pastoral peoples are forced to resort to cash purchases, and yet do not view their herds as a commercial asset to be invested in the market system. Some of the most wealthy who are attuned to market possibilities certainly do so, and they are included in these figures. In their case, the sale of surplus stock at the best time is not necessarily aimed towards culling the herds of fertile animals, but towards acquiring further stock for breeding, often from poorer herders at times when prices are low. The less wealthy have good reason to mistrust the vagaries of the market system. Trapped in their poverty, they too see a growing family and herd as offering the only realistic form of security.[40]

Those that are edged out of pastoralism have traditionally resorted to foraging, and the margins of the cash economy have offered a new niche for casual labour and have almost entirely replaced hunting and gathering in the region. In a chain reaction, the emigration of younger men seeking work has increased the pressures on women and older men who remain behind, especially when labour resources are stretched to their limit during the dry season. This may open up new opportunities for some women who find themselves managing a household for the first time; but those who are still bound by obligations to the parental generation may have even less rather than more freedom. Without the means to tend their already inadequate herds, poorer families have drifted to settle near the permanent sources of water to eke out a living, and famine relief camps have tended to grow around these points. Among the traditional pastoralists in the 1980s, about one-third of the Turkana, up to 40 per cent of the Uaso Booran, and 45 per cent of the Rendille proper were said to be permanently settled in newly formed towns, depending substantially on some form of relief. More recently a figure of 30 per cent has been suggested for the urban population living inside the Samburu district.[41]

The problem of these camps follows the same pattern as subsidized schemes in general whereby destitute pastoralists become trapped in their dependency, even against the intentions of the funding agencies, who are trapped in their commitment. The process has been vividly illustrated for the Turkana by Vigdis Broch-Due (1990). As noted in Chapter 1, the Turkana area is

[40] Parkipuny (1979: 138); Dahl and Hjort (1979: 16); Perlov (1983: 129–30); Hogg (1986: 322); Spencer (1988: 23); Fratkin (1991: 8, 110); Ndagala (1992: 74); Little (1992: 158). Cf. P. R. Baker (1975: 197–8) and Gartrell (1988: 205–6) for northern Uganda. I am particularly grateful to David Western for permission to borrow the format used in Fig. 7.1 and the data for the Loitokitok Maasai, which have been adapted from his doctoral thesis (Western 1973: 139, Fig. 49). The market for cattle in Western's study was not affected by quarantine restrictions during 1970; however, cattle sales over the winter period appear more pronounced than might be expected during a relatively short drought. Among the Kenya Maasai, the rainy seasons are normally heavy in the spring and relatively light in the autumn, but few years are exactly normal.

[41] Dahl (1979*a*: 273); Stiles (1983: 3); Adams (1986: 317); Hogg (1986: 322–3; 1987: 49); Fratkin (1991: 130); Little (1992: 66, 151–2). Cf. Talle (1988: 239–40). Jonathan Lodompui (personal communication) has provided the locally accepted estimate for urbanization in Samburu.

particularly barren and this has inhibited the development of extended families. Stock-owners are relatively independent and remain mobile in small family units. Their poverty accentuates the need for collaboration, but this is best served by building up an extensive network of friends—stock associates— scattered over a wide area and with access to different resources. These bonds are maintained by gifts and favours as the need arises. Instead of claiming status as a member of a worthy 'marriageable' family, as among the Maasai, a Turkana needs to build up his own personal network of trust from boyhood, nurturing his reputation through good will and shrewd calculation in his giving and begging.[42] Broch-Due argues that this is not a contractual system that can be expressed in terms of precise credit and debt, but a system of vague obligation where stock-owners are judged by their associates according to their broad record of performance. Those who fail to maintain credibility destroy their network by default and are forced into some form of dependency from which they cannot easily escape. From this viewpoint, resort to a famine relief camp is just a new form of dependency. Ostensibly, a destitute Turkana at the camp can maintain a minimum livelihood for the duration of the drought. However, attempts by the relief agency to help him return with his family to his former pastoral life with the gift of a small herd are undermined by his loss of credibility. Having withdrawn and remained apart from his personal network, these bonds cannot be reactivated at once. The returnee is isolated until he rebuilds his credibility among a viable number of associates, with little to give and only a discredited claim to beg. In the short term, he cannot call on sufficient resources to tide over his family in an emergency, and the next downturn in fortune forces him to return with them to the refugee camp as a dependant, cutting himself off again from any network he has tried to revive.[43]

In effect, one has a dual system operating within the district, the humanitarian dependency of the refugee centres close to permanent water supplies contrasting with the dynamics of enterprise within the pastoral system in the more arid areas. However, as these centres grow and encourage subsistence farming, they also take up the best dry-season pasture, increasing the pressure on the nomadic sector to seek support in the next drought. Like the pastoralists, the aid agencies and development planners are caught up in a neo-Malthusian trap. In seeking to give preference to their dependants as against the fully pastoral nomads and systematically taking up the best land in a worsening situation, they too subscribe to the Tragedy of the Commons.

Conclusion: Pastoralism and the Reckoning of Growth

Pastoralists in East Africa are caught up in an ecological impasse that extends to the whole region. Analyses of the problem range from a Malthusian concern

---

[42] P. H. Gulliver (1955: 196–9, 209–13). See also p. 37.
[43] Broch-Due (1990: 147–54); Storas (1990: 138–40). Cf. Stiles (1983: 2); Hogg (1987: 49–53).

for overpopulation to a neo-Malthusian concern over more fundamental environmental issues. In Kenya and Tanzania, population growth has exceeded economic growth, implying deteriorating standards of living, and they have been locked in balance-of-payments crises since the 1970s.[44] Reliable data are not available for neighbouring countries, but the endemic droughts and sporadic civil wars that have characterized their recent history suggest increasing pressures in a deteriorating situation. The availability of Western medicine has shifted the problem, but at the cost of intensifying rather than resolving it: the ability of medical knowledge to save life in remote areas exceeds the ability of technical knowledge to sustain it.

An alternative perspective, put forward by such writers as Ester Boserup, considers a more positive approach towards development. This upturns the Malthusian view by regarding population pressure as a prime stimulus for technological progress rather than its casualty. The two views pose the question: under what conditions does private interest ultimately serve public good, and under what conditions does it undermine it, as in the Tragedy of the Commons? Like development planners, Boserup views progress from the vantage point of success in an environment that has the potential for benign exploitation. Individuals and groups respond to the increasing or decreasing pressure of circumstance, but generally the trend with the growth of population is towards intensification of effort and the upward thrust of civilization with increasing knowledge. Her argument upholds the liberal philosophy of progress through competition and places even the most primitive technologies and landscapes within a broad evolutionary struggle for survival. She notes the relevance of family enterprise (cf. Chapter 1), but this does not extend to pastoralism, which is confined to the most dispersed regions. Along with hunting, gathering, and forest fallow agriculture, pastoralism is doomed to extinction as a way of life by the increasing pressure of population growth.[45]

The position of the Malthusian argument in Boserup's model is largely hidden. She directs attention towards the growth phases of the rise and fall of populations, acknowledging the limits to growth in certain circumstances, but constantly reverting to the opportunity for intensification elsewhere and the availability of relevant knowledge within the wider region. It is not simply people who migrate under necessity, but technologies that diffuse also in response to need.[46] Her argument shifts between contemporary examples from the Third World and the chequered progress of economic history, and the analysis concentrates on the more productive centres of growth. There is only a tacit acknowledgement that those living at the fringe face a struggle for survival due to overpopulation; and there is no consideration of the role of modern medical technology in promoting population growth. In other words,

[44] See n. 26 above.
[45] Boserup (1965: 105; 1981: 23, 205).
[46] Boserup (1965: 23, 29, 41, 56, 61, 72; 1981: 3–4, 41, 75).

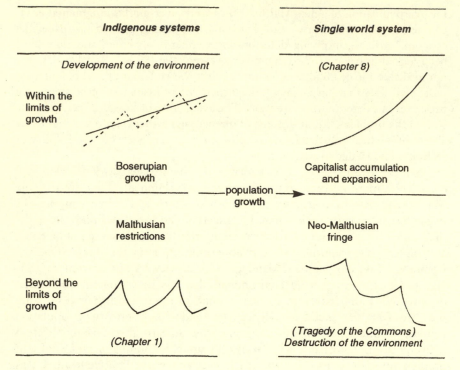

Indigenous systems	Single world system
Development of the environment	(Chapter 8)

Within the limits of growth

Boserupian growth — population growth → Capitalist accumulation and expansion

Malthusian restrictions — Neo-Malthusian fringe

Beyond the limits of growth

(Chapter 1) — (Tragedy of the Commons) Destruction of the environment

FIG. 7.2. *Profiles of growth and disaster*

the Malthusian argument is displaced from the centre to the periphery.[47] Higher mortality rates due to the ravages of epidemic, famine, and war are acknowledged as reasons for the more sluggish growth and reversals in the past, but the possibility of contemporary downturns is hardly considered. This is to disregard the less privileged sectors of the population who live or lived in areas with little potential, or without the requisite knowledge to intensify their production, or at times of epidemic and population decline. The technical knowledge that might resolve the dilemmas facing those that are progressively marginalized is elusive, and the search for ways of coping with a worsening situation then becomes the critical issue. It is precisely such situations that are central to a Malthusian concern for overpopulation, and in the neo–Malthusian model they are the byproduct of development elsewhere. The criticism against development planners is that Western expertise alone is inadequate and their attempts at partial solutions can only exacerbate the problem.

Fig. 7.2 summarizes the various aspects of this argument. On the left-hand side are two views of indigenous systems, showing the unending Malthusian

[47] Boserup (1965: 14, 37, 41, 49, 56, 74, 99, 114, 118; 1981: 86).

sawtooth pattern of growth and disaster as outlined in Chapter 1 (bottom left); and this contrasts with a generally upward gradient in Boserup's model for historical development (top left). With intensification, these are transformed respectively into a downward gradient in the neo-Malthusian model of ecological decline (bottom right); and the notion of take-off to sustained growth to which Boserup's model logically leads (top right). The question for development then is: given the worldwide premiss of economic take-off, can the neo-Malthusian cost of underdevelopment in backward areas ever be eliminated? This draws attention to the interaction between the upper and lower right-hand sectors and is a topic that is considered further in Chapter 8.

More can be said on the issue of public interest which is so badly served in each of the viewpoints. A major problem posed in the present chapter concerns the neo-Malthusian Tragedy of the Commons, in which the possibilities of shared adaptation are undermined by immediate self-interest. When this phrase was coined by Garrett Hardin (1968), the overgrazing of unrestricted pastureland was taken as an allegory of human excess in general, with wider relevance for the contradiction between short-term and long-term interests. This may arguably apply to pastoralism in East Africa under modern conditions, but its application to the traditional setting can be questioned. The Tragedy of the Commons in East Africa is not simply that the environment is doomed by any short-term desire to maximize herds; it is also that official policies have ignored and even undermined some exemplary characteristics of traditional societies that upheld community values and long-term interests. Putting to one side the limits of ecological understanding in traditional husbandry, there is a general emphasis on restrictions that protect what are seen to be critical resources from individual abuse.[48] Even the ideological commitment to growth is modified in situations of severe ecological constraint. This occurs among the pastoral Rendille, whose camel herds increase only at a sluggish pace if at all, and the irrigation Sonjo who use all available water to its fullest extent.

---

[48] There is a premiss of free access to all pasture and water throughout the region, but subject to local variation. The most frequent communal control concerns maintenance of and access to water points (P. H. Gulliver 1955: 37–8; Spencer 1965: 5–6; 1988: 17; N. Dyson-Hudson 1966: 59, 112–13; Legesse 1973: 86–7; Ensminger 1992: 131–2), and limiting the access to pasture by neighbouring peoples (N. Dyson-Hudson 1966: 151; Spencer 1988: 18) or during times of scarcity (Spencer 1965: 5; Little 1985*b*: 139; Hogg 1993: 68). Beyond these restraints, indigenous systems of grazing control appear to have been absent and would probably be unworkable (cf. Swift 1977*a*: 173; 1977*b*: 464; Ensminger 1992: 130). The bases for claims that there were elaborate traditional systems of grazing rotation among the Maasai and Samburu are not clear (Jacobs 1980: 287; Sperling and Galaty 1990: 80; cf. Niamir 1995: 247, 255). In my own researches, both the Samburu and Maasai viewed such systems as administrative impositions that were wholly at variance with their own traditional practices. They pointed out that any system that closed off grazing to allow grass to grow would simply attract herds of wild game at the expense of their cattle. Moreover, among the Samburu, where clans were interspersed, autonomous, and generally nomadic, there would have been no indigenous means of controlling any elaborate scheme. Such patterns of grazing as existed were matters of individual preference and expedience rather than of prescription (Spencer 1973: 182–91).

In different ways, each of these societies appears to place customary limits on population growth, matching their ideals to the reality of their environment and implying a cultural adaptation on the part of the community at large when confronted with a stark Malthusian choice.[49]

Nomadic pastoralists are faced with similar constraints because stock-owners depend heavily on each other and need to maintain a mutual trust. A recurrent theme in this work has concerned the pattern of constraints on the individual through kinship, age systems, and networks of trust, curbing the opportunities of individuals to exploit others for personal gain. In the traditional setting, the resolution of the Tragedy of the Commons lies in the strength of community bonds; and such indigenous concepts as 'marriageability', 'trustworthiness', or 'credibility' reflect the reputations of individuals and families on which their future collaboration depends. Institutions are based on trust. If this is strained to its limit at times of severe crisis—the downturn of the sawtooth profile—then it is necessary to restore trust to ensure a return to a buoyant future in easier times: in other words, to return to the ethics of traditional husbandry that are underpinned by longer-term interests. Maintaining trust and reputation is the insurance against the next downturn. While much has been made of the pressure on common land caused by uncontrolled pastoralism—and this is considered further in the final chapter of this work—the spirit of community among African pastoralists traditionally rises above the undiluted self-interest that has created the current situation.[50]

[49] For the Rendille, Spencer (1973: 11, 35, 137, 142–4); cf. Ch. 1 n. 36 above. A similar interpretation of Robert Gray's account of the Sonjo is impressionistic. In comparison with other societies of this region, such as those considered in Chapter 1, there is an emphasis on the strict limitations of their (irrigation) economy, and the circumscribed nature of the villages which would seem to give little scope for expansion. Again, the circumscribed sense of history associated with their religion appears to preclude any notion of development beyond the seasonal cycle. There is a general desire for children, but there is also evidence of population decline. The tendency towards monogamy coupled with late marriage for men could indicate a later marriage for women also than Gray suggests, limiting their span of fertility, as among the Rendille (R. F. Gray 1963: 12, 58–63, 67, 97–8, 108, 159, 167). Quite apart from this, population limitation would follow from the steady flow of surplus Sonjo women (and their children) to the pastoral Maasai. This provides 'an unfailing market' in exchange for goats, which occupy a 'crucial position in the [Sonjo] exchange system' (R. F. Gray 1960: 42–3; 1962: 486–9).

[50] See pp. 17–18, 37, 43, and 201.

8

Pastoralists and the Threshold of
Change and Inequality

The topic of social inequality was considered in Chapter 2 with reference to variation in polygyny as an index. In that context, the unequal distribution of wives among elders in the pastoral samples reveals a continuous distribution of prestige. Men do not automatically accrue wives with age, but there do not appear to be insurmountable hurdles holding back any elder with ability and a certain luck. The non-pastoral samples, however, are more likely to show a distinct discontinuity between a privileged élite and an underprivileged majority with breaks in the distribution of prestige. It is the difference between conditions encouraging a degree of social mobility and the hurdles of class difference impeding this.

Little's analysis of recent Chamus experience reveals a distinct shift from the pastoralist model. There is increasing polarization as a new category of individualists have broken away from traditional obligations, investing in new opportunities in the monetary economy. Cattle herds and wives remain an important means of storing wealth and a source of prestige, but the critical resource has now shifted to land rather than cattle. A similar trend has been recorded in a wide variety of recent studies among East African pastoralists.[1] Generally, what Richard Hogg (1986) has described as 'the new pastoralism' in Northern Kenya has involved the fragmentation of traditional bonds that underpinned community existence. Corresponding to those who have benefited from change are others whose herds have dwindled, edging them towards marginal forms of agriculture and unskilled wage labour. This again is a recurrent feature of these studies.[2]

This chapter considers aspects of change affecting pastoralists in three stages. The first considers a source of confusion associated with the rift between

---

[1] Kenyan Maasai: Hedlund (1979: 30–1); Galaty (1981: 82); Graham (1988: 3–6); Kituyi (1990: 153–96). Tanzanian Maasai: Parkipuny (1979: 147); Arhem (1985: 68); Ndagala (1992: 74, 82–4, 172). Samburu: Hjort (1979: 144–6); Sperling (1987b: 188–9). Turkana: Hogg (1986: 321), Broch-Due (1990: 154–7). Ariaal: Fratkin (1991: 62, 65–8). Rendille: Fratkin (1991: 105). Uaso Booran: Dahl (1979a: 198–200, 219–29, 254–6). Obbu: Oba (1990: 40–1). Orma: Ensminger (1992: 123–4, 132–3). Somali: Graham (1988: 8); Swift (1979: 463–4).
[2] Chamus: Little (1992: 104–16, 155). Maasai: Kituyi (1990: 76–81, 106–7, 134–7, 159–61, 178–91); Ndagala (1992: 76–8, 171–3). Samburu: Perlov (1983: 128–30); Sperling (1987b: 187–9). Turkana: Hjort (1979: 132–4, 141). Uaso Booran: Dahl (1979a: 214–20). Orma: Ensminger (1992: 84–8). New townships: Hjort (1979: 128–32, 139–71); Hogg (1986: 323).

successive generations. The second then examines the articulation between traditional pastoral society and the spread of the market economy. And the third explores the relevance of notions of underdevelopment and dependency for nomadic pastoralist societies in the region.

Social Change and the 'Problem of Generations'

The topic of change is dogged by a methodological problem that is especially marked in the analysis of preliterate societies with no archival base. Age systems, for instance, concern the dual process of ageing and of historically changing relations between young and old. What appears to be a novelty in one context may emerge as a time-honoured aspect of the system at another level. The ethnographer is confronted with evidence of both and an uncertain overlap, and has then to rely on a personal judgement to decide which is analytically more appropriate. In this work so far, historical explanations seemed to explain the Jie generation-set paradox in Chapter 3 and the shifting pattern of relations between Chamus elders and young men in Chapter 5; whereas an ahistorical model of succession seemed more appropriate for interpreting the Karimojong and Nyakyusa generation systems in Chapter 3, and also the patterns of ageing in Fig. 2.3. Or should the fluctuating profiles for the Mursi and Kipsigis in Fig. 2.3*d* perhaps have suggested some historical explanation? A dynamic model of change gives a very different slant on the data from one that stresses the persistence of tradition. The problem then becomes a matter of disentangling real historical change from the processes of ageing and the persisting structure of relations between old and young.[3]

This poses the question: to what extent do young people shift towards the traditional outlooks of their elders as they mellow; or to what extent do they carry the novel subculture and expectations of their youth with them and incorporate these into their view of 'tradition'? The interpretation of historical change then becomes a 'problem of generations', as it was dubbed by Mannheim (1952)—not to be confused with generation-sets. Each 'generation' has a unique perspective of history that may involve a constant redefinition of 'traditional' values. The visiting anthropologist has a snapshot view of a scene that has never remained still; and the historian is faced with the inscrutable problem of deciding how far oral traditions are genuine history as against a construct of the older 'generation'. Even the next generation of anthropologists and historians can only bring further hindsight to bear on this dilemma, which can never be finally resolved.

This has a bearing on studies of the transition towards a modern market economy in East Africa, with a rising tide of individualism and the progressive erosion of tradition. The weight of evidence clearly points towards radical

---

[3] See pp. 80, 116, 121, 127, 168, and 195. Cf. Mannheim (1952: 278–9).

change. Nevertheless, there remains the problem of discerning between novel features that are historically unique, and recurrent aspects that are characteristic rather than unique. Expressing this as a 'problem of generations' is to suggest that earlier transitions may also have involved independent striving among younger men at the expense of their obligations to their seniors and a recurrent aspect of career patterns. One is then led to ask: to what extent should the moral boundary that separates tradition from innovation be viewed also as an aspect of the persisting structure of relations between a privileged senior generation and an opportunistic junior generation? The problem facing the interpretation of ethnography is to strike a balance between novelty and persistence, and to ascertain how far 'change' is no more than traditional society in modern dress.

Peter Little's analysis of the recent transition within Chamus society again provides a useful illustration. The sense of an impending crisis in the 1980s highlights chronic food shortages, the marginalization of those edged into wage employment to service the irrigation sector, and the innovations of young men challenging tradition.[4] Yet each of these has its counterpart in earlier times. Chronic food shortage is a theme that has characterized reports on the area ever since the earliest accounts of the 1880s. The Chamus hired paupers to work the irrigation system in the 1880s, and this was reiterated in an early administrative record in 1914. Earlier innovations had also been spearheaded by young men, when they built up cattle herds (Peles age-set), when they subsequently adopted the Maasai warrior-village system to defend these herds (Kiliako age-set), and then when they progressively defied the constraints of *moranhood*, arranging their own premature initiations and marriages.[5] In these respects, the crisis of recent change can arguably be read as confirming some deep-seated pattern, and the boundary between tradition and innovation remains uncertain.

Another study of the crisis of change among an agro-pastoral people that has similarities to the Chamus concerns the Giriama in south-eastern Kenya. David Parkin's earlier work on these people (1972) focused on those living in the palm belt and the emergence of enterprising young men who evaded the 'gerontocratic' obligation that required them to produce palm wine for sharing among traditional elders. This evasion enabled them to extract coconut copra as an alternative product that could be sold to traders. These young 'accumulators' would then add to their capital by using their profits to buy palm trees from less enterprising 'losers'. In this way, the accumulators not only evaded traditional expectations, but also made it harder for the losers with dwindling assets to produce palm wine. Again, this provides an instance of growing self-interest in the cash economy undermining the authority of the elders. Parkin's

---

[4] Little (1985*a*: 255; 1992: 9, 43–4, 53, 57, 67–8, 107, 116, 126–34).
[5] Cf. pp. 151–2, 163, 179, 182, and 211, and Anderson (1984: 119–20). The Baringo District Annual Report for 1914 describes the Chamus as capable of hiring labour when they need it.

subsequent study of the Giriama (1991) switches to their more traditional pastoralist area in the west; and as with the Chamus, one notes successive changes in their economic base and the innovative role of young men at various stages. In pre-colonial times, the Giriama had lived in a large fortified village because of the threat of raids by the Maasai and Oromo. With the establishment of peace in the area, they dispersed with their herds into small clan settlements and relied increasingly on shifting cultivation. This was a radical transition that appears comparable to the Chamus response when they too dispersed from their two fortified villages under the colonial umbrella. Further dispersal occurred as ambitious young men sought to secure their independence by hiding their surplus cattle among friends beyond the grasping reach of senior kin, and this became an established practice among the pastoralists. These evasions provide a foretaste of the later stage, when many Giriama moved into the palm belt and younger men again tried to evade traditional obligations. It is evident that the trappings of 'tradition' have shifted repeatedly. The tradition of producing and sharing palm wine could have been no older than the senior elders who had planted the palm trees in the first place, some of whom were still alive; while the sale of copra appears to be almost as long-standing as the production of palm wine for redistribution. Similarly, the earlier tradition of dispersed pastoralism was itself relatively shallow, reaching back only a further generation or so. The 'problem of generations' then poses the following questions. Is the recent crisis of change a novelty in every sense or can it also be seen as the reiterated play of tension between generations that is endemic among Giriama? Might it be that young men have pioneered change not once but three times within the space of a century—first as dispersed herders, then producing palm wine, and then engaging in trade? As they accumulate wealth and grow old, might these same men find themselves obliged to fulfil obligations, as has occurred among their seniors both within the palm belt and in the traditional pastoral area? As a basis for political organization, is the premiss of 'gerontocracy', of power traditionally in the hands of older men, undermined, not so much by new 'accumulators' and outside market forces, as by an inherent contradiction, as among the Samburu?[6]

The evidence of change in the region is overwhelming. There can be no question that population growth has increased pressure on the land, that many pastoralists have been forced to settle, and that social life has been transformed first by colonial intervention and then by the growing market economy. However, in what follows, there remains the caveat that the privileged position of the ethnographic present in anthropological and other writings may exaggerate

---

[6] Parkin (1972: 8, 17, 23, 55–62, 83–6; 1991: 20, 33, 49, 58–70, 80–1, 87–8, 211–12). Cf. Brantley (1978: 260), who suggests that the undermining of Giriama gerontocracy was evident by 1912. Parkin does not explicitly suggest that tapping the palm trees for wine in Giriama inhibits the production of coconuts. However, this seems a necessary inference, or those who 'accumulate' through the sale of copra would have no problem in fulfilling their traditional obligations also.

the novelty of certain changes; and oral traditions of 'change' may conceal changing 'oral traditions' and the persistence of underlying patterns.

Shifting Traditions and the Moral Threshold

With reference to the threshold between tradition and the spread of the market economy, it is useful to elaborate the right-hand part of Fig. 7.2. The aim here is to construct a 'gravity model', stemming from earlier analyses by Clyde Mitchell on labour migration (1970) and Fredrik Barth on the role of the entrepreneur (1963). In Fig. 8.1 the traditional pastoralist sector and the emerging capitalist alternative are again shown in the lower and upper parts of the diagram. In this model, each has its attraction, pulling pastoralists in opposite directions, rather like opposed gravitational fields. Individuals are placed somewhere in the intervening space. Those in the lower part are more strongly attracted to the traditional setting and those higher up are drawn towards the capitalist alternative. The hyphenated threshold across the centre represents a zone where these 'gravitational' forces exactly balance and there is no net pull in either direction; or to borrow a term from economics, it is the 'line of indifference' along which the individual has no definite inclination either way. Or better still, this midline may be regarded as a boundary between the two opposed cultures; far from being indifferent, pastoralists may be sensitively aware of a moral dilemma when crossing this threshold. In this sense, it is a moral threshold. If they were to lose this sensitivity and become truly indifferent, then there would be no dilemma, the boundary would no longer exist, and the two cultures would have merged.

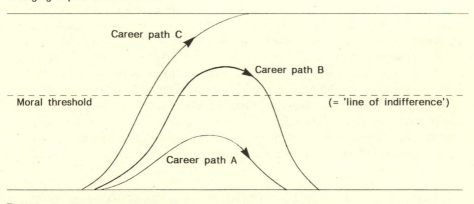

Emerging capitalist alternative

Career path C

Career path B

Moral threshold   (= 'line of indifference')

Career path A

Traditional pastoralist sector

FIG. 8.1. *The gravity model and career trajectories*

This model may be used to trace different career profiles among pastoralists in their encounters with the capitalist alternative. These may broadly follow one of three trajectories or career paths, labelled *A*, *B*, and *C* in the diagram. Labour migration from a traditional setting may be taken as an apt example for these paths, which represent degrees of involvement in the cash economy. Trajectory *A* applies to those who might be tempted to migrate in their youth but find themselves increasingly and then irrevocably involved in managing the family herd: the career path begins to veer upwards but returns towards the base before it has crossed the moral threshold. Among the Chamus this would describe the path followed by the majority of the Merisho age-set, who were reluctant to enter the wage economy, even on a seasonal basis. This career path represents the pull of new opportunities on those nomadic pastoralists who have resisted the intrusion of Western influence more decisively than those in the more settled areas, and to this extent they have retained a greater sense of cultural integrity.

Trajectory *B* is typified by those who are impelled towards migration to the extent that they actually cross the moral threshold, possibly in response to a domestic crisis. At this point, the prospects of wage labour are more attractive than those of staying behind and they leave for a spell until the pull of returning home brings them back across this threshold and they return: a process that may be repeated several times. This was typical of the next Chamus age-set, the Meduti, who began to migrate seasonally in order to use their wages to build up their own herds. This career path also applies to those pastoralist groups that have established their own tradition of joining the police or army as a modern alternative to warriorhood, such as the Samburu, and also to the Booran practice of encouraging younger sons to migrate for a period to diversify the economic viability of the family as a whole. In their lives away from home, pastoralist ethnic minorities may associate with their peers and maintain an enclave of tradition that communicates with the home area through the two-way flow of migration, as occurs among the Oromo or Maasai in Nairobi: the resilience of the traditional sector has its own localized gravitational pull, even in an urban environment.[7]

Trajectory *C* applies to those who have drifted towards the townships and never return, having become increasingly caught up with an alternative life style and social network. What might initially have been intended as trajectory *B* in a time of crisis merges into *C* by default, and they have achieved an irreversible transition between cultures.[8] The dispersal of the Turkana, especially, appears to be a vivid illustration of this one-way drift from the independ-

[7] Spencer (1973: 163–4); Dahl (1979*a*: 213); Hjort (1979: 141–2, 158); Hogg (1986: 326); Sperling (1987*b*: 178).
[8] Dahl (1979*a*: 104–5, 213); Hjort (1979: 5, 28–9, 106, 141, 144–6, 151–8); Kituyi (1990: 179, 182–4, 207); Baxter (1993: 151).

ent nomadic life style of pastoralism. The southward drift of Turkana in search of work is long-standing, but more recently many families have settled as refugees in the newly established townships within their own area and are trapped by their loss of a credible network if they try to return to the traditional pastoral sector.[9] In terms of the gravity model, it is as if the prevailing options for Turkana are trajectories *A* or *C*. For those who leave the pastoral nomadic economy, there is little hope of return (*B*), and they become increasingly sedentarized (*C*). It is, as Little has argued for Chamus who seek wage employment, only a further instance of the 'sloughing off of poor herders from Africa's pastoral sector [that] predates colonialism'.[10]

The model applies equally to non-migrants who are tempted to compromise their traditional ideals as the capitalist alternative becomes established within their home area. Path *A* applies to those who sell stock to buy essential goods but have no investment in the market itself. Path *B* describes the career of those that have set up their own minor enterprises within their home area—perhaps a local business based on acquired skills or wages—and find their entanglement with kin and demands for credit drives them out of business with a certain tragic inevitability. Path *C* applies to successful local entrepreneurs whose education or experience inures them to traditional demands, and their business survives through the developing market economy. These career paths are identified in various studies of creeping change among non-migrants as monetary values dislodge traditional expectations. Three key examples in David Parkin's earlier study of Giriama illustrate successive steps up the entrepreneurial ladder, and these can be broadly traced along trajectories *A*, *B*, and *C*. Similarly, Mukhisa Kituyi's study of recent change among the Maasai compares three such instances. They provide a cross-section of the variety of experience in a time of change.[11]

Among these trajectories, it is *B* that acts as the Trojan horse, shifting the base of tradition. In so much as the returning migrant brings new ideas, investing his savings in a business enterprise or taking some unprecedented initiative, this poses a threat to traditional constraints and may be perceived as unethical and even a challenge by those within the traditional culture. Each of the major transitions experienced by the Chamus from the time that they converted to pastoralism, and especially the most recent trend towards individualism, can be seen as a crisis of change of this sort. As Fredrik Barth (1963) has noted, the entrepreneur is an innovator who bridges the threshold between tradition and new opportunity to personal advantage. As each innovation becomes accepted practice, the definition of 'traditional society' and the moral threshold between old and new shifts, and the local culture becomes

---

[9] See p. 226; Broch-Due (1990: 154–7).
[10] Little (1992: 115). See also pp. 132 and 208.
[11] Parkin (1972: 88–95); Kituyi (1990: 134–7).

increasingly part of a wider regional system. The point to emphasize is the relativity of the model, and this relates to the 'problem of generations'. Tradition inevitably changes, and each time a Chamus labour migrant has returned to exchange his savings for cattle, for instance, 'tradition' has shifted towards the monetary economy. Elders may regard themselves as the guardians of 'traditional' values associated with pastoralism. However, by encouraging their sons and sons-in-law to bring back cash for their own use, they are shifting the initiative towards a younger generation that has access to the money market. In this way, trajectory *B* infuses 'tradition' with new expectations. In effect, through the constant compromise with change, the whole diagram shifts upwards: 'tradition' and the moral threshold move upwards, while the emerging capitalist alternative moves further up still as the whole area becomes increasingly involved in the world economy.

Underdevelopment and the Pastoralist Fringe

Market forces and successive government strategies have combined to transform local economies throughout East Africa. In Kenya and Tanzania, with different approaches to development, this has led to an extended critique to account for the failings of official policies in each country. In this debate, the role of the peasantry has been central to the main argument, whereas nomadic pastoralists have been peripheral. Following Chayanov, such writers as Shanin have drawn attention to the narrow concern of traditional peasant households who produce for their own consumption and extend only passively to fulfil wider obligations beyond their immediate needs. The family is identified as the principal unit of production, as among pastoralists, but there is no suggestion of an expansive orientation towards growth: production is restricted to the level of necessity, with diminishing returns for labour beyond that level.[12] This contrasts with the pastoralist model, outlined in Chapter 1, where labour is altogether less demanding and the returns for extra care are generally expected to pay off with increased capital. Pastoralists appear to have a different kind of labour–reward curve, with an emphasis on the strategic use of effort and a longer-term interest. Even following a catastrophic loss of stock due to some epidemic or when a young elder exhausts himself to feed his growing family, there is normally a vision of an investment rather than of diminishing returns beyond a certain point. This then raises the question: to what extent is the passive element in peasant economies the product of political and economic repression rather than an inherent characteristic?

In Kenya, the broad strategy for economic development has followed the Swynnerton Plan (1955). This was a response to the fragmentation of land holdings due to population pressure in the more fertile areas. It envisaged a new

---

[12] Chayanov (1966 (cf. Hyden 1987: 120)); Shanin (1972 (cf. Njonjo 1981: 27–8)). Cf. p. 19.

economic infrastructure that amalgamated unviable farms into larger units, creating an energetic class of landowning Africans. This would reduce the less successful to a landless workforce, but they would ultimately benefit from the wealth generated by commercial cropping.[13] The plan provided a charter for capitalist development which was further pursued after Independence in 1963, and in essence it focused wholly on the upper part of Fig. 8.1 (and the upper right of Fig. 7.2).

The extended critique of this strategy has been in the mainstream of dependency theory, which is at the core of Peter Little's analysis of the recent emergence of classes among the Chamus, but transposed onto a national and international stage. As in colonial times, the same major business interests are seen to continue dictating the terms of trade for their own benefit, creating a chain of dependency that penetrates to the remotest areas and perpetuates underdevelopment. Instead of wealth trickling downwards through employment and trade, as envisaged in the Swynnerton Plan, there has been an upward flow, with wealth becoming concentrated at one extreme and poverty increasing at all lower levels. The surplus produce of these rural areas—cash crops, meat, and unskilled labour—feed into a system with restricted competition that is geared to an external market, buying cheap and selling dear. As in Chamus, smallholders are lured into wage labour during the more lucrative peak periods of the agricultural cycle to feed their families, and this diverts them from their own herds and crops at this critical time and leads them ultimately to sell their stock and holdings to stave off famine. The upward flow of capital from those trapped at the bottom is replicated at each level through the operation of a restricted market, and people everywhere are dependent upon self-interest at a higher level. Viewed from above, the domination of world markets over Third World countries is replicated within these countries by striking inequalities in wealth. In Kenya, for instance, there has emerged an affluent class of bourgeoisie with one of the most concentrated patterns of landownership in the world today.[14]

The initial thrust of this model (referred to here as Dependency Theory I) concerned the dispossession of the peasantry, who have played a critical role in generating the surplus and reproducing the conditions that have made the centralization of power and of capital accumulation possible. The central debate has not extended to nomadic pastoralists, where the tenacity of tradition has prevailed and attempts at development have a chequered history (Chapter 7). Pastoralists are implicitly relegated to a limbo, even beyond the landless peasants that have been edged into migrant labour: they are not just an underclass but an outer fringe. However, creeping dependency, as peasants are edged out of their traditional niche, is also the very general experience of

---

[13] Leys (1975: 52–3, 69); Carlsen (1980: 23–7).
[14] Leys (1975); Carlsen (1980: 75–7, 190–2); Njonjo (1981: 27, 36, 39).

pastoralists. The literature on this aspect of modern pastoralism in East Africa—Richard Hogg's 'new pastoralism'—may be regarded as a worm's-eye view of Dependency Theory I. In this model, one cannot speak of a pastoralist mode of production any more than of a peasant mode of production. The whole region merges into the dominant mode of capitalism. Recent accounts of the condition of pastoralists in Kenya reiterate the points, with growing polarization between the rich and the dispossessed, increasing commerce, creeping claims to pasture and herd-ownership extending to powerful absentee owners, corruption, and the emergence of new local élites, perpetuated through unequal access to education.[15]

In Tanzania as in Kenya, the ideal of development among pastoralists has been overshadowed by the problem of increasing poverty and the loss of good grazing land to marginal agriculture. However, the socialist policies that have been pursued since Independence have at least inhibited the emergence of a privileged estate-owning élite and some of the other more flamboyant trappings of capitalism. There is an undertone of growing commercialism and inequality in the pastoralist areas, but these trends are significantly more moderate than in Kenya, and to this extent there appears to be a greater persistence of tradition in certain respects.[16] A similar situation holds in the agricultural sector, with the peasantry retaining the ideal of family holdings and a primary concern for the productivity of their own small farms; but this too is modified by a growing element of individual enterprise, as farmers have weighed the advantages of pursuing self-interest against the risks of denying traditional obligations.[17] It has been argued that these tendencies towards personal gain in rural Tanzania are the residue of an earlier colonial influence coupled with the steady infiltration of commercial attitudes from Kenya.[18] This is in effect to appeal to Dependency Theory I to explain the shortcomings of official policy. However, it ignores the extent to which the traditional ideal of growth among pastoralists was also shared among agricultural communities where polygyny and a measure of inequality were common (Chapter 2 and contra-Chayanov). As compared with the official state policies that sought to reinstate traditional values of self-sufficiency, revitalizing 'traditional' village life and communal landownership, the tradition that has proved stronger at the local level has been oriented

---

[15] e.g. Hedlund (1979: 32); Dahl (1979*a*: 198–200, 213, 224–5, 255–6, 259); Hogg (1986: 321–2); Sperling (1987*b*: 185–9); Graham (1988: 3–4); Kituyi (1990: 10–12, 155, 160, 206–15); Kelly (1990: 88–9); Fratkin (1991: 8, 106, 127); Galaty (1994: 193–5). Cf. Little (1992: 69–70, 101, 103, 106, 139–42). See also pp. 212 and 216.

[16] e.g. Parkipuny (1979: 147–8, 156); Arhem (1985: 27); Hurskainen (1990: 85–6); Ndagala (1990: 57, 59; 1992: 82–3, 140–2, 157, 171–2). A useful indication of the contrast between the two countries is given by comparing Mukhisu Kituyi (1990) with Daniel Ndagala (1992). These studies are of pastoral change in the 1980s among the Maasai of Kenya and Tanzania respectively.

[17] Feldman (1969: 87–9, 98–111); Ingle (1972: 3–10); Hyden (1980: 123–4, 156–7, 179).

[18] Shivji (1976: 34, 160); Parkipuny (1979: 148); Hyden (1980: 123, 156); Rigby (1992: 99, 148, 159). Cf. Graham (1988: 3).

towards family enterprise coupled with traditional obligations rather than 'community' in the sense imposed uniformly from above. What is officially regarded as a Tragedy of the Commons, in which self-interest has defeated a return to community values, seems rather to be a continuation of a more fundamental tradition, albeit modified up to a point by new commercial opportunities. State policies may have fallen short of their objectives of encouraging the development of self-sufficient community enterprises, but ironically there appears to be greater continuity with the past as a result of this protection, preserving up to a point the very aspect of rural society that capitalist penetration has undermined in Kenya.

The Tanzanian experience of the persistence of local tradition bears on a critique of Dependency Theory I in such countries as Kenya. Dependency Theory II argues that the theory in its original form has underestimated the extent to which this element of persistence serves to sustain underdevelopment, even among those whose livelihood is largely integrated into the cash economy. In this revised version of the theory, capitalism is seen to have penetrated only to an extent that is directly relevant to its own expansion: in exploiting cheap labour and materials, it nurtures rather than destroys the underdeveloped sector. It dominates at the centres of economic growth, while customary forms of transaction and exchange remain viable at the periphery. Local bonds within the traditional milieu provide an essential safeguard against the impact of poverty, indirectly subsidizing the centre.[19] Dependency Theory I suggests the systematic debilitation of tradition which may be expressed as the irreversible trend of trajectory *C* in Fig. 8.1. Dependency Theory II draws attention to the strength of trajectory *B*, representing an accommodation of both capitalism and tradition away from the centres of growth. There is transaction and compromise rather than an overwhelming transition, shifting the threshold of Fig. 8.1 rather than destroying it. The debate focuses especially on the peasantry, but the thrust of the argument clearly applies also to pastoralists, albeit that they are a stage further removed from the forces of change. The shift in emphasis between the two theories is summarized in Fig. 8.2.

Thus, the critiques of both socialism in Tanzania and Dependency Theory I in Kenya (which is itself a critique) point in the same direction, noting a certain resilience of family enterprise among the peasantry, albeit in a situation of continuing underdevelopment. This is even more pertinent for pastoralists, given that their scope for innovation is limited by their nomadic life style.

The principal question concerning the future of pastoralists lies in their boundary with the peasantry, and increasingly so as some of their best dry-season grazing close to permanent sources of water is systematically encroached by farming and settlement. Answers to this suggest three possibilities. An

---

[19] Wolpe (1972: 437); Laclau (1977: 32, 39); Long (1977: 85–8, 94–5); Hyden (1980: 4, 9, 18–23, 182; 1987: 118); Leys (1982: 186–7).

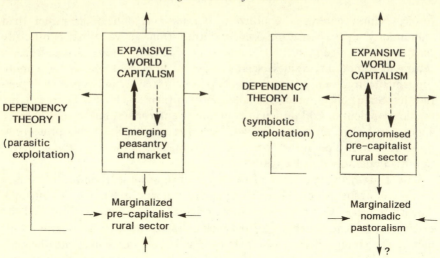

FIG. 8.2. *Dependency theories of unequal exchange and the pastoralist anomaly*

unmodified Dependency Theory I denies nomadic pastoralists any independent future: they would be no more than the client herdsmen of the flocks and herds owned by an absentee élite. A revised Dependency Theory II is the 'Chamus solution': this would switch the initiative from attaining pure pastoralist ideals to accommodating pastoralism as a semi-autonomous fringe activity within an underdeveloped peasant economy. A third possibility is that nomadic pastoralism could survive in the bleakest possible areas beyond the reaches of the world market, as they always have. This would be the 'Turkana solution', which is well adapted for those who are most resilient, but offers little chance of growth or of a return to pastoralism for others who are forced out. The scope for these three possibilities is taken up in Chapter 9.

Conclusion: Confidence and the Threshold of Change

Two Western views of pastoralism in East Africa are expressed in popular representation. The first is ethnographic, written or filmed, perceived from within a traditional culture, and elaborated in Part I of the present work. The other is a more world-weary view, typical of the tourist visiting the Maasai, for instance, with glimpses of a decaying culture: initially as unemployed vagrants near the bus station in Nairobi; then fleetingly as aimless onlookers at the small townships along the motor road; and then finally at the end of the trip as a contrived model village where a performance of women's or *moran* dancing is mounted for a fee and photographs are allowed, again at a price. It is a view of this kind that has emerged in Part III. In the first representation, the threshold of Fig. 8.1 is emphasized, separating a self-contained nomadic life style from civilization, which belongs to another world of cultural dissonance beyond the horizon; while the second representation in effect traces trajectory C backwards to the realization that perhaps there is no threshold.

Dependency theory corresponds broadly with the second view, and there is also a sense in which it falls within the tradition of Western scholarship. Early travel books and administrative records also reflect an orientation from civilization looking outwards, and (neo-)colonial histories tend to place early development and encounters with local dignitories within the individualistic and even heroic setting of the pioneering frontier of Western expansion. Development economists tend similarly to presuppose Western economic ideals and to apply Western models. In contrast to these, dependency theory questions the ideals of development and presents an altogether more hard-edged approach to history. Yet it too is oriented radially along the routes of trade, labour migration, and development, tracing the forces that emanate from international urban centres of commerce and growth to the satellites and beyond.

From this viewpoint, the capitalist system displays a relentless pattern. There is also a monotonous uniformity in its various manifestations that contrasts with the rich variety of traditional systems as one examines them in finer detail. Elaborating Fig. 8.1, one is not just concerned with a simple model of two poles separated by a single threshold, but rather with Western innovation dominating the economic arena at the centre and surrounded by a halo of thresholds and an outer ring of traditional societies beyond. In Dependency Theory I, the capitalist market economy is endowed with the gravitational force of a black hole, ingesting non-capitalist societies irreversibly as the thresholds dissolve. In Dependency Theory II, the critique argues that non-capitalist forms persist, but as client satellites on the fringe of capitalism. Their traditions appear to retain an integrity of sorts, but the restrictions inhibit adaptation and growth, and this encourages the supply of cheap labour and raw materials, perpetuating the inequalities of underdevelopment.

This view of the persistence of non-capitalist traditions recalls the notion of moral thresholds, discussed in Chapter 1, where it was applied to the separation of traditional activities and roles into clearly demarcated domains: age systems, extended families, exchange networks, women's gatherings, and so on.[20] These domains have their own institutional subcultures, and, to this extent, the boundaries between them are also sensitive. The elaboration of Fig. 8.1, with the capitalist core surrounded by a halo of thresholds and an outer ring of semi-traditional satellites, can be further extended by superimposing the configuration of domains (Fig. 1.2) on each of the satellites, providing a whole range of sub-thresholds. Viewing this array from the capitalist centre outwards, dependency-theory literature has been concerned with the articulation between

[20] See p. 44.

modes of production, focusing almost entirely on the historical process whereby capitalism exploits various non-capitalist modes with the penetration of cash. It dominates as an irresistible economic infrastructure that erodes the ideological framework of tradition and can intrude across thresholds and sub-thresholds with impunity when there is profit to be made.[21]

Viewed from the periphery, however, each domain has its own gravitational pull as it were: it is ethically charged and dominated by ideological factors, and the sub-thresholds delineating the distribution of power are perceived in ethical terms of traditional expectation. The limitation of dependency theory at the periphery is that the penetration of the market economy can only be as viable as the confidence it inspires, and its advance may be impeded by a residual confidence in the indigenous system of exchange and expectation. Even money can become endowed with a non-capitalist significance. In a traditional domain, it may undergo a moral transformation, ceasing to have a generalized market value and taking on characteristics appropriate to that domain. Thus, when Maasai elders give money to a group of dancing women for their blessing, this has a different connotation to money given by tourists. It becomes an aspect of the relationship between elders and wives in general and a substitute for other gifts in the past. Similarly, when these women press their takings on a particularly destitute member of their group, this becomes an aspect of their solidarity and the purchases of the recipient take on the character of a gift and not merely a commodity. Turning to the Nuer, Sharon Hutchinson has shown how cash has substituted for cattle in their system of exchange, but only up to a point and only when it has been gained in an appropriate way. To this extent, instead of being a wholly impersonal medium, money can acquire a certain 'pedigree', like cattle, and enter into the traditional sphere of exchange. Purchased guns too have entered this sphere among the Nuer, but they have also introduced a new element of impersonality and destructiveness into homicide, modifying the critical role of feud in the political system: there has been change but not exactly Westernization.[22] In other pastoralist societies, where money is substituted for cattle in the payment of bride-wealth, this is less immediately concerned with the commoditization of women than with maintaining the power differentials between older and younger men. The younger men are the principal wage-earners, bringing money back to their home societies, while the older men control the marriages of their daughters as an important source of income. A common feature of this exchange has been the inflation of bride-wealth: as money accumulates, so the older men ask higher prices. Money is a novelty, but the underlying differentials of power persist, and to this extent confidence in the traditional system of exchange persists.

[21] Meillassoux (1972: 98, 102); Dupré and Rey (1973: 132–7, 142); Long (1977: 72, 86–103); Foster-Carter (1978: 216–19, 222–3). Cf. Asad (1979: 420–2); Bradburd (1984: 3–5).
[22] Hutchinson (1996: 73–111, 140–4, 150–7).

Where tradition has been subverted, as among the Chamus, thresholds become blurred. Yet, there is clearly an element of accommodation on both sides even here. Any outsider who wishes to establish an economic base has to generate confidence by local standards. Local businessmen are forced to choose between the hazards of mistrust and the need to cultivate bonds of reciprocity within the local tradition, deferring to local expectations (trajectory *B* in Fig. 8.1). By marrying further wives in the process of establishing position locally, they take on the expectations of further affines. By accepting credit and the possibility of bad debts, they display a measure of good faith. Even absentee owners who employ impoverished herdsmen to tend inflated herds have to extend a trust that is normally confined to kinsmen.[23] Innovators have to generate confidence through gestures that are meaningful within the traditional system.

In Chapter 1 the reiterated point concerned the need to cultivate networks of exchange and marriage as an insurance against the inevitability of loss from time to time. Creditworthiness and marriageability are not based on contractual agreements that specify the conditions of each gift and eventual repayment. It is trust and credibility rather than investment that are emphasized, and in this spirit there is give and take rather than precise calculation. It is Sahlins's 'generalized reciprocity' that typifies a non-capitalist mode of behaviour as against the 'balanced reciprocity' of the market.[24] However, a system that operates through a loose network of association is not simply an aspect of pastoralist or other non-capitalist societies alone. It is characteristic also of the informal infrastructure of capitalism itself, where gifts may be used to cement relations, undercutting the principle of a 'free' market but serving to generate confidence on which any market depends. The informal system extends throughout the network of dependency relations from the local level to the national and beyond. It is an aspect of patronage at all levels, an informal old-boy network that complicates the distinction between patron and client, since both are dependent on the other, and also between capitalist and non-capitalist systems. To the extent that trust has to be maintained in both directions, there cannot be domination. Where this trust becomes attenuated, so does the penetration of capitalism, and those on the periphery have to look to one another for support rather than towards the market.

This raises uncertainties concerning the future of capitalism in remoter parts of East Africa. To the extent that resources for commercial exploitation become attenuated in remoter areas, so too do the communication links with the outside world and the infrastructure of commerce and government. The concern of development agencies has been with the settled margins of the developing

---

[23] Dahl (1979*a*: 77; 1979*b*: 272–3); Hjort (1979: 39–40); Little (1992: 87). See also pp. 47 and 213.

[24] See p. 17. Sahlins (1974: 193). Cf. Hyden (1987: 119–24); Broch-Due (1990: 158–9); Sobania (1991: 130–1).

world, where the growing populations are heavily subsidized because of the barrenness of the local terrain. Apart from supplying cheap labour, those trapped in these marginal settlements are a drain on resources rather than an asset, a stagnating underclass in a situation of underdevelopment. This lays bare the limits of capitalist growth as it reaches out towards extensive waste-lands that are too sparse for investment and in a region noted for political instability.

It is a situation in which nomadic pastoralists in the semi-arid hinterland and beyond have to look after themselves. To the extent that they have to rely on their own enterprise for survival in these least promising areas, the resilience and integrity of their commitment are major assets. Their future is inscrutable, of course, but there is a further strand to this analysis if one steps back to consider the development of pastoralism from a broader evolutionary perspective. It is to this that we now turn.

9

The Shadow of Islam and the Spread
of the Desert

Pastoralism and agriculture are overlapping forms of adaptation that can be viewed as a phenomenon of history and, beyond that, as products of some major climatic shifts. Geological evidence suggests that savannah ecosystems evolved over millions of years, during which they became adapted to severe fluctuations in climate, including periods of glaciation when conditions were cooler and intensely arid. Around 12,000 BC in the Middle East and somewhat later in northern Africa, the most recent interglacial period brought warmth and humidity that lasted some 4,000–5,000 years.[1] Archaeological evidence suggests that it was during this moister phase that cereals and livestock were first domesticated in various parts of the Middle East. These included sheep and goats, long-horned cattle, and then short-horned cattle, possibly through selective breeding around 7,000 BC.[2] This was a period when the Sahara, which had previously been uninhabitable, became a grassland with lakes, streams, and fauna typical of the East African savannah today, and attracting human settlement. Over this period also, the lakes of eastern Africa rose to very high levels and supported large settlements based on fishing, possibly comparable with the earliest traditions of the proto-Chamus.[3]

This bland period was followed by what may be described as dampened oscillations in the climate alternating between moist and arid phases along an increasingly arid trend. In northern Africa, there was a sharp and severe arid period around 5,000 BC, and the steady onset of another more prolonged but less severe arid period from around 3,000 BC as the Sahara degenerated progressively into desert.[4] It was during the moist phase between these two periods that agriculture and pastoralism spread into northern Africa. The spread of pastoralism was hindered by the tsetse fly that bred in these moist conditions, broadly where the annual rainfall was above 500 mm. Only as the tsetse belt moved southwards with increasing aridity could pastoralism spread to the Sahel and eastern Africa; and cattle appear to have reached northern Kenya by

---

[1] Stiles (1981: 376); Lamprey (1983: 645); Gowlett (1988: 32–3); Sadr (1991: 31).
[2] Lamprey (1983: 646–8); Gowlett (1988: 35, 45); A. B. Smith (1992: 40, 52–3).
[3] Stiles (1981: 376); Gowlett (1988: 33–4); Sadr (1991: 30); A. B. Smith (1992: 65).
[4] Stiles (1981: 376; 1983: 1); Gowlett (1988: 38–40); Sadr (1991: 31, 95, 42–3); A.B. Smith (1992: 44, 51, 65, 67, 73). Sadr's chart (on p. 31) appears augmented by a more recent moist period up to the nineteenth century (Gowlett 1988: 42–4).

2,000 BC or later, concentrated especially in areas that were too arid for agriculture.[5] Camel pastoralism was a more recent addition to this mix, following a similar route. Single-humped camels were domesticated in the Middle East around 2,000 BC during an increasingly arid phase, and then spread to northern Africa with the drier conditions, and reached the remoter parts of eastern Africa around perhaps the fourteenth century AD.[6] The history of pastoralism in Africa is thus bound up with climatic trends towards aridity.

These major fluctuations in the climate along a trend towards decreasing rainfall in northern and eastern Africa seem to have affected the movements of population and modes of adaptation. With new techniques and increasing population pressures, there has been a reduction in biodiversity, leading to a more fragile balance of life, and extending to the planet as a whole.[7] The question then arises: were the increasing aridity of the soil and fundamental changes in the local ecosystems due to the activities of the pastoralists, or to some combination of agriculture and pastoralism, or would they have occurred even without human interference? To what extent did indigenous pastoral practices create or respond to changing ecological conditions?[8]

Pastoral Adaptation: The Benign Model and the Hidden Hand

Evidence concerning cause and effect in the process of land degradation is sufficiently ambiguous to support diverging views.[9] There are two basic models of the relationship between nomadic pastoralists and their environment: a benign model and one that is doom-laden. These recall the two views expressed in the lower half of Fig. 7.2 (p. 228): the benign view is Malthusian, struggling at the rough end of a balance with nature, and the other is neo-Malthusian, tumbling inescapably towards disaster.

The benign view that pastoral nomadism is naturally and inherently adjusted to environmental constraints broadly follows the Unesco pronouncement on the pastoral continuum that was cited at the outset of this volume. There is the presumption of some 'hidden hand' that would ensure the survival of pastoralism, but for outside interference. Expressed by one ecologist: 'traditional nomadic society was approximately in equilibrium with natural resources on which they entirely depended; any mistake in land use was penalized by reduction of the land carrying capacity for human and animal populations. Hence,

---

[5] Phillipson (1977: 76, 84); Lamprey (1983: 645–8); Stiles (1983: 1); Collett (1987: 130); Gowlett (1988: 31, 42); Sadr (1991: 31, 79); A. B. Smith (1992: 52, 56–7, 66, 72–3, 79–80); F. Marshall (1994: 33–4, 36).

[6] Lamprey (1983: 648); Stiles (1983: 1); Gowlett (1988: 44).

[7] Gowlett (1988: 28, 45).

[8] Stiles (1981: 377–8); Lamprey (1983: 645); Gowlett (1988: 38–40, 44–5).

[9] Allan (1965: 321); Sandford (1983: 12–16). Cf. Spencer (1973: 180–2, 189–90); Grove (1974: 144–6); Prothero (1974: 164); Baker (1974: 173–4); Horowitz (1981: 67–75); Homewood and Rodgers (1987: 111–13).

they had to learn sound land-use practices in order to survive.'[10] This is to argue that the pastoralists left to themselves are closer to the natural forces that shape their decisions than Western advisers with only a partial knowledge. It even assumes that the evolutionary acquisition of indigenous knowledge by trial and error in these non-literate societies is on a par with the adaptation of savannah ecosystems over millions of years prior to human habitation. The benign model emphasizes the virtue of adaptability, and the extent to which pastoral nomadism as a way of life has surmounted periods of regional instability and fluctuations of climate or tsetse infestation, well above the threshold of environmental degradation.[11]

The implicit notion of some hidden hand has an affinity with a functionalist approach in anthropology, which is well represented in pastoralist studies that emphasize the robustness of tradition, irrespective of the inevitability of change. These are, after all, remarkably resilient societies and this resilience deserves explanation. A recurrent theme in the present work has concerned the notion of tradition, not merely as some immutable practice, but as an expression of collective wisdom and accumulated experience that adapts to changing situations. Ethnographies of the region repeatedly note the role of discussion among elders in pooling their ideas and experiences on matters of common concern in a search for some acceptable solution. In a key position are those with a flare for bringing together different points of view into some imaginative synthesis that stretches beyond parochial interests. It is evident from Part I that the focus of community concern extends beyond the accommodation of change at a technological level to the institutional context of pastoralism controlled by the elders. In Chapters 1 and 2, kinship was seen to be concerned with the organization of pastoralism as a joint family enterprise extending to the ideal of polygyny and growth. Age systems were viewed as a key factor in the organization of community affairs beyond the family, and hence concerned the wider context of pastoral production. The systems opposed individualistic opportunism and the upthrust of youth, but they too were subject to review and modification. In Chapter 3, it was seen how elders, as the guardians of tradition, could generate a radical step towards unprecedented change in times of crisis. This was illustrated among the Jie, when the elders modified their generation-set system in response to the pressures of events, and also among the Oromo by the role of *gada* assemblies in resolving anomalies in customary law. Successive adaptations among the Chamus, considered in Part II, provided an extended example of how practices could respond to new situations. A Darwinian process of natural selection seemed to underlie the deliberations of the elders in the course of pooling their points of view and variety of experience, emerging with creative innovations and compromises that responded to the collective interest

[10] Houerou (1986: 140). See also Spooner (1971); Baxter (1993: 157).
[11] Baier (1976: 5); Kjekshus (1977: 67–8); Swift (1977*b*: 457); Homewood and Rodgers (1987: 122–4); Gowlett (1988: 44).

(Chapter 6).[12] This is to emphasize the robustness of pastoral cultures in response to opportunity and hence the benign aspect of adaptability. However, a benign model that places the weight of functionalist adaptability on the shoulders of conscious human experience does not address the broader historical issue regarding damage caused by the non-conscious and unintended consequences of action.

Pastoral Maladaptation: The Neo-Malthusian Critique

Chapter 7 questioned whether the Tragedy of the Commons applies to indigenous systems where individual families rely on community support and share a common interest. However, this does not preclude unwitting forms of destruction that lie beyond popular understanding and foresight in the longer term. Thus, if one considers indigenous knowledge concerning cattle management and ethno-veterinary medicine, then this may be benign and sound, stemming from the accumulated feedback of direct experience. But wisdom derived from the care of livestock is altogether more immediate than a wider ecological understanding. The process of experiencing the link between the care of common land and nomadic herding strategies is more extended, and the benign argument is harder to sustain at this level.[13] The problem concerns the limits of collective experience in an unpredictable environment. The severity of the epidemics in East Africa in the 1880s, for instance, were held to be quite unprecedented. If each pastoralist had to rely on his own knowledge and the consensus of wisdom in coping with periods of hardship as they occurred, how should he respond to one that developed into a catastrophe beyond living experience? And if this was part of a long-term trend, say some major climatic shift, then how far would even this further experience be relevant for those who survived and attempted to rebuild their herds?[14] To take a parallel from Chapter 3, the analysis of the Karimojong–Jie generation-set system suggested the operation of an extended cycle that lay beyond the adult experience of any living elder. Problems inherent in the system led to a very uncertain response among the Karimojong, and even to an unprecedented initiative by Jie elders that eventually undermined the whole system. If the collective wisdom of elders at large cannot guarantee the survival of their system (or agreement among the ethnographers), then can one assert with confidence any 'approxi-

---

[12] See p. 200–1.

[13] In a comprehensive survey of forty-seven studies of indigenous knowledge in developing countries (Warren *et al.* 1995), only two are directly relevant to pastoralism. The essay on ethnoveterinary medicine is packed with a detailed breakdown of the topic from a wide range of sources (Mathias-Mundy and McCorkle); whereas the essay concerned with the indigenous management of (semi-)arid land provides a sweeping outline of other sources, but evades the critical issues of indigenous understanding and usage (Niamir). This suggests that the fund of pastoralist knowledge has built up around the care of livestock rather than of the land itself. Cf. p. 229 n. 48.

[14] Dyson-Hudson and Dyson-Hudson (1982: 234–5); Gowlett (1988: 45).

mate equilibrium [in which pastoralists] had to learn sound land-use practices in order to survive'? Over this extended period of deteriorating conditions, one appears to be more in the province of an untamed cosmos than of some ecological balance with nature or a Boserupian tendency towards realistic adaptation (Chapter 7).

A neo-Malthusian approach views the irreversible loss of diverse forms of flora and fauna as a direct result of the process of human adaptation and population growth since the transition from hunting and gathering. In its starkest form, this critique argues that agriculture in parts of northern Africa and the Sahel led to the progressive degradation of marginal areas where rainfall levels were steadily decreasing. Such areas were then occupied by pastoralists who could survive through their mobility, but degraded the land further. By protecting young and sick animals from predators, pastoralists could even increase their herds, but only at the expense of destroying their habitat even further. Foliage became grazed to a point where it failed to reproduce itself: annual plants could not form seed and perennials could not transfer nutrients to their roots for storage.[15] This view places pastoralism at the tail-end of a sequence of destruction, adapted to conditions of ecological decline, shifting to better areas where possible, or adopting more hardy types of stock as whole areas became colonized by more arid plant communities. The sawtooth profile of growth and decay, in other words, appears skewed towards degradation in the longer term, as indicated in Fig. 7.2, and expressed in the assertion that the nomad is not so much a son of the desert as its father.[16] From this point of view, pastoralism even in its traditional setting is presented as maladapted, caught up in a slow self-defeating vicious spiral.

This critique identifies the whole thrust of human domestication in marginal conditions as the source of degradation, and not simply pastoralism as such or the domesticated goat in particular. Agriculture also plays a part. In the benign model, historical evidence of opportunistic switching between pastoral, agricultural, and foraging niches may be regarded as a more inclusive demonstration of human adaptiveness.[17] However, in the neo-Malthusian critique, this switching also provides a more inclusive view of land degradation. The critique challenges, for instance, the (benign) view that pastoral populations have shown altogether less tendency to grow than in agricultural areas—until they too settle to cultivate.[18] To the extent that the trend appears to have been for the pastoral overspill to settle down to agriculture and not the reverse, pastoralists do not contain their own growth, and to that extent they contribute indirectly to the pressure on the environment elsewhere.

---

[15] Lamprey (1983: 643, 653, 656, 658–9, 663). Cf. Stebbing (1938: 5–10, 13, 19, 21); Allan (1965: 292, 320–1); Ingold (1980: 75–8); Stiles (1981: 374–5; 1983).

[16] Cited by Markakis (1993: 10).

[17] See pp. 20–1 and 209.

[18] Allan (1965: 319); Swift (1977a: 173–4; 1977b: 465–71); Dahl and Hjort (1979: 7); Stiles (1983: 3).

The neo-Malthusian critique presents a sombre assessment, but in one major respect its relevance to East Africa may be questioned. The evidence derives largely from research in the Sahara and Sahel. While drought in East Africa since the 1970s seems to echo the earlier Sahel pattern, where comparable policies had been previously applied, it remains that the two regions were associated with different cultural traditions, and different forms of adaptation may conceivably have applied. To this extent the earlier experience of pastoralism in northern Africa is not necessarily relevant to eastern Africa. The Sahara and Sahel belonged to the Islamic world which had its own identity, ideology, and patterns of social organization that extended to the Middle East. It is useful, therefore, to consider ways in which pastoralism in these Islamic areas had their own distinctive stamp that diverged from the broad pattern of the East African model.

Islamic Pastoralism and the Extension of Business Enterprise

Pastoral nomads everywhere appear to have an ambiguous status, but this differs in a number of ways in the Islamic areas as compared with East Africa. In various parts of the Middle East and northern Africa, for instance, a popular view in the literature relegates pastoralism to the sparse borders of civilization. It is perceived as offering a more primitive life style, reliant on the resources of the settled areas and always under threat from environmental factors. The notion that the overspill from agricultural populations drifts into pastoralism is even the reverse of the situation in East Africa, where the pastoral niche has been fully exploited, both in earlier times and more recently.[19]

Historically, however, a more robust reputation attaches to the nomadic Bedouin as an expanding, conquering force who exacted tribute from settled populations and held the military balance of power in unstable regions. This more positive view is also associated with the strategic position that Bedouin held in the development of the overland caravan trade, which created a major shift in the pattern of commerce once camels had been harnessed after the third century AD. In the areas that they dominated, Bedouin bred the stock and provided the guards and caravaneers. New towns and cities emerged on the sites of some of their settlements, centred on the place where the camels were unloaded, and associated with pastoral culture. This development gave Bedouin access to new wealth and opportunities. Yet only those that settled down to an urban life could exploit this advantage, taking the initiative in the development of the state and commerce as rulers, soldiers, or merchants. Those that remained as pastoral nomads never rose above an ancillary role, resisting domination, but dependent increasingly on urban patronage. Even their link

---

[19] Spooner (1971: 201, 206; 1972: 260–7); Bates and Lees (1977: 832); Swift (1977*b*: 460); Swidler (1980: 21–9); Sadr (1991: 1, 127–8); Cribb (1991: 10, 27).

with the ruling dynasties who claimed Bedouin origins was largely ideological. They were separated by a vast gulf in their wealth and life style.[20]

The spread of Islam from the Middle East into Africa from the seventh century followed the network of trade routes, again taking a similar course to the spread of stock in an earlier period. Islam, trade, and urban civilization fed upon one another, and where conditions encouraged long-distance trade and notably in the towns, Islam established itself.[21] Beyond the territories controlled by Bedouin and Berbers in the Mediterranean hinterland, the penetration of Islam southwards followed the trade routes through areas that were also dominated by camel nomads, to the savannah belt associated especially with Fulani cattle pastoralism in West Africa. Beyond these, further south still, the prevalence of the tsetse fly limited pastoralism, and in these southern areas, Islam has remained a minority religion. Among the Islamic pastoralists of sub-Saharan Africa, this general pattern may be traced historically with reference to three broadly representative groups: the Tuareg, Fulani, and Somali. The following thumbnail sketches are intended to illustrate the extent to which these peoples were involved in a regional network of business enterprise interwoven with social stratification. This was a different order to the more egalitarian systems of family enterprise outlined for the non-Islamic pastoralists of East Africa in Chapter 1.

The Tuareg were Islamic camel nomads who ranged over the sparse wastelands of the Sahel along the southern reaches of the Sahara, placing them in a strategic position for control over the trans-Saharan caravan trade in precolonial times. Their military dominance over this area took the form of a highly stratified confederation, headed by powerful noble families and warrior tribes whose ambitions were held in check by internal rivalries. Other Tuareg were reduced to various levels of servility, ranging from less wealthy camel nomads to cultivators on semi-feudal vassal estates. In the course of their annual cycle of transhumance, the Tuareg serviced the Sahel stretch of the trans-Saharan caravan trade, providing Islamic merchants and agents from the north with transport and protection to the south. At the more fertile and populated southern end of this cycle, the Tuareg also traded surplus stock and desert products for grain on their own account, transporting and retrading these opportunistically in response to local differences in supply and demand, especially with regard to the profits that could be obtained from mineral salts. It was the developing economy of the southern towns that provided their source of wealth, enabling them to maintain a relatively high standard of living—in food and clothing—despite their nomadic life style. For the more ambitious Tuareg in times of peace, their patronage diversified through a commercial infrastructure, with specialist craftsmen, farming estates, and a

---

[20] Asad (1973: 62, 64, 68, 71–2; 1979: 424–6); Bulliet (1980: 34–45); Cribb (1991: 26).
[21] I. M. Lewis (1966: 4, 15); Trimingham (1968: 37–9).

trading network of agents in the various towns and cities. Meanwhile, those who remained nomadic took care to maintain a separate ethnic identity, pitching their camps outside the towns, and avoiding involvement in urban affairs. The most successful business leaders were drawn from a few aristocratic Tuareg families, whose power lay in their commanding position over the opportunities offered by short- and long-distance transportation through their network of clients. To this extent, and also the extent to which they were forced to settle temporarily among their dependent estates in times of severe drought, the Tuareg were part of a regional economic system. Their strength lay in retaining control over a lucrative regional niche that spanned the ecological zones from the nomadic regime of the Sahel to these southern areas where it was spread broadly rather than linked to any single urban centre.[22]

While the Tuareg enhanced their livelihood by spanning diverse ecological zones from north to south, the pastoral Fulani were confined by their cattle herds to the savannah belt from west to east. Historically, they originated in Senegal in the far west around the tenth century and their migratory tracts tended to expand eastwards until they extended halfway across Africa to Chad and beyond. Those that lost their herds were forced to settle as agriculturalists, forming scattered settlements at points along the broad trail pioneered by the pastoralists. In any area, they were an ethnic minority. However, at times of discontent against an established pagan regime and inspired by Islamic holy men, it was the settled and nomadic Fulani who took the initiative in transforming any popular uprising into a *jihad*, an Islamic holy war that consolidated their position and control over pastureland. The outcome was to establish Fulani systematically as the dominant culture, headed by Fulani rulers within the urban capitals, and with Islam as the official religion and principle of government. In this process, the pastoral Fulani held an ambiguous position. They provided the disciplined warrior force in times of state formation and insurrection and were the ideological confreres of the urban élites. Nevertheless, as pastoralists they remained elusively nomadic, and in normal times their allegiances to state and to Islam were tenuous. They did not mix easily with the local populations, who regarded them as essentially pagan and uncivilized. Yet, their claims to be the true repositors of Fulani culture and defenders of Islam politically were impeccable, and they in their turn scorned the settled populations. The pastoral Fulani, then, like the Bedouin, held a potent role historically in the spread of Islam and the establishment of Islamic states, but became an increasingly irrelevant minority as the dominance of urban civilization became established. Moreover, they could not altogether shake themselves free of the influence of the towns. The towns had developed as market centres and the nodal points of power, interlinked by trade routes and the pilgrim

---

[22] Nicolaisen (1963: 209–19); Lovejoy and Baier (1976: 145–7, 150–3, 155, 160–6); Bernus (1990: 152–4).

traffic between West Africa and Arabia (pioneered by Fulani even as far east as Ethiopia). Fulani culture dominated, and, while the pastoralists did not accommodate to settled or urban values, their diet was mixed, and they were frequent visitors to the cities and towns where they had their own networks of kin.[23]

Further east, on the coast of the Horn of Africa and southwards, Islam again followed trade routes to become established along the network of ports, and again typically in association with urban culture, dominated by ruling élites and trading interests.[24] In the pastoral hinterland along the northern strip of the Horn, Islam also spread, associated with the camel-owning Somali, who claimed traditional links with Arabia across the Gulf of Aden. According to their oral traditions, it was Islam that provided a unifying ideal in the southward expansion of the Somali into land previously occupied by non-Islamic Oromo pastoralists. As they expanded further south still into the more fertile area around Juba, the Somali assimilated the indigenous populations, and a form of stratification developed comparable with the settled Fulani. However, the unity that the Somali displayed along their frontiers was undermined internally by the disarray of lineage politics and endless competition for control over local resources. Rather than a balance between predation and husbandry, noted in Chapter 1 for the non-Islamic inland pastoralists, there was a volatile array of feuding that tended to override the Islamic ideal of unity. Lineage solidarity was only achieved at a relatively low level, with somewhat tenuous contractual agreements between rival lineages at higher levels, mediated by their religious leaders.

Against this background of feuding, inland trade from the coastal ports involved a more peaceful aspect of Somali society. In return for gifts and a share in the profits, influential leaders of strong clans would ensure protection for non-Somali caravans passing through their territories. This linked Somali pastoralism to the development of trade and a taste for exotic commodities, providing an urban dimension to their life style as trading enterprises worked their way inland with the expansion of Somali borders. Small towns scattered throughout the Somali region were clearly well established by the time of Ioan Lewis's study in the 1950s: a period when viable urban centres did not exist in the more inland non-Islamic pastoral areas and were as yet unthinkable. Pastoralism and urbanism were complementary aspects of the Somali pattern of transhumance. In the dry season from April to September, their camel herds dispersed into small mobile camps, while a major sector of the human population migrated towards the towns and these became the focal points of the pastoral system, dominated by pastoral values and lineage politics. A tendency towards stratification is evident. Poorer families who remained confined to a nomadic existence away from the towns at this time became more peripheral

---

[23] Stenning (1959: 11–23); Azarya (1993: 42–50); Shimada (1993: 88–96).
[24] Spaulding (1991: 28–34).

and were held in disregard along with those whose poverty had forced them to settle as cultivators. Influence within the towns and the means to power were underpinned by wealth in camels and success in trading, and these in turn were enhanced by strength of character and the privilege of birth. With the onset of the rains, there was a twin movement away from the towns. Families were reunited with their camel herds. At the same time, it was precisely this monsoon season that facilitated overseas trading with the Middle East, and business opportunities and labour migration shifted towards the coast.[25]

The boundary between the Somali especially and the non-Islamic pastoralists inland, principally the Booran, has a direct relevance for the present study. A distant affinity between the Booran (Oromo) and Islam was noted in Chapter 1, with less emphasis on the polygynous family and more concern for differences of status between families and of wealth and success.[26] However, Booran identity clearly relates to the sensitivity of the Somali boundary and their differences with Islam, rather than to any similarities. Today, they regard the assemblies of their *gada* age/generation organization as the principal means of upholding traditional values based on *nagaa*, 'the peace of Booran', in contrast to *jihad*, which is perceived not so much as a 'holy war' waged by the Somali against non-believers, but rather as an expression of the belligerence of Somali society within itself, rent by constant factionalism and feuding. *Jihad* is opposed to *nagaa*, as the Somali are to the Booran. It is *gada*, they argue, that is primarily responsible for confronting the threat of Somali expansion. Without this discipline to uphold their traditions and the ideal of Oromo unity, it is said, the Somali would already have expanded far inland and as far south as Tanzania.[27]

The eastern flank of Boorana is characterized by a patchwork of groups with identities that have shifted between Somali and Oromo. Local historical traditions are of conversion to and from Islam in this border area with a general trend towards 'Somalization' as Oromo groups have transferred their pastoralism from cattle to camels, and for the Booran this implies also the volatile disarray of lineage politics.[28] However, not all camel pastoralists in this area ally

---

[25]   I. M. Lewis (1961: 31, 82, 90–4, 100, 124, 197; 1994: 114–16, 126, 128).

[26]   See p. 49.

[27]   Getachew Kassa (1990, and personal communication during a visit to the Oromo area in 1994). This Booran view of their ability to confront Somali expansion may be compared with Trimingham (1968: 128), who has made a similar point concerning the limits of the spread of Islam in this region due to the age organization. However, more consistent with Trimingham's principal thesis (n. 21 above), one may note that the age systems survived in areas that were not exposed to long-distance trade; and this suggests that it has been trade that has brought in Islam rather than age systems as such that have kept Islam at bay. Again, I. M. Lewis (1961: 25) has expressed this boundary of Islam in terms of the balance of political strength between the Somali and Oromo. Yet the Rendille at least retained their independence of either, and their isolation from Islam seems again explicable in terms of the absence of established trade links inland.

[28]   According to Getachew Kassa (1990: 2, and personal communication), the Booran refer to those sectors of Oromo that have recently taken up both camel husbandry and Islam as *Bupi*, 'balloons' that easily burst when pricked, because without *gada* they are quarrelsome and constant victims to infighting. Cf. the Samburu attitude towards the camel-owning Rendille, who also are regarded as prone to anger (Spencer 1973: 105).

themselves ideologically with the Somali. The traditions of such Kenya pastoralists as the Rendille, Gabbra, and Sakuye, which linked them culturally to the Somali in various ways, did not extend to Islam itself. Instead of the fragile balance between rival warrior lineages and charismatic priestly lineages as among the Somali, it was the principle of seniority within the family that influenced behaviour and status as among their allies and neighbours who were cattle pastoralists, with younger men as warriors and older men bearing the charisma of a closeness to God that increased as they aged.[29]

That Islam did not penetrate beyond the Somali frontiers or inland from the Swahili coast in the south seems primarily due to the fact that markets further inland did not begin to establish themselves historically until new conditions were created during the nineteenth century. These markets involved the emergence of (Islamic) mercenary states associated with slave-trading from the Tanzanian coast to the south of the Maasai, and simultaneously the southward penetration of (Islamic) trade from the Sudan into Uganda. Together these formed a pincer movement that bypassed the non-Islamic inland pastoralists for a while yet.[30] Sporadic attempts at trading by Islamic as well as Kamba pioneers occurred, even as far inland as Baringo (Chapter 6). However, the increasing involvement of European colonial powers at this stage altered the course of history throughout the region. It remains a moot point whether in other circumstances the trading and then Islam might have spread among the various inland pastoral peoples and what forms this might have taken.

The Islamic Model of Pastoral Development

The need to view pastoralism as part of a regional ecological system has been stressed by Fredrik Barth, noting the dynamic interplay between herders and sedentary peoples.[31] While the context of Barth's analysis is the Middle East, this approach clearly has relevance for Islamic Africa where pastoralists and farmers are enmeshed in a common history and ecological setting. It is a history that extends to the development of commerce, long-distance trade, urbanization, and state infrastructures. The common history and ecology extends beyond pastoralists and cultivators to the process of civilization itself.

In this respect, there is a sharp difference within the non-Islamic pastoral continuum in East Africa that has been the concern of the present volume. Trading between pastoralists and farmers was certainly an aspect of their

---

[29] See p. 126. While the Rendille claim a distant link with the Somali, they could also have affinity with the Yibir, who, according to Somali myth, were the previous rulers of their land but are now reduced to an inferior caste of bondsmen. The Yibir still claim magical powers and a potent curse, and this suggests a parallel with the *iipire*, who are the dominant lineages of all respected Rendille clans and claim similar powers (I. M. Lewis 1961: 14, 263–4; Spencer 1973: 61–2, 147).

[30] Low (1963: 314–17); Tosh (1970); Schneider (1979: 232–9); Jones (1980: 15–18).

[31] Barth (1973: 11). Cf. Spooner (1972: 261); Lovejoy and Baier (1976: 145–6); Bates and Lees (1977: 825–7); Swift (1977*b*: 460–1).

pattern of survival, and also a degree of diffusion and intermigration, as among the Chamus. However, there was a distinct shift from the Islamic patterns in the scale of this trading and the lack of urban civilization. Such states as existed further inland were characterized by a very rudimentary division of labour. There were no regular caravans across the region, and for the pastoralists such trading as existed was essentially an *ad hoc* response to seasonal shortages: it was for food when their own supplies had run low and the occasional luxury item.[32] The ideal, if not always the practice, was of self-sufficiency within each pastoral group as a confederation of family enterprises, albeit subject to times of hardship. The notion of enterprise is clearly also present among the Islamic pastoralists, but it is altogether more developed to incorporate larger groupings than the family and into a more complex network that bears on commercial relations externally. It surmounts the successive generational crises (Chapter 1) to build up into altogether more developed businesses, with wealthy men in key positions to exert influence ranging from patronage among the Somali (and the Baggara, Kababish, and Afar) to a highly developed form of stratification among the Tuareg.[33] The pastoral Fulani were perhaps a partial exception to this pattern, with less patronage, a more casual adherence to Islam, and more independence for the family. But they too depended on trade and were closely associated along a continuum with settled Fulani, who in turn were part of the stratified system of Fulani theocratic states. The historical trend was for pastoral Fulani to be drawn towards Islamic civilization.[34]

For the non-Islamic pastoralists, the route towards a more urbane life style simply did not exist. Their purview was more limited and the networks of credit and debt were concerned with marriage negotiations and the exchange of women for livestock as an aspect of family and herd development. This generated certain inequalities between the more and the less successful herd-owners and polygynists (Chapter 2), but it did not reach towards a stratified system of patronage, apart from the subordination of women and children. The limitation of the small family enterprise was a problem of reconciling the ideal of independence among maturing sons with the father's interest in keeping his estate together as a viable concern. There was no basis for diversifying the necessary skills and acumen appropriate to a growing organization. Sons had certain automatic rights regardless of aptitude; while client-herdsman from outside the family, who might have more aptitude, would only be trusted to a limited extent, limiting their potential. The Islamic pattern, on the other hand, was

---

[32] Dahl (1979*b*: 266); Hjort (1981*a*: 137); Oba (1990: 39); Sobania (1991: 124–9, 133–6); Johnson (1991: 110); Little (1992: 13).

[33] Cunnison (1966: 3, 28, 36, 114–17); Asad (1970: 184–93; 1972: 133–9). A visit to the Afar in 1994 during Getachew Kassa's fieldwork there seemed to confirm every major point of this section concerning the Islamic model. As opposed to the Somali, there was also a certain parallel to the Fulani in the Afar's loose adherence to Islamic principles in the more nomadic areas and a closer adherence in the settled areas.

[34] Stenning (1959: 21–4); Azarya (1993: 49); Shimada (1993: 94–5).

adapted to development. It involved a greater measure of meritocratic fluidity. Successful clients—even slaves—could earn the trust of their patrons, and a network of dependency could develop into a dispersed labour force and a network of support, extending the range of competence and trust beyond the family.[35]

Ernest Gellner has drawn a similar distinction that elaborates the point. This is between the world-views of what he terms 'marginal' as against 'primitive tribalism'.[36] 'Marginal tribalism' refers to tribes without rulers in the Islamic world, and these are typically pastoralists inhabiting the margins of established states. The involvement of such peoples with their own type of social order is comprehensive, but there is also an element of symbiosis with the more populated areas across their borders and they are aware of an alternative social order. Moreover, they all share the same religion and to this extent they embrace a loftier ideal and the legitimacy of a wider civilization that extends from the authority of those at the centre to the independence of those on the margins who have chosen to reject political overrule by living in a less accessible area. 'Primitive tribalism', on the other hand, is a description of people without rulers who have no conception of any alternative to their own type of society. It fills their horizon and they are 'culturally islands unto themselves'—a phrase that appears an apt characterization of societies within the non-Islamic pastoral continuum of East Africa. Historically, there has been no overarching religion nor a neighbouring state authority to whom they had to relate—until recently.

This recent transition raises the question of how far the colonial/post-colonial experience of non-Islamic pastoralists in East Africa places them in a comparable position to Islamic pastoralists elsewhere over a very much longer period. To what extent does the recent process of development and change in East Africa echo a much earlier development in the Islamic areas further north? The Chamus exemplify these trends very clearly, and Chapters 7 and 8 indicate that Chamus experience is characteristic of the whole region.

The Islamic Model and Recent Trends among Non-Islamic Pastoralists

Some parallels between the established Islamic pattern and more recent trends in East Africa are quite striking.

The elaboration of trade

Trade has become increasingly important in the remoter pastoral areas that have only recently been directly exposed to Western economic forces. Historically, the contrast between such areas and those that have engaged in long-distance trade in pre-colonial times is widely acknowledged.[37] In the Islamic

---

[35] Lovejoy and Baier (1976: 164–5). See pp. 47 and 50.
[36] Gellner (1969: 1–3).
[37] Gray and Birmingham (1970: ch. 1). Cf. Spooner (1971: 202).

TABLE 9.1.   *Profiles of involvement in the cash economy*

Survey group (and source)	Wealth in stock compared with the average (= 1.00)	Proportion of income derived from stock (%)	Proportion of expenditure on			
			food (%)	stock (%)	clothes (%)	other (%)
Average						
Maasai (Evangelou)	1.00	91	16	80	2	2
Chamus (Little)	1.00	65	84	6	8	2
Fulani (Sutter)	1.00	62	64	5	14	17
Tuareg (Bernus)	1.00	89	20	11	26	43
Stratified by wealth						
Chamus (Little)						
richest 10%	4.29	93	69	19	7	5
mid-range	0.88	44	90	1	8	1
poorest 30%	0.13	47	92	—	7	1
Fulani (Sutter)						
richest 13%	3.21	80	56	5	13	26
mid-range	0.82	59	66	6	14	14
poorest 21%	0.18	31	70	4	13	13

Islamic societies italicized.

pastoral areas, the passage of long-distance trade offered a source of revenue and also opportunities to exchange stock products for a more general range of non-pastoral goods. These brought a taste for higher standards of living and were popularly associated with a superior way of life. In the non-Islamic areas, pastoralists confined their trading to the purchase of bare essentials with only the occasional luxury. The implications of recent trends are illustrated in Table 9.1.[38]

The table displays some characteristic features of four pastoral societies for whom comparable data are available concerning involvement in the growing cash economy. Dotted lines subdivide the table into four quarters. The upper-left quarter indicates the extent to which two of these societies (the Maasai and Tuareg) are the more purely pastoral, with a larger proportion of their cash incomes derived from and spent on their herds (notably the Maasai), and a

[38] The data in table 9.1 have been collated in a form that makes the separate surveys directly comparable. Evangelou (1984: 145–8, 155) refers to the Kenyan Maasai within two group ranches who would be more involved in the market economy than those outside. His data on levels of wealth do not extend to all the categories of the table, and hence have not been incorporated here. For the Chamus, data provided in two separate sources by Little (1985a: 253; 1992: 65, 113, 123) have been combined to reproduce them in the present form. For the Fulani, Sutter (1987: 200, 202, 205) refers to the agro-pastoralists in north Senegal. In collating Sutter's data, six small stock have been equated with one cow (following Little 1992: 65). For the Tuareg, Bernus (1990: 165) refers primarily to cattle-owners of Kel Denneg with no indication of stratification by wealth. The broad pattern of expenditure for the Tuareg is not substantially changed if one removes the heavy tax burden from Bernus's data and clothing is the heaviest item of purchase (the percentages for expenditure then become: 26 14 : 34 26).

lesser proportion spent on purchasing food. The lower-left quarter provides a finer breakdown of this pattern according to the distribution of wealth in the other two societies with a more mixed economy (the Chamus and Fulani). This reveals the extent to which the richest sectors, with over three times the average herd, display a more 'pastoral' pattern, while the poorest sectors invert this pattern (notably the Chamus). The slightly higher proportion of income derived from stock in the poorest sector of Chamus is at the expense of running down their remaining herds to survive, and this is matched by the high expenditure of the richest sector who buy up these stock to add to their own herds.[39] On the left-hand side generally, to the extent that income is derived from stock, there is no need to supplement this through wage labour. The upper-right quarter of the table reveals different degrees of involvement in the purchase of clothes and other non-essential goods. The two non-Islamic societies score least in this quarter (notably the Maasai) and the two Islamic societies score most (notably the Tuareg). It is this part of the table that indicates most clearly the extent to which the Islamic societies are enmeshed within the cash economy, relying to a greater extent on non-essential commodities, and to this extent they are (and have been) more integrated into the world economy. Among the Tuareg, for instance, the table illustrates the extent to which their involvement with long-distance trade has been associated with higher standards of living and a heavy involvement with clothing, which they themselves contrast with the semi-clothed state of their pastoral Fulani neighbours.[40] No doubt the Fulani would have a similar attitude towards the Chamus and more especially towards the frugal Maasai. The order of listing in Table 9.1, in other words, reflects the extent to which these peoples have resisted integration into the market economy, with the Maasai heading the list. Generally, conversion to Islam appears to lead to enhanced expectations for a higher standard of living. Among the Uaso Booran and the Orma, for instance, the process of turning to Islam has accompanied an increased involvement in trade and consumer goods, orienting their life style towards the Islamic Somali, and they regard as commonplace what their non-Islamic Booran cousins further north would consider luxuries.[41]

The development of towns

The process of urban growth was noted in Chapter 7 in relation to the development of administrative centres, missions, and refugee camps into permanent townships that housed a growing proportion of the population, even up to one-third or more. As they have developed, these have taken on the characteristics of urban areas elsewhere, serving as commercial centres for the surrounding

---

[39] Little (1992: 92, 101). See p. 212.
[40] Bernus (1990: 156, 168).
[41] Baxter (1966: 242); Ensminger (1992: 59–60, 68, 96–7).

region. Because they have to be sited close to permanent sources of water and (ideally) land suitable for cultivation, this has deprived the nomadic pastoralists of their most reliable dry season pastures. Increasingly, the pastoralists are exposed to drought, precipitating further migrations of stockless refugees to these centres. This process has shifted the balance of advantage away from the pastoralists, and pastoralism itself has become regarded as an archaic form of existence, out of touch with the modern world and with no future. One of the most striking developments in the non–Islamic areas of East Africa is this devaluation of pastoralism from a respected ideal throughout the region to what is now regarded as a backward-looking irrelevance, suitable only for areas that are too marginal for any alternative economic venture. Further north, it is precisely this type of transformation that has been described historically among the Bedouin, Fulani, and other Islamic pastoralists on the periphery of developing towns as the new centres of commerce and power. The Tuareg and Somali may have sustained the pastoral ideal to a greater extent, but they too were integrated into a wider commercial network, and recent trends have shifted the balance further away from pastoralism as an ideal and towards the towns.[42] To the extent that even the remotest pastoralists have been drawn into the margins of the world economy, there is no longer any 'primitive tribalism' cut off from alternative forms of existence.

Increasing social differentiation

The development of new urban areas accompanies the polarization of wealth. The non-Islamic towns have developed their own infrastructure, which is mobilized around an emerging élite of connected insiders and outsiders, opening up new opportunities ranging from business enterprise for the ambitious to marginal employment for the impoverished coupled with precarious forms of cultivation. Traditionally among East African pastoralists, there were considerable differences in wealth between rich and poor. Surplus stock could be converted to wives, and, with growing families and dispersed herds, there was no theoretical limit to this wealth (Chapter 1). It is this that accounts for the high incidence of polygyny in many of these societies (Chapter 2). However, the wealth of polygynists would be dispersed among a larger number of sons in the next generation; and there was always a pressure on wealthier stock-owners to share their good fortune, converting it to prestige and insuring themselves against a downturn in their luck. To a very considerable extent, each successive generation had to build up its own fortunes in societies where the principal form of stratification was by age (Chapter 3). Modern commercial forces have shifted this traditional pattern to a new form of social differentiation (Chapter 8). Those pastoralists that have held to earlier ideals have found themselves

---

[42] Swift (1979: 463–4); Graham (1988: 9); Bernus (1990: 171–2); Doornbos (1993: 111–17).

TABLE 9.2. *Pareto's Law in stock and polygyny*

Survey group (and source)	Proportion of stock owned by the most wealthy 20% (%)	Proportion of wives accrued by the most polygynous 20% (%)
Chamus (Little)	67 (1980–1)	37 (1980–1)
Orma (Ensminger)	60 (1987)	—
Fulani (Sutter/Hopen)	57 (1981–2)	35 (1952–5)
Tuareg (Bernus)	56 (1969)	—
Mukogodo (Herren/Cronk)	53 (1987–8)	33 (1986)
Orma (Ensminger)	51 (1979)	—
Maasai (Evangelou/Spencer)	50 (1980–1)	36 (1977)
Samburu (Spencer)	40 (1958)	35 (1958)

Islamic societies italicized.

edged to the margins of a changing world, unable to compete and witnessing the polarization of their society. It has been notably the younger men who have accommodated to the changing opportunities, entering the competition for control over key resources and building up their patronage and personal estates. This increasing gap between those with wealth and influence and those reduced to poverty is again reminiscent of the Islamic pattern, where influence is associated with striking inequalities in wealth and personal charisma rather than age as such.

Table 9.2 draws on available data to compare the distribution of wealth as a measure of stratification among certain pastoralist groups.[43] The percentages used here invoke Pareto's Law once again, as in Chapter 2, indicating the scale of the lion's share controlled by the most successful 20 per cent of elders. With regard to the distribution of stock, there is a particularly striking contrast between the comparatively early estimate of differentiation among the Samburu and the more recent estimate for the Chamus, who may well have been similar to Samburu in earlier times (cf. Table 6.4, p. 196). The contrast between the earlier and more recent Orma surveys points in the same direction with an increasing gap between rich and poor in the process of their recent conversion to Islam.

[43] Bernus (1974: 68); Evangelou (1984: 137); Little (1985a: 253; 1992: 65); Sutter (1987: 200); Herren (1990: 120); Ensminger (1992: 84, 89). Details of the Samburu sample of herd distribution are given in Dahl and Hjort (1976: 30). Following the argument on p. 65, the negative binomial series that corresponded to the distribution of recorded classes most closely provided a profile from which the stock owned by the wealthiest 20% could be estimated. Again following Little (1992: 65), six small stock have been counted as equivalent to one cow. The final column of this table refers to *all* wives and not to *further* wives (or to implied prestige) as in Chapter 2.

The final column of Table 9.2 indicates the Pareto percentage for the distribution of wives (taken from Table 2.5). This shows a marked uniformity between samples, irrespective of differences in their average levels of polygyny or of degrees of inequality in stock-ownership. The clear implication is that differences in wealth that have emerged recently have concerned stock rather than wives as such. Average polygyny rates and the distribution of wives with age may have changed, but not apparently the share of wives among the most polygynous elders. In the Islamic model, polygyny is not given prominence. Correspondingly, there is little evidence that this provides a critical index of change in the non-Islamic samples.

In these trends, there is a certain inversion of traditional values discussed in Chapter 1 and summarized in Fig. 1.2. Instead of a general principle of equality, notably between peers of the same age-set, and respect for age, there is an individualistic disregard for traditional ideals. Instead of a general notion of creditworthiness as a path towards influence and success, there is an emphasis on wealth itself as a means towards influence, patronage, and more wealth. Stratification is in the process of enveloping the pastoral continuum into a wider society reaching towards the townships, and the national and international economy. As the non-Islamic pastoralists have become ensnared by the pressure on resources, they are edged further towards the drought-ridden margins, and forced increasingly to switch to being cultivators, hired herdsmen, migrant labourers, or very occasionally with a degree of charismatic flare and luck to becoming aspiring members of the emerging élite. It presents a pattern that is more familiar in the more northern Islamic areas.

The changing status of women

While Table 9.2 obscures any shift in the patterns of polygyny due to change, it is clearly possible that gender relations have changed with the process of sedentarization and the spread of urban culture. In a survey of this topic, Gudrun Dahl (1987) has pointed to a loss of status among women in pastoral societies, which has followed from a shift in attitude towards stock. In the traditional system, a woman had definite rights and responsibilities in her stock and played an essential role in the self-sufficiency of her household. With the development of the market, the subsistence value of stock and stock products has been increasingly edged out by their commercial value, and the principal trading has been essentially in the hands of men, undercutting the women's domain. In addition, as men are increasingly obliged to leave home as labour migrants and children are sent to school, the workload of women extends from their traditional domestic routines to a heavier involvement in herding and caring for stock. With increased stratification, the wives of a few wealthy elders may be relieved of some of this extra burden, but at the expense of their links with the network of support among other women, while the clear majority find themselves further burdened. To emphasize the point, Dahl notes that women's rights are even more depressed in pastoral societies of the Middle East where the market is stronger.[44]

The argument is consistent with the other trends noted here, with Islamic experience again providing a vision of the impact of a more developed market economy on traditional pastoral systems. There is a double process of stratification that affects families at one level, and gender relations at another. However low the status of women in some pastoral societies, it appears to be lower for the majority in the transition towards a less self-reliant life style so long as they remain tied to pastoralism.

The spread of camel husbandry

Camel husbandry spread from the Islamic north to the hot lowland areas of the Horn of Africa, where it is primarily associated with the Somali and neighbouring peoples.[45] In the nineteenth century, it spread to the Ariaal and Turkana, and successive accounts of the Turkana reveal an increasing sophistication in their management techniques in the process of adaptation.[46] More recently, limited numbers of camels have been acquired also by the Samburu, Pokot, and Uaso Booran, possibly in response to the loss of some of the best grazing land for their cattle under modern conditions. The pioneers have been wealthier stock-owners who are able to afford the costs of purchase and of managing the camels separately. Just as there is a certain exclusiveness among those Rendille or Somali who can afford to remain inside the camel economy as against those that are squeezed out, so that diversification of herds to incorporate camels can be viewed as an aspect of growing economic differentiation.[47]

There is a more pessimistic slant to the spread of camel pastoralism. The use of camels for transportation is limited by the rough terrain that typifies the most marginal parts of East Africa. They are hard to manage in comparison with cattle, and are more susceptible to disease, stunting the prospects for herd growth. In the context of political instability which bedevils some of these remoter areas, the slow growth rate of camels impedes recovery from armed attack (notably the lethal destruction of modern warfare), whereas cattle herds with greater resilience and growth can recover. With these points in mind, the

---

[44] Dahl (1987: 257, 261, 270–2, 274). Cf. Obeler (1985: 278–80); Ensminger (1987: 35–6, 39–42, 46–7). Two surveys of the position of women among Islamic pastoralists adopt diverging views. Beck and Keddie (1978: 331–2, 363, 367–9, 382–4) suggest a pattern consistent with Dahl. Nelson (1973: 43–55) presents a looser argument and appears more concerned with women in settled communities.

[45] Stiles (1983: 1–2); Gilles (1983: 5); Hjort and Dahl (1984: 18–21).

[46] The adaptation to camels among the Turkana involved a transition from treating them like cattle (P. H. Gulliver 1955: 30, 39, 260) to a process of specialization, with separate skills and migratory tracts, extending the network of trust in caring for one another's stock (Storas 1990: 139). The Turkana have developed their herds to the point that they now actually sell camels to their neighbours (Sperling 1987a: 6–7).

[47] I. M. Lewis (1961: 100–1); Dahl (1979a: 51–3); Stiles (1983: 2); Sperling (1987a: 6–7, 9–10); Bollig (1992: 35). See p. 25.

camel may be regarded as the animal of last resort, and its spread is viewed by some commentators as a gauge for the dessication of the environment. The process of desertification, which is largely associated with the spread of the Sahara into the Sahel, is held from this point of view to apply increasingly to East Africa.[48] The neo-Malthusian argument extends from the Islamic areas in the northern half of Africa to the non-Islamic eastern parts.

Conclusion: Pastoralism and the Wake of Civilization

Ambivalence towards the spread of camel pastoralism is characteristic of diverging views concerning environmental degradation. The parallels between the recent experience of non-Islamic pastoralists in East Africa and the historical pattern in the Islamic areas are striking and they can be interpreted either way. On the one hand, there is the Boserupian view of population pressures leading towards technological progress (for some) combined with the darker Malthusian side of surplus populations driven to the margins. On the other hand, there is the neo-Malthusian view that emphasizes the devastating effect on the environment caused by growing misuse and mismanagement. This accepts that pastoralists may be responsible for the degradation of their land, but only as part of a more general trend. It again posits the Tragedy of the Commons, not because pastoralists are alone in exploiting common resources for personal gain, but because they are drawn under modern conditions into a wider economy that offers no alternative and implicates everyone. It is the tragedy of the process of civilization.

This leaves unresolved the question concerning the extent to which the traditional pattern of nomadic pastoralism in East Africa might have been adapted to some ecological balance. There appears to be no clear evidence to confirm that the recurrent Malthusian damage to herds due to overgrazing in the pre-colonial period was matched by a lasting neo-Malthusian damage to the land. The absence of evidence of earlier cultivation in areas now associated with pastoralism in East Africa suggests that they have always been semi-arid.[49] Without clear evidence, it is tempting to assume some viable Malthusian balance in pre-colonial times, as implied in Chapter 1 and outlined more fully at the beginning of Chapter 7. From this point of view, it is the phenomenon of pastoralism that has displayed a remarkable resilience, even in the face of major climatic shifts.

However, this is to elevate traditional pastoralism to some self-contained

---

[48] Asad (1973: 70); Dahl (1979*a*: 16); Stiles (1983: 1–2); Hjort and Dahl (1984: 15–17); Schlee (1989: 19); Oba (1990: 40).

[49] Homewood and Rodgers (1987: 122–4); F. Marshall (1994: 33–4, 36). There is, however, evidence in northern Somalia of terraced agriculture near ruined towns (I. M. Lewis 1960: 214), and oral traditions in pastoral Karamoja also refer to earlier agricultural settlement (Lamphear 1976: 81–4; cf. Gartrell 1988: 197).

niche and to ignore that it has belonged to a wider continuum, geographically and historically. It is to overlook the extent to which new technologies have crept into the area over the centuries, with pastoralism itself as just one of these in its time. As it spread from northern to eastern parts of Africa, pastoralism appears to have been better adapted than agriculture to the semi-arid areas already inhabited by hunting and gathering foragers. In such conditions and with its inordinate capacity for growth, pastoralism was able to leap ahead of the slow expansion of civilization from which it originated, dominating the regions unsuitable for agriculture for several millennia perhaps, but not indefinitely. In the period just before European contact, trade (with or without Islam) was expanding into the area, and firearms were poised to be the next major acquisition, transforming the political balance. Even without colonial intervention, the overall trend appears to have been towards a growing economic infrastructure and a pattern similar to those well established in the Islamic areas further north.

In this scenario, as an urban-based culture spreads into surrounding regions, 'primitive tribalism' merges into 'marginal tribalism'. Near the towns, every known ecological niche becomes further exploited in response to growing demands for agricultural and pastoral produce, increasing the pressure on the environment. As economic pressures work outwards, this is experienced in remoter areas as an increasing incidence of drought, while more and more people, pastoralists included, become enmeshed in the wider regional economy and the growth of urban society. For the successful, family enterprise merges into business enterprise, luxuries become regarded as basic needs, while pastoralists who cannot compete turn to cultivation or to the urban areas in search of work; so stratification gathers pace, reaching out to the remoter parts. As pastoralists become increasingly involved in the regional economy, their life style becomes increasingly differentiated and dependent on non-pastoral products. Pastoralism is no more the cause of this trend than any other sector, but the pastoralists are caught up in a wider continuum along with all others.

This is to argue that recent trends may in a sense have been predestined in a historical process that replicates Islamic experience, creating the opportunities for pastoralism in the first place and now raising fundamental issues concerning its future. Meanwhile, in remoter parts and within limits set by the modern world, the traditional pastoral continuum persists in many ways. So long as it persists, there is still the opportunity to gauge its relevance for understanding an enduring way of life and the dilemmas of those caught in the wake of the process of civilization.

References

Adams, M. E. (1986), 'Merging Relief and Development: The Case of Turkana', *Development Policy Review*, 4: 314–24.

Adams, W. M., and Anderson, D. M. (1988), 'Irrigation before Development: Indigenous and Induced Change in Agricultural Water Management in East Africa', *African Affairs*, 87: 519–36.

Allan, W. (1965), *The African Husbandman* (Edinburgh: Oliver & Boyd).

Almagor, U. (1978), *Pastoral Partners: Affinity and Bond Partnership among the Dassanetch* (Manchester: Manchester University Press).

——(1979), 'Raiders and Elders: A Confrontation of Generations among the Dassanetch', in Fukui and Turton (1979), 119–45.

——(1985), 'The Bee Connection: The Symbolism of a Cyclical Order in an East African Age System', *Journal of Anthropological Research*, 41: 1–17.

Alsaker-Kjerland, K. (1995), 'Cattle Breed, Shillings Dont: The Belated Incorporation of the AbaKuria into Modern Kenya', thesis submitted for Dr Philosophiae, University of Bergen.

Anderson, D. M. (1984), 'Some Thoughts on the Nineteenth Century History of the Il Chamus of Baringo District', *Mila: A Journal of Cultural Research*, 7: 107–25.

——(1988), 'Cultivating Pastoralists: Ecology and Economy among the Il Chamus of Baringo, 1840–1980', in Johnson and Anderson (1988), 241–60.

——(1989), 'Agriculture and Irrigation Technology at Lake Baringo in the Nineteenth Century', *Azania*, 24: 84–97.

——and Grove R. (1987) (eds.), *Conservation in Africa: People, Policies and Practice* (Cambridge: Cambridge University Press).

Arhem, K. (1985), *Pastoral Man in the Garden of Eden: The Maasai of the Ngorongoro Conservation Area, Tanzania* (Uppsala: University of Uppsala, Department of Cultural Anthropology).

Asad, T. (1970), *The Kababish Arabs: Power, Authority and Consent in a Nomadic Tribe* (London: Hurst).

——(1972), 'Political Inequality in the Kababish Tribe', in Cunnison and James (1972), 126–48.

——(1973), 'The Beduin as a Military Force: Notes on Some Aspects of Power Relations between Nomads and Sedentaries in Historical Perspective', in Nelson (1973), 61–72.

——(1979), 'Equality in Nomadic Social Systems? Notes towards the Dissolution of an Anthropological Category', in L'Équipe Écologie (1979), 419–28.

Ashton, H. (1952), *The Basuto* (London: Oxford University Press).

Austin, H. H. (1899), 'From Njemps to Marich, Save, and Mumia's (British East Africa)', *Geographical Journal*, 14: 307–10.

Azarya, V. (1993), 'Sedentarization and Ethnic Identity among the Fulbe: A Comparative View', in Eguchi and Azarya (1993), 35–60.

Baier, S. (1976), 'Economic History and Development: Drought and the Sahelian Economics of Niger', *African Economic History*, 1: 1–16.

Baker, P. R. (1975), 'Development and the Pastoral Peoples of Karamoja', in Monod (1975), 187–205.

Baker, R. (1977), 'Polarisation: Stages in the Environmental Impact of Alien Ideas on a Semi-Pastoral Society', in O'Keefe and Wisner (1977), 151–70.

Baker, S. J. K. (1974), 'A Background to the Study of Drought in East Africa', *African Affairs*, 73: 170–7.

Banton, M. P. (1957), *West African City* (London: Oxford University Press).

Barber, J. P. (1968), *Imperial Frontier: A Study of Relations between the British and the Pastoral Tribes of NE Uganda* (Nairobi: East African Publishing House).

Barnard, A. (1992), *Hunters and Herders of Southern Africa* (Cambridge: Cambridge University Press).

Barnes, J. A. (1949), 'Measures of Divorce Frequency in Simple Societies', *Journal of the Royal Anthropological Institute*, 79: 37–62.

——(1951), *Marriage in a Changing Society* (Rhodes–Livingstone Paper No. 20; London: Oxford University Press).

Bartels, L. (1970), 'Studies of the Galla in Wallaga', *Journal of Ethiopian Studies*, 8: 135–60.

Barth, F. (1963) (ed.), *The Role of the Entrepreneur in Social Change in Northern Norway* (Bergen: Universitetsforlaget).

——(1967), 'Economic Spheres in Darfur', in Firth (1967), 149–74.

——(1973), 'A General Perspective on Nomad–Sedentary Relations in the Middle East', in Nelson (1973), 11–21.

Basutoland, (1937), *Basutoland Census 1936* (Pretoria: Government Printer).

Bates, D. G., and Lees, S. H. (1977), 'The Role of Exchange in Productive Specialization', *American Anthropologist*, 79: 824–41.

Baxter, P. T. W. (1954), 'The Social Organisation of the Galla of Northern Kenya', D.Phil. thesis, University of Oxford.

——(1966), 'Acceptance and Rejection of Islam among the Boran of the Northern Frontier District of Kenya', in I. M. Lewis (1966), 233–50.

——(1978), 'Boran Age-Sets and Generation-Sets: *gada* a Puzzle or a Maze?', in Baxter and Almagor (1978), 151–82.

——(1979), 'Boran Age-Sets and Warfare', in Fukui and Turton (1979), 69–95.

——(1993), 'The "New" East African Pastoralist: An Overview', in Markakis (1993), 143–62.

——(1996), 'Towards a Comparative Ethnography of the Oromo: The Importance of Affines', in Baxter *et al.* (1996), 178–89.

——and Almagor, U. (1978) (eds.), *Age, Generation and Time: Some Features of East African Age Organisations* (London: Hurst).

——and Hogg, R. (1990) (eds.), *Property, Poverty and People* (Manchester: Department of Anthropology, University of Manchester).

——Hultin, J., and Triulzi, A. (1996) (eds.), *Being and Becoming Oromo: Historical and Anthropological Enquiries* (Uppsala: Nordiska Afrikainstitutet).

Beck, L., and Keddie, N. (1978) (eds.), *Women in the Muslim World* (Cambridge, Mass.: Harvard University Press).

Benedict, B. (1968), 'Family Firms and Economic Development', *Southwestern Journal of Anthropology*, 24: 1–19.

Bernard, F. E. (1982), 'Rural Population Pressure and Redistribution in Kenya', in

Clarke and Kosinski (1982), 150–6.

Bernardi, B. (1952), 'The Age-System of the Nilo-Hamitic Peoples: A Critical Evaluation', *Africa*, 22: 316–32.

——(1985), *Age Class Systems: Social Institutions and Polities Based on Age* (Cambridge: Cambridge University Press).

Berntsen, J. L. (1976), 'The Maasai and their Neighbors: Variables of Interaction', *African Economic History*, 2: 1–11.

——(1979), 'Economic Variations among Maa-Speaking Peoples', in B. A. Ogot (ed.), *Hadith 7: Ecology and History in East Africa* (Nairobi: Kenya Literature Bureau), 108–27.

Bernus, E. (1974), *Les Illabakan* (Paris: Mouton).

——(1990), 'Dates, Dromedaries, and Drought: Diversification in Tuareg Pastoral Systems', in Galaty and Johnson (1990), 149–76.

Bohannan, P. (1954), *Tiv Farm and Settlement* (London: HMSO).

——(1955), 'Some Principles of Exchange and Investment among the Tiv', *American Anthropologist*, 57: 60–70.

——(1966), *African Outline* (Harmondsworth: Penguin).

——and Dalton, G. (1962) (eds.), *Markets in Africa* (Evanston, Ill.: Northwestern University Press).

Bollig, M. (1992), 'East Pokot Camel Husbandry', *Nomadic Peoples*, 31: 34–50.

Boserup, E. (1965), *The Conditions of Agricultural Growth: The Economics of Agrarian Change under Population Pressure* (London: Allen & Unwin).

——(1981), *Population and Technology* (Oxford: Blackwell).

Bradburd, D. (1984), 'Marxism and the Study of Pastoralists', *Nomadic Peoples*, 16: 3–14.

Brain, R. (1972), *Bangwa Kinship and Marriage* (Cambridge: Cambridge University Press).

Brandstrom, P., Hultin, J., and Lindstrom, J. (1979), *Aspects of Agro-Pastoralism in East Africa* (Research Report No. 51; Uppsala: Scandinavian Institute of African Studies).

Brantley, C. (1978), 'Gerontocratic Government: Age-Sets in Pre-Colonial Giriama', *Africa*, 48: 248–64.

Bray, W. (1973), 'The Biological Basis of Culture', in C. Renfrew (ed.), *The Explanation of Culture Change: Models of Prehistory* (London: Duckworth), 73–92.

Broch-Due, V. (1990), '"Livestock Speak Louder than Sweet Words": Changing Property and Gender Relations among the Turkana', in Baxter and Hogg (1990), 147–63.

Brown, G. G., and Hutt, A. M. B. (1935), *Anthropology in Action* (London: Oxford University Press).

Bulcha, M. (1996), 'The Survival and Reconstruction of Oromo National Identity', in Baxter *et al.* (1996), 48–66.

Bulliet, R. (1980), 'Sedentarization of Nomads in the Seventh Century: The Arabs of Basra and Kufa', in Salzman (1980), 35–47.

Burling, R. (1962), 'Maximisation Theories and the Study of Economic Anthropology', *American Anthropologist*, 64: 802–21.

Buxton, J. (1963), *Chiefs and Strangers: A Study of Political Assimilation among the Mandari* (Oxford: Clarendon Press).

——(1973), *Religion and Healing in Mandari* (Oxford: Clarendon Press).

Campbell, D. J. (1984), 'Response to Drought among Farmers and Herders in Southern Kajiado District, Kenya', *Human Ecology*, 12: 35–64.

Carlsen, J. (1980), *Economic and Social Transformation in Rural Kenya* (Uppsala: Scandinavian Institute of African Studies).

Chambers, R. J. H. (1973), 'The Perkerra Irrigation Scheme: A Contrasting Case', in R. Chambers and J. Moris (eds.), *Mwea: An Irrigated Rice Settlement in Kenya* (Munich: Weltforum Verlag), 344–64.

Chapple, E. D., and Coon, C. S. (1947), *Principles of Anthropology* (London: Jonathan Cape).

Charsley, S. R. (1969), *The Princes of Nyakyusa* (Nairobi: East African Publishing House).

Chayanov, A. V. (1966), *The Theory of Peasant Economy* (Homewood, Ill.: Irwin).

Childs, G. M. (1949), *Umbundu Kinship and Character* (London: Oxford University Press).

Clark, D. (1952), 'A Karamojong Wedding', *Uganda Journal*, 16: 176–7.

Clarke, J. I., and Kosinski, L. A. (1982) (eds.), *Redistribution of Population in Africa* (London: Heinemann).

Clignet, R. (1970), *Many Wives, Many Powers* (Evanston, Ill.: Northwestern University Press).

Collett, D. (1987), 'Pastoralists and Wildlife: Image and Reality in Kenya Maasailand', in Anderson and Grove (1987), 129–48.

Colson, E. (1958), *Marriage and Family among the Plateau Tonga* (Manchester: Manchester University Press).

Cordell, D. D., and Gregory, J. W. (1987) (eds.), *African Population and Capitalism: Historical Perspectives*, Boulder, Colo.: Westview).

Cowen, M. (1982), 'The British State and Agrarian Accumulation in Kenya', in Fransman (1982), 142–69.

Cribb, R. (1991), *Nomads in Archaeology* (Cambridge: Cambridge University Press).

Crosby, K. H. (1937), 'Polygamy in Mende Country', *Africa*, 10: 249–64.

Culwick A. T., and Culwick, G. M. (1938), 'A Study of Population in Ulanga, Tanganyika Territory', *Sociological Review*, 30: 365–79.

Cummins, S. L. (1904), 'Subclans of the Bahr-el-Ghazal Dinka', *Journal of the Royal Anthropological Institute*, 34: 149–66.

Cunnison, I. (1966), *Baggara Arabs: Power and Lineage in a Sudanese Nomad Tribe* (Oxford: Clarendon Press).

——and James, W. (1972) (eds.), *Essays in Sudan Ethnography* (London: Hurst).

Curley, R. T. (1973), *Elders, Shades and Women* (Berkeley and Los Angeles: University of California Press).

Dahl, G. (1979a), *Suffering Grass: Subsistence and Society in Waso Borana* (Stockholm: Department of Social Anthropology, University of Stockholm).

——(1979b), 'Ecology and Equality: The Boran Case', in L'Équipe Écologie (1979), 261–81.

——(1987), 'Women in Pastoral Production', *Ethnos*, 52: 246–79.

——(1996), 'Sources of Life and Identity', in Baxter *et al.* (1996), 162–77.

——and Hjort, A. (1976), *Having Herds: Pastoral Herd Growth and Household Economy* (Stockholm: Department of Social Anthropology, University of Stockholm).

————(1979), *Pastoral Change and the Role of Drought* (Stockholm: SAREC).

Darling, F. F., and Farvar, M. A. (1972), 'Ecological Consequences of Sedentarization of Nomads', in M. A. Favar and J. P. Milton (eds.), *The Careless Technology: Ecology and International Development* (New York: Natural History Press), 671–82.

Darwin, C. (1871), *The Descent of Man, and Selection in Relation to Sex* (London: J. Murray).

Dawson, M. H. (1987), 'Health, Nutrition, and Population in Central Kenya, 1890–1945', in Cordell and Gregory (1987), 201–17.

de Jonge, K. (1985), 'Demographic Developments and Class Contradictions in a "Domestic" Community: The Nyakyusa (Tanzania) before Colonial Conquest', in W. van Binsbergen and P. Geschiere (eds.), *Old Modes of Production and Capitalist Encroachment: Anthropological Explorations in Africa* (London: Routledge & Kegan Paul), 39–70.

Doornbos, M. (1993), 'Pasture and Polis: The Roots of Political Marginalisation of Somali Pastoralism', in Markakis (1993), 100–21.

Dorjahn, V. R. (1959), 'The Factor of Polygamy in African Demography', in R. B. Bascom and M. J. Herskovits (eds.), *Continuity and Change in African Cultures* (Chicago: University of Chicago Press), 87–112.

Douglas, M. (1967), 'Primitive Rationing: A Study of Controlled Exchange', in Firth (1967), 119–47.

Dundas, K. R. (1910), 'Notes on the Tribes Inhabiting Baringo District', *Journal of the Royal Anthropological Institute*, 40: 49–73.

Dupré, G., and Rey, P. P. (1973), 'Reflections on the Pertinence of a Theory of the History of Exchange', *Economy and Society*, 2: 131–63.

Durkheim, E. (1951; orig. 1897), *Suicide: A Study in Sociology*, trans. J. Spaulding and G. Simpson (New York: Free Press).

——(1964; orig. 1893), *The Division of Labor in Society*; trans. Simpson (New York: Free Press).

Dyson-Hudson, N. (1966), *Karimojong Politics* (Oxford: Clarendon Press).

——and Dyson-Hudson, R. (1982), 'The Structure of East African Herds and the Future of East African Herders', *Development and Change*, 13: 213–38.

Edgerton, R. B. (1971), *The Individual in Cultural Adaptation: A Study of Four East African Peoples* (Berkeley and Los Angeles: University of California Press).

Eguchi, P. K., and Azarya, V. (1993) (eds.), *Unity and Diversity of a People: The Search for Fulbe identity* (Senri Ethnological Studies No. 35; Osaka: National Museum of Ethnology).

Eisenstadt, S. N. (1954), 'African Age Groups', *Africa*, 25: 100–11.

——(1956), *From Generation to Generation* (London: Routledge & Kegan Paul).

Elam, Y. (1973), *The Social and Sexual Roles of Hima Women* (Manchester: Manchester University Press).

Ensminger, J. (1987), 'Economic and Political Differentiation among Galole Orma Women', *Ethnos*, 52: 28–49.

——(1992), *Making a Market: The Institutional Transformation of an African Society* (Cambridge: Cambridge University Press).

L'Équipe Écologie et Anthropologie des Sociétés Pastorales (1979), *Pastoral Production and Society* (Cambridge: Cambridge University Press).

Evangelou, P. (1984), *Livestock Development in Kenya's Maasailand: Pastoralists' Tran-*

sition to a Market Economy (Boulder, Colo.: Westview).

Evans-Pritchard, E. E. (1940), *The Nuer* (Oxford: Clarendon Press).

——(1951), *Kinship and Marriage among the Nuer* (Oxford: Clarendon Press).

——(1956), *Nuer Religion* (Oxford: Clarendon Press).

Fadiman, J. A. (1982), *An Oral History of Tribal Warfare: The Meru of Mt Kenya* (Ohio: Ohio University Press).

Fallers, L. A. (1956), *Bantu Bureaucracy* (Chicago: University of Chicago Press).

Fedders, A., and Salvadori, C. (1980), *Peoples and Cultures of Kenya* (Nairobi: Transafrica).

Feldman, D. (1969), 'The Economics of Ideology: Some Problems of Achieving Rural Socialism in Tanzania', in Leys (1969), 85–111.

Firth, R. (1967) (ed.), *Themes in Economic Anthropology* (London: Tavistock).

Forde, C. D. (1941), *Marriage and Family among the Yako* (London: London School of Economics).

Fortes, M. (1949), *The Web of Kinship among the Tallensi* (London: Oxford University Press).

——(1954), 'A Demographic Field Study in Ashanti', in F. Lorimer (ed.), *Culture and Human Fertility*, (Paris: Unesco), 253–339.

——(1958), 'Introduction' to Goody (1958), 1–14.

Fosbrooke, H. A. (1948), 'An Administrative Survey of the Masai Social System', *Tanganyika Notes and Records*, 26: 1–50.

——(1956), 'The Masai Age-Group System as a Guide to Tribal Chronology', *African Studies*, 15: 188–206.

Foster-Carter, A. (1978), 'Can we Articulate "Articulation"?', in J. Clammer (ed.), *The New Economic Anthropology* (London: Macmillan), 210–49.

Fraenkel, M. (1964), *Tribe and Class in Monrovia* (London: Oxford University Press).

Fransman, M. (1982) (ed.), *Industry and Accumulation in Africa* (London: Heinemann).

Frantz, C. (1975), 'Contraction and Expansion in Nigerian Bovine Pastoralism', in Monod (1975), 338–53.

Fratkin, E. (1991), *Surviving Drought and Development: Ariaal Pastoralists of Northern Kenya* (Boulder, Colo.: Westview).

——Galvin, K. A., and Roth, E. A. (1994) (eds.), *African Pastoralist Systems* (Boulder, Colo.: Lynne Rienner).

Froggatt, P., Dudgeon, M. Y., and Merrett, J. D. (1969), 'Consultation in General Practice, Analysis of Individual Frequencies', *British Journal of Preventive and Social Medicine*, 23: 1–11.

Fukui, K., and Turton, D. (1979) (eds.), *Warfare among East African Herders* (Senri Ethnological Studies No. 3; Osaka: National Museum of Ethnology).

Galaty, J. G. (1980), 'The Maasai Group-Ranch: Politics and Development in an African Pastoral Society', in Salzman (1980), 157–72.

——(1981), 'Land and Livestock among Kenyan Maasai', *Journal of Asian and African Studies*, 16: 68–88.

——(1984), 'Cultural Perspectives on Nomadic Pastoral Societies', *Nomadic Peoples*, 16: 15–29.

——(1994), 'Rangeland Tenure and Pastoralism in Africa', in Fratkin *et al.* (1994),

185–204.

——Aronson, D., and Salzman, P. C. (1981) (eds.), *The Future of Pastoral Peoples* (Ottawa: International Development Research Centre).

——and Bonte, P. (1991) (eds.), *Herders, Warriors and Traders: Pastoralism in Africa* (Boulder, Colo.: Westview).

——and Johnson, D. L. (1990) (eds.), *The World of Pastoralism: Herding Systems in Comparative Perspective* (London: Guilford Press).

Galletti, R., Baldwin, K. D. S., and Dina, I. O. (1956), *Nigeria Cocoa Farmers* (London: Oxford University Press).

Gamble, D. P. (1957), *The Wolof of Senegambia* (Ethnographic Survey of Africa; London: International African Institute).

Gartrell, B. (1988), 'Prelude to Disaster: The Case of Karamoja', in Johnson and Anderson (1988), 193–217.

Gellner, E. (1969), *Saints of the Atlas* (London: Weidenfeld & Nicolson).

Gibson, G. D. (1958), 'Herero Marriage', *Rhodes–Livingstone Journal*, 24: 1–37.

Gilles, J. L. (1983), 'A Reaction to "Desertification and Pastoral Development in Northern Kenya"', *Nomadic Peoples*, 13: 15–16.

——and Jamtgaard, K. (1982), 'Overgrazing in Pastoral Areas', *Nomadic Peoples*, 10: 1–10.

Gluckman, M. (1950). 'Kinship and Marriage among the Lozi and Zulu', in Radcliffe-Brown and Forde (1950), 166–206.

——(1965), *Politics, Law and Ritual in Tribal Society* (Oxford: Blackwell).

Goldschmidt, W. (1972), 'The Operations of a Sebei Capitalist: A Contribution to Economic Anthropology', *Ethnology*, 11: 187–201.

——(1976), *Culture and Behaviour of the Sebei* (Berkeley and Los Angeles: University of California Press).

——(1981), 'The Failure of Pastoral Economic Development Programs in Africa', in Galaty *et al.* (1981), 101–18.

Goody, E. (1973), *Contexts of Kinship* (Cambridge: Cambridge University Press).

Goody, J. R. (1958) (ed.), *The Development Cycle in Domestic Groups* (Cambridge: Cambridge University Press).

——(1973), 'Bridewealth and Dowry in Africa and Eurasia', in J. R. Goody and S. J. Tambiah, *Bridewealth and Dowry* (Cambridge: Cambridge University Press), 1–58.

Gough, K. (1971), 'Nuer Kinship: A Re-Examination', in T. O. Beidelman (ed.), *The Translation of Culture* (London: Tavistock), 79–121.

Gowlett, J. A. J. (1988), 'Human Adaptation and Long-term Climatic Change in Northeast Africa: An Archaeological Perspective', in Johnson and Anderson (1988), 27–45.

Graham, O. (1988), 'Enclosure of the East African Rangelands: Recent Trends and their Impact', ODI Pastoral Development Network Paper 25a.

Grandin, B. E., and Lembuya, P. (1987), 'The Impact of the 1984 Drought in Olkarkar Group Ranch, Kajiado, Kenya', ODI Pastoral Development Network Paper 23e.

Gray, R., and Birmingham, D. (1970) (eds.), *Pre-Colonial African Trade: Essays on Trade in Central and Eastern Africa before 1900* (London: Oxford University Press).

Gray, R. F. (1960), 'Sonjo Bride-Price and the Question of African "Wife Purchase"', *American Anthropologist*, 62: 34–57.

——(1962), 'Economic Exchange in a Sonjo Village', in Bohannan and Dalton (1962),

469–92.

——(1963), *The Sonjo of Tanganyika* (London: Oxford University Press).

——(1964), 'Introduction', to Gray and Gulliver (1964), 1–33.

Gray, R. F., and Gulliver, P. H. (1964) (eds.), *The Family Estate in Africa* (London: Routledge & Kegan Paul).

Greenwood, M., and Yule, G. U. (1920), 'An Inquiry into the Nature of Frequency Distributions', *Journal of the Royal Statistical Society*, 83: 255–79.

Gregory, J. W. (1896), *The Great Rift Valley* (London: John Murray).

Grove, A. T. (1974), 'Desertification in the African Environment', *African Affairs*, 73: 137–51.

Gulliver, P., and Gulliver, P. H. (1953), *The Central Nilo-Hamites* (London: International African Institute).

Gulliver, P. H. (1952), 'The Karamojong Cluster', *Africa*, 22: 1–21.

——(1953), 'The Age Organization of the Jie Tribe', *Journal of the Royal Anthropological Institute*, 83: 147–68.

——(1954), 'Jie Agriculture', *Uganda Journal*, 18: 65–70.

——(1955), *The Family Herds* (London: Routledge & Kegan Paul).

——(1958), 'The Turkana Age Organization', *American Anthropologist*, 60: 900–22.

——(1962), 'The Evolution of Arusha Trade', in Bohannan and Dalton (1962), 431–56.

——(1963), *Social Control in an African Society: A Study of the Arusha* (London: Routledge & Kegan Paul).

——(1964), 'The Arusha Family', in Gray and Gulliver (1964), 197–229.

Haaland, G. (1972), 'Nomadism as an Economic Career among the Sedentaries in the Sudan Savannah Belt', in Cunnison and James (1972), 149–72.

——(1977), 'Pastoral Systems of Production: The Socio-Cultural Context and Some Economic and Ecological Implications', in O'Keefe and Wisner (1977), 179–93.

Hardin, G. (1968), 'The Tragedy of the Commons', *Science*, 162: 1243–8.

Hart, K. (1986), 'Heads or Tails? Two Sides of the Coin', *Man*, 21: 637–56.

Hartmann, W. (1991), *Das Politische System der Nyakyusa* (Fort Lauderdale: Verlage Breitenbach).

Haugerud, A. (1989), 'Land Tenure and Agrarian Change in Kenya', *Africa*, 59: 61–90.

Heald, S. (1989), *Controlling Anger: The Sociology of Gisu Violence* (Manchester: Manchester University Press).

Hedlund, H. (1979), 'Contradictions in the Peripheralization of a Pastoral Society: The Maasai', *Review of African Political Economy*, 15/16: 15–34.

Henin, R. A. (1969), 'Marriage Patterns and Trends in the Nomadic and Settled Populations of the Sudan, *Africa*, 39: 238–59.

Herren, U. J. (1990), 'Socioeconomic Stratification and Small Stock Production in Mukogodo Division, Kenya', *Research in Economic Anthropology*, 12: 111–48.

Herskovits, M. J. (1926), 'The Cattle Complex in Africa', *American Anthropologist*, 28: 230–72, 351–80, 494–528, 533–54.

Hjort, A. (1979), *Savanna Town: Rural Ties and Urban Opportunities in Northern Kenya* (Stockholm: Department of Social Anthropology, University of Stockholm).

——(1981*a*), 'Herds, Trade, and Grain: Pastoralism in a Regional Perspective', in Galaty *et al.* (1981), 135–43.

——(1981*b*), 'Ethnic Transformation, Dependency and Change: The Ilgira Samburu of Northern Kenya', *Journal of Asian and African Studies*, 16: 50–67.

——(1982), 'A Critique of "Ecological" Models of Pastoral Land Use', *Nomadic Peoples*, 10: 11–27.

Hjort, A., and Dahl, G. (1984), 'Significance and Prospects of Camel Pastoralism', in M. A. Hussein (ed.), *Camel Pastoralism in Somalia: Proceedings from a Workshop Held in Baydhabo April 8–13, 1984* (Mogadishu: Somali Academy of Sciences and Arts), 11–35.

Hogg, R. S. (1981), 'The Social and Economic Organisation of the Boran of Isiolo District, Kenya', Ph.D. thesis submitted to the Faculty of Economics and Social Studies, University of Manchester.

——(1986), 'The New Pastoralism: Poverty and Dependency in Northern Kenya', *Africa*, 56: 319–33.

——(1987), 'Development in Kenya: Drought, Desertification and Food Scarcity', *African Affairs*, 88: 47–58.

——(1993), 'Continuity and Change among the Boran in Ethiopia', in Markakis (1993), 68–82.

von Hohnel, L. (1894), *Discovery by Count Teleki of Lakes Rudolf and Stephanie* (vol. ii) (London: Longman).

Hollis, A. C. (1905), *The Masai: Their Language and Folklore* (Oxford: Clarendon Press).

Holy, L. (1974), *Neighbours and Kinsmen: A Study of the Berti People of Darfur* (London: Hurst).

Homewood, K. M., and Rodgers, W. A. (1987), 'Pastoralism, Conservation and the Overgrazing Controversy', in Anderson and Grove (1987), 111–28.

————(1991), *Maasailand Ecology: Pastoral Development and Wildlife Conservation in Ngorongoro, Tanzania* (Cambridge: Cambridge University Press).

Hopen, C. E. (1958), *The Pastoral Fulbe Family in Gwandu* (London: Oxford University Press).

Horowitz, M. M. (1981), 'Research Priorities in Pastoral Studies: An Agenda for the 1980's', in Galaty *et al.* (1981), 61–88.

Houerou, H. N. Le (1986), 'The Desert and Arid Zones of Northern Africa', in M. Evernari, Noy-Meir, I., and Goodall, D. W. (eds.), *Ecosystems of the World 12B: Hot Deserts and Arid Shrublands* (Amsterdam: Elsevier), 101–47.

Howell, P. P. (1951), 'Notes on the Ngork Dinka of Western Kordofan', *Sudan Notes and Records*, 32: 239–93.

——(1954), *A Manual of Nuer Law* (London: Oxford University Press).

Hoyle, S. (1977), 'The Khashm el Girba Agricultural Scheme: An Example of an Attempt to Settle Nomads', in O'Keefe and Wisner (1977), 116–31.

Hultin, J. (1979), 'Political Structure and the Development of Inequality among the Macha Oromo', in L'Équipe Écologie (1979), 283–93.

Hunt, D. (1984), *The Impending Crisis in Kenya: The Case for Land Reform*, (Aldershot: Gower).

Huntingford, G. W. B. (1950), *Nandi Work and Culture* (London: HMSO).

Hurskainen, A. (1984), *Cattle and Culture: The Structure of a Pastoral Parakuyo Society* (Studia Orientalia 56; Helsinki: The Finnish Oriental Society).

——(1990), 'Levels of Identity and National Integrity: A Viewpont of the Pastoral Maasai and Parakuyo', *Nomadic Peoples*, 25–7: 79–92.

Hutchinson, S. E. (1996), *Nuer Dilemmas: Coping with Money, War and the State* (Berkeley and Los Angeles: University of California Press).

Hyden, G. (1980), *Beyond Ujamaa in Tanzania: Underdevelopment and an Uncaptured Peasantry* (London: Heinemann).

——(1987), 'Capital Accumulation, Resource Distribution and Governance in Kenya: The Role of Economy of Affection', in Schatzberg (1982), 117–36.

Ingle, C. R. (1972), *From Village to State in Tanzania: The Politics of Rural Development* (Ithaca, NY: Cornell University Press).

Ingold, T. (1980), *Hunters, Pastoralists and Ranchers: Reindeer Economies and their Transformations* (Cambridge: Cambridge University Press).

Jacobs, A. H. (1968), 'A Chronology of the Pastoral Maasai', in B. A. Ogot (ed.), *Hadith 1* (Nairobi: East African Publishing House), 10–31.

——(1979), 'Maasai Inter-tribal Relations: Beligerent Herdsmen or Peaceable Pastoralists?', in Fukui and Turton (1979), 33–52.

——(1980), 'Pastoral Maasai and Tropical Rural Development', in R. H. Bates and M. F. Lofchie (eds.), *Agricultural Development in Africa* (New York: Praeger), 275–300.

Johnson, D. H. (1991), 'Political Ecology in the Upper Nile: The Twentieth Century Expansion of the Pastoral "Common Economy"', in Galaty and Bonte (1991), 89–117.

Johnson, D. H., and Anderson, D. M. (1988) (eds.), *The Ecology of Survival: Case Studies from Northeast African History* (London: Lester Crook Academic Publishing).

Johnston, H. H. (1902), *The Uganda Protectorate* (London: Hutchinson).

Jones, W. O. (1980), 'Agricultural Trade within Tropical Africa: Historical Background', in R. H. Bates and M. F. Lofchie (eds.), *Agricultural Development in Africa: Issues of Public Policy* (New York: Praeger), 10–45.

Kassa, Getachew (1990), 'Islam, Trade and Pastoralism in the Southern Province of Ethiopia', paper presented at the Islamic Annual Seminar: Middle Eastern and Islamic Study Centre, Tokyo.

Kawai, K. (1988), 'The Residential Patterns and Kinship Relations among the Il Chamus of Northern Kenya', in S. Sato and H. Umehara (eds.), *Comparative Study on the Socio-ecological Adaptation Mechanism among Pastoral Peoples in Northern Kenya* (Tokyo: Rikkyo University), 11–27.

Kelly, H. (1990), 'Commercialization, Sedentarization, Economic Diversification and Changing Property Relations among Orma Pastoralists of Kenya', in Baxter and Hogg (1990), 80–94.

Kelly, R. C. (1985), *The Nuer Conquest: The Structure and Development of an Expansionist System* (Ann Arbor, Mich.: University of Michigan Press).

Kenya, Select Committee on Unemployment (1970), *Report* (Nairobi).

Kenya (1971), 'The Future Growth of Kenya's Population and its Consequences', *Kenya Statistical Digest*, 9(2): 1–3.

Kenya Land Commission: Evidence and Memoranda (1933) (London: HMSO).

Kenya, Republic of (n.d.), *1979 Population Census, ii. Analytical Report* (Nairobi: Central Bureau of Statistics, Ministry of Finance and Planning).

Kenyatta, J. (1938), *Facing Mount Kenya* (London: Secker & Warburg).

Kertzer, D. I., and Keith, J. (1984) (eds.), *Age and Anthropological Theory* (Ithaca, NY: Cornell University Press).

Keya, G. A. (1991), 'Alternative Policies and Models for Arid and Semi-Arid Lands in Kenya', in P. T. W. Baxter (ed.), *When the Grass is Gone: Development Intervention in African Lands* (Uppsala: Scandinavian Institute of African Studies), 73–80.

Kituyi, M. (1990), *Becoming Kenyans: Socio-Economic Transformation of the Pastoral Maasai* (Nairobi: African Centre for Technology Studies).

Kjaerby, F. (1983), *Problems and Contradictions in the Development of Ox-Cultivation in Tanzania* (Research Report No. 66; Copenhagen: Centre for Development Research).

Kjekshus, H. (1977), *Ecology Control and Economic Development in East African History: The Case of Tanganyika 1850–1950* (London: Heinemann).

Klima, G. J. (1970), *The Barabaig: East African Cattle-Herders* (New York: Holt, Rinehart & Winston).

Konczacki, Z. A. (1978), *The Economics of Pastoralism: A Case Study of Sub-Saharan Africa* (London: Cass).

Konter, J. J. (1974), 'Changing Marital Relations among the Nyakyusa, Rangwe District, Tanzania', MS, Leiden: Africastudiecentrum.

Kuper, H. (1947), *An African Aristocracy* (London: Oxford University Press).

Laclau, E. (1977), *Politics and Ideology in Marxist Theory: Capitalism—Fascism—Populism* (London: New Left Books).

Lamphear, J. (1976), *The Traditional History of the Jie of Uganda* (Oxford: Clarendon Press).

——(1992), *The Scattering Time: Turkana Responses to Colonial Rule* (Oxford Studies in African Affairs; Oxford: Clarendon Press).

——(1993), 'Aspects of "Becoming Turkana": Interactions and Assimilation between Maa- and Ateker-Speakers', in Spear and Waller (1993), 87–104.

Lamprey, H. F. (1983), 'Pastoralism Yesterday and Today: The Over-Grazing Problem', in F. Bourlière (ed.), *Tropical Savannas* (Ecosystems of the World, No. 13; Amsterdam: Elsevier), 643–66.

Leakey, L. S. B. (1977), *The Southern Kikuyu before 1903* (London: Academic Press).

Legesse, A. (1973), *Gada: Three Approaches to the Study of African Society* (New York: Free Press).

Lewis, B. A. (1972), *The Murle* (Oxford: Clarendon Press).

Lewis, I. M. (1955), *Peoples of the Horn of Africa* (Ethnographic Survey of Africa, N. E. Africa part I; London: International African Institute).

——(1960), 'The Somali Conquest of the Horn of Africa', *Journal of African History*, 1: 213–29.

——(1961), *A Pastoral Democracy* (London: Oxford University Press).

——(1962), *Marriage and Family in Northern Somaliland* (Kampala: EAISR).

——(1966) (ed.), *Islam in Tropical Africa* (London: International African Institute).

——(1975), 'The Dynamics of Nomadism: Prospects for Sedentarization and Social Change', in Monod (1975), 426–42.

——(1994), *Blood and Bone: The Call of Kinship in Somali Society* (Lawrenceville, NJ: The Red Sea Press).

Leys, C. (1969) (ed.), *Politics and Change in Developing Countries: Studies in the Theory and Practice of Development* (Cambridge: Cambridge University Press).

——(1975), *Underdevelopment in Kenya: The Political Economy of Neo-Colonialism*

1964–71 (London: Heinemann).

—— (1982), 'Accumulation, Class Formation and Dependency: Kenya', in Fransman (1982), 170–92.

Lienhardt, G. (1958), 'The Western Dinka', in J. Middleton and D. Tait, *Tribes without Rulers* (London: Routledge & Kegan Paul), 97–135.

—— (1961), *Divinity and Experience: The Religion of the Dinka* (Oxford: Clarendon Press).

Little, P. D. (1983), 'The Livestock-Grain Connection in Northern Kenya: An Analysis of Pastoral Economics and Semiarid Land Development', *Rural Africana*, NS 15–16: 91–108.

—— (1985*a*), 'Social Differentiation and Pastoralist Sedentarization in Northern Kenya', *Africa*, 55: 243–61.

—— (1985*b*), 'Absentee Herd Owners and Part-Time Pastoralists: The Political Economy of Resource Use in Northern Kenya', *Human Ecology*, 13: 131–51.

—— (1987*a*), 'Land Use Conflicts in the Agricultural/Pastoral Borderlands: The Case of Kenya', in P. D. Little and M. M. Horowitz (eds.), *Lands at Risk in the Third World: Local-Level Perspectives* (Boulder, Colo.: Westview), 195–212.

—— (1987*b*), 'Woman as Ol Payian (Elder): The Status of Widows among the Il Chamus (Njemps) of Kenya', *Ethnos*, 52: 81–102.

—— (1992), *The Elusive Granary: Herder, Farmer, and State in Northern Kenya* (Cambridge: Cambridge University Press).

Livingstone, I. (1977), 'Economic Irrationality among Pastoral Peoples: Myth or Reality?', *Development and Change*, 8: 209–30.

Long, N. (1977), *Introduction to the Sociology of Development* (London: Tavistock).

Lovejoy, P. E., and Baier, S. (1976), 'The Desert-Side Economy of the Central Sudan', in M. H. Glantz (ed.), *The Politics of Natural Disaster: The Case of the Sahel Drought* (New York: Praeger), 145–75.

Low, D. A. (1963), 'The Northern Interior 1840–84', in R. Oliver and G. Mathew (eds.), *History of East Africa*, i (London: Oxford University Press), 297–351.

McCulloch, M., Littlewood, M., and Dugast, I. (1954), *Peoples of the Central Cameroons* (Ethnographic Survey of Africa; London: International African Institute).

Mace, R. (1993), 'Transitions between Cultivation and Pastoralism in Sub-Saharan Africa', *Current Anthropology*, 34: 363–82.

McKenny, M. (1973), 'The Social Structure of the Nyakyusa: A Re-Evaluation', *Africa*, 43: 91–107.

Mair, L. P. (1953), 'African Marriage and Social Change', in Phillips (1953), 1–171.

Manger, L. O. (1988), 'Traders, Farmers and Pastoralists: Economic Adaptations and Environmental Problems in the Southern Nuba Mountains of the Sudan', in Johnson and Anderson (1988), 155–72.

Manners, R. A. (1962), 'Land Use, Trade and Growth of Market Economy in Kipsigis Country', in Bohannan and Dalton (1962), 493–519.

Mannheim, K. (1952; orig. 1929), 'The Problem of Generations', in *Essays on the Sociology of Knowledge* (London: Routledge & Kegan Paul), 276–320.

Markakis, J. (1993) (ed.), *Conflict and the Decline of Pastoralism in the Horn of Africa* (London: Macmillan).

Maro, P. S., and Mlay, W. F. I. (1982), 'Population Redistribution in Tanzania', in

Clarke and Kosinski (1982), 176–81.

Marris, P., and Somerset, A. (1972), *African Businessmen* (London: Routledge & Kegan Paul).

Marshall, F. (1994), 'Archaeological Perspectives on East African Pastoralism', in Fratkin *et al.* (1994), 17–43.

Marshall, L. (1976), *The !Kung of Nyae Nyae* (Cambridge, Mass.: Harvard University Press).

Marx, E. (1977), 'The Tribe as a Unit of Subsistence', *American Anthropologist*, 79: 343–63.

Mathias-Mundy, E., and McCorkle, C. M. (1995), 'Ethnoveterinary Medicine and Development: A Review of the Literature', in Warren *et al.* (1995), 488–98.

Maybury-Lewis, D. (1984), 'Age and Kinship: A Structural View', in D. I. Kertzer and J. Keith (eds.), *Age and Anthropological Theory* (Ithaca, NY: Cornell University Press), 123–140.

Mbithi, P. M., and Barnes, C. (1975), *The Spontaneous Settlement Problem in Kenya* (Nairobi: E. A. Literature Bureau).

——and Wisner, B. (1973), 'Drought and Famine in Kenya', *Journal of East African Research and Development*, 3: 113–43.

Mead, M. (1937) (ed.), *Cooperation and Competition among Primitive Peoples* (New York: McGraw-Hill).

Meillassoux, C. (1964), *Anthropologie économique des Gouro de Côte d'Ivoire* (Paris: Mouton).

——(1972), 'From Reproduction to Production: A Marxist Approach to Economic Anthropology', *Economy and Society*, 1: 92–105.

Merker, M. (1904), 'Die Masai', MS, trans. Buxton (Berlin: Dietrich Reimer).

Miller, D. (1983), *A Pocket Popper* ([London]: Fontana).

Mitchell, J. C. (1970; orig. 1959), 'The Causes of Labour Migration', in J. Middleton, *Black Africa: Its Peoples and their Cultures Today* (London: Macmillan), 23–37.

——(1980) (ed.), *Numerical Techniques in Social Anthropology* (ASA Essays in Social Anthropology No. 3; Philadelphia: ISHI).

Mitchell, J. C., and Barnes, J. A. (1950), *The Lamba Village* (Cape Town: University of Cape Town).

von Mitzlaff, U. (1988), *Maasai-Frauen* (Munich: Trickster).

Monod, T. (1975), *Pastoralism in Tropical Africa* (London: Oxford University Press).

Moore, H. L. (1986), *Space, Text and Gender: An Anthropological Study of the Marakwet of Kenya* (Cambridge: Cambridge University Press).

Moore, S. F. (1986), *Social Facts and Fabrications: 'Customary' Law on Kilimanjaro, 1880–1980* (Cambridge: Cambridge University Press).

Moris, J. R. (1981), *Managing Induced Rural Development* (Bloomington, Ind.: International Development Institute).

——and Hatfield, C. R. (1982), 'A New Reality: Western Technology Faces Pastoralism in the Maasai Project', in *Report of an Exploratory Workshop on the Role of Anthropologists in Interdisciplinary Teams Developing Improved Food Production Technology* (Lagua: International Rice Research Institute), 43–61.

Muriuki, G. (1974), *A History of the Kikuyu 1500–1900* (London: Oxford University Press).

Nadel, S. F. (1942), *A Black Byzantium* (London: Oxford University Press).

——(1947), *The Nuba* (London: Oxford University Press).

Native Labour Commission, East African Protectorate (1913), *Report and Evidence* (Nairobi).

Ndagala, D. K. (1990), 'Pastoralists and the State in Tanzania', *Nomadic Peoples*, 25–7: 51–64.

——(1992), *Territory, Pastoralists and Livestock: Resource Control among the Kisongo Maasai* (Studies in Cultural Anthropology 18; Uppsala: University of Uppsala, Department of Cultural Anthropology).

Nelson, C. (1973) (ed.), *The Desert and the Sown: Nomads in the Wider Society* (Berkeley and Los Angeles: University of California Press).

New, C. (1873), *Life, Wanderings and Labour in Eastern Africa* (London: Cass).

Niamir, M. (1995), 'Indigenous Systems of Natural Resource Management among Pastoralists of Arid and Semi-Arid Africa', in Warren *et al.* (1995), 245–57.

Nicolaisen, J. (1963), *Ecology and Culture of the Pastoral Tuareg* (Copenhagen: The National Museum of Copenhagen).

Njonjo, A. L. (1981), 'The Kenya Peasantry: A Reassessment', *Review of African Political Economy*, 20: 27–40.

Nukunya, G. K. (1969), *Kinship and Marriage among the Anlo Ewe* (New York: Athlone Press).

Nyangira, N. (1987), 'Ethnicity, Class and Politics in Kenya', in Schatzberg (1987), 15–32.

Oba, G. (1990), 'Changing Property Rights among Settling Pastoralists: An Adaptive Strategy to Declining Pastoral Resources', in Baxter and Hogg (1990), 38–44.

Obeler, R. S. (1985), *Women, Power, and Economic Change: The Nandi of Kenya* (Stanford: Stanford University Press).

O'Keefe, P., and Wisner, B. (1977) (eds.), *Land Use and Development* (African Environment Special Report 5; London: International African Institute).

O'Leary, M. (1984), *The Kitui Akamba* (Nairobi: Heinemann).

Ominde, S. H. (1968), *Land and Population Movements in Kenya* (Evanston, Ill.: Northwestern University Press).

Onyemelukwe, C. C. (1974), *Economic Development: An Inside View* (London: Longman).

Ornas, A. H. af, and Dahl, G. (1991), *Responsible Man: The Atmaan Beja of North-Eastern Sudan* (Uppsala: Stockholm Studies in Social Anthropology/Nordiska Africainstitutet).

Osogo, J. (1970), 'The Significance of Clans in the History of East Africa', in B. A. Ogot (ed.), *Hadith 2* (Nairobi: East African Publishing House), 30–41.

Oxby, C. (1981), 'Group Ranches in Africa', MS report prepared for FAO (Rome).

Packard, R. M. (1981), *Chiefship and Cosmology: An Historical Study of Political Competition* (Bloomington, Ind.: Indiana University Press).

Paine, R. (1971), 'Animals as Capital', *Anthropological Quarterly*, 44: 157–72.

Parkin, D. J. (1972), *Palms, Wine and Witnesses: Public Spirit and Private Gain in an African Farming Community* (London: Intertext Books).

——(1974), 'Congregational and Interpersonal Ideologies in Political Ethnicity', in A. Cohen (ed.), *Urban Ethnicity* (London: Tavistock), 119–58.

——(1978), *The Cultural Definition of Political Response* (London: Academic Press).

——(1991), *Sacred Void: Spacial Images of Work and Ritual among the Giriama of Kenya* (Cambridge: Cambridge University Press).

Parkipuny, M. L. Ole (1979), 'Some Crucial Aspects of the Maasai Predicament', in A. Coulson, (ed.), *African Socialism in Practice: the Tanzanian Experience* (Nottingham: Spokesman), 136–57.

Peristiany, J. G. (1939), *The Social Institutions of the Kipsigis* (London: Routledge & Kegan Paul).

Perlov, D. C. (1983), 'The Role of Commercial Livestock in Samburu Economic Strategies—Research Notes', *Rural Africana*, 15–16: 127–30.

Peters, C. (1891), *New Light on Dark Africa* (London: Ward, Lock & Co.).

Phillips, A. (1953) (ed.), *Survey of African Marriage and Family Life* (London: Oxford University Press).

Phillipson, D. W. (1977), *Later Prehistory of Eastern and Southern Africa* (London: Heinemann).

Popper, K. R. (1963), *Conjectures and Refutations: The Growth of Scientific Knowledge* (London: Routledge & Kegan Paul).

Powell-Cotton, P. H. G. (1904), *In Unknown Africa* (London: Hurst & Blackett).

Prothero, R. M. (1974), 'Human Perspectives on Drought in West Africa', *African Affairs*, 73: 162–9.

Radcliffe-Brown, A., and Forde, D. (1950) (eds.), *African Systems of Kinship and Marriage* (London: Oxford University Press).

Richards, A. I. (1939), *Land, Labour and Diet in Northern Rhodesia* (London: Oxford University Press).

——(1940), *Bemba Marriage and Present Economic Conditions* (Rhodes–Livingstone Paper No. 4; London: Oxford University Press).

Rigby, P. (1968), 'Some Gogo Rituals of "Purification": An Essay on Social and Moral Categories', in E. R. Leach (ed.), *Dialectic in Practical Religion* (Cambridge: Cambridge University Press), 153–78.

——(1969), *Cattle and Kinship among the Gogo* (New York: Cornell University Press).

——(1992), *Cattle, Capitalism, and Class: Ilparakuyo Maasai Transformations* (Philadelphia: Temple University Press).

Roth, E. A. (1993), 'Re-Examination of Rendille Fertility Regulation', *American Anthropologist*, 95: 597–612.

Routledge, W. S., and Routledge, K. (1910), *With a Prehistoric People: The Akikuyu of British East Africa* (London: Cass).

Royal Commission on East Africa 1953–1955 (1955), *Report*, Cmnd. 9745 (London: HMSO).

Sadr, K. (1991), *The Development of Nomadism in Ancient Northeast Africa* (Philadelphia: University of Pennsylvania Press).

Sahlins, M. (1974), *Stone Age Economics* (London: Tavistock).

Salih, M. A. M. (1993), 'Pastoralists and the War in Southern Sudan: The Ngok Dinka/Humur Conflict in South Kordofan', in Markakis (1993), 16–29.

Salzman, P. C. (1980) (ed.), *When Nomads Settle* (New York: Praeger).

Sandford, S. (1983), *Management of Pastoral Development in the Third World* (Chichester: Wiley).

Sankan, S. S. Ole (1971), *The Maasai* (Nairobi: East African Literature Bureau).

Sato, S. (1980), 'Pastoral Movements and the Subsistence Unit of the Rendille of Northern Kenya: With Special Reference to the Camel Ecology', in S. Wada, and P. K. Eguchi (eds.), *Africa 2* (Senri Ethnological Studies No. 6; Osaka: National Museum of Ethnology), 1–78.

Schapera, I. (1940), *Married Life in an African Tribe* (London: Faber & Faber).

Schatzberg, M. G. (1987) (ed.), *The Political Economy of Kenya* (New York: Praeger).

Schlee, G. (1989), *Identities on the Move: Clanship and Pastoralism in Northern Kenya* (Manchester: Manchester University Press).

Schneider, H. K. (1968), 'Economics in East African Aboriginal Societies', in E. E. LeClair Jr and H. K. Schneider (eds.), *Economic Anthropology* (New York: Holt, Reinhart and Winston), 426–45.

——(1979), *Livestock and Equality in East Africa: the Economic Basis for Social Structure* (Bloomington, Ind.: Indiana University Press).

Shanin, T. (1972), *The Awkward Class* (Oxford: Clarendon Press).

Shell-Duncan, B. K. (1994), 'Child Fostering among Nomadic Turkana Pastoralists', in Fratkin *et al.* (1994), 147–64.

Shimada, Y. (1993), 'Jihad as Dialectical Movement and Formation of Islamic Identity among the Fulbe', in Eguchi and Azarya (1993), 87–117.

Shivji, I. G. (1976), *Class Struggles in Tanzania* (London: Heinemann).

Siegel, M. (1940), *The Mackenzie Collection* (Memoir of the American Anthropological Association No. 55; Supplement to the *American Anthropologist*, 42 (4, Part 2).

Smith, A. B. (1992), *Pastoralism in Africa: Origins and Development Ecology* (London: Hurst).

Smith, M. G. (1955), *The Economy of Hausa Communities of Zaria* (London: HMSO).

Sobania, N. W. (1980), 'The Historical Traditions of the Peoples of the Lake Turkana Basin *c*.1840–1925', Ph.D. thesis, University of London.

——(1991), 'Feasts, Famines and Friends: Nineteenth Century Exchange and Ethnicity in the Eastern Lake Turkana Region', in Galaty and Bonte (1991), 118–42.

Sorbo, G. M. (1977), 'Nomads on the Scheme: A Study of Irrigation Agriculture and Pastoralism in Eastern Sudan', in O'Keefe and Wisner (1977), 132–50.

Spaulding, J. (1991), 'An Historical Context for the Study of Islam in Eastern Africa', in K. W. Harrow (ed.), *Faces of Islam in African Literature* (Portsmouth, NH: Heinemann), 23–36.

Spear, T., and Waller, R. (1993) (eds.), *Being Maasai: Ethnicity and Identity in East Africa* (London: James Currey).

Spencer, P. (1965), *The Samburu: A Study of Gerontocracy in a Nomadic Tribe* (London: Routledge & Kegan Paul).

——(1973), *Nomads in Alliance: Symbiosis and Growth among the Rendille and Samburu of Kenya* (London: Oxford University Press).

——(1974), 'Drought and the Commitment to Growth', *African Affairs*, 73: 419–27.

——(1976), 'Opposing Streams and the Gerontocratic Ladder: Models of Age Organisation in East Africa', *Man*, NS 11: 153–75.

——(1978), 'The Jie Generation Paradox', in Baxter and Almagor (1978), 131–49.

——(1980), 'Polygyny as a Measure of Social Differentiation in Africa', in Mitchell (1980), 117–60.

——(1984), 'Pastoralists and the Ghost of Capitalism', *Production pastorale et société*, 15: 61–76.

——(1988), *The Maasai of Matapato: A Study of Rituals of Rebellion* (Manchester: Manchester University Press).

——(1989), 'The Maasai Double-Helix and the Theory of Dilemmas', in D. Maybury-Lewis and U. Almagor (eds.), *The Attraction of Opposites: Thought and Society in Dualistic Mode* (Ann Arbor, Mich.: University of Michigan Press), 297–320.

——and Wright, J. J. (1971), 'Consultation Frequencies in General Practice', in P. Spencer, *General Practice and Models of the Referral Process* (Health Report No. 6; London: Institute for Operational Research), 31–45.

Sperling, L. (1987a), 'The Adoption of Camels by Samburu Cattle Herders', *Nomadic Peoples*, 23: 1–17.

——(1987b), 'Wage Employment among Samburu Pastoralists of Northcentral Kenya', *Research in Economic Anthropology*, 9: 167–90.

——and Galaty, J. G. (1990), 'Cattle, Culture and Economy: Dynamics in East African Pastoralism', in Galaty and Johnson (1990), 69–98.

Spooner, B. (1971), 'Towards a Generative Model of Nomadism', *Anthropological Quarterly*, 44: 198–210.

——(1972), 'The Iranian Deserts', in B. Spooner (ed.), *Population Growth: Anthropological Implications* (Cambridge, Mass.: MIT), 245–68.

Stebbing, E. P. (1938), 'The Man-Made Desert: Erosion and Drought', *Journal of the Royal African Society*, 37 (suppl.): 3–40.

Steinhart, E. (1979), 'The Kingdoms on the March: Speculation on Social and Political Change', in J. B. Webster (ed.), *Chronology, Migration and Drought in Interlacustrine Africa* (New York: Africana Publishing), 189–213.

Stenning, D. J. (1958), 'Household Viability among the Pastoral Fulani', in J. R. Goody (1958), 92–119.

——(1959), *Savannah Nomads* (London: Oxford University Press).

Stewart, F. H. (1977), *Fundamentals of Age-Group Systems* (New York: Academic Press).

Stiles, D. N. (1981), 'Relevance of the Past in Projections about Pastoral Peoples', in Galaty *et al.* (1981), 370–8.

——(1983), 'Desertification and Pastoral Development in Northern Kenya', *Nomadic Peoples*, 13: 1–14.

Storas, F. (1990), 'Intention of Implication: The Effects of Turkana Social Organization on Ecological Balances', in Baxter and Hogg (1990), 137–46.

Sutter, J. W. (1987), 'Cattle and Inequality: Herd Size Differences and Pastoral Production among the Fulani of Northeastern Senegal', *Africa*, 57: 196–218.

Swidler, N. (1980), 'Sedentarization and Modes of Economic Integration in the Middle East' in Salzman (1980), 21–33.

Swift, J. J. (1977a), 'Desertification and Man in the Sahel', in O'Keefe and Wisner (1977), 171–8.

——(1977b), 'Sahelian Pastoralists: Underdevelopment, Desertification, and Famine', *Annual Review of Anthropology*, 6: 457–78.

——(1979), 'The Development of Livestock Trading in a Nomad Pastoral Economy: The Somali Case', in L'Équipe Écologie (1979), 447–66.

Tait, D. (1961), *The Konkomba of Northern Ghana* (London: Oxford University Press).

Talle, A. (1988), *Women at a Loss: Changes in Maasai Pastoralism and their Effects on Gender Relations* (Stockholm: Department of Social Anthropology, University of Stockholm).

Taylor, B. K. (1969), *The Western Lacustrine Bantu* (Ethnographic Survey of Africa, London: International African Institute).

Thomas, N. W. (1913), *Anthropological Report on the Ibo-Speaking Peoples of Nigeria: Part 1, Law and Custom* (London: Harrison & Sons).

Thomson, J. (1885), *Through Masai Land* (London: Samson Low).

Throup, D. W. (1987), 'The Construction and Destruction of the Kenyatta State', in Schatzberg (1987), 33–74.

Titherington, G. W. (1927), 'The Raik Dinka of Bahr El Ghazal Province', *Sudan Notes and Records*, 10: 159–209.

Tornay, S. (1979), 'Générations, classes d'âge et superstructure', in L'Équipe Écologie (1979), 307–27.

Torry, W. I. (1976), 'Residence Rules among Gabra Nomads: Some Ecological Considerations', *Ethnology*, 15: 269–85.

Tosh, J. (1970), 'The Northern Interlacustrine Region', in R. Gray and D. Birmingham (1970), 103–18.

Trimingham, J. S. (1968), *The Influence of Islam upon Africa* (London: Longman).

Tucker, A. N., and Mpaayei, J. T. Ole (1955), *A Maasai Grammar* (London: Longman).

Turnbull, C. M. (1965), *Wayward Servants: The Two Worlds of the African Pygmies* (London: Eyre & Spottiswoode).

Turner, V. W. (1957), *Schism and Continuity in an African Society* (Manchester: Manchester University Press).

Turshen, M. (1987), 'Population Growth and the Deterioration of Health: Mainland Tanzania, 1920–1960', in Cordell and Gregory (1987), 187–200.

Turton, D. (1973), 'The Social Organisation of the Mursi', Ph.D. dissertation, London School of Economics.

——(1975), 'The Relation between Oratory and the Exercise of Influence among the Mursi', in M. Bloch (ed.), *Political Language and Oratory in Traditional Society* (London: Academic Press), 163–83.

——(1980), 'The Economics of Mursi Bridewealth: A Comparative Perspective', in J. L. Comaroff (ed.), *The Meaning of Marriage Payments* (London: Academic Press), 67–92.

Unesco (1970), *Use and Conservation of the Biosphere* (Paris: Unesco).

Wagner, G. (1940), 'The Political Organization of the Bantu of Kavirondo', in M. Fortes and E. E. Evans-Pritchard (eds.), *African Political Systems* (London: Oxford University Press), 197–236.

——(1949), *The Bantu of North Kavirondo* (London: Oxford University Press).

Wakefield, T. (1870), 'Notes on the Geography of Eastern Africa', *Journal of the Royal Geographical Society*, 15: 303–99.

Waller, R. (1976), 'The Maasai and the British 1895–1905: The Origins of an Alliance', *Journal of African History*, 17: 529–53.

——(1993), 'Acceptees and Aliens: Kikuyu Settlement in Maasailand', in Spear and

Waller (1993), 226–57.

Ward, B. (1969), 'The Poor World's Cities', *Economist*, 233 (6589): 56–70.

Warren, D. M., Slikkerveer, L. J., and Brokensha, D. (1995) (eds.), *The Cultural Dimension of Development: Indigenous Knowledge Systems* (London: Intermediate Technology Publications).

Weber, M. (1930; orig. 1922), *The Protestant Ethic and the Spirit of Capitalism*, trans. Parsons (London: Allen & Unwin).

Western, D. (1973), 'The Structure, Dynamics and Changes of the Amboseli Ecosystem', Ph.D. thesis, University of Nairobi.

Wienpahl, J. (1984), 'Women's Role in Livestock Production among the Turkana of Kenya', *Research in Economic Anthropology*, 6: 193–215.

Wilson, M. (1950), 'Nyakyusa Kinship', in Radcliffe-Brown and Forde (1950), 111–39.

——(1951), *Good Company* (London: Oxford University Press).

——(1957), *Rituals of Kinship among the Nyakyusa* (London: Oxford University Press).

——(1959), *Communal Rituals of the Nyakyusa* (London: Oxford University Press).

——(1975), 'Letter', to *Africa*, 45: 202–5.

——(1977), *For Men and Elders: Change in the Relations of Generations and of Men and Women among the Nyakyusa–Ngonde People 1875–1971* (London: International African Institute).

Wilson, R. T., Diallo, A., and Wagenaar, K. (1985), 'Mixed Herding and the Demographic Parameters of Domestic Animals in Arid and Semi-Arid Zones of Tropical Africa', in A. G. Hill (ed.), *Population, Health and Nutrition in the Sahel* (London: K.P.I.).

Winter, E. H. (1956), *Bwamba* (Cambridge: Heffer).

Wisner, B. (1977), 'Man-Made Famine in Eastern Kenya: The Interrelationship of Environment and Development', in O'Keefe and Wisner (1977), 194–215.

Wolff, K. H. (1950), *The Sociology of Georg Simmel* (Glencoe, Ill.: Free Press).

Wolpe, H., 1972, 'Capitalism and Cheap Labour-power in South Africa: From Segregation to Apartheid', *Economy and Society*, 1: 425–56.

Wood, A. P. (1982), 'Spontaneous Agricultural Resettlement in Ethiopia, 1950–74', in Clarke and Kosinski (1982), 157–84.

World Bank (1986), *Population Growth and Policies in Sub-Saharan Africa*, Washington: World Bank.

SUBJECT INDEX

NAME INDEX